SHORT
HISTORIES

Short Histories are authoritative and elegantly written introductory texts which offer fresh perspectives on the way history is taught and understood in the 21st century. Designed to have strong appeal to university students and their teachers, as well as to general readers and history enthusiasts, *Short Histories* comprise novel attempts to bring informed interpretation, as well as factual reportage, to historical debates. Addressing key subjects and topics in the fields of history, the history of ideas, religion, classical studies, politics, philosophy and Middle East studies, these texts move beyond the bland, neutral "introductions" that so often serve as the primary undergraduate teaching tool. While always providing students and generalists with the core facts that they need to get to grips with, *Short Histories* go further. They offer new insights into how a topic has been understood in the past, and what different social and cultural factors might have been at work. They bring original perspectives to bear on current interpretations. They raise questions and—with extensive bibliographies—point the reader to further study, even as they suggest answers. Each text addresses a variety of subjects in a greater degree of depth than is often found in comparable series, yet at the same time in a concise and compact handbook form. *Short Histories* aim to be "introductions with an edge." In combining questioning and searching analysis with informed historical writing, they bring history up-to-date for an increasingly complex and globalized digital age.

For more information about titles and authors in the series, please visit: https://www.bloomsbury.com/series/short-histories/

A Short History of . . .

A SHORT HISTORY OF FLORENCE AND THE FLORENTINE REPUBLIC

Brian Jeffrey Maxson

BLOOMSBURY ACADEMIC
LONDON • NEW YORK • OXFORD • NEW DELHI • SYDNEY

BLOOMSBURY ACADEMIC
Bloomsbury Publishing Plc
50 Bedford Square, London, WC1B 3DP, UK
1385 Broadway, New York, NY 10018, USA
29 Earlsfort Terrace, Dublin 2, Ireland

BLOOMSBURY, BLOOMSBURY ACADEMIC and the Diana logo are
trademarks of Bloomsbury Publishing Plc

First published in Great Britain 2023
Reprinted 2023

ISBN: HB: 978-1-7883-1488-6
PB: 978-1-7883-1489-3
ePDF: 978-0-7556-4014-0
eBook: 978-0-7556-4012-6

Series: Short Histories

Typeset by Deanta Global Publishing Services, Chennai, India
Printed and bound in Great Britain

To find out more about our authors and books visit www.bloomsbury.com and
sign up for our newsletters.

Contents

Figures

Acknowledgments

This book has been written in the early morning hours of days spent working as an assistant dean; in afternoon and evening hours of days spent working as a faculty member; and in all hours of days spent in quarantine during the Covid-19 pandemic. Fellowships from I Tatti (the Harvard University Center for Italian Renaissance Studies), the ETSU small RDC program, the ETSU School of Graduate Studies, and the ETSU History Department have provided the funds to research and write this book. Ideas for the book were presented at the Ferrari Humanities Symposium at the University of Rochester; the Medieval and Renaissance Conference at the University of Virginia at Wise; the Renaissance Society of America; and the Mid-Atlantic Renaissance and Reformation Conference at Virginia Tech University. My thanks and gratitude to the organizers of those events and the audience members at each session. At ETSU, my thanks to my colleagues, especially Julie Fox-Horton, Josh Reid, and Michael Fowler, who co-organize our "Appalachian Premodernists" group, and my chair Doug Burgess, who has continually supported my work on Italy from the Appalachian Highlands of northeast Tennessee. My MA students Heather Alexander, Keri Blair, Seth Walker, Margaret Hayden, and Alexis Doutrich each helped edit and provided feedback. Outside ETSU, many colleagues have offered ideas and feedback. At Bloomsbury, my thanks to Abigail Lane for her patience and encouragement. In the fields of medieval, Renaissance, and early modern history I have incurred far too many debts to repay them all here—space rather than forgetfulness limits the names that follow. Nicholas Baker provided honest comments and corrected many errors. Monique O'Connell listened to many ideas for this book across both online and in-person conversations. Kanisorn Wongsrichanalai read and provided feedback on a manuscript far outside of his specialty on the American Civil War. Chris Celenza provided support and encouragement for me and this book in many different ways. When I was first invited to write this book, Pablo González Tornel listened to my hesitations and helped me decide that I could at least try to write a book like this. I also want to thank a handful of people outside of the academy: Massimo Auguardi, Derek Court, Matteo Garbuglia, and Moreno Meneghetti have each given me much more than I can repay over the past several years of friendship and conversation. My extended family, David and Linda Maxson, Kathy Van Zuuk, Vivian Roach, and Michael Schmidt each provided important inputs. My parents, Ron and Cathy, my wife, Jennifer, and my daughter, Alex, create and fill a home that makes work like this possible. Thank you as always and as ever.

All errors in the book, obviously, are my own.

This book is dedicated to my parents, Cathy and Ronald Maxson, with love and gratitude.

INTRODUCTION

THE BIRTH OF FLORENCE, ORIGINS TO 1250

The city of Florence lies within the shadow of Filippo Brunelleschi's towering dome. Centuries after the dome's completion the structure still commands the attention of astonished observers. Viewed from the quiet gravel square in front of the church of San Miniato al Monte, the red-bricked dome pulls eyes from the urban buildings out to the Apennines rolling beyond the city (Figure 1). Where once some of Europe's greatest minds, artists, wealthiest merchants, and most cunning politicians lived their lives, today *fiorentini*, tourists, and students marvel at the endless wonder found within the city on the Arno. It is a city whose progeny included Dante, Petrarch, Donatello, Lorenzo de' Medici, Michelangelo, Galileo, and many, many others.

But it is also a city whose impressive chapter in European history seems implausible. Unlike other Italian cities like Venice, Genoa, or Pisa, the city lacks a natural port. Moreover, for most of Florentine history, the Arno River was as much a destructive monster, patiently awaiting the fall rains to unleash its merciless floods, as it was an artery pumping the blood of the Florentine economy. Unlike Rome, Florence had no pope to inject wealth and visitors into the city. Unlike Naples—where Greek, Latin, and even Arabic interwove the cultural fabric characteristic of a major Mediterranean coastal city—no prince with vast European holdings established long-term rule in Florence. Unlike Milan to the north, Florence lacked a rich tradition as leader of its neighbors. Even as late as 1100, very little about Florence suggested its future successes. In fact, most of what remains of Florence's past and all that made the city famous dates to later centuries. This book tells the unlikely story of Florence from its humble origins as a colony during the late Roman Republic until the current city of bustling tourists. The majority of the

Figure 1 View of Florence from San Miniato al Monte, 2010. Author's Photo. Florence.

book, however, focuses on Florence's greatest centuries of influence between 1250 and 1600.

Most people first encounter Florence through beautiful pictures of the city's majestic dome (*il Duomo*), the Ponte Vecchio, or perhaps through its most famous resident, Michelangelo's towering *David* (*il Gigante*). Even so, Florence has always competed with other Italian cities for popular interest. Visitors to Venice are drawn to the promise of a moonlight gondola ride through that city's canals. Less the city's history, it is the strange serendipity of Venice itself that draws onlookers. To the south, visitors to Rome are shocked at the city's past and present size: the distance between the Roman Coliseum and Vatican City quickly upends plans "to just make a daytrip" and see the city. Under the hot summer sun, visitors marvel at historical strata burrowing 20 feet below the modern metropolis. It is 3,000 years of buildings, religious pilgrimage, and the centers of modern Italian political power that beckon visitors. Florence too has unique features woven into its urban fabric, and it too has millennia of history awaiting the curious.[1] But it is the treasures of the Renaissance above all that draw visitors to the city. Unlike the timeless canals of Venice or the endless historical strata of Rome, Florence exploded into prominence in the late medieval period, burned brightly for about four hundred years, and then largely receded from view. In short, people come to Florence to see the Renaissance. Where did that city originally come from? Why did its light shine so brightly? And when and why was the city eclipsed by other powers?

Historians have been arguing about the answers to those questions since the Renaissance itself. The most influential answer appeared during the mid-1800s. At that time, Jacob Burckhardt's book *The Civilization of Italy during the Renaissance* contended that Renaissance Italians discovered the light of modernity after years stranded within the opaque superstition of medieval darkness. For Burckhardt, modernity meant secularism, the discovery of the individual, and the creation of stronger states. Burckhardt credited these accomplishments to Italians from across the peninsula, but he reserved particular praise for the Florentines. Fifteenth-century Florence, Burckhardt contended, "deserves the name of the most modern state in the world."[2] It was "in advance of other cities."[3] Even grander, it was "in advance of the rest of Italy."[4] But Burckhardt thought that the triumphant march of Italian progress was short-lived. In the sixteenth century, he claimed that the Spanish occupied the Italian peninsula and the Catholic Church imposed the Counter Reformation upon Italians. These actions locked the Florentines back within their medieval prison, and the flame of modernity was temporarily extinguished.

Although still resilient in popular conceptions of the period, historians long ago abandoned Burckhardt's fantasies about individuals, modernity, and the medieval period.[5] Individualism obviously existed long before the 1300s in Italy, and the so-called Middle Ages (or "Dark Ages") were just as dynamic and culturally rich as earlier and later periods. Moreover, even apparent similarities between our world and that of many centuries ago mask vital differences. Yet, even as scholars have revised old assumptions, Florence has retained a special and prominent place in European history, especially within the Italian Renaissance. The art of men like Verrocchio, Leonardo, Michelangelo, and Cellini continues to appear in popular culture and continues to draw countless students and tourists to Florence. For specialists, the city lends itself to study: millions of original manuscripts and archival records survive from late medieval, Renaissance, and early modern Florence, more than any other premodern European city.[6] When and why did the city of Florence prosper, and what do its cultural monuments still tell people about its past?

Florence began as an Ancient Roman settlement on the shores of a troublesome river that meanders through the rolling hills of Tuscany. But the Romans did not enter empty lands. The Etruscans already inhabited the region that came to bear their name. Their hilltop town of Fiesole already overlooked the location of modern Florence. The growing strength of the Roman Republic in the 300s BCE ended Etruscan power in the area. At first, Fiesole prospered under its new Roman rulers: even today people can take a short bus ride from Florence to explore the well-preserved ruins of ancient Fiesole. Under Roman rule, people from Fiesole expanded their community to a site down the mountain on the banks of the Arno River. The community was short-lived. A civil war broke out in the tumultuous late Roman Republic, and the people at Fiesole's new settlement supported the losing side. Consequently, Fiesole's fledgling sister city was leveled in 82 BCE.

The current city of Florence traces its origins to around thirty years later, sometime in the 50s or 40s BCE. At that time, a new, small Roman colony was founded a short distance from the old site.[7] The imprint of this square Roman colony, in fact, can still be seen overtop the streets in the oldest parts of modern Florence. Roman Florence never became a city of significance in Antiquity. Like the people in many Ancient Roman cities, Florentines sought entertainment at their amphitheater, the outline of which can still be traced in the curving streets near the church of Santa Croce.[8] Florence seems to have outgrown its original square plan and had buildings outside its original city walls. It was probably a bustling medium-sized town by around 300 CE. Late ancient Florence might even have grown enough to be a regional capital![9]

However, the Roman Empire had many such towns. The few ancient sources that mention Florence grant it little importance.[10] One such source, for example, claims that around the year 250 CE an Armenian named Minias was martyred in the city and buried on a hill outside town. San Miniato al Monte, the church whose unparalleled panoramas of Florence began this chapter, was later built on that site.[11] In another source, in 393 CE Bishop Ambrose of Milan took temporary refuge in the city. During his stay he both appointed the bishop Zenobius—reputedly the first Florentine bishop and consequently a civic icon for the city—and consecrated the city's first cathedral at San Lorenzo.[12] As was common in towns in late Antiquity, the church of San Lorenzo was built outside the city's walls. It was only later, during the ninth and tenth centuries, that episcopal power grew enough in Florence that the different, newer, more centrally located church of Santa Reparata began to replace San Lorenzo as a central place for worship.[13]

The Roman Empire increasingly lost control over the Mediterranean, Europe, Italy, and Florence during the fifth century. The Italian peninsula became divided into many different political units. Legend has it that the armies of Alaric and Attila obliterated Florence in the 400s. Historians tell a more complicated story. It is true that most structures outside the town's small enclosed center were destroyed around that time.[14] But it is also true that the destruction was far from total. Enough survived, for example, for one literary source to relate that the Florentines opened their gates to a Byzantine commander during the 500s.[15] Nevertheless, over the next centuries, the city dwindled. Trade dried up. Roman buildings fell into disuse, decay, and desolation. Florentines were born, lived their lives, and died in the shadows of the city's ancient past. The Lombard kings of Italy used the city for defense and probably built the Florentine Baptistery (Figure 2).[16] Frank and Saxon rulers took over the city from 774 until 962. They used the nearby city of Lucca as their regional capital and left Florence on its own.[17] Thus, by the year 1000 Florence had existed for over a millennium, but its history was unremarkable. The city possessed little political influence, and whatever literature or art its citizens produced has long since been lost.[18]

Figure 2 The Baptistery, *c.* 1890–1900. Anonymous Photomechanical Print. Florence.

The history of Europe changed after the first millennium and fortune's winds favored the Florentines. By that time a splintered empire based in northern Europe continued to claim sovereignty over the lands that had formerly made up the Ancient Roman Empire. Meanwhile, Christianity had spread throughout Europe and was overseen by a complex hierarchy of churchmen. These churchmen oversaw wealthy plots of land. Moreover, those churchmen fell under a separate legal system than other people: when churchmen committed crimes, they went to different courts than other people. Additionally, churchmen paid taxes to the Church rather than to local governments. For these reasons, in the past, emperors and noblemen had filled church offices in and around their lands with family members and loyal friends. They could then work with those friends and family members to control both secular and church components within and around their holdings. But, during the 1000s Europeans began seeking spiritual and institutional changes within the Church. These men and women wanted holy people to lead more exemplary lives. They wanted their local priests to be more educated. They wanted church officials to be more interested in saving souls than making money. They began to claim that members of the Church should be able to choose pious people to fill empty church offices. In addition to religious concerns, some members of the Church saw an opportunity to weaken their political rivals by installing men loyal to the current pope rather than the local lord. Obviously, emperors and noblemen resisted these changes as infringements upon their prerogatives. These contests between rulers and church officials, sometimes written by candlelight, sometimes pursued by the glint of a sword, lasted for centuries.

These broader changes in piety and politics coincided with dramatic changes in Florence. In 978 a noblewoman named Willa supposedly endowed the foundation of a Benedictine Abbey in the city. This endowment reflects Willa's piety even as it also shows a new preference for Florence over other Tuscan cities as a seat of power. Willa's son Hugo followed his mother's lead. Upon his death, Hugo chose to be buried in the Badia in Florence. Modern visitors to the Badia can still, in fact, see Hugo's final resting place, although the extant tomb dates somewhat later to the 1400s.[19] Renewed religious sentiments brought other changes to Florence. Probably between 1014 and 1018 Bishop Hildebrand inaugurated the first of several stages of building for the church of San Miniato al Monte.[20] Some of the earliest surviving literature from Florence soon followed: Hildebrand commissioned a life of Saint Minias to try to prove that the relics in his new church were genuine.[21] New buildings, new writings, new piety, new political importance: Florence was beginning a new period of history.

One key change occurred during the papacy of Pope Gregory VII. The election of Pope Gregory in 1073 ushered in decades of armed disputes over who had the right to fill vacant church offices across Europe.[22] At that time Florence was a city within the lands of the countess Matilda of Canossa. When hostilities broke out between the emperor and the pope, Matilda not only chose to support the papal side, she even invited Pope Gregory to shelter in her personal castle at Canossa. There, Pope Gregory excommunicated Emperor Henry IV and, consequently, released Henry's vassals from their oaths of allegiance to him. Chaos erupted in Henry's lands. Safe behind the castle walls Pope Gregory waited for those rebellions to ruin his rival. In 1077 Emperor Henry traveled to Canossa and begged—barefoot, in the snow, over several days—forgiveness from the pope. The penitential ploy worked. The pope was victorious. Even centuries later the papacy remained grateful for Matilda's help: during the mid-1600s her bones were moved to St. Peter's Cathedral in Vatican City. There, a tomb by Bernini still commemorates her.[23]

Matilda's pro-papal support brought the broader papal-imperial dispute into Florence (Figure 3). When Matilda threw her support behind the papacy, she also robbed the emperor of the resources and revenues from her extensive lands and cities on the Italian peninsula. In the past those areas had looked to the emperor as Matilda's political superior. As Matilda's lord, incomes from a city like Florence flowed to Matilda and then, in part, across the Alps to imperial coffers. Matilda's action, however, proclaimed opposition to the emperor. Florentine wealth stopped reaching the emperor. Moreover, the Florentines began to think of the emperor as an enemy to be fought, not a superior to be obeyed.[24] Consequently, Florence and other Tuscan cities became, in both theory and practice, increasingly independent.

Florence was changing. Previously Lucca and Pisa had been the most important cities in Tuscany. Additionally, although Florence technically had overseen the lands and towns in its immediate vicinity—called a *contado*—the people in those areas had not viewed Florence as powerful enough to obey.[25] However, during the second half of the 1000s Florence began to separate itself from other Tuscan towns. By mid-century Florence had grown enough both to host a church council and temporarily serve as an administrative capital for the region.[26] Matilda and her successors bestowed numerous new rights and privileges that enabled the Florentines to make their own decisions and keep more of

Figure 3 William R. Shepherd, *The Holy Roman Empire under the Hohenstaufen,*
1138–1254 © Wikimedia Commons.

their own wealth.[27] Old noble families from the countryside moved in to exploit the city's growing political agency. They found many spaces already taken: within the city, Florentine urban families were expanding their investments in property; creating innovative banking techniques; and building continental trade networks. That new wealth bought them access to political decisions.[28] Soon the city walls were no longer big enough to hold the burgeoning population and growing economy.[29]

The reasons for Florence's rise remain ambiguous: a widespread economic network, demographic growth, political changes, leadership, a critical geographical position for peninsula trade, religious importance, and other factors all played roles. But many Italian cities were growing during that time; many were experiencing political changes; and many were founded on important trade routes. It simply remains unclear why the specific Florentine combination of factors proved so fertile. What is easier to outline are the consequences of the city's growth. Florence conquered its smaller neighbors. Fiesole, for example, fell in 1125.[30] Florence's government grew in power. For example, consuls—named after their Ancient Roman counterpart—became the leading office in the republic around that time.[31] Florentines fought for power in their growing city. Different factions formed around new merchants and noble rural families. These factions then fought among themselves and against each other. Families built massive defensive towers to protect their persons and possessions. The city fragmented into semiautonomous zones centered around each medieval skyscraper. Viewed from the Piazza di San Miniato the hundreds of towers would have seemed like quills on an angry porcupine. Few of these towers survive to testify to their former power, and the late medieval vista has disappeared under the modern city.[32]

During the second half of the 1100s Florence became the central power in Tuscany. Compare, for example, the Florentine response to Emperor Frederick I in the 1160s versus that to Emperor Henry VI in 1197. In the 1160s the emperor Frederick I was attempting to consolidate his power over the cities of northern Italy. The northern Italian cities resisted him by joining together in the "Lombard League." Florence played a minimal role in that association.[33] In 1197, the situation was similar, but Florence's influence had increased. The emperor Henry VI arrived in Italy, like his ancestor, to press imperial claims over the cities of the Italian peninsula. This time, Florence led its neighbors into a "Tuscan League." The Tuscan League petitioned the empire to let each community rule itself. Henry VI ignored the request. The members of the Tuscan League interpreted his silence as approval for their demands.[34]

With an increased position came even more innovations and developments. Internally, the Florentines established new taxes and changed their government. They tried to limit factional corruption by appointing a non-Florentine to come to the city and serve as chief executive for a one-year term, a position called the *podestà*.[35] The Florentines received formal jurisdiction over their city plus a three mile radius from Emperor Henry VI.[36] They began keeping better records, records that reveal a new sense of a common Florentine identity.[37] During these years of change, the Florentines even altered the ways that they bequeathed goods to their heirs![38] The expansion of the city walls paralleled this growth and change. In 1172 the walls of Florence encompassed about 80 hectares. However, by 1284 the work began to expand the walls eightfold to 630 hectares.[39] Some of that wall still survives in the modern city. Just outside the *oltrarno* quarter of the city people can enjoy a peaceful walk along the narrow Via di Belvedere. The steep road runs parallel to an extant section of wall before leading into a later sixteenth-century fortress. Pedestrians must dodge the occasional car, but they are rewarded with tranquility, greenery, historical stonework, and even the occasional animal, both wild and domesticated.

The growing city continued to expand. Urban merchants began to cast wider trading and banking nets farther into the European continent. By 1211 there were Florentine merchants in Champagne, France. By 1220 they were in Sardinia. By 1223 they were in Britain. Provence followed by 1248. Back in Florence, the wool industry grew by focusing on finishing and exporting garments. By 1250 Florence formed a trading, textile, and banking hub for a continental network. To continue and facilitate future growth the Florentines minted a new gold currency in 1252, called the Florin, which by the fourteenth century had become the standard unit of currency across Europe.[40] Those people exchanging Florins saw yet another change in the city. Instead of earlier civic saints like Saint Minas or Saint Zenobius, late medieval Florentines had placed their community under the patronage of Saint John the Baptist. Consequently, a likeness of John the Baptist graced the Florin.[41] Around the same time many of the city's industrial and commercial workers formed into groups called guilds. These guilds, in turn, soon became the basis for picking officeholders in the Florentine government.[42] The job of the government grew in complexity as additional neighbors fell within the city's dominion.[43]

Volatile factions intermixed with these economic successes, population growth, and political developments. People plotted. People counterplotted. They proceeded to live their lives. They holed up in their towers, bonded with their allies, and attacked their enemies. The factions exploded in 1216. At that time another emperor, this time Frederick II, had again brought armies to reestablish imperial control over the Italian peninsula. Pope Innocent III opposed him. The communes of Italy like Florence were both caught in the middle and active propagators of the conflict. Cities and citizens became divided between Guelfs—those individuals supporting the papacy—and Ghibellines—those supporting the emperor. The Buondelmonti faction in Florence took up the cause of the pope and his champion. The Uberti faction in Florence joined Frederick II. Fighting erupted in, outside, and all around the city. In the 1240s Frederick enjoyed a moment of ascendancy. Ghibellines came to power in Florence. They sought to revoke the concessions to Florence dating to the Tuscan League. By doing so, they sought to return the city to the imperial fold.[44]

The Ghibelline victory was, however, short-lived. In 1250 Frederick II died. A new government, called the *Primo Popolo*, came to power in Florence.[45] This new government consisted of officeholders drawn from the city's merchants and artisans. In fact, surviving electoral rolls from 1250 to 1260 suggest a clear attempt to remove nobles from high-level governmental posts and replace them with new men.[46] Additionally, they sought to minimize the role of Guelf and Ghibelline partisans at home, and disentangle the city from those conflicts abroad. The government added twenty militia companies with an elected "Captain of the People" to lead them. It kept the *podestà* in place with the understanding that he would be more sympathetic to the demands of more groups of people. Additionally, it created a new governmental body, the *anziani*. The *anziani* consisted of twelve men who represented six different geographical sections of the city.[47] The advent of the *Primo Popolo*, in short, opened a new chapter in the history of Florence: in 1250 Florence was over 1,200 years old, but the city's story was just beginning

1

LATE MEDIEVAL FLORENCE, 1251–1378

In ancient times Rome had started off as an unremarkable Italian town some distance from the coast. Over time its republican government solidified and the Romans began conquering their neighbors. Eventually, they exercised control over the entire Mediterranean Sea, in addition to lands in northern Europe, northern Africa, and the Middle East. To an outside observer in 1330, there were plenty of reasons to believe that the economic, political, and cultural influence of late medieval Florence might lead the city down the same mighty path as the past greatness of Rome. Already by 1300 Florence was the second largest city in Europe, behind only Paris.[1] Late medieval Florentine bankers and merchants fueled a transcontinental European economy. In the arts, Florentines like Cimabue, Brunetto Latini, Giotto, and Dante were introducing the city's cultures to the broader continent. Florence was conquering its neighbors, and it bought those neighbors that it could not conquer. Growth bred ambition. The Florentines began to argue that their city descended from Julius Caesar. As Rome's heir, Florentines claimed, their city owed allegiance to no one.

But things collapsed in the mid-fourteenth century. The Black Death decimated Florence between 1348 and 1350. The initial outbreaks of the plague killed roughly half of the city's population. Repeated new outbreaks meant that by 1427, Florence had dropped to less than 40,000 people, roughly a third of its former size.[2] Almost simultaneously, Florentine bankers and merchants met with unexpected setbacks abroad. Families that had financed kings now faced red ledgers and empty treasure chests. The city's political connections contracted. Certainly, the weakened position of Florence contributed to that contraction. Another part of the change, however, was determined for them: in 1305 the papacy moved to Avignon; in 1313 the emperor lost his last serious attempt to reassert control over Italy; and from 1337 the French focused their fighting on the English rather than the Italians. Consequently, Florentine politics became more regional. Florentine struggles were hardly unique in the chaotic fourteenth century. Yet, what set Florence apart from other cities was that the city's cultural influence, despite so many other setbacks, continued to grow. From 1382 Florentine culture increasingly gained influence, even as the city's politics were increasingly restricted to north-central Italy.

The *Primo Popolo* set Florence on a course to perhaps match the power of Ancient Rome. The *Primo Popolo* took steps to enhance their control over the city. They ordered the city's families to lower their towers to less than half of their former height. Weaker fortifications made it more difficult for families to create semi-independent enclaves within the city. As noted in the last chapter, they pressed the first gold Florin and stacked government offices with new men, rather than the noble lines more directly enmeshed in Guelf and Ghibelline conflicts. By 1254 at the latest the city's conquests, political reforms, and economic might made them the dominant city in Tuscany.[3] The Florentines also added new symbolism to their recent years of practical political independence. The city selected its own unique coat of arms—a red lily on a white field. In addition, they picked the lion (later called a *Marzocco*) as its civic symbol.[4] In fact, a sculpted *Marzocco* holding that coat of arms still holds silent vigil in front of the Palazzo Vecchio in Florence.

New power meant the city needed a new political space. In 1255 the *Primo Popolo* began construction on a building to house government officials.[5] That building still exists. Now a museum called the *Bargello*, most people today enter it through a doorway on the Via Ghibellina. Through the door a large loggia surrounded by late thirteenth-century columns opens before us (Figure 4). We can choose our own adventure. If we walk through the ground-floor archway we catch glimpses of some of the original mid-thirteenth-century architecture. Perhaps, instead, we choose to ascend the large staircase. As we climb, to the left lies the courtyard, to our right looms an ancient wall covered with countless coats of arms. Each coat of arms dates to the late medieval and Renaissance periods; each commemorates the tenure of a foreign official who temporarily lived in the building while he was charged with settling legal disputes. When we reach the top of the staircase, we find another colonnade, this one dating to 1317–20. To the right is a large room now stuffed with sculptures by Donatello, Michelangelo, and many others.[6]

Figure 4 Royal Museum, the court (i.e., Bargello Museum, the courtyard).
Anonymous Photomechanical Print. Florence. Library of Congress.

A bit farther on we find a chapel decorated with a fragmentary fresco of the Last Judgement. Tradition states that the fresco includes portraits of Dante Alighieri and his teacher Brunetto Latini. Unfortunately, in this case, tradition is probably wrong.[7]

The size of the Bargello implied the unlimited dreams of the *Primo Popolo*; an exterior inscription on the building made those ambitions explicit.[8] The inscription placed a prosperous Florence in a European context: "When most revered Alexander, to whom the world does homage, was pastor of the world, along with King William." Florence, thus, was more than just a city within north-central Italy. It was a city that coexisted with pan-European rulers Pope Alexander IV and the German King William of Holland. The inscription continued. Within that context, the city enjoyed just and noble rule. In particular, a Florentine official, the Captain of the People, is "resplendent to behold, renowned, and distinguished for his honesty. His battle standards identify him, and his banners express the badge of the people." Indeed, "His banner confers the enjoyments of life on those who want their city to rise up to the heaven. May Christ favor that city, and preserve it in a covenant of peace, because Florence is abounding in riches."[9] The wealth of this pan-European city had a great future. Florence's riches, its able governors, and military successes meant that it "has defeated its enemies in war and in a great uprising. It enjoys *fortuna*, distinctions, and a powerful people. The city confirms and acquires; inflamed it now safely extends its battle camps. It rules the sea, the land, and possesses the entire world."[10] The outcome of this empire was beneficial: "Through the rule of that city all of Tuscany becomes prosperous." The expanding Florentine empire harkened back to the greatness of Rome, for "Just like Rome, the city remains forever to lead triumphant men. It sees all things, bringing them together under certain law."[11] That is, Florence in 1255 was "just like Rome," and its growing status and good fortune was clearly a reward for its just leaders and Christian state. Invested with the authority of Rome it was only for now that the city shared the continent with the pope and the emperor. Under the *Primo Popolo* Florence was setting its sights on bigger things.

To turn inscription into reality Florence first had to calm its own factions. Different groups fought violently for power during those years, a combustible situation illustrated by the career of the chancellor in the *Primo Popolo* government, Brunetto Latini, which mirrored Florentine infighting during the latter 1200s.[12] Latini was born in Florence between 1220 and 1230. After training in Bologna, he was appointed chancellor of the *Primo Popolo* in 1250. In 1255 he wrote the inscription found on the wall of the Bargello. By the later 1250s it was clear that the city had failed to disentangle itself from broader Guelf and Ghibelline struggles. Thus, Latini was sent as a diplomat to France to seek aid against the city's Ghibelline enemies.[13] As Latini negotiated abroad the Florentine forces faced off against the Ghibelline armies of Manfred, skilled son of Frederick II. On September 4, 1260, the Ghibellines, led by Manfred's allies from Siena, decimated the Florentine-led Guelfs.[14]

A fourteenth-century manuscript reveals the slaughter. There, Florentine foot-soldiers, each holding a shield with the city's new lily, hold their spears against the advancing forces. The Ghibellines swing their swords. Their horses leap from Siena's fortified doors. The viewer needs little imagination to see what happens next: the bell on the proud Florentine cart in the background, called a *caroccio*, will soon fill the air, but not with swaggering sounds of victory. Instead, its tolls will mournfully mingle with the rancid reek of total defeat.[15] After the battle, the Ghibellines took over Florence and exiled the Guelfs. Legend has it that some Ghibellines even sought to raze Florence. In doing so, they hoped to remove the city from any future Guelf and Ghibelline struggles. Only the eloquence of the Ghibelline leader, Farinata degli Uberti, supposedly dissuaded his allies from their destructive plan.[16]

The diplomat Brunetto Latini heard about the defeat at Montaperti and the conquest of his city. Not surprisingly, he decided to stay in France.[17] During his time abroad he wrote several original and enduring literary works. Each reflected his interest in classical rhetoric. For example, he finished translations of texts by Cicero, Aristotle, Sallust, and others from Latin into French and Italian. In addition, he wrote his *Book of the Treasure*, first in French and then in Italian. This encyclopedic work featured a history of the world; Latini's guidance for governing well; and instructions for eloquent expression.[18] Latini's works fit into broader cultural trends in northern Italy. Specifically, in the late 1200s individuals called humanists were reading long-ignored classical authors and Latin texts. These humanists were incorporating ideas from these classical works into their own original Latin writings. They even were trying to imitate the Latin style of their favorite classical poets and historians! But the center of these new studies was in the Veneto, not in Florence.[19] Despite their shared interests, Brunetto Latini had little contact with these early humanists. In fact, not only Florence but all of Tuscany seems to have been tangential to the earliest humanist movement.[20] Mid-thirteenth-century Florence may have been a key player in international politics, but it was hardly a leading cultural center.

Ghibelline power in Florence was short-lived. After Montaperti Pope Urban VI joined forces with an ambitious but poor French noble Charles of Anjou (a patron, in fact, of Brunetto Latini). Pope Urban and Charles eyed the defeat of Ghibelline power in southern Italy, but they needed money to accomplish their goals. They turned to the exiled Florentine Guelfs: those Guelfs were far from home, but they still had access to piles of money. The pope, the French noble, and the Florentines reached an agreement. The Florentine Guelf exiles supplied cash to Charles; in exchange, Charles promised to them lucrative trading deals throughout southern Italy. The investment paid off. In 1266 Charles defeated Manfred at the Battle of Benevento. In 1267 the Florentines expelled the Ghibellines from their city and appointed Charles as *podestà* for ten years.[21] Guelf rule was established over significant parts of Italy. And Guelf rule began to mean French rule.

What happened to Brunetto Latini? Latini probably accompanied Charles to Florence, although he only rose to prominent government posts during the 1280s. During the 1280s or 1290s he may have been one of Dante's teachers, or at least Dante viewed him as an inspiration.[22] In late 1293 Latini died and was buried in the church of Santa Maria Maggiore, where a column may still mark what is left of his tomb.[23] In Florence today, Santa Maria Maggiore is a noticeably ancient church along the busy Via de' Cerretani. Most people quickly pass it by; its doors are often closed. Those leaving the *stazione* rush past it on their way to the Piazza del Duomo and the majesty of Brunelleschi's dome. Those walking in the other direction often have too little time for an ancient church, however intriguing: a train awaits to take them on another adventure.

Back in the 1270s, Charles of Anjou's ten-year term as *podestà* threatened to end the Florentine Republic. Certainly, between 1267 and 1277 the republic still functioned, and more urban merchants and less landed nobles were holding political offices.[24] But even a glance outside the city gates revealed how this political story usually ended. During the 1200s most northern Italian republics succumbed to the rule of one family. Ordinarily, a family seized power and then quickly changed the law. Those new laws always appeared to keep most of the old republican systems intact. In practice, however, the laws were careful to consolidate all real power in the hands of a single person.[25] It seemed that mighty Florence too would follow that path. In 1277 Charles's ten-year term ended. Predictably, he refused to relinquish power.

The coup may have worked—it had, after all, worked for similar nobles in other Italian cities. But in 1282 the people of Sicily revolted against Charles's rule over their island.[26] The revolt drew Charles's time, attention, and resources away from Florence. Amid the chaos, the Florentines moved out from under Charles's authority. They then turned to ironing out a new, hopefully more stable government. The establishment of the "Ordinances of Justice" in 1293 marked a critical moment. The Ordinances of Justice established six and then later eight representatives, called priors. Above the priors was a single Standard Bearer of Justice, who set the political agenda for the city. The terms of these and other offices were usually two, three, or four months. Additionally, dozens of families were labeled as "magnates" and banned from holding political office.[27]

Late medieval Florence continued to grow in power and influence under the new Ordinances of Justice. The exiled Guelfs in 1267 had used their money to overturn Ghibelline rule of their city. After returning to power the Guelfs sought to ensure that the newly exiled Ghibellines could not do the same. Consequently, a section of Ghibelline towers, houses, and property were destroyed to reduce the exiles' assets and to make space for a new declaration of Florentine power and independence. In 1298 the Florentines set the foundation stones for a new government palace atop the blackened rubble of Ghibelline fortunes.[28] For a design they chose to tie the building's style back to Ancient Roman traditions.[29] Even today people can walk past the inscription on the Bargello, which proudly proclaimed Florence's similarities with Ancient Rome, and then proceed to the Palazzo Vecchio, which announced the same basic message: Florence derived its power from Antiquity and had set its eyes on recreating the might of its ancestor.

The Palazzo Vecchio proclaimed other characteristics of the late medieval city. A series of crests line the building just below its primary outcropping. These coats of arms include the city's own crest, a token of Florentine collective identity and independence from others. In addition, the city continued to proclaim its allegiance to Guelf causes: both the papacy and the Angevins appear among the shields.[30] The problems with Charles of Anjou had done little to separate the Florentines from their Guelf allies.[31] In fact, the perceived connections between Florence, the French, and the papacy formed a long-lasting civic identity that helped shape the city's history for centuries to come. Over time terms like "Guelf" and "Ghibelline" became more amorphous. Over the decades the Florentines certainly antagonized the French; fought wars against the papacy; created alliances with emperors; and fought among themselves. But in late medieval Florence a basic assumption—one that overlay the daily, weekly, monthly, and annual hum of politics and diplomacy—arose that the city was pro-papal, pro-French, and pro-Guelf. The Palazzo Vecchio still proclaims those loyalties (Figure 5). Today, visitors usually look up to the building's soaring bell tower from the hot Piazza della *Signoria*. There, they join thousands of others who pause and pace across the paved square, frantically following umbrellas that demarcate different tour groups. The tower seems off-center from that viewpoint. However, if the centuries are stripped away our vantage turns to a historical space that is both similar and different. Originally people entered the building from doors on north side. When we view the structure from that point of view the tower appears symmetrical.[32]

The Ordinances of Justice brought some political stability, but it did little to quell the factions of late medieval Florence. In addition to individual fighting, family feuds, neighborhood disputes, and partisan pugnacities, two larger groups consistently competed for political power. On the one hand were the *popolo*. These Florentines enjoyed

Figure 5 Palazzo Vecchio. Photo by Dimitris Kamaras, April 22, 2016. Photo
accessed at Palazzo Vecchio, Florence | Dimitris Kamaras | Flickr.

guild membership and benefited from the city's unusually high-literacy
levels. They typically sided with the papacy in diplomatic disputes.
They favored political reforms that opened government offices to more
people. They tended to be from newer families. On the other hand, the
grandi encompassed both those elites dubbed magnates and other very
wealthy individuals. The *grandi* often descended from the oldest families
in Florence. They preferred that the government be limited to fewer
people. The *grandi* admired European court cultures. The *popolo* often
blamed Florentine social and political instabilities on feuds erupting
between extended *grandi* families. In the 1290s the Ordinances of Justice
represented a temporary victory for the *popolo*, even as these groups
fought over power for decades.[33]

By the early 1300s the powerful late medieval city remained pitted against itself. The *grandi* had taken control of the government. The exiled Ghibellines were not a serious threat, and thus the Guelfs in Florence split into two rival factions, the Whites and the Blacks. It did not take long for the Whites and Blacks to begin to follow old political fault lines. Around 1300 the Blacks appealed to Pope Boniface VIII to help them defeat their rivals. The pope, in turn, appealed to his French allies. To oppose the traditional papal/French/Guelf alliance, the Whites sought support from Ghibelline exiles and their allies. In the struggle, the Blacks proved victorious. They seized control over Florence and exiled their opponents. In exile, those Whites continued to strengthen their bonds with Ghibellines. They began to argue that the emperor needed to re-establish rule over Florence.[34] The most famous exiled member of the Whites was Dante Alighieri.

Dante Alighieri exemplifies the culture and politics of late medieval Florence. Like Brunetto Latini before him, Dante learned about a change of power in Florence while he was out of town. But, unlike Latini, Dante never returned to Florence. Instead, he spent more than twenty years in exile. Dante, like Latini, became a strong advocate for the potential of Italian as a written language. Most famously, Dante spent the years of his exile writing, editing, and perfecting his poetic masterpiece the *Divine Comedy.* In that work, Dante told of his journey through hell (*Inferno*), purgatory (*Purgatorio*), and paradise (*Paradiso*). Along the way Dante damned his enemies to horrific tortures while placing his allies in more amenable situations. The poem also reveals Dante's evolving political outlook. His *Inferno*, written first, remained heavily indebted to the Florentine Guelf civic outlook. However, in his *Purgatorio,* written sometime later, Dante embraced a Ghibelline vision of the emperor as a savior of Italy. In his last years of exile, as he wrote his *Paradiso*, Dante continued to promote an imperial perspective, even as he seems to have grown increasingly disillusioned that he would live to see the emperor enact God's righteous plan on earth.[35]

The political fights between the Blacks and Whites fit into continental contests over papal and imperial power. Odds favored the Whites and the Ghibellines by the early 1310s. At that time the emperor Henry VII seemed poised to do what Frederick I "Barbarossa," Frederick II, and Manfred all could not: conquer the Italian peninsula for the empire.[36] From exile, Dante wrote a new work, *On Kingship*, to build the imperial case to rule over Italy. Dante argued that God had chosen the emperor to rule over this world. He presented his case using the style of Latin, systematic argumentation, and authority of authors popular in European universities. His argument that the emperor, by rights, should rule the world had implications far beyond north-central Italy, and thus it was a text theoretically as accessible to a person at Oxford as it was one at Bologna. Perhaps it could be read back in Florence! After all, Florentine schools were gaining prestige in the first decades of the 1300s.[37] Indeed, the first push, albeit unsuccessful, to found a university in Florence came in 1321.[38] Meanwhile, at least one thinker, Geri d'Arezzo, was introducing the new humanist studies to Tuscany.[39] If the emperor was successful, late medieval Florence could become a central cog in a new continental Ghibelline network, and a leader in vernacular and maybe even humanist culture. Whether Guelf or Ghibelline, the future seemed wide open for the once minor Roman town.

That promise for the future transitioned to harbingers of disasters to come. Emperor Henry VII died before his plans could fully germinate. In practice, few people read Dante's *On Kingship*.[40] Neither man died in Florence. Dante lived out his life in exile. To this day his tomb receives international homage in Ravenna. Emperor Henry VII's final resting place is somewhat less well-known. Interested readers can take a short train trip from Florence to Pisa. In Pisa, they can walk or take a short bus ride from the train station to the cathedral complex. After a quick stop to pretend to hold up the Leaning Tower, they can enter the large cathedral itself, its walls still holding fragmentary inscriptions from plundered ancient monuments. Therein lies Henry VII, the would-be Ghibelline conqueror of Florence.

Ultimately, Dante's vernacular works helped shape the form of the modern Italian language, but in the fourteenth century Dante's use and defense of the vernacular marked the end of an era for Florence. Despite spending his last years in exile living in the same cities as the early Italian humanists, Dante's engagement with their studies seems to have been distant. He does not seem to have explored the same new classical sources that they were using; he does not seem to have adopted their new critical approach to texts; and he does not seem to have striven to emulate the new Latin style adopted in their poetry and historical writings.[41] Those humanists, in turn, did not share Dante's embrace of the vernacular. In the decades that followed it was the classical studies of the early humanists that became more popular than Dante's advocacy of the vernacular. It was not that vernacular writing stopped or that debates over its use ended. But from the mid-fourteenth century Latin gained prominence and cultural advantage over the vernacular that did not end until the early sixteenth century.[42] The early Italian humanists were the start of something new, while Dante symbolized an end to something else.

Of course, few saw the deaths of Dante or Henry VII as foreshadowing much of anything for late medieval Florence. The city continued to increase its power. Internally, government reforms aimed to increase stability. During the early 1300s two new government bodies, the Twelve Good Men and the Sixteen Standard Bearers, were created to advise the priors and the Standard Bearer of Justice. Collectively, these powerful offices became known as the *Signoria* and its Colleges, or just the *Signoria* for short. The *grandi* worked to ensure that the addition of more offices did not mean more people were involved in the government. Before the 1310s all guildsmen had helped elect the next priors. However, during that decade current priors began to handpick their successors. Even the two big legislative bodies in the government became closed off to most Florentines as former officeholders automatically joined a legislative assembly. Thus, in practice, specifically selected priors proposed new laws. Then, the people who had handpicked those priors were charged with approving or rejecting their proposals. Political power effectively coalesced around a small oligarchy.[43]

This increasingly oligarchic Florence seemed destined to fulfill the bold claims carved into the Bargello. The estimated 120,000 people living in Florence meant that it was an enormous late medieval city. The city's wool industry alone employed 10,000 people. Florentine banking and trading companies financed large and small-scale operations across Europe and beyond.[44] For example, the Bardi and Peruzzi families played no small role in bankrolling Edward III's opening salvos of the Hundred Years between 1337 and 1340.[45] It bears repeating: the companies of two Florentine families—not the city, not most of the city, just two families and their associates—were bankrolling the king of England. In politics, new growth opened opportunities for expansion. The papacy had left Rome in 1305 and moved its base of operations to Avignon, a papal territory in what is now southern France. Florentine Guelfism certainly did not prevent the Florentines from expanding their influence to fill the ensuing power vacuum in the territories to the city's south and east.[46] The Florentine chronicler Giovanni Villani foretold that "Florence, the daughter and creature of Rome, was in the ascendancy and destined for great things."[47]

The urban topography of Florence began morphing into the capital of a budding empire. By 1330 nearly 4,000 people in the city were employed in construction.[48] Four massive, surviving structures trace their origins to the promise of the late medieval city. The Florentines began work on a new cathedral. In the past the Baptistery had held central religious focus for most Florentines.[49] For example, the earliest extant view of Florence, dating to the mid-1300s, emphasized the Baptistery. In the image, men and women flank and pray to the Virgin Mary. The city of Florence shelters underneath the Virgin's cloak. Many churches are recognizable. Other buildings, like the Palazzo Vecchio, appear, but they all blend in a mashup of similar windows, towers, and colors. Yet, noticeable amid the structures is the distinct and demarcated Florentine Baptistery, a point to which the eye keeps returning (Figure 6).[50] By 1330, the city was outgrowing its ancient Baptistery. Thus, Arnolfo di Cambio began overseeing the construction of a new, massive cathedral that could accommodate around 30,000 people. It was to far exceed the size of churches in rival cities like Pisa or Siena. On September 8, 1296, a cardinal representing Pope Boniface VIII ceremonially laid the first stone of Santa Maria del Fiore.[51]

Other projects were also restructuring the urban topography of Florence. In the western part of town, now across the street from the bustling train

Figure 6 *Madonna della Misericordia—Detail of a View of Florence, c.* 1340–50. Fresco. Photo by Sailko. Museo del Bigallo, Florence.

station that shares its name, in 1280 the city's Dominican friars began building another massive church devoted to the Virgin Mary, called Santa Maria Novella. They began an expensive facade for the church and placed stylistic, pointed gothic arches as they worked their way up from the ground. Across town to the east, the Franciscan order, not to be outdone, began rebuilding Santa Croce to match and exceed their cross-town rivals in 1295. It was their third expansion of the church during the thirteenth century![52] Both Santa Maria Novella and Santa Croce anticipated huge crowds of worshippers. Plans for both churches included open squares out front to accommodate the growing Florentine population.[53] Around the same time, not far from the Baptistery, miracles began happening at the city's grain market. The structure—Orsanmichele—was rebuilt and repurposed to accommodate the increasingly important religious shrine.[54] In the 1330s the government assigned exterior spaces to important guilds. Each guild was to fix an image—painted or sculpted, permanent or portable—of their patron saint.[55]

These buildings enshrined innovative artistic styles. Even as plans were afoot to renovate Santa Croce, the artist Bencivieni di Pepo, called Cimabue, painted a crucifix to assist its worshippers. Little is known about this once-famous artist. Indeed, he is among the earliest Florentine artists whose name has survived time's relentless onslaught against historical memory.[56] On his crucifix Cimabue emphasized the divine nature of Christ and made use of forms popular throughout much of Europe. For example, the genre of the crucifixion scene was hardly unusual for a late thirteenth-century church. A visiting merchant, a friar, or a political figure would also have recognized the s-shape eloquence of Christ's body, a style common among period pieces. Thus, Florentines and foreigners found a common visual vocabulary in the painting.

Both Florentines and foreigners also saw some things that were new. The artist wanted viewers to see the human side of their savior. Cimabue's crucified Christ contorted his body from the tortures on the cross. Christ's loin cloth appears almost real: the painting becomes a window through which viewers could marvel at and contemplate Christ's sacrifice. Today, unfortunately, that window has lost much of its transparency. In 1966 the Arno drowned Santa Croce under meters of mud and water. After offering comfort to the faithful through seven hundred years of historical change, Cimabue's crucifixion, his masterpiece, was damaged.[57] Only old photographs remain (Figure 7).

The Florentine Giotto da Bondone further popularized the humanizing innovations by Cimabue and lesser-known painters, especially artists

Figure 7 Cimabue. *Crucifix, c.* 1285. Paint on wood. Heavily damaged version remains in Santa Croce, Florence. Anonymous Photo, pre-1966.

from Rome. Slightly younger than Cimabue, Giotto was born shortly before or after 1270 and died in 1337.[58] Like Cimabue, little about Giotto's life is known for certain. He was famous in his own lifetime. Dante claimed in his *Inferno*, in fact, that Cimabue had once been the talk of Italy, but now all look to Giotto.[59] Giotto may have been witty. About fifteen years after Giotto had died the writer Giovanni Boccacio told a story about him. Giotto and Forese da Rabatta, a Florentine lawyer and statesman renowned for his learning, were riding run-down horses to their properties in the Mugello, an area just north of Florence.[60] A rainstorm turned the road to mud. The cloaks of the lawyer and the artist became filthy. Forese looked at Giotto's sorry state and remarked, "Giotto, supposing we were to meet some stranger who had never seen you before, do you think he would believe that you were the greatest painter in the world?" Giotto replied to his equally disheveled colleague, "Sir, I think he would believe it if, after taking a look at you, he gave you credit for knowing your ABC."[61]

Over a long career Giotto popularized the new humanizing style in and outside of Florence. His masterpiece were his frescoes for the Arena Chapel in Padua. In Padua, the banker Enrico Scrovegni had inherited and then further built a fortune through usury. Usury was a sin, and consequently, Enrico worried about the state of his soul. After the Jubilee year in 1300 he temporarily decided to change his ways. Thus, he paid to build a chapel and hired Giotto to cover its walls with frescoes. On one wall Giotto painted the Last Judgement. In that image, Christ rules over the court of heaven. Below him to the right are saved souls anticipating their ascent to the heavenly crowd of angels. To Christ's left the damned regret their earthly choices as Satan inflicts eternal punishments. Between the saved and damned, directly below Christ, Giotto painted a cross. At its foot, a penitent Scrovegni hands his chapel to angels. The implication is clear: Scrovegni could afford to construct a chapel, and through that action he hoped the angels could persuade Christ to place him on the right side.

Many of Giotto's frescoes in the Arena Chapel depict scenes from the life of Christ. Within them, images repeatedly suggest Scrovegni's penitent rejection of usury. For example, late medieval Christians associated the figure of Judas with the sin of usury. His presence, mistakes, and punishments are unusually prominent throughout the frescoes. In one fresco depicting the betrayal of Christ by Judas, Judas's yellow cloak centers the scene. The size and color of the cloak continually bring the viewer's eyes back to Judas's face: his lips are puckered, shortly before or after he has kissed Christ in friendship. Perhaps his monstrous face reveals a dawning realization of the gravity of his mistake. Christ clearly knows what is coming: unlike Judas's treacherous features, Christ's face reveals stoic resignation.[62] Giotto carried his style across the Italian peninsula, working in Rome, Assisi, Naples, and of course Florence. His chapels for the Bardi and Peruzzi families in Santa Croce contain the same emphases on humanizing divine figures.[63] It was a perfected version of an increasingly popular style, and a Florentine was at the front of it. But it was a shared style and visual vocabulary that spoke to and responded to people far beyond Florence.

By around 1330, in short, late medieval Florence was prosperous, growing, and powerful. Under the Ordinances of Justice, factions and a decreasing number of families dominated politics, but those realities did not hinder the city's expansion. The city's merchants traded the city's wool across Europe. Its bankers were the backers of kings. Its building projects bespoke a capital of continental aspirations. Could late medieval Florence, like Ancient Rome before it, build a powerful, lasting empire? With the benefit of hindsight such aspirations might seem laughable. But remove the layers of history and resituate late medieval Florence in its own context. Had not Rome itself started as a small Italian republic before shockingly expanding its might over the Mediterranean and beyond? The wealth was there. Politics were solidifying. Florentine cultural influence was growing.

One proud illustration within Giovanni Villani's *Chronicle* left little doubt about Florence's potential for the future. In that illustration, a bearded Julius Caesar stands outside stout city walls. He gives the command to found Florence. Another central figure looks heavenward, either thanking God for the foundation or receiving benediction for the action.[64] Although Villani used other sources to write about those earliest days of Florentine history, he wrote the latter parts of his *Chronicle* as the events happened. In 1348 he recorded that a great sickness had struck his city. He then left a blank so he could return later to fill in when the pestilence ended. He died before he had the chance.[65]

Florentine's demographic, economic, and political possibilities crashed in the 1330s and 1340s.[66] During those decades, Florentine banking companies became overextended. Creditors began cashing out their investments. Those withdrawals, in turn, made it impossible to cover other financial gambles. For example, the Bardi and the Peruzzi families had loaned the king of England, Edward III, over a million florins to finance his wars against the French. However, Edward had no ability to repay those debts. The families thus lost the money. The losses then spooked other major clients. The pope, fearing the Florentines families lacked capital, removed most Florentine bankers from papal banking accounts.[67] Things became so bad by 1340 that the Bardi family attempted a coup in Florence to force the government to assist with their financial affairs. By early 1342 the city of Florence was in a full-blown economic crisis. Something had to be done.

The Florentines invited the noble, Walter of Brienne, to come to their city and fix their problems.[68] Walter had been the city's mercenary captain—called a *condottiere*—in their recent failed attempt to conquer Lucca. Moreover, Walter was well-connected in southern Italy and in Avignon. He could, they hoped, use his influence to alleviate some of their economic stresses.[69] Walter, however, had bigger plans for his role in Florence. By September he had declared himself *signore* of Florence for life. As *signore,* he turned to the city's economic woes. He changed taxation laws in Florence and in its countryside. He sought to save money through ending a regional war. Despite Walter's initial support from the *grandi,* many of his policies most benefited the *popolo.* Consequently, Walter's rule was brief. On July 26, 1343, he was removed from office and thrown out of the city. For a second time Florence had narrowly avoided succumbing to rule by one person. By September the Ordinances of Justice had been reestablished. By October the Florentines had opened office-holding to include more new men and their families. By December they sought to roll all public debt in Florence into a single *"monte"* (literally "mountain") to deal with Florentine economic problems.[70] But things kept getting worse. More debts, famine, political unrest, and territorial losses struck the city.[71]

Then came the Genoese ships. These mercantile ships sailed back to Italy from the Black Sea. In addition to their goods, they carried a pathogen on the fleas of rats and, in an even deadlier form, through human fluids. Sick individuals developed buboes on their bodies. Those even unluckier developed severe pneumonic symptoms. From the ports, down the roads, through the mountains, it spread. During the spring and summer of 1348 some 50,000–60,000 Florentines, half the population, died.[72] People struggled to make sense of the seemingly merciless and random killing. The pious and the impious died alike. Perhaps God had abandoned the world: some started to disregard the laws of people and God as irrelevant in the face of the inevitable onslaught of death. Perhaps God was angry: others hoped extreme measures of piety could appease Him. Flagellants, for example, walked through streets littered with unimaginable sights, smells, and sounds, hoping to gain the penance of the population by whipping themselves. Explanations for what was happening also came from proto-scientists and astrologers.[73] One catastrophe compounded another. The plague continued to come back through the fourteenth and later centuries. Sometimes it even mirrored the demographic decimation of the original pathogen.[74]

The Black Death frosted a crumbled cake of catastrophes that mocked earlier Florentine ambitions. City walls now encircled fallow fields and abandoned houses. Cavernous churches echoed the few surviving voices of the faithful. Before the plague the Florentines had laid the foundations for Santa Maria del Fiore, which they planned to become the biggest cathedral in Europe. Giotto himself had designed its bell tower. That tower was shaded with half-built, stagnant walls. After all, who survived to build them? Who was going to pay for it? The external niches of Orsanmichele lay, with few exceptions, empty. The Florentines had opened office-holding to new families; however, half of those newly eligible men were dead. A political stalemate ensued in which individuals, families, and factions fought over how open to make the city's government. Neither *popolo* nor *grandi* possessed enough power to sway the political pendulum one way or the other. The diminished size of Florence meant that once-promising regional conquests failed to lead to further expansion.[75] The Hundred Years' War and the papal residence at Avignon separated Florence from traditional Guelf allies. For over 150 years Florence became a regional power with regional aspirations.

Yet, paradoxically, the city's cultural influence increased even as so much else in Florence declined. Francesco Petrarch played a primary role in that development. The Florentines had exiled Petrarch's father in the same Black and White Guelf troubles that had afflicted Dante.[76] Petrarch was born during his father's exile. He initially attended law school but despised it. Thus, he dropped out and instead focused on literature. In the mid-1300s each part of Italy spoke similar but different versions of a single language. Petrarch wrote over 300 poems in the version of Italian spoken in Florence. In line after line Petrarch wrote of his lost love Laura, fame, and salvation. Simultaneously, Petrarch described his conversion from a worldly man to a man of faith.[77] The book proved enormously popular and influential. After Petrarch, poets tried to emulate his forms and style. Petrarch's imitators included men, women, rich, poor, famous, and forgotten. Sometimes the works were highly original. Sometimes derivative.[78] But it was the Florentine form of Italian at the center of those poems.

Petrarch's fame and impact extended beyond his Italian poems. He helped transfer the center of the new humanist studies from their traditional homes in Padua, Verona, and Bologna to Florence. Inspired by a teacher in Bologna, Petrarch cemented his scholarly reputation by creating a new edition of the Ancient Roman historian Livy.[79] Petrarch established a vast network of admirers and followers interested in a deeper knowledge of the classical past, classical authors, and classical styles.[80] In works such as *On His Own Ignorance and that of Many Others* he claimed that humanists focused on practical concerns, whereas university philosophers, theologians, and proto-scientists studied esoteric minutia. In his *Ascent of Mt. Ventoux* Petrarch used a religious allegory to express appreciation for the beauty of the world. He popularized long-forgotten classical texts. He even, somewhat hypocritically, wrote a letter to the Roman patrician Cicero to scold that man for his obsession with civic honors and wealth![81] Peripatetic Petrarch's many correspondences with Florentines planted the seeds of humanist learning in Florence, although he himself never visited the city.[82] Giovanni Boccaccio began to cultivate those seeds into a Florentine forest.[83]

Giovanni Boccaccio served as a crucial link to popularize humanism among members of the Florentine patriciate. Boccaccio grew up in the *oltrarno* quarter of Florence before spending significant time in the Kingdom of Naples, where his family had business contacts. In Naples, Boccaccio began his literary career, but it was after his return to Florence that his star began to glow most brightly.[84] Back at his family's ancestral home, he wrote his vernacular masterpiece the *Decameron* between the latter 1340s and early 1350s. The *Decameron* pretended to tell the tale of a group of young people who had fled the plague in Florence by escaping to a country estate. There, they passed the time by telling 100 reused, revised, and/or original stories. The stories were written to entertain, but Boccaccio also lodged frequent attacks against hypocrisy, greed, and corruption among his contemporaries.[85] In one story, a thief made his final confession to a priest. In the story, the man confessed to a multitude of made-up trivialities instead of his numerous very real crimes. The priest was so convinced of the thief's blameless life that he sought his posthumous beatification.[86] In another story, a prioress prepares to punish one of her nuns for sexual improprieties. The nun, however, points out that the prioress has the pants of a priest on her head. Thus, the entire convent is permitted to enjoy future dalliances.[87]

In the long run Boccaccio's *Decameron*, like Petrarch's poems, centered both writers in the history of Italian literature. But in the more immediate surroundings, Petrarch and then Boccaccio's humanist studies earned the respect of and influence on their contemporaries. After the 1350s Boccaccio began writing original Latin writings in emulation of classical models. Weighty encyclopedic tomes emerged from his pen. One work collected known knowledge about the pagan gods. Another sought to complement Petrarch's *On Famous Men* with a companion piece, *On Famous Women,* in which Boccaccio crafted over a hundred short and long biographies of women from Antiquity to the present.[88] Just as importantly, Boccaccio collected classical books. He bequeathed them to the church of Santo Spirito, the largest church in the *oltrarno* quarter in Florence. Petrarch and Boccaccio's correspondences show that humanism was hardly absent from Florence prior to the 1370s. But their books, their writings, and the writings of their followers helped morph Florence into a center for humanist studies.[89]

As humanist studies grew Florence continued its descent into factional infighting and regional politics. Around 1350 two families emerged to lead the city's most powerful factions.[90] The groups continued to follow the lines associated with the *popolo* and *grandi*. On the one side, the Albizzi, the Strozzi, the Rucellai, and others worked to restrict office-holding to fewer families. They advocated to continue the city's traditional Guelf alliances with the papacy and the French. Their leading opponents were members of the Ricci family. The Ricci were more sympathetic to demands for a more open political structure. Additionally, they were more willing to explore diplomatic options beyond the usual Guelf allies. Families like the Medici and the Alberti allied with the Ricci. Both major factions competed for allies in Florence. The stalemate between them continued throughout the 1350s, 1360s, and early 1370s.[91]

However, these two factions encompassed only a fraction of the Florentine population. The Albizzi, the Ricci, their allies, and their enemies coexisted with many other social and political groups. Most people only tangentially associated themselves with either faction. Instead, they primarily looked out for their own security, honor, power, piety, and wealth. Francesco Datini, for example, became one of the richest people in Europe in the late 1300s. Tens of thousands of letters and documents survive by, to, and about him. These unparalleled documents include information about Datini's businesses, his friends, his family, and even his personal life. For example, in 1386, his wife Margherita wrote to inform her absent husband about the state of his businesses. She was blunt: "You have left two fellows in charge of the warehouse here in Florence who don't have half a brain between them" and "It seems a place run by children. I would suggest that if you have another incompetent over there, send him here, because this is how you seem to prefer things."[92] Letters like these unveil a portrait of a late fourteenth-century businessperson. Datini and his friends combined too much wealth with ambition to totally avoid politics, but their primary concerns clearly lay elsewhere.[93]

Florentines began to explore new ways to convince others to their points of view. By the 1360s and 1370s this motivation, at least in part, led some to start emulating Petrarch's humanist studies. Specifically, they emulated Petrarch's own writings and followed his recommendations to learn new styles and content from classical books. For example, Luigi di Teri di Nello Gianfigliazzi crafted a synopsis of rhetorical books by

Cicero. Contemporaries, in turn, praised Luigi Gianfigliazzi's learning. Lapo da Castiglionchio the elder, meanwhile, tried to emulate Petrarch's letters. Lapo even tried applying some of his new classical learning in a speech to the pope in 1366.[94] Both Lapo and Luigi were hardly literary giants during the late 1300s. But both men took the new humanist studies and applied them in practical situations. It was those sorts of humanist studies, especially in Latin, that came to underlie so much of the culture of Renaissance Florence in the years to come.

The stalemate between the Albizzi and Ricci factions ended during the 1370s. After years of fighting, the two factions agreed to form an alliance to keep government offices restricted to fewer people. Other coalitions formed to oppose them. These opposition groups won. The Ricci, the Albizzi, the Strozzi, the Ridolfi, and others were all banned from office. Office-holding, once again, was expanded. In addition, the new people in power were less devoted to Guelf loyalties.[95] During the decades of papal absence in Avignon, the Florentines had taken control over Pistoia, Prato, San Gimignano, Volterra, and other communities. Already in the 1360s that expansion had begun to run against renewed papal interest in their own lands to the south and east of Florence.[96] Those simmering conflicts and the diminished Guelpism of the government opened a war between the papacy and Florence in 1375. In the conflict, Florence, whose government palace proclaimed its Guelf loyalties, allied with Ghibelline Milan against the pope.[97]

It was a consequential conflict. For the pope, the conflict encouraged efforts underfoot to return from France to Rome. From Rome, Pope Gregory XI hoped to be able to better lead the war effort.[98] But in 1378 the pope had hardly returned to Rome before he unexpectedly died. Pro-French cardinals opposed the election of his successor Urban VI and elected their own rival pope. Faced with a split in the Church, Urban concluded a peace agreement with the Florentines. For the next forty years there were two and at times even three competing popes.[99] Papal weakness prolonged the period in which Florence enjoyed a weak power to their south and east. At times Florence declined to take advantage of the situation. At other times the Florentines expanded their territory further, to include Arezzo, Montepulciano, Pisa, and others.[100]

Within Florence itself, the empowerment of new men, wartime tensions, and economic problems created yet another combustible brew in the volatile city. In May 1378, Salvestro de' Medici became Standard Bearer of Justice. From that platform he worked with individuals still barred from governmental offices to demand enfranchisement and greater economic equality.[101] On July 21, 1378, 7,000 people stormed the Bargello. The next day they seized the government palace.[102] By July 31 they had created new electoral bags that provided greater inclusion for people from even the poorest guilds. Their government was short-lived. By September members of the lowest of the guilds, the Ciompi, had once again been deemed ineligible for government office. Other new men retained their eligibility for a time, but they too lost most of their power by 1382. Florence was set to embark on a new chapter in its internal political affairs.[103] In this new chapter, Florentines dressed their internal politics, diplomatic regionalism, and changing civic identity in the guises of humanism and new art. Renaissance Florence was a city juxtaposed between thwarted political ambitions and cultural influence beyond its wildest dreams

2

OLIGARCHS IN THE EARLY RENAISSANCE, 1379–1433

Buonaccorso Pitti's horse gave way from the punishment. Again. Pitti had been entrusted on November 22, 1394, to carry a secret mission to the Duke of Orleans in Paris. The success of Pitti's mission hinged upon arriving to the duke before a rival diplomat carrying a contrary message.[1] It is impossible after 600 years to know exactly what Buonaccorso looked like as he raced across the French countryside—historians do not have even an approximation of Pitti's height, his weight, his facial features, or his body structure. Such is the nature of men and women dead long before the invention of widespread portraiture, let alone photographs. Yet, whatever his facial features they were soon beaming: Pitti claims in his self-congratulatory chronicle that his mission was a success.

Buonaccorso Pitti exemplifies a leading patrician in early Renaissance Florence. The Pitti family benefited from a new constriction of political power around a small oligarchy. Although no known artistic works survive from a Pitti-paid commission, Buonaccorso must have joined other Florentines in paying for a religious icon, a painted decoration, a sculpture, or some other piece. He had many fashionable artistic styles to choose from in early Renaissance Florence. Each style spoke a dialect within the transcontinental cultural languages spoken in early fifteenth-century Europe. Finally, like his contemporaries, Pitti dabbled in enough humanist studies to appear learned. Pitti's letters and orations no longer exist, but in them he would have used new sources and styles to make arguments similar to traditional Florentine claims: Florence was heir to Rome and thus rightly looked to expand its territory and influence. By 1400, however, such claims ran hollow. The political reach of Florence increasingly became limited to Tuscany and the Italian peninsula. Florentines continued to send occasional diplomats, like Buonaccorso Pitti, to distant places like France or the empire. But the continental centrality and political promise of late medieval Florence had ended.

The Florentine patriciate reacted to the challenges of the Ciompi in 1378 by limiting access to real political power. Throughout the 1300s, the Florentines had quarreled over how many people ought to share political power in their city. After 1382, the number of people theoretically eligible to hold political office greatly expanded. By 1433, in fact, two out of every three Florentine males theoretically could hold a political office.[2] Thus, at first glance it looked like the pendulum had swung back to the side of a more inclusive government. However, things were not as they seemed. The apparent openness masked the transition of political power to a smaller group of citizens.

From the 1380s controls were created to consolidate power and limit the numbers of people serving in a few specific offices. The system was complicated. People became eligible for political office by paying their taxes, joining guilds, and reaching a certain age. People in one government office, called the *accoppiatori*, were charged with filling electoral bags with the names of Florentines deemed eligible for important government positions. Lots of Florentines met the basic requirements and so lots of names went into the bags. At a later date, different people then drew the names of new officeholders from the prepared bags. Starting in 1387, the *accoppiatori* gained new powers. They still filled one election bag with all the eligible names; however, they also created a second electoral bag. In the second bag, the *accoppiatori* placed a small number of handpicked names. Then, at election time, six of the priors came from the first bag and two of them came from the second bag. In effect, the changes meant that allies of the *accoppiatori* always made up at least 25 percent of the priors. The system was not perfect. Specifically, the *accoppiatori* were limited by the lists of people deemed eligible for office. Such lists contained both their allies and their enemies. Even if the *accoppiatori* could always pick friends for two seats, that still meant that rivals could fill the six others. Thus, in 1393, the *accoppiatori* were provided the authority to create a new list of eligible names. From those new lists they filled both the big and the smaller election bags. Even better, the law allowed them to increase from two to three the number of names pulled from the smaller bag.

These changes fundamentally altered the Florentine government. The *accoppiatori* placed the names of thousands of Florentines into the big election bag. Any one of them could theoretically fill a seat on the city's most powerful governmental body! However, actually, about sixty people and their close allies began making policies and decisions for the city. Those few dozen people routinely held office; advised others then in office; and served as diplomats or other appointed positions. Most Florentines consented to the system because they knew that they were eligible for office. They knew that the *accoppiatori* had placed their names in the bigger electoral bag. They dreamed of the honors that awaited them on the day that, hopefully soon, their names were drawn for office. Although the influence of the office itself might be limited, the honor of holding that office would be much longer lasting. So, they waited. So, in place of the fourteenth-century swings between open and closed office-holding, Florentine politics in the early Renaissance became about accepting a theoretically open government that in reality was closed to only a few.[3]

One key to the system was the assumption that office-holding itself was a primary component to measure a person's social status. Florentines at the top of the Florentine social ladder had all held the top offices in the Florentine Republic. Within that group, the most prestigious could trace generations of officeholders back to the original Ordinances of Justice in 1293. These men complemented their family traditions with wealth.[4] They recognized each other's status by intermarrying. Marriage was complex in Renaissance Florence. Each daughter in each family possessed a dowry that a bride bought to a marital match. The value of the dowry reflected the family's status and ambitions. The dowries for elder daughters usually, but not always, were higher than for younger children. Dowries in elite families far exceeded those of women from poorer families. Florentines from newer families could use marriage to make up for their shorter family histories. Sometimes individuals from illustrious lineages fell on hard times. A newly wealthy family, thus, could make their matches more desirable by increasing the size of their dowries. Additionally, their wealth meant that they could explore matches with less dowered younger daughters than less wealthy, but more established, families.[5] Marriage connections could, in turn, both help and be helped by holding political office.

Gregorio Dati provides one example of this new consensus politics and social mobility in action. Dati's early life reflected his modest means and middling social status. Dati joined a trading company in 1385 as a junior partner. All the partners had invested money up front, but Dati lacked the funds to do so. Thus, the other partners agreed to loan him his share. In return, Dati agreed to receive only 1/12 of the company's profits. As a junior partner, Dati traveled to distant Valencia to do the company's legwork while the more senior investors stayed in Florence. Dati was clearly good at his job. Already in 1387 the company revised its charter. Now Dati invested 500 florins of his own money while retaining the same 1/12 share of the profits. Six years later a third renegotiation occurred. This time Dati invested 1,000 florins and slightly increased his profit share. Then, in 1395 a further adjustment was made. In that year Dati created a new company in which he enjoyed a senior role. Dati invested money and remained in Florence. The son of one of his partners traveled abroad to manage the company's daily operations. By 1403 Dati was diversifying his portfolio to include rental properties. Over twenty years he had risen a long way from his previous humble origins!

Dati used his acumen and wealth to help increase his social status. His marriages reflect some of these changes. First, he married Bandecca di Buonaccorso Berardi, who was the daughter of one of his first business partners. The marriage tied Dati to a family of modest standing in Florence.[6] It also added a marital bond to the financial ones in the business partnership. Berardi's untimely death unfortunately ended the short marriage. Dati, a widower, married again, this time to Isabetta di Mari Vilanuzzi. The Vilanuzzi family were neither among the wealthiest nor most political families in Florence. Thus, the match again shows Dati's middling social status even into the early 1390s. But things changed as Dati's finances improved over the next decade. After Isabetta's death, Dati married Ginevra Brancacci, a woman from a leading Florentine family, in 1403. Several factors made the match between a Brancacci bride and parvenu Dati possible. One, Dati's wealth made him a possible match. Two, the Brancacci noticed Dati's rising position because they both lived in the same neighborhood in Florence. Three, Ginevra was a 21-year-old widower. Her status for a second marriage was less than it had been for her first.

The Dati family continued their rise. After forming a marital connection with a leading Florentine family, Dati was elected to the *Signoria* for the first time. While Gregorio Dati was in office, Ginevra Brancacci gave birth to a son. Dati's colleagues in government were chosen as the child's godparents. Through that action, Dati reinforced his bonds with these colleagues. The bond also ensured that Dati's son would enjoy powerful allies later in life. The Dati family also benefited from the ecclesiastical career of Gregorio's brother Leonardo. The Church provided a different path for some people to devote their lives to God and also to improve their social standing. Successful members of the church could become renowned for their piety. They also could find the ear of powerful people. They could themselves receive incomes, lands, and positions of direct political and spiritual power. Although a churchman probably lacked a direct heir, he could share the fruits of his success with his extended family members. That was what Leonardo did. In 1411, Ginevra Brancacci died. By that time, Gregorio's brother Leonardo Dati had achieved enough standing in the Church that he requested and obtained absolution for her sins from the pope himself.[7] The action reflected both the brothers' pious concern for Ginevra's soul and their new social position. From humble origins, Gregorio Dati had climbed the Florentine social ladder and obtained the economic, social, and political standing of a Florentine patrician.

Dati was not alone. In fact, Florentines enjoyed a surprising degree of social mobility during the early 1400s.[8] Florentine society possessed a robust middle class with a more equitable wealth distribution than the twenty-first-century United States.[9] Florentines used their money, in part, to purchase paintings, furniture, architecture, sculpture, manuscripts, and other commodities.[10] Certainly, much of this material culture aimed to secure the salvation of pious patrons. Yet, culture, then and now, always simultaneously speaks many different languages to many different people. As people sought to save their souls, they also tried to impress their neighbors with their displays of wealth. As people showed off their fortunes, they also tried to convince others that this specific commission was only the latest addition to a long familial tradition of such largesse. In short, people could increase their social status in early Renaissance Florence, but they needed money, political power, and a good marriage to do it. They then used the multiple languages of art and literature to present their respective cases for that status. Culture became, in part, a form of competitive, common, and conspicuous consumption.

Humanist learning became a tool to proclaim, and in some cases improve, a person's status. Petrarch and Boccaccio had encouraged enough interest in humanist studies to secure the election of Coluccio Salutati as chancellor of the Florentine Republic in 1375. As chancellor, Salutati was charged with writing letters from Florence to other rulers, overseeing diplomatic commissions, and other similar tasks. He also possessed an incalculable amount of unofficial influence gained from his stable position in the government over three decades. That long tenure made his institutional knowledge and extensive familiarity with Florentine allies, antagonists, and issues an essential resource for the transitory office holders. Salutati used his humanist studies to implement major changes to the style and content of official Florentine letters. He wrote state dispatches that emulated classical examples. He drew upon his classical studies to better defend Florentine actions.[11] These changes drew the attention of other leaders and learned people. They responded to Salutati's claims and made their own. What had begun as a literary fad in the Veneto had morphed into a key language of statecraft, and the Florentines were leading the conversation.

Humanist studies continued to gain popularity within Florence itself. Salutati's successes inspired more Florentines to explore classical studies. Salutati joined forces with the friar Luigi Marsili. The two men encouraged their contemporaries to make use of Boccaccio's book bequest to Santo Spirito.[12] The scope of humanist studies was expanding. By the late 1300s Greek was little read in most areas of Europe and Greek manuscripts were hard to come by. Thus, in the 1390s Salutati and the patrician Palla di Nofri Strozzi spearheaded the hire of the Byzantine Greek Manuel Chrysoloras. Chrysoloras arrived from Byzantium to teach Greek from a house in Florence. He brought Greek works that humanists had read about but previously never seen. He began receiving payments from the city to teach Florentines and non-Florentines alike.[13] By 1399 these students began publishing translations of these newly rediscovered Greek texts into Latin.[14] Gifted students found positions in bureaucracies and courts across the Italian peninsula. The peripatetic papal curia proved particularly supportive of these learned, eloquent men. For a time in the early 1400s the most talented humanist scholars worked for the pope![15]

By the 1410s and 1420s humanism had become a cultural phenomenon that stretched across social classes. Thousands of Florentines—both men and women, were literate, meaning that they could read their local dialect of Italian. Many also, although certainly not most, could also read Latin. Additionally, daily life of all but the poorest Florentines involved writing materials for contracts, receipts, inventories, and other practical matters. Florentines used those writing materials to copy popular and useful texts: model speeches, historical accounts, popular sermons, sections from the Bible, or a favorite vernacular story. Starting in the 1410s and 1420s Florentines became increasingly interested in humanist studies in classical eloquence, history, and virtue. They began to include translations and summaries of new texts from Byzantium in their small literary compilations.

Most of these Florentines were undoubtedly interested in the texts they were reading, to one degree or another. Yet, another reason that

Florentines dabbled in humanism was to be or at least appear learned, impress others, and, hopefully, one day attain the honor of political office. By the early 1420s people began to equate learning and eloquence with an ability to emulate the complicated rhetoric of classical authors and refer to their writings. Eloquence was beneficial in all aspects of daily life, from business negotiations to after-dinner conversations. Better rhetoric helped people to make more persuasive arguments. Thus, the most eloquent individuals, even if they lacked more traditional marks of social status, became sought after for civic and political positions previously reserved for men from the oldest and wealthiest Florentine families.[16]

By the 1420s Florence was a leader in humanist studies becoming popular throughout Europe. Notable scholars in France copied manuscripts and delivered eloquent orations. Centers of learning formed around the royal court, French dukes, and major cities.[17] People in the Holy Roman Empire adopted classical rhetoric to correspond with Italian humanists.[18] Humanist studies were developed and catered to local situations across the continent.[19] As such, humanism in early Renaissance Florence participated in a shared literary culture, continually influencing and being influenced by neighbors near and far. Certainly, other important learned foci continued unabated, in and outside Florence. Philosophers and theologians, for example, continued to create innovative works that cared little for the humanist studies of eloquence, ethics, and the classical world.[20] But by the 1420s the popularity of humanism was on the rise.

While social competitions helped promote the popularity of humanism in Renaissance Florence, key humanist works reflected the city's changing external political situation. The Great Schism in the papacy meant that rival French and Italian popes vied for recognition from the powers of Europe. Additionally, rivals to the throne of Naples each claimed descent from the House of Anjou. In place of traditional Guelf support for French and papal policies, leading Florentines promoted policies of demurral. They tried to support Italian claimants to the papacy while avoiding offense to the French. Many Florentines began to promote the idea of limited expansion for themselves and policies that encouraged stability among the other powers of Italy. Guelfism certainly was not dead in the city, but Florentines increasingly disagreed about how much support to offer traditional Guelf allies or even what Guelfism meant.[21] Instead of conflicts with transnational impact, the Florentines focused on the nearby Romagna.[22]

Works by Coluccio Salutati reflected these changes. For example, during the war with the papacy between 1375 and 1378, Salutati turned away from the language of Guelfs and Ghibellines. Instead, he argued that Florence was an independent republic with republican traditions predating the struggles between the popes, the French, and the emperors.[23] In another example, by the late 1390s the Florentines were seeking an alliance with the emperor to fight against Milan. In that context, Salutati wrote a treatise, *On Tyranny*, in which he defended the rights and authority of the Ancient Roman emperor. Because the emperor in 1399, in theory, derived his own authority from Caesar, Salutati's defense implicitly assisted the arguments of Florence's would-be Ghibelline ally.[24] Not all Florentines agreed with these changes, and fights over Florentine civic identity became yet another source of contention in Renaissance Florence. These competitions between Florentines are seen in the city's visual culture.

The church of Orsanmichele reflects the piety of the city as well as the varied visual languages in which Florentines made their arguments for power and status (Figure 8) in the early fifteenth century.[25] Since the disasters of the mid-fourteenth century the exterior niches on the building had remained empty. During that same time, Orsanmichele had become a citywide holy shrine.[26] In 1365 its image of the Virgin Mary, for example, had been designated a protector of the city.[27] The Standard Bearer of Justice was required to swear allegiance to the city of Florence within the building. In a 1386 law that government official was also required to go to Orsanmichele to offer fruit to St. Anne, who the Florentines believed had helped them expel Walter of Brienne.[28] Thus, the state of the building reflected upon the city itself. The giant open-air vaults that once had stored towering mounds of grain were filled in with delicate gothic windows. A beautiful tabernacle enclosed the holiest space within the building.[29] But the exterior niches on the building remained empty.

In April 1406, the Florentine government ordered the city's guilds to decorate their assigned niches or lose them to a different group.[30] The law spurred a flurry of activity. Each guild chose an artist to sculpt its patron saint. Each guild wanted its sculpture to boast its piety, wealth, and cultural sophistication. Simultaneously, so many different patrons meant that the sculptures on Orsanmichele made use of a range of then fashionable visual languages.[31] The sculptures reinforced the consensus structure of the Florentine government. At Orsanmichele, the sculpted patron saints reflected the same guilds run by the same people who ran the city. When Florentines used the sculptures to facilitate a prayer, they also implicitly accepted the central role of those saints and their guilds as powerbrokers over Florence. The sculptures guarded the holy sites

Figure 8 Orsanmichele. Photo by Jordiferrer, August 8, 2016. Florence.

within Orsanmichele in the same way that the guildsmen in Florentine offices guarded Florentine liberty.[32] That monolithic message masked the fierce competition for honors among Florentines.

The sharp differences between visual styles at Orsanmichele reveal the fissures and competitions among Florentines. For example, the Cloth-Merchants' Guild commissioned Lorenzo Ghiberti to create a bronze statue of St. John the Baptist for their niche (Figure 9). Bronze cost roughly ten times as much as stone. Consequently, nobody had used it for a free-standing sculpture since the Ancient Romans. A sculpture of the patron saint of Florence blurred the boundaries between the city as a whole and the specific guild of the Cloth-Merchants.[33] Moreover, Ghiberti and his guild patrons chose to depict St. John in a way popular in courts across Europe. For example, St. John's clothes elegantly sway in deep, designed

Figure 9 Lorenzo Ghiberti (copy of). *St. John the Baptist*, 1414–16. Bronze sculpture.

folds rather than conforming to the figure's body.[34] It was a style that Ghiberti probably learned from a Spanish painter.[35] A Florentine artist; a Spanish influence: the Cloth-Merchants' presentation of wealth, piety, power, and civic prominence reached across the Florentine population and far beyond.

Other visual languages could make the same kinds of statements. For a different niche on Orsanmichele, Donatello created a stone

Figure 10 Donatello (copy of). *St. Mark*, 1411–13. Marble sculpture.

sculpture of St. Mark for the guild of Linen-makers and Used-Clothes
Dealers (Figure 10).[36] St. Mark's grave contrapposto stance and close-
fitting garments contrasted with the elegant St. John the Baptist and his
swooping drapery folds. St. Mark's beard mimics classical busts. The
torso at first glance seems too long: Donatello elongated it to try to
accommodate the most common viewer angle several feet below. Thus,
Donatello's St. Mark differed from Ghiberti's figure on the same building.
But, like Ghiberti's work, Donatello and his patrons tapped into a visual
language spoken across Florence, Italy, and beyond. Instead of the power
and status of a contemporary court, here was the power and status of
Ancient Rome.

The juxtaposition between the sculptures might seem like Donatello's work was avant-garde, while Ghiberti's one was old-fashioned.[37] But early fifteenth-century Florentines did not view the sculptures that way. The sculpture of St. John the Baptist, in fact, was placed *after* Donatello's St. Mark.[38] Moreover, later guilds sought to commission sculptures to express their piety and to compete against the wealth and courtly elegance of Ghiberti's St. John the Baptist.[39] By contrast, the initial responses to Donatello's St. Mark were critical. According to a later story, Donatello revealed his sculpture to his patrons. They were unimpressed and told him that it was unacceptable. Donatello asked if he could try to change their opinions after making some revisions. They agreed. During the next two weeks Donatello placed the sculpture higher in the air to change its viewer angle. He made no other alterations. At the second unveiling it met with universal praise.[40] During these decades an evaluation of Florentine visual culture that uses classicism as its measure misses the rich variety of options available to artists and patrons. Each of those options made bold claims to the Florentine and foreign passersby on the busy streets below.[41] Orsanmichele symbolized the translational languages of culture, the consensus republican ideal of Florentine politics, Florentine collective piety, and their competitions for status in the 1410s and 1420s.

During that same time Florence began to tell new stories about its past to reflect its new present. Previous Florentine histories had contended that Julius Caesar had founded their city; Attila the Hun had destroyed it; and then Charlemagne had refounded it. Those stories had worked well to explain actions by late medieval Florentines, who had claimed the inheritance of Ancient Rome because they were the heirs of the first Roman emperor. Their alliance with the French—that is their devoted Guelfism—stretched back to Charlemagne's foundation centuries ago. Those stories, however, worked less well in the changed situations of the early 1400s. The Great Schism and the near-total defeat of the French forces at Agincourt in the Hundred Years War made overt connections to the two traditional Guelf allies impractical.[42] The Ghibelline threat in the city no longer seemed urgent. The official, institutional arm of the Guelf Party in Florence increasingly seemed redundant: it seemed a social club for aristocrats without a practical function. Some Florentines continued to call for adherence to old papal and French alliances, but such voices were harder to hear over others arguing for a focus and response to more regional concerns.[43] In 1415 the Florentine government thus commissioned the humanist Leonardo Bruni to write a new history of Florence.[44]

Bruni wrote a history that explained a Florence that was neither an afterthought Roman colony nor a promising late medieval powerhouse. The city was instead governed by consensus politics, focused on regional affairs, and enjoying a rapidly expanding interest in humanism. Bruni's *History* told of Florentine families that lived in harmony within the political system rather than opposing it. They didn't need real political power because they gained honor and status through holding occasional political offices.[45] Bruni argued that the warlord Sulla had founded Florentine during the late Roman Republic, not Julius Caesar as others had previously claimed. Moreover, Attila the Hun had not destroyed the city. Consequently, Charlemagne could not have refounded Florence: he merely helped rebuild parts of it. These arguments loosened the ties between the Florence and the French. Moreover, they rejected claims by the emperors and others to be theoretical rulers over Florence. Instead, the *History* asserted that Florence was an independent republic that had inherited the mantle of the Ancient Roman Republic. The argument, theoretically, meant that Florence was staking claim to all the old Roman Republic lands across Europe, the Mediterranean, and beyond. But the emphasis was upon Florence's rights to conquer and rule its regional neighbors.[46]

The Florentines aimed to make Bruni's *History* rise above their constant competition and instead become the official, unanimous version of their city's past. They turned to God for assistance. In 1428 the Florentines paraded their most precious icon through their city. This image, called Our Lady of Impruneta, was brought into the city streets whenever the city needed an especially direct line to beseech God. The specific context was an attempt to ensure God's help to preserve a new peace with their enemy Milan. When the civic ritual reached its climax in front of the Palazzo Vecchio, the *Signoria* asked Leonardo Bruni to present the first six books of his *History* to them. God, their most precious religious image, the Florentine government, and most of the city consented to Bruni's version of the city's past. After the ritual, the *Signoria* placed Bruni's volume in their chapel within the Palazzo Vecchio. There it lay amid other precious items in that special holy place.[47]

Unfortunately, no icon possessed enough power to fill in the chasms cracking across the Florentine urban fabric. The city had become stretched across countless, interconnecting patronage networks. In these networks, the most powerful people in a neighborhood offered their neighbors access to their resources. These neighbors, in turn, implicitly or explicitly agreed to perform actions or offer loyalty at some near or future date. All people were tied by myriads of complementary and competing obligations to people with more or less power than they had. During the 1420s the largest, wealthiest, and most resourceful patronage network formed around Cosimo de' Medici, who had made a fortune through papal banking. Most of the Medici clients lived in the streets and blocks around the Medici home near the church of San Lorenzo. These clients tended to come from newer families and were usually bound together by marriages and business connections.[48]

Other families formed their own patronage networks, but these other networks were usually smaller and less tight knit than that of the Medici family. Like the Medici, these other patronage groups sought enrichment and power and were drawn together through obligatory bonds.[49] For example, across town the newcomer Agnolo Pandolfini amassed wealth and gained status from frequent office-holding. Throughout the 1410s and 1420s he argued for passivism in Florentine affairs: sometimes he agreed with Medici allies, sometimes he opposed them. He laid a foundation for his sons and grandsons to become leaders in their Florentine neighborhood near the Badia. Unlike the well-documented clients of Cosimo de' Medici, the specifics of Agnolo Pandolfini's patronage network are lost to time. Yet Agnolo, like most Florentine patricians, spent his life consolidating his wealth, power, piety, and status for himself, his heirs, and his allies. The result was a city defined by complicated webs of polycentric patronage networks.[50]

A series of disagreements ripped across these patronage webs during the 1420s and early 1430s. For example, people continued to argue about what role, if any, Guelfism and the Guelf Party should still play in the Florentine Republic. Several key leaders in the Florentine government also enjoyed leadership roles in the Florentine Guelf Party.[51] These leaders sought to revive the party's fortunes in Florence despite the French setbacks against England and tensions with the papacy.[52] After all, In 1388 the Florentines had declared the French St. Louis of Toulouse as an official protector of their city. Then, the Guelf Party had used recent wars against Milan as an opportunity to revive rhetoric about Florentine "Guelfs" versus Milanese "Ghibellines."[53] During the 1410s the Guelf Party sought to increase their status by commissioning Leonardo Bruni to rewrite their official statutes.[54] To those literary efforts the party added major renovations for their palace in the city.[55] But their boldest claim to continue shaping Florentine policies came in a magnificent bronze sculpture of St. Louis of Toulouse by Donatello for the Guelf Party's niche on Orsanmichele (Figure 11).[56]

Figure 11 Donatello. *St. Louis of Toulouse, c.* 1421–5. Bronze sculpture.

Donatello's work asserted the continued status of the Guelf Party in Florence and their devotion to French and papal causes. St. Louis of Toulouse had been brother to the king of France and a member of the Angevin family. He had initially rejected his inherited privilege in favor of joining the order of the Franciscan friars. He, however, was appointed a bishop, and it is possible that the ostentatious weight of his clothes and miter in Donatello's depiction may symbolize Louis's episcopal burden.[57] The sculpture was placed within a niche designed to refer to classical architecture.[58] The placement of the gilded bronze work on the east side of the building meant that each morning it reflected the rays of the rising sun.[59] Classical columns; expensive materials; a stylish visual language: here was a statue by a pious and powerful organization within Florence.[60] Even more, all viewers looked up at the Guelf Party's commitment to their traditional French and ecclesiastical allies. Decades before, perhaps, that statement would have drawn little comment. But by the 1420s the

Guelf Party and its ideas were one group among many competing for space in an increasingly hostile political environment.

By the latter 1420s disagreements between factions were spilling into the open. In 1427 the Florentines passed a new form of taxation, called the *Catasto*. The *Catasto* promised a more equitable distribution of taxes across the citizenry. Unlike previous taxes, the *Catasto* required individuals within Florence and its subject territories to submit a detailed account of their wealth and assets. That information was then used to make a tax assessment.[61] Some people opposed the legislation as too radical. Others saw it as a necessary innovation. The legislation barely passed.[62] In 1429 disagreements again broke out over a war to conquer the city-state of Lucca. The outlay of cash for the conflict was enormous. Factional fighting meant the city constantly vacillated between its approaches to the war. Things became so bad that the government created a new governmental body tasked with rooting out factions![63] By late 1430 the Florentines were losing the war. Losing only made things in the city worse. The war dragged on until a victory at the Battle of San Romano in 1432 provided the opportunity to make a less humiliating peace. Lucca remained independent. Florence remained divided against itself.

Peace abroad wilted under factional war at home. On September 5, 1433, a Florentine *Signoria* allied with a factional coalition led by Rinaldo degli Albizzi called Cosimo de' Medici to the Palazzo Vecchio. Cosimo was supposedly needed for a deliberative council. Instead, he arrived, was arrested, and was locked in the building's tall tower. The government appointed 200 citizens—a group called a *Balìa*—to make changes to the government. Five hundred foot-soldiers were brought into the city to maintain order. The *Balìa* voted to exile Cosimo and several other family members to different parts of Italy. They implemented policies to try to seize Medici assets at home and abroad. But otherwise they left the existing government structures intact. Institutions remained the same. Eligibility for office remained the same. Even the lists of people deemed eligible for office were left the same. Rinaldo and his allies sought to maintain the consensus order within Florence while removing key members of the increasingly powerful Medici faction.[64]

Over the next several months Rinaldo and his allies sought to continue influencing Florentines in office to direct the city's affairs. But their factions had waited too long to act against the Medici patronage network. Cosimo had been supplying the Florentine government with enormous sums of money to support Florentine policies at home and abroad. That money dried up after his exile. In addition, Cosimo had gained numerous and powerful allies throughout his neighborhood. Those men continued to have a voice in government affairs and even remained eligible to hold office in the city. By 1433 the Medici family had gained powerful allies abroad. Specifically, they had served as primary bankers for the pope for much of the fifteenth century. Rinaldo and his allies had clearly hoped that they could seize enough Medici assets to cover their government's financial losses. They thought that removal of the heads of the Medici faction would kill its body in Florence. They expected any external support for the Medici exiles to be inconsequential. But they were wrong.

A series of events in the summer of 1434 informally placed the Medici family at the top of the Florentine political hierarchy for the next sixty years. The events started with the pope. The Great Schism may have ended in 1417, but Pope Eugenius IV was still facing challenges to his power as pope as well as hostility to his presence in Rome. His power reached a nadir in the summer of 1434: an uprising in the Eternal City forced Pope Eugenius to flee the city in disguise. His lands in Italy were in shambles, his support outside Italy in question. To where could he flee? Florence offered haven; but would the situation there be better than in Rome? Florence too was riven with factions, and the pope's largest financer, the Medici family, had been exiled. A pope in a boat in disguise had few options. In late June he arrived in Florence and established residence in Santa Maria Novella. The many Medici allies in Florence began plotting and looking for the right opportunity. In September the *accoppiatori* pulled the names of a *Signoria* full of Medici loyalists.[65]

The pieces were then in place. Exiled in Venice, Cosimo anticipated both that the friendly *Signoria* would attempt to recall him to Florence and that Rinaldo and his allies would oppose those efforts. Cosimo knew he might need allies in the struggles ahead. Thus, he issued an enormous loan to the Venetian government. Through that loan, he sought to make sure that Venice—a key Florentine ally in their diplomatic and bellicose affairs—supported him instead of Rinaldo's coalition. On September 25 the *Signoria* requested that all Florentines convene outside the Palazzo Vecchio—an action called a *parlamento*—on September 29. At the *parlamento* they planned to request that the Florentines approve the return of the exiled Medici family members and their allies. Rinaldo and his coalition had to act. On September 26 they gathered around 1,000 men in what is now the Piazza San Firenze in Florence. Their goal was to stop the *Signoria* by taking the Palazzo Vecchio by force. Five hundred men gathered in the Palazzo Vecchio to defend it. By 1434 Florentine factions had become so complicated that the civil strife turned families and neighbors against one another: Rinaldo's own brother, Luca, lined up to fight against him from within the government palace.

No pitched battle ultimately erupted between the two small armies. Rinaldo had counted on many partisans who failed to bring themselves, their networks, and their resources to the Piazza. Without their support Rinaldo knew that he lacked the means to take over the fortified Palazzo Vecchio. From across town the pope offered to mediate the conflict. In theory it was the perfect solution: the vicar of Christ was not a part of a Florentine faction and, seemingly by good fortune, was living in Florence. He would be the perfect third-party judge and negotiator. It was an offer that could not be refused: the opposing sides agreed to let Pope Eugenius help sort out their differences. In practice, all knew that the pope was dependent upon Medici money. The next events were a surprise to no one. A *parlamento* convened in the Piazza della Signoria. The Florentine population had to push through armed guards surrounding the Piazza to obey the summons. The *Signoria* requested approval of a new *Balìa* to make changes to the government. The armed guards ensured that the population voted to approve the request. The *Balìa* revoked the exile of the Medici and their allies. They then banished dozens of powerful Florentines whom the Medici allies deemed as threats.[66] Would the exiles hold? Would the republic continue? Would the Medici become tyrants?

By 1434 Florence had changed from the city of the failed Ciompi revolt. The contests about how open to make real political power in Florence had transitioned to a system of consensus politics. In consensus politics, a few dozen families guided the city's main decisions, while all others sought the honor and social status of holding an occasional political office. The consensus ideal overlay an increasingly factionalized city. People formed competing and complementary factional networks among their neighbors. They each sought more status for themselves and their allies through marriages, money, and other means. Humanism and a range of visual languages offered new ways to express piety and create objects of beauty. They also became tools to persuade others to a range of points of view. Although the city's culture spoke to audiences in and beyond the city, Florentine politics shifted to more regional affairs. The pro-French and pro-papal Guelf voices still existed, but they were one voice in a crowd of competing ideas. In the early 1430s that crowd no longer could contain everyone's ambitions. Those tensions reached their peak; exiles ensued; opponents were crushed; and the faction of Cosimo de' Medici emerged victorious. Time would tell if that victory was temporary, permanent, pyrrhic, or empowering.

3

THE REPUBLIC CONTESTED, 1434–65

On September 6, 1441, the mercenary captain Baldaccio d' Anghiari was thrown from a window of the Palazzo Vecchio. Baldaccio's contorted body was decapitated. The head was displayed to the general populace.[1] This Florentine mercenary was a victim of the struggles for advantage and honor that continued after the return of the Medici family from exile. Cosimo and his allies kept most pieces of the Florentine government in place. However, they installed increasingly overt mechanisms to ensure their people possessed the most political power. Baldaccio fell in with too many people outside of the Medici faction and thus he was killed. Between 1434 and 1465 that extreme fate was unusual. Most ambitious Florentines threaded a passage through the Scylla of political marginalization and the Charybdis of total subservience as Medici loyalists. The problem was that, as the Medici's power continued to increase, options other than ostentatious opposition or subjugation decreased. The window for familial and individual social, economic, political, and cultural actions was closing. Gaining honor through office without the Medici family became harder and harder. Was Florence to be a consensus-based oligarchy or a Medici tyranny?

The answer to that question blurred further as the Medici faction shaped external policies and co-opted the visual and literary arts to defend its powerful position. The Medici faction backed the formal enshrinement of political regionalism through the Peace of Lodi in 1454. That agreement required the powers of Italy to pledge each other support from all aggressors. Thus, in theory, the states of the entire peninsula agreed to exist within their own borders. In addition, they all agreed to fight against any northern power that crossed the Alps. It was a far cry from late medieval Florence's dreams of conquest and professed Guelf loyalties. It was not supported by all Florentines any more than the Medici faction itself possessed unanimous support. Like in the early 1400s, Florentines made use of humanism and the visual arts to create beautiful objects as well as to express piety and to make arguments about their status and points of view for people in their city and beyond. But the power of the Medici faction in Florence was making it harder to hear the voices of anyone else.

Recent and distant Florentine history had taught the Medici faction that Florentine governmental victories often proved transitory. Thus, they immediately tweaked the government to stay in power. The Medici faction inherited a political system where the *accoppiatori* were handpicking some officeholders, while others were picked by chance. Rinaldo degli Albizzi and his allies in 1433 had been content to remove a few powerful Medici family member and allies while keeping the rest of the system intact. The Medici faction, by contrast, exiled far more of their most powerful real and perceived opponents. Next, they extended the power of the *accoppiatori* to handpick people for office. They knew that the lists of eligible officeholders still included people who remained loyal to the exiled Medici enemies. Thus, they destroyed all the old lists of eligible officeholders and created new ones. In short, the *accoppiatori* would still be handpicking loyalists to some offices. Simultaneously, for offices picked by chance, the new lists ensured that the Medici faction had at the very least taken away the eligibility of their most problematic opponents.[2] The people left in the drawing bags obviously included Medici partisans. Most names, however, were men looking for their own honors in whatever system was in place at the moment.

The system worked to keep the Medici faction in power while maintaining the republican form of government. But it was a delicate artifice. There were two major problems. One, the ability of the *accoppiatori* to handpick people for office was a temporary power. Every few years the Florentine legislative councils had to approve extensions of those powers. It was far easier to control the small, powerful executive powers in the government than those bigger approval bodies. Thus, the system temporarily broke down in 1441, 1443, and 1449, even as the legislative bodies did eventually approve the powers for the *accoppiatori* in each case. The other major problem was that the system depended upon powerful families to work *with* the Medici family. They did not work *for* them. Those allied families possessed wealth, ancient lineages, reputations, ambitions, and patronage networks of their own. They each had their own specific agendas. They served as *accoppiatori* and benefited from the electoral machinations. But they were partners, not dependents; allies, not henchmen.[3]

Neri Capponi serves as one notable example of the type of man working with, but not for, the Medici faction. The Capponi family were an old and wealthy Florentine family based in the *oltrarno* quarter of the city. Neri inherited additional prestige from this father, Gino, who had been a Florentine war hero in the conquest of Pisa in 1406. Neri became a prominent officeholder and himself an expert in military affairs. Like his father, Neri was deemed a war hero after his role in the Battle of Anghiari in 1440. Neri became so popular and powerful in Florence that people began to see him as Cosimo's chief rival in the city. Baldaccio d'Anghiari, whose defenestration began this chapter, was one of Neri's allies, and people viewed Baldaccio's death as an attack at Neri's power base. But, notably, Neri continued to play a leading role in the Florentine government until his death in 1457. Neri supported some initiatives while opposing others. Despite contemporary gossip, he lacked the power and probably the desire to orchestrate a coup. Thus, he worked within the political framework in which he found himself. He used military glory, wealth, culture, and office-holding to carve out honors for himself, his family, their allies, and their clients. He avoided toadyism and rebellion through a more middle course.[4] That middle, however, was shrinking.

The cultural patronage of Cosimo de' Medici began to transform the city into continual reminders of his piety as well as of his premier power and position. Already in the 1430s the Medici family had begun paying for a committee to oversee the rebuilding of the ancient church of San Lorenzo (Figure 12). By 1442 Cosimo took over the project. Designed by Filippo Brunelleschi and others, the building blended ancient and more recent Tuscan visual traditions. For example, its ceiling design derives from the ruins of Roman baths, while its central colonnade refers to both Ancient and Tuscan models (Figure 13).[5] The power dynamic was clear enough: neighborhood families around San Lorenzo could commission culture for their individual family chapels; the Medici would fund the church itself. If they missed the point, within view of the San Lorenzo construction site the Medici brothers hired the architect Michelozzo di Bartolomeo Michelozzi to build a new palace. It was to be a home worthy of their status. Florentines during the 1440s marveled that the builders dug a foundation as big as a city block. By contrast, other wealthy palaces, like the still extant Palazzo Davizzi-Davanzati, in Florence seemed quaint in comparison.[6] The rusticated first floor left little doubt that the building was a formidable fortress and a monument to Medici money.

Figure 12 Exterior of San Lorenzo.

Figure 13 Interior of San Lorenzo.

Next Cosimo set his sights on rebuilding a second large church in his part of Florence. Just down the road from his new palace, near the fringe of the city, was a Dominican church dedicated to San Marco. The structure had fallen into disrepair and thus Michelozzo was again commissioned as the architect to rebuild it. Additionally, the talented and holy Fra Angelico was hired to paint the main altarpiece for the church. The altarpiece seamlessly blended artistic beauty, religious piety, family status, and political power. In the image, details such as the drawn curtain, masterful use of new perspective techniques, and attention to bodily space make the illusion that a real court scene is opening before the viewer. Several saints serve as courtiers before the classical, heavenly throne, upon which sit the Virgin and her infant son. Cosimo de' Medici's patronage was unmistakable. Cosimo's name saint, for example, kneels in the forefront and looks out at the viewer. The *palle* from Cosimo's heraldic device decorate the vegetation in the background (Figure 14).[7]

San Marco provided a growing number of Florentines even more overt statements to Medici power. In 1437 the Florentine humanist Niccolò Niccoli died. Over the course of his life Niccolò had bankrupted himself in his quest to amass a peerless library.[8] Upon his death, Niccolò left instructions that a small group of trustees use his books to create a library open to "all studious citizens."[9] The trustees consigned their authority to one of their number, Cosimo de' Medici. Cosimo took care of Niccolò's debts, donated the books to San Marco, and asked Michelozzo to create a space within the new church for their perusal.[10] The library combined classical architecture with Niccolò's classical books. Together the space and manuscripts took readers back in time to Antiquity itself. Yet, the room also reminded readers who had sponsored their time-travel. A wall slab placed in the reading room explicitly proclaimed the patronage of Cosimo de' Medici.[11] Like the Ancient Romans of old, Cosimo offered his patronage to the world of culture. More than one powerful man in Florence, Cosimo embodied Rome reborn. More than a pious patron of a single painting, Cosimo's faith built entire churches. By 1450 it was impossible to live, worship, or visit the San Giovanni quarter of Florence without seeing and reading those messages. But Medici ambition extended far beyond control over one neighborhood.

Medici patronage made the same arguments for piety, power, and status on a citywide scale. The completion of the Florentine *Duomo* marked the pinnacle of Cosimo's success. After the city's fourteenth-century collapse, work on a central cathedral for the city had slowed. It was not until the latter 1350s and 1360s that the pace of work increased.[12] By 1367 the

Figure 14 Fra Angelico. *San Marco Altarpiece*, *c.* 1438–40.

builders needed ideas about how to construct a dome wide enough and at such a height to cover the huge opening drawn into the plans for Santa Maria del Fiore. Nobody had a good solution. One group suggested that transalpine builders had used flying buttresses to solve somewhat similar problems. Perhaps that might work? Another group contended that Ancient Romans had constructed large domes without those sorts of buttresses. Thus, there must be a different solution and one that they deemed would be more beautiful. The Florentines decided to avoid the buttresses. However, without buttresses the dome simply could not be built.[13] For years rain poured through the opening in the roof onto the interminable construction site below. A wall was built in 1380 so people could at least use the building's finished sections without getting wet.[14]

By 1400 sunlight, moonlight, rain, and occasionally snow continued to fall through the gaping hole in the roof.[15] The Florentines were undeterred. This time, they extended an invitation to the world's architects to come to Florence to study the problem. Several ideas were put forth. One person suggested that the cathedral be filled with a mixture of dirt and coins. The workers, then, could stand on the dirt to work on the dome. Once it was finished, all interested could remove the dirt and keep whatever coins that they found.[16] The idea was politely declined. Another individual, Filippo Brunelleschi, presented more complicated solutions.[17] The men overseeing the project were convinced. On April 16, 1420, Brunelleschi was tasked with putting his ideas into the actual construction of the dome.[18]

Brunelleshi used a unique approach indebted to Florentine traditions. Unlike other domes the *Duomo* proudly showed its octagonal shape: it mirrors the number of sides of the nearby Baptistery. The steep upward slant of the dome facilitated weight distribution across the cavernous space. Additionally, the dome has two sets of parallel walls to lighten its load. Brunelleschi developed new tools and machines both to make the dome possible and to make its construction site run smoother. Instead of building scaffolding from the floor, the builders hung scaffolding from the rising walls. The builders set herringbone bricks to help support the structure.[19] To get supplies to the workers, Brunelleschi developed a hoist that oxen could power while always moving in the same direction.[20]

By March 25, 1436, work had progressed enough to formally consecrate the building's altar. Pope Eugenius IV, still living in Florence, walked the short distance from his apartments at Santa Maria Novella.[21] Rituals followed. The Standard Bear of Justice received a knighthood. Mass followed. Then, indulgences were offered for six years to those visiting the impressive structure. Cosimo de' Medici requested that the number be ten. The Florentine *Signoria* had previously made a similar request but had been denied. Cosimo's appeal, by contrast, was approved.[22] It was a use of influence worthy of a man seeking salvation.[23] But it also was a demonstration of influence that tied him to the Florentines' mightiest architectural marvel. It was even more than that. Fifteenth-century Florentines associated religious piety with material rewards. God actively rewarded the just and punished the wicked, even if His reasons sometimes remained hidden. By ostentatious displays of Medici wealth on religious structures, decorations, and altarpieces, Cosimo was both expressing his piety and reinforcing the view of just how much God had rewarded him. Divine favor underlay Cosimo's wealth, position, and political system.

The increasing power of the Medici faction necessitated a new story about the Florentine past. Leonardo Bruni's official history of Florence had only reached the expulsion of Walter of Brienne when he presented it to the city government in 1428. He continued to work on the decades of the 1300s as he lived through the factional violence and precarious victory of the Medici and their allies. Bruni's overall approach in these new sections remained the same as his had used in earlier parts. However, in these new chapters he was careful to promote the historical accomplishments of the Medici family while exonerating them from potential areas of criticism.[24] The central role over Florence that the Medici were promoting for themselves now was enshrined in the official history of Florence.

In 1439 Bruni presented this new version of the Florentine past to the Florentine government amid another ritual embraced by the Medici faction. The story begins, again, with the pope. Pope Eugenius IV had left Florence in 1437 to live in Bologna. From Bologna, he negotiated an ecumenical council to reunify the Greek and Latin churches. The council opened in Ferrara in 1438. However, in 1439 the pope claimed that the plague threatened the council's participants and thus would need to move to another city.[25] He did not say that Cosimo's brother Lorenzo de' Medici had negotiated the transfer. He left out that the Medici family financed the move for the cash-strapped pope. And perhaps Pope Eugenius feigned surprise when Cosimo de' Medici, conveniently serving a term as Standard Bearer of Justice, greeted the papal and Greek entourages upon their arrival in Florence.[26] Regardless, Pope Eugenius moved back into his apartments in Santa Maria Novella. After months of negotiation the Greek and Latin delegations reached an agreement to smooth out their theological differences. The pope issued an official proclamation. The Florentines held a celebration. At the peak of the celebration for the Medici-sponsored council Leonardo Bruni presented his new, more Medici-favorable version of fourteenth-century Florence. The Florentines then placed that volume and its version of the past within the *Signoria*'s chapel. There, God and the saints could both sanction and protect it.[27]

After the Council of Ferrara-Florence Cosimo and his faction increasingly tied Florence to alliances with the mercenary captain Francesco Sforza at the expense of traditional alliances with the papacy, the French, and in recent decades the Venetians. The Papal Great Schism and the weakness of early fifteenth-century popes meant that, in practice, no central power controlled the pope's lands in central Italy. At the same time, cities throughout the Italian peninsula relied upon mercenary captains and their companies to fight their wars. The most successful mercenary captains tried to turn their wealth and military glory into permanent bases for operations. The Papal States offered the obvious choice for these men: the pope lacked the resources to exert control over those lands, thus towns could be conquered and then defended while surrounding zones could provide necessary resources. During the 1440s Francesco Sforza was one mercenary waging wars of conquest with the Papal States. Cosimo de' Medici helped finance Sforza's actions. Sforza in turn offered a reliable and talented man to promote Medici efforts in and outside Florence. Additionally, Sforza oversaw a reliable supply of grain from his conquered lands into Florence. After all, people with satiated stomachs were less likely to want the Medici to stop controlling things in their city.[28]

The entire situation made Pope Eugenius furious. Pope Eugenius hired Baldaccio d'Anghiari to help reassert control over his lands. Baldaccio was thrown out a window. The pope blamed Cosimo and his faction. Not by coincidence, the pope soon after judged that Rome was safe enough to return to. From Rome, he looked for allies to fight against Sforza's growing power in the Papal State.[29] The situation came to a head in 1447. In that year the Duke of Milan died without a clear successor. Francesco Sforza argued that, by rights, Milan was his because he had married the Milanese duke's daughter Bianca. Other Italian powers rejected the argument and put forth their own claims. Peninsular-wide war ensued. Cosimo de' Medici continued to supply Sforza with cash. Sforza successfully conquered Milan in 1450. The conquest did not stop the war. Italian powers lined up to support or contest Sforza's conquests and claims to powerful Milan. Florence, led by Cosimo's faction, threw their lot in with Sforza. It was a move that placed the city against traditional allies like the papacy, the French, and the Venetians. It was not a move that gathered unanimous Florentine support.

The Florentine Giannozzo Manetti opposed Cosimo's shift of Florentine alliances toward Milan and Francesco Sforza. Manetti was considered one of the leading humanists in Italy during the 1440s and 1450s. Although most modern readers find his prolix Latin verbose, hundreds of Manetti's contemporaries flocked to his hour-long orations.[30] And Manetti had many opportunities to speak through his years of unbroken service in government offices in and outside Florence. By 1450 Manetti had made enemies within the Medici faction. Manetti, moreover, began vocally opposing Florentine support of Francesco Sforza and urging that the city return to its more traditional allies in Venice. It was still possible in 1450 in Florence to have a successful political career without ostentatiously supporting every Medici initiative. Office-holding still meant honor, and electoral controls still left many opportunities for ambitious Florentines. But Giannozzo Manetti pushed too far.

By 1452 Manetti knew that his political problems were such that he was no longer welcome in Florence. While in office outside the city he wrote a long panegyric to Alfonso, king of Naples, a man who was opposing Francesco Sforza and whom Manetti had befriended some years earlier.[31] Along with the long laudation Manetti sent a copy of his original work *On Human Worth and Excellence*. The work ostensibly avoided politics. In it, Manetti rejected previous writers who had argued that sin made human life miserable. Instead, Manetti claimed that people had a unique, privileged role in God's plan.[32] The content pertained to philosophy; but the dedication of the text also spilled its contents into the social and political world. Manetti was reminding the king of his learning. He was offering his words of praise as a gift. Manetti hoped for some form of reciprocity. The effort paid off. In exchange for adding learned prestige to Alfonso's court, Manetti received a comfortable stipend and a refuge from the Medici faction in Florence. But his efforts to push against the new direction in Florentine external affairs had ended in failure.

The fall of Constantinople in 1453 cemented Florentine political regionalism as well as Cosimo's shift in Florentine alliances away from the papacy, the French, and the Venetians. In what is now modern Turkey the emperor Constantine had founded a capital for the Ancient Roman Empire in 324 CE. For nearly 900 years that city, called Constantinople, had served as the capital of the eastern half of the Roman Empire, called the Byzantine Empire. For 900 years its unrivaled walls had deflected even the most terrible siege engines born by the most aggressive armies. For 900 years the size of the Byzantine Empire had ebbed and flowed with the waxing and waning power of its neighbors as well as the competence or craziness of its own emperors. Then, in 1204 the city fell to an army of French and Venetian crusaders. The resilient Byzantines took their capital back in 1261. They returned to an empire in shambles, but they had suffered near defeats before. Byzantium always bounced back.

The timeless quality of Constantinople made its fall to the Ottoman Turks in 1453 shocking. By the fourteenth and fifteenth centuries the Ottomans had conquered most of what is now Turkey and Greece. They had effectively diminished the ancient Byzantine Empire to its capital city and a few scattered territories. The Byzantines sought aid from the

Christians to their west. Manuel Chrysoloras, the Greek teacher from the last chapter, and the Council of Ferrara-Florence, addressed in this chapter, were both part of those efforts. But little tangible help arrived. After all, Constantinople had always been there. It always would be. What war engine could penetrate its impregnable walls? Gunpowder. In 1453 those thick medieval walls became easy targets for giant Ottoman cannons. Walls that had once encompassed a city of hundreds of thousands of people—maybe even a million!—were defended by a few thousand men. The city fell to the Ottomans. Shock fell upon the cities and kingdoms of Europe: an ancient player in their politics was dead, and a new one was born.[33]

The fall of Constantinople spurred the Peace of Lodi in 1454 and then an Italian League in 1455 (Figure 15). In those accords the powers of Italy agreed to stop warring and instead defend one another. The League signatories agreed that if one of them attacked a different signatory then all the other League members were required to come to the defender's aid. In practice, the Italian League formalized the regionalized political focus of Florence. By the League agreement, neither the Florentines nor any other Italian power could aim to establish a sprawling empire. Instead, each power had to remain content within its own existing borders. Even more, the defensive pact within the Italian League meant that if any transalpine power attempted to attack a League member then all other signatories had to help. A city like Florence, which had for so long cherished its connections with the French, now was legally required to stop asking them for assistance and to fight against the French if they happened to arrive anywhere in Italy.[34] Pope Nicholas V, Francesco Sforza, and Cosimo de' Medici were the chief architects of the League. It made permanent Cosimo's changes to Florentine external affairs. French coats of arms still hung near papal ones on the Palazzo Vecchio, but the massive Medici palace across town had no such permanent decorations.

The Italian League seemed to promise peace for Italy after decades of nearly unending warfare. The pope was calling for a new crusade to retake Constantinople and beyond. Maybe the Italians could turn their arms in that direction. In Florence, the League marked a controversial shift in the city's external affairs. For people opposed to the Medici machinations of the Florentine government it also, however, created an opportunity. From 1434 until 1455 the Medici faction had continually argued that government controls had to be renewed because of external threats or open warfare. The Italian League supposedly ended those threats. Calls came forth to open more Florentine offices to more people

Figure 15 Reginald Lane Poole. *Italy after the Peace of Lodi* (originally published as plate 68 in *The Historical Atlas of Europe*). © Wikimedia Commons.

again, and to pick more offices by chance again. One Florentine wrote to Giannozzo Manetti that he thought the peace would bring about a "revival of the republic." Manetti, then, could return to Florence, return to office-holding, and help the republic return to form.[35] But those things were not to be.

A series of events soon after that time provided the Medici faction with an opportunity to further strengthen their control over the city of Florence. The powerful Florentine patrician Neri Capponi had died in 1457. Capponi seems to have been a moderating voice within Florentine politics. Without his voice, tensions began stretching across the city, across the peninsula, and beyond. The Florentine Girolamo Machiavelli attempted a coup to overthrow the Medici-controlled government.[36] He failed and the response was swift and conclusive. A new *parlamento* of Florentine citizens was called to the square in front of the Palazzo Vecchio. Like in 1434 armed men surrounded the Florentine citizens to ensure that they provided the desired answers to all questions asked. The citizens approved the creation of new lists of men eligible for office. They also approved of a new governmental body, the Council of 100. The Council of 100 was to serve as a permanent check on the passage and enforcement of all legislation in the city. It was also to be packed with members of the Medici faction and their allies.[37]

Cosimo used his tighter control over Florence to manage external events. In the same summer as Girolamo Machiavelli's failed coup, Pope Callixtus III died. A mercenary captain named Jacopo Piccinino seized the opportunity provided by the period between popes to conquer the town of Assisi in the Papal State. A new pope, Pius II, was then elected in Rome. Pope Pius called upon the other members of the Italian League to help him repel Piccinino from the town. The Italian powers, including Florence, demurred.[38] Then, soon after, Alfonso, king of Naples, also died. Alfonso's bastard son Ferrante was to inherit the Kingdom of Naples, but Ferrante's claim was disputed. Pope Pius argued that, in the absence of a legitimate heir, the Kingdom of Naples reverted to its papal overlord. Thus, Pope Pius II declared Ferrante's claim invalid and instead declared himself the new king of Naples. Nobles within the Kingdom of Naples used the pope's ruling to justify a rebellion against Ferrante's rule. They were not alone. Since the 1200s the Angevin dukes—dukes like Charles of Anjou from Chapter 1—in France had claimed and fought to possess southern Italy. King Alfonso from Aragon had beaten René of Anjou in 1442 to take sole possession of the Kingdom of Naples. In 1458 René's son, John, began prepping an invasion force to right that perceived wrong: Duke John sought to remove Ferrante and reinstall Angevin rule over southern Italy.

The Florentines had to decide between their old traditional ties to France and their newer obligations to the Italian League. In 1459 John of Anjou arrived in Italy with an army to take Naples. He called upon the Florentines, as ancient friends of the French, to assist his cause. King Ferrante also called upon the Florentines, as members of the Italian League, for assistance. Cosimo and Francesco Sforza publicly stalled. In secret, they funneled resources to Ferrante.[39] It was a continuation of Cosimo's embrace of regional politics as well as flexibility toward France and the papacy. And by 1459, on the foundation of the Council of 100, Florence increasingly was Cosimo's city. It was harder and harder to differentiate between the policies pursued at the Palazzo Vecchio and those pushed by the Medici in their grand *palazzo*. Rulers outside Florence began thinking of Cosimo as the ruler of the city, rather than a person in a republic. Visiting dignitaries went through the motions of meeting the *Signoria* before meeting with Cosimo at his house to discuss the issues at hand. Citizen advisory meetings at the Palazzo Vecchio began concluding that the best solution was to go to Cosimo's house and ask his opinion.

Cosimo's stronger position in Florence was embodied in Benozzo Gozzoli's *Adoration of the Magi* frescoes painted in the 1450s and 1460s (Figure 16). The Medici family commissioned Gozzoli to paint the

Figure 16 Benozzo Gozzoli, *Adoration of the Magi, View of the Procession of the Youngest King, c.* 1459–63. Fresco.

frescoes within the private chapel of the new Medici palace. The stunning images show a long train of the faithful traveling the countryside to pay homage to the newborn Christ. It was at one level a pious fantasy. Portraits of Cosimo and his sons appear among the first men riding behind the youngest of the three Magi. Behind Cosimo are other family portraits, such as his grandsons Lorenzo (later called "the Magnificent") and Giuliano.[40] All ride their finest mounts—except for humble Cosimo, who rides a mule—to pay homage to the newborn Savior.[41]

The fresco also expressed the power of the Medici faction by the late 1450s. By that time Cosimo was sometimes greeting visiting dignitaries within the chapel.[42] It was a setting rife with symbolism. Within fifteenth-century diplomacy, diplomats sometimes adopted the biblical story of the Magi as a parallel for their own missions. For example, diplomats to a new emperor might claim that, like the Magi of old, they too had seen a star in the east and come to adore it.[43] Visitors to the Medici Chapel saw the central location of the Medici family in Gozzoli's frescoes. They saw the family on their way to worship the baby Christ. They also received reminders that the Medici's own power was supplemented by powerful friends and allies. In the fresco, also on a fine horse, rode Galeazzo Maria Sforza, son of Cosimo's friend Francesco. Riding next to him was Sigismundo Malatesta. Malatesta was hated by the pope, but he was a mercenary whom the Medici could count on.[44] In a different part of the fresco, some of Cosimo's principal allies in Florence appear: Neri Capponi, Dietisalvi Neroni, and others. The image depicted the power of Cosimo's faction, its external supports, and its promise for more Medici in the future. But the savviest of viewers might have whispered that Cosimo was getting older. The men depicted did not owe nearly as much to loyalty to Cosimo's heir apparent Piero. The Medici family controlled the Florentine Republic, but how long would it be before other Florentines wanted a bigger piece of the pie?

The political changes of 1458 did not whisk away the ambitions of other Florentines. In fact, despite the narrowing of political space around Cosimo de' Medici, several options remained for people to seek out honor and power without overtly opposing or obeying Cosimo. In one example, the patrician Agnolo Acciaiuoli tried to replace Cosimo as Francesco Sforza's preferred Florentine ally. Agnolo failed.[45] In another example, the patrician Piero de' Pazzi tried to return the city to its pro-French allegiances. Piero overtly supported John of Anjou's efforts in Italy. Piero even tried to create a new alliance between Milan and France to break the Italian League and return the Angevins to Naples. Piero also failed.[46] In a final example, the patrician Niccolò Soderini tried to combine support for the Medici-Sforza alliance with attempts to remove some of the electoral controls within Florence. He failed too.[47]

Most Florentines sought to earn whatever honors they could within the changing system. The Pandolfini family serve as one example. Agnolo Pandolfini, introduced in last chapter, managed to stay aloof from most factional fighting during the 1420s and 1430s. As a result, his sons Carlo and Giannozzo inherited a powerful position that was neither beholden nor opposed to the Medici faction. Both sons had successful political careers: Giannozzo in particular became a leading diplomat and officeholder. Giannozzo passed down his standing to his eldest son Pandolfo, who sought to augment it further. During the latter 1450s and 1460s Pandolfo viewed the Medici faction as powerful, clearly, but also as a dominant faction within a republic—not a faction synonymous with the government itself. During his career Pandolfo worked to thwart further consolidation of the government by the Medici family. He praised efforts that sought to remove existing governmental controls. He viewed some of those controls as benefiting his friends but also thought such changes would be for the greater good. Florentines, including the Medici faction, mourned Pandolfo's premature passing in 1464.[48] Cosimo was powerful, but options remained for ambitious Florentines within the corrupted republic.

Pandolfo and his brothers have left a telling visual statement of their ambitions, political ambiguity, and filial devotion. After their father Giannozzo died, the brothers sought to construct a tomb in his honor. Even more, Florentine practice meant that spouses were often buried together, and thus the tomb could actually be for both parents. The brothers commissioned an artist to make a tomb in direct emulation of one made for a Medici family member across town. In their finished forms the two tombs are virtually identical. The Pandolfini tomb in the Badia told all viewers about the family's wealth, cultural sophistication, and devotion to their father. Savvy viewers, meanwhile, recognized it as a near copy of the Medici tomb in the church of Santissima Annunziata. It was a statement of ambition, imitation, and even rivalry, but it offered no challenge to the most powerful family in the city.[49]

The Rucellai family tried a similar tactic. The Rucellai were an older Florentine family than the Pandolfini. They lived across town in the Santa Maria Novella quarter. They were married to families that the Medici faction exiled in 1434. They even helped at least one exile manage his affairs from abroad.[50] Giovanni Rucellai kept a private book in which he praised problematic people like the exile Palla di Nofri Strozzi and the person non grata Giannozzo Manetti.[51] With such friends and relatives, it is not surprising that Giovanni Rucellai was kept out of the city's lists of eligible officeholders during the 1440s and early 1450s.[52]

Without the ability to gain honor from office Giovanni turned to other means to increase his status and return to an active role in the Florentine Republic. As the Medici palace rose near San Lorenzo, Giovanni hired the learned polymath Leon Battista Alberti to design a new palace for the Rucellai family. Unable to simply level a city block, Giovanni tried to buy all the houses around his building site. In the home itself the cobbled properties were renovated and connected as best as they could be. On the exterior, Alberti fashioned a unified facade to mask the architectural chaos within. Alberti made use of the visual languages of Antiquity to profess Rucellai power. For example, ancient examples had used increasingly ornate columns on higher floors: Doric on the ground floor; Ionic on the second; and the most ornate column type, Corinthian, on the third. Alberti adopted the same basic scheme for the Rucellai palace floors. He also used classical instructions to help guide the proportions of his different types of columns. The result was an elegant facade that professed Rucellai status while tying them to the Ancient Romans. In the decades that followed thirty more Florentines constructed family palaces, even as they tended to prefer more traditional architectural models.[53] Each was a statement of wealth; an expression of beauty. Each also proclaimed power within the Medici system in Florence.

In addition to palaces and the visual arts, Florentines continued to use humanism to pursue curious lines of inquiry and as a means to augment their social status within and beyond their city. By the 1450s humanism had become common among Florentines. Classical books, even ones written in Ancient Greek, were becoming easier to find. One consequence was that standard classical texts no longer satiated minds hungry for new knowledge. Another consequence was that simply dabbling in a bit of classical studies no longer impressed anyone: people assumed that elites or would-be elites knew the basics of Antiquity. A third consequence was that people began to prize the most gifted people in their city in new ways. These men, thus, could use their learned reputations to supplement more traditional marks of status. Thus, the leading humanist scholars increasingly explored more esoteric and complicated philosophical topics. They were often most interested in new works by Plato and his followers.[54]

Cosimo de' Medici sought to associate himself with these trends. Greek delegates to the Council of Florence had brought many ancient Greek texts that had not been read outside of Byzantium and the Middle East for centuries. Men formed learned circles in Florence to meet to discuss the ideas in some of those texts.[55] Cosimo offered patronage to the doctor, priest, and humanist Marsilio Ficino to translate all the known works of Plato from Greek into Latin. At the time, most of those works existed only in Greek or Arabic translation. Ficino set to work. However, as he toiled away Cosimo came into possession of a work attributed to a certain Hermes Trismegistus. People in the mid-fifteenth century believed that Hermes lived long before Plato. Cosimo asked Ficino to switch texts, and thus Ficino set Plato aside to work on the writings of Hermes.[56] Ironically, years later it was proven that Hermes Trismegistus probably never existed. Several different unnamed classical writers during the 100s wrote the texts that Ficino translated. But to Cosimo and Ficino, the corpus of Hermes Trismegistus represented old knowledge: older than Athens, maybe even older than Moses himself.

Florentines far beyond just Cosimo de' Medici embraced Marsilio Ficino's more metaphysical approach to humanist studies. In addition to Plato and Hermes Trismegistus, Ficino translated and commented upon many other writers in the Platonic tradition.[57] He wrote a long work, the *Platonic Theology*, in which he sought to reconcile the teachings of Plato with Christianity.[58] In another work, his *Three Books on Life*, Ficino proposed a series of recommendations for readers to live healthier lives. He included recommendations for sleep and waking, rest and work, and many other topics. He also included advice drawn from more controversial sources. Ficino suggested that people could use astrology, image magic, and astral forces to improve their health.

Fifteenth-century Florentines accepted many forces as part of their world that are unfamiliar to many people in the twenty-first century. They knew that God played a direct role in shaping lives, down to influencing daily events. They knew that God rewarded the just and punished the wicked. They knew that magical forces were a given, and that demons and witches were a real danger. They knew that the earth was at the center of the universe and that the heavens were immutable. Thus, any change in the sky had to portend something. Period medicine took for granted that the balance of four bodily humors—blood, black bile, yellow bile, and phlegm—determined a person's health, personality, and mood.[59] The natural world directly impacted that balance. Thus, doctors like Ficino needed to restore proper bodily balances with different plants, spices, gems, and other objects. These assumptions meant that people sometimes struggled to draw the line between acceptable use of such forces and items versus an unacceptable avocation of them.[60] In the *Three Books on Life* Ficino pushed too far. His work was condemned. In response, Ficino wrote a defense of his work dedicated to three powerful Florentine friends.[61] The dedicatees were not literary luminaries—they were Florentine patricians. By the second half of the fifteenth-century Florentines continued to stand at the center of the humanist movement, and the humanist movement was moving in new directions.

Words of Ficino, Manetti, and Bruni; images by Gozzoli and Fra Angelico; buildings by Michelozzi and Brunelleschi: Florentines and foreigners alike understood these cultural languages. They read each protestation to power, pious pronouncement, assertion of alliance or enmity, and declaration of status. Some were better at reading these languages than others. For example, Alessandra Macinghi had married Matteo Strozzi in a match that joined two powerful families. Matteo was exiled in 1434. He died shortly after. Alessandra became a young single mother. When her sons came of age, they were subject to the same exile imposed upon their father. Thus, they went to work with extended family members in Naples and in Bruges. Savvy Alessandra, as well as her keen son-in-law, kept them updated on Florentine politics. She even used codes to describe the most sensitive matters.[62]

Not all Florentines were as keen or interested as Alessandra Macinghi-Strozzi. Giovanna Valori lived around the same time as Alessandra, and the two women probably knew each other.[63] Like Alessandra, Giovanna married a Florentine active in government affairs, in this case Giannozzo Pandolfini. Unlike Alessandra, Giovanna seems to have kept her distance from politics. For example, Giannozzo Manetti had served in political offices with Giannozzo Pandolfini. The two men would have had frequent and regular opportunities for conversation. When Manetti wrote a eulogy for Pandolfini's funeral, however, he did not know Giovanna's name and had to ask for it from a mutual friend, Vespasiano da Bisticci. Bisticci knew Giovanna well from his frequent interactions with the Pandolfini family. When he wrote a short biography of Giovanna, he praised her personal virtue and piety as well as how well she had passed those traits onto her children.[64] It is possible that Giovanna's separation from political matters reflected misogynistic tendencies in some households. Most men thought that family patriarchs ought to mold their wives into models of submission and obedience. They proclaimed that women ought to be sequestered at home, hidden from sight, and removed from the masculine work of making money and gaining honor.[65] But perhaps Giovanna's interests just lay elsewhere. After all, there were plenty of women in fifteenth-century Florence who were helping to manage household finances, offering prayers, indirectly moving political affairs, serving as cultural patrons, and even creating their own cultural works.[66]

Women were banned from holding political offices, but they were the lynchpins of Florentine politics and society. Women bonded families and factions together through marriage. As such, marriages tended to begin as contracted arrangements between parties. At times the spouses knew each other well enough before the wedding. But at other times they were complete strangers.[67] For example, Alessandra Macinghi-Strozzi's son Filippo in Naples reached marital age. Thus, his relatives back in Florence began looking for a bride. Alessandra wrote letters to Filippo describing options. She relayed the willingness of different families to wed an exile. She described different potential matches in terms of their looks and potential to assist in a household.[68] Filippo had never met or seen any of the women. That husband and wife could exchange first greetings and permanent marriage vows on the same day was simply a part of life.

Women carried the honor of their families into the Florentine marriage market. They were expected to be chaste to ensure the best possible marital match and to avoid the dishonor of an illegitimate pregnancy. Lived experience often was more complicated. For example, in the mid-1400s a certain Lusanna had a romantic affair with her neighbor Giovanni. Giovanni possessed much more social status than his lover. After some time, the two were married in secret: a secret marriage could avoid the dishonor for Giovanni's family from wedding a woman with less status, while it also could allow the affair to continue. More time elapsed, and Giovanni reached an age when his family needed him to create a marriage bond with another powerful family in the neighborhood. Giovanni, thus, denied that he had ever married Lusanna. Instead, he claimed they had simply exchanged the usual sorts of empty promises between transitory lovers. Lusanna took the matter to court. The case was appealed all the way to the pope himself for a ruling. Lusanna lost.[69]

Women tied families together in fifteenth-century Florence; their bodies embodied their family's honor; and their lives made households function. Married women in Florence were usually much younger than their husbands. Many married women faced the annual dangers of childbirth. Many died. Almost a third of women received enough of an education to have basic literacy. They used those skills for a range of activities. Women helped manage their households. When their husbands were away, they took sole possession of economic and other decisions. Women taught and oversaw the elementary education of their children, both for girls and boys. If a husband died, widows even gained some level of legal rights in Florentine courts. They gained some financial independence because their marital dowries were returned to them. All of these activities kept the household functioning and kept women abreast and involved in the world around them.

Women who did not marry also played vital roles in family strategies. Many such women entered convents. Certainly, the woman and the family's religious piety played a central role in the decision to become a nun. Yet, there were also other considerations. A woman could offer a much smaller dowry to join a convent than a marriage. Florentines viewed such cost-saving arrangements as honorable, especially for younger daughters. Once in a convent, a fifteenth-century nun continued to play an active role in the fabric of the city. Convents owned and rented properties throughout Florence. Powerful nuns in the convent consequently became powerful landlords outside their religious house. Nuns performed important functions in the production of goods, especially silk. They were permitted to do tasks and visit people outside of the convent. The life of a nun, in short, remained continually intersected with her family and with the city of Florence itself. One daughter might create a marriage alliance in the neighborhood. Another might join the local convent to help direct its affairs to ends favorable to the family.[70] In mid-fifteenth-century Florence, both women and men observed the political world and its languages around them. Simultaneously, they pursued strategies aimed at honor and piety, as well as to augment their status within a world increasingly dominated, but not yet closed, by the Medici family.

In 1464 Cosimo de' Medici died. The funeral ceremonies ostentatiously emphasized that a great patrician had passed but nothing more. Cosimo's heirs buried him under a floor slab near the main altar in San Lorenzo. It was a prized position, but all wealthy people pursued prized burial spots in their neighborhood church.[71] The tomb professed that Cosimo was part of the system. He was not a despot, not a king. The Florentine government voted to dub Cosimo posthumously the *"pater patriae"* of Florence. The Ancient Roman title accentuated that Cosimo was at most first among equals. He was pious, humble, and a patron of the arts. He helped guide the republic rather than ruling it alone.[72] It was partially false: everyone knew that Cosimo had no equals in Florence. But it was also partially true: Cosimo did rule through making changes to, but while overall keeping, the republican system. He depended on the continued loyalty of allies. Would Cosimo's changes in and outside of Florence continue after he was gone?

Speeches are ephemeral, tombs can be stepped over, and paint only covers underlying cracks for so long. Men like Agnolo Acciaiuoli, Luca Pitti, and Dietisalvi Neroni had been content to work in Cosimo's system. As allies, they benefited from it. After all, whether or not resistance was an option, support was the path of least resistance. After Cosimo died his allies had to decide if Cosimo's son, Piero, deserved the same deference. His enemies had to determine if now was the moment to strike. A clean dynastic succession could maintain the status quo for friend and foe alike. A more open government promised obvious benefits for Cosimo's enemies. For friends the status quo promised continued benefits, but also a consolidating ceiling upon their ambitions. Perhaps a return to forms less controlled might yield to them greater rewards and greater honors. Was it really the Sforza in Milan with whom the Florentines should ally in external affairs? Should the Italian League continue? Maybe the French would be better partners? Was Florence a republic to be dominated by one family helped by others? Was Florence a republic with equitable sharing of honors and power? Florence seemed to be at another turning point.

4

THE MEDICI CONSOLIDATED, 1466–92

In the 1500s Francesco Guicciardini argued that Italy had enjoyed a golden age under the leadership of Lorenzo de' Medici, called Lorenzo the Magnificent. Lorenzo, Guicciardini claimed, had used the Peace of Lodi from 1454 to create decades of peace and stability for Florence and for all of Italy. During Lorenzo's golden age, warfare vanished, culture boomed, states prospered, and transalpine powers left Italy alone. Some centuries later, Voltaire showered similar praises upon Lorenzo and his Florence. But Voltaire went even further. He claimed that the second half of the fifteenth century marked one of the four great apices in European history.[1] Even today Lorenzo often appears in fictional and nonfictional historical accounts as a benevolent patron of the arts motivated by nothing else than the good of all and the beautification of his city. In those tales, his enemies were greedy men, too wicked to appreciate the age in which they lived.

The history of Florence between the deaths of Cosimo de' Medici in 1464 and that of his grandson Lorenzo in 1492 reveals a much more complicated story. Internal politics sped faster around the Medici center point. The Italian League continued to restrict external politics to regional affairs. Some Florentines continued or created new alliances with the Medici faction. Others resisted their approach to both internal and external affairs. Most Florentines did neither. They lived their lives as best they could within the changing systems in their city. For all of them, different visual and literary cultures offered tools to make claims to piety, status, and power. Even as the Italian League meant regional politics, Florentine culture spoke transcontinental languages. Florence seemed to be becoming synonymous with the Medici family. It also was an important source for cultural trends far beyond the Arno River.

The death of Cosimo de' Medici left his adult, sickly son Piero in charge of family, faction, and Florence. Piero had spent years watching Cosimo use economic might, patronage, culture, and allies to dominate Florence. Now it was Piero's turn.[2] But Cosimo's death provided an opportunity for his friends and enemies to reevaluate their respective situations. Hundreds of people began clamoring to return the city's political space to more people. They feared that the Medici might be setting up the sort of tyranny under which most other former Italian republics suffered. Had the Florentines evicted Charles of Anjou and Walter of Brienne only to suffer despotism under a would-be local lord? They demanded that the government return to its pre-Medici forms.

Momentum favored them. In the fall of 1465, the handpicked selections by the *accoppiatori* came to an end. Traditional elections by lot resumed. Debates about how open to make the government picked up where they had left off some decades earlier.[3] Things only got worse for Piero. In March 1466 Francesco Sforza died. Challenges to Piero's standing in Florence became more overt. Within two months around 400 people signed an oath to support traditional governmental forms and the end of electoral shenanigans. A standoff ensued. The Milanese offered Piero military support. Piero supplemented their force with a private army packed with thousands of men. The Florentine Luca Pitti emerged as the leader of the opposition. Luca received military backing from the Duke of Ferrara. He too amassed a large personal army.[4] The Tuscan hills threatened to run with more than just red wine in the summer of 1466.

Luca Pitti headed one of the old families in Florence that had calculated that support for Cosimo was in their interest while support for Piero was not. Already by the late 1300s, the Pitti were a leading Florentine family. The diary of Luca's father Buonaccorso Pitti, which began Chapter 2, tells of nights at the gambling tables; duels with French nobles; and drunken dances at death's door. In Florence, Buonaccorso Pitti's ties to the French set him apart from others. He even served as a diplomat from the Queen of France to Florence![5] Luca's son, also named Buonaccorso Pitti, continued the family's ties to France. In 1461–2, for example, Luca's son joined a handful of other Francophile Florentines to congratulate the new king of France, Louis XI.[6]

Like other Florentines, Luca Pitti proclaimed his status by building a new palace. He started constructing it during the 1450s. The building survives, even as later inhabitants greatly altered and expanded it.[7] Even so, a copy of a drawing of Florence during the 1480s suggests its

Figure 17 Francesco Rosselli (attributed). Florence (view from the chain) (copy of). Anonymous photo of nineteenth-century reproduction. Florence.

original audacious size (Figure 17). In the image, the palace marks the end of the Florentine cityscape in the *oltrarno* quarter of the city. Behind it roll the Pitti's extensive properties before butting up against the city wall. The Pitti Palace and two churches serve as the three landmarks that overshadow all the other smaller, interchangeable buildings in the quarter.[8] A painting from some decades later offers a similar view. In the painting, Luca Pitti wears red robes emblematic of patrician status in the city. His two sons stand behind him. They wear the same garments. They promise the future of the family line. Behind the men, the imposing Pitti Palace reminds viewers of the scale of Pitti power. Simultaneously, the fortress-like palace deters any would-be challengers to the Pitti's position.[9] Thus, even before its later additions, the original Pitti Palace was an ostentatious statement of family power and status. By 1466 Luca Pitti was welcoming allies to his house as if he were a noble holding court.[10]

The situation exploded in August 1466. With opposing armies in the surrounding areas, the *Signoria* ordered Luca Pitti and Piero de' Medici to reach an accord and disperse their supporters. Piero refused. Armed conflict seemed inevitable and people prepared for the worst. Money, not arms, carried the day. On August 29 Piero bribed Luca to change sides. Luca agreed to help Piero remain in power. In exchange, Piero offered three things. One, in Piero's government the *accoppiatori* would again handpick officeholders and Luca would be appointed to be among these new *accoppiatori*. Two, Luca's brother would also receive a prominent spot in the newly formed government. Three, Piero agreed to a marital tie with a Pitti daughter, thus formally uniting the interests of the two families.

Luca's betrayal of his allies turned the tide of the conflict. On September 1, Piero de' Medici summoned his private army of between 6,000 and 8,000 people to enter Florence. A second army packed with Piero's Milanese supporters, meanwhile, waited outside the city. Once again, a *parlamento* of citizens was called to the Piazza della Signoria. Once again, an armed guard watched the vote to ensure its outcome. Once again, the Florentines approved the *accoppiatori* to handpick officeholders. Luca Pitti's former allies fled town soon after.[11] They tried and failed to use alliances with other powers to aid their cause. Ultimately, when Piero de' Medici died in 1469 his sons Lorenzo and Giuliano inherited a state that left little ambiguity about who was in charge (Figures 18 and 19): four hundred Florentines had signed on to remove Medici controls after Cosimo's death in 1464; after Piero's death just five years later 700 Florentines signed an agreement to pass Piero's position down to his sons.[12] After 1469 it seemed the Florentines would need to be content to try to influence decisions rather than realistically to hope to outlive or outshine the young Medici patriarchs.

Figure 18 Andrea del Verrocchio (probable). *Bust of Lorenzo de' Medici*. Sixteenth-century copy of the original. Terracotta. National Gallery of Art, Washington D.C.

Figure 19 Andrea del Verrocchio. *Bust of Giuliano de Medici, c.* 1475–8. Terracotta. National Gallery of Art, Washington D.C.

Changes at Orsanmichele reflected the increasing strength of the Medici and the Italian League. In Chapter 2, Donatello's statue of St. Louis of Toulouse at Orsanmichele had shown the range of dissonant voices within the pre-1434 republic. For nearly fifty years that precious bronze sculpture had professed the continued power of the Guelf Party and their Francophile loyalties. After several years of the Medici-supported, anti-French Italian League, in 1463 the Guelf Party sold their niche at Orsanmichele to the Merchant's Tribunal, a civic body tasked with adjudicating trade disputes. The pretense was the Guelf Party's financial strains. However, the Medici faction had spent years seeking ways to minimize the Guelf Party's influence within and outside Florence. By contrast, they had actively promoted partisans to help run the Merchant's Tribunal.[13] Donatello's bronze was taken down. In its place, by the mid-1480s the artist Verrocchio placed a new bronze sculpted set of Christ and the Doubting Thomas, a copy which still fills Donatello's original niche. The new work replaced a sculpture with deep ties to France with a different story with long-time associations with the Medici family.[14]

The continued use of visual culture for at least partial political ends brought members of the Medici faction into contact with a young Leonardo da Vinci. Leonardo was the illegitimate son of a notary from a nearby town. He moved to Florence around 1464. Soon after his arrival he joined Verrocchio's workshop. As some people in the busy workshop

Figure 20 Andrea del Verrocchio and workshop. *Baptism of Christ, c.* 1470s. Oil and tempera on wood. Uffizi Gallery, Florence.

made progress on the Christ and the Doubting Thomas statues, Leonardo was assisting with several paintings.[15] Most strikingly, he worked with others to complete an image of the Baptism of Christ in the early 1470s (Figure 20). In workshops, apprentices learned to imitate the style of their master, and thus it is often difficult to identify the parts of pieces done by the master versus those done by assistants and apprentices. In this case, however, on the viewer's left, the profile of the angel and the landscape behind her reveal Leonardo's unmistakable *sfumato* style.[16]

In Verrocchio's workshop Leonardo assisted on projects commissioned to project Medici's artistic taste, power, and position. For example, in late January 1475, the Florentine government held a joust to commemorate the creation of a new agreement with Venice and Milan. It was a civic celebration for the Florentine state. However, the cultural images at the event informed all that Florence was becoming synonymous with Medici power. Giuliano was the Medici family representative. For the event he dressed to impress, wearing "pearls and jewels valuing more than 60,000 florins."[17] Like a stereotypical medieval knight, Giuliano supposedly fought for his beloved mistress Simonetta Cattaneo-Vespucci.[18] He brought forth two banners. One was made by the famed artist Botticelli. The other was sketched by Verrocchio but finished by Leonardo da Vinci. On the standard, a woman lounges on her arm after an exhausting day picking flowers. Cupid attempts to wake her from her slumber. The joust awaits. Several people held supporting roles in the event, but it was clearly Giuliano de' Medici who played the lead.[19]

In 1471, Lorenzo and Giuliano took measures to formalize further their primary position in Florence. Since 1458 and again in 1466 the Medici has been influencing the composition of the Council of 100. The Council of 100 in turn had handpicked the men who served as *accoppiatori*. The *accoppiatori* had then handpicked the *Signoria*. The *Signoria* had then run the state. It was cumbersome and different officeholders at times were showing signs of greater independence. Thus, a new change was made. Around forty people were charged with reforming the operations of the different Florentine legislative councils. The elder Medici brother, Lorenzo, was careful to handpick each of these forty people. The Council of 100 were assigned full power over matters of taxation, elections, and military affairs. Then, the group of forty handpicked individuals to be lifetime members of the Council of 100. The changes meant that the Medici family no longer had to worry about the larger, more traditional legislative bodies that used to approve legislation and that, because of their size, were harder to control. Control of the *accoppiatori* and the Council of 100 was now enough.[20] The Medici vice over political power was tightening.

Still Florentines tried to stop the doors closing on their republic.[21] At times people resisted through peaceful means. For example, in 1476 Alamanno Rinuccini was sent to Rome as a Florentine diplomat to the pope. Rinuccini was from an ancient Florentine family. Many of his friends in recent years had been moving from the Florentine middle to more overt support of Lorenzo and Giuliano. Perhaps Rinuccini would follow their example.[22] As a diplomat, Rinuccini was expected to inform Lorenzo directly of business in Rome. He was to conduct Lorenzo's wishes. He was also to keep the Florentine government informed of many matters, but only partially and only after he told Lorenzo. While abroad

Rinuccini ignored these expectations. Instead, he sent his diplomatic dispatches directly to the government. Lorenzo was furious. Rinuccini's political career effectively ended.[23] Embittered at the Medici's monopoly over honorable political pursuits, Rinuccini channeled his anger into a humanist dialogue on the nature of governments and tyranny. The dialogue offered a critique of Lorenzo de' Medici and the shenanigans of his allies.[24] Rinuccini's private family diary was even more pointed. There, from the *studio* within his own home, Rinuccini openly fumed about the tyranny of Medici control.[25] A family like the Rinuccini belonged in office and in charge or, at the very least, as partners in political control. Subservience to another family meant dishonor.

Other people used more violent means to oppose the political controls of the Medici during the 1470s. In 1471 a conflict broke out over who could profit from a valuable alum deposit near the town of Volterra. Lorenzo and Giuliano wanted to control it. The Medici family already possessed a monopoly over an alum deposit within papal lands. If they could add the Volterran deposit to their portfolio then they could both avoid a potential competitor and effectively corner the market in Italy and beyond. The Volterrans, by contrast, were interested in more local control. Without the Medici's influence, the town and its protectors could keep most of the profits. Thus, Volterra revolted. Lorenzo and Giuliano hired the mercenary captain Federico da Montefeltro to put down the revolt. In 1472 Volterra negotiated their surrender to that captain. Federico and his armies sacked the city anyway.[26]

Florentine families themselves continued to resist Medici control over the Florentine Republic. In 1478 one family and its allies were almost successful. The Pazzi family were another old Florentine family that had determined to work within the Medici system after 1434. At times the partnership worked very well. The two families even formed a marriage alliance to encourage future collaborations. However, tensions already were forming while Cosimo de' Medici was still alive. For example, in 1462 Alessandra Macinghi-Strozzi warned her exiled sons to stay distant from the Pazzi's offers of help and alliance. In her view, the Pazzi were simply no match for the Medici and their allies.[27]

The pressure built with Lorenzo and Giuliano's steadily increased control over political honors. No Pazzi were among the forty men picked in the governmental changes in 1471.[28] In 1473, the archbishop of Florence died. Just like in earlier centuries churchmen in Florence were big property owners and powerbrokers, but ones who existed within the Church hierarchy rather than the one controlled by the Florentine government. The Pazzi family wanted to choose a replacement so they could increase their power in Florence, their family status, and their access to an intercessor with God. The Medici brothers wanted the same things. Pope Sixtus IV sided with the Pazzi. Then he went a step farther. Pope Sixtus removed the Medici family from their lucrative position as papal bankers. In their place, the pope appointed the Pazzi.

The Pazzi were emboldened. They were buoyed by financial and political successes. They enjoyed explicit and implicit support from regional powers as well as the king of France. They were aggrieved at political controls that made their ancient lineage subservient to another Florentine family. Now was the time to remove the Medici from their perch and end the unnatural Italian League. A conspiracy was laid. Pope Sixtus IV, King Ferrante in Naples, Federico da' Montefeltro, and the Pazzi family joined together to plot the fall of Lorenzo and Giuliano from power.[29] The conspiracy was hatched in April 1478. The Pazzi and their allies attended mass at Santa Maria del Fiore. Lorenzo, Giuliano, and their supporters were also present. The priest raised the host during the mass. The Pazzi and their allies struck. Giuliano was killed. Lorenzo was wounded, but his supporters helped him escape to a separate room. They barred the door from the chaos outside. Time went by. Lorenzo escaped the cathedral and reached the safety of the Medici palace. Hours passed. The Pazzi tried to summon the populace to arms. Few came out to offer support: either the Medici or the Pazzi would pull the strings of Florentine political power. Did it really matter which one? Most Florentines, one way or another, would work within whichever system shook out.

The Medici allies took the advantage. Pazzi family members and their allies were hunted down and executed. No distance was far enough to escape Lorenzo's wrath. The man who had delivered the killing blows to Giuliano fled to Constantinople. There he was captured in 1479 and sent back to Florence. The murderous conspirator was hung by the neck, his body left to sway by a rope thrown from the ramparts of the Palazzo Vecchio. No less than Leonardo da Vinci drew an image of his corpse.[30] Who could draw the line between family vendetta and civic justice? The Pazzi's family palace was looted. Today, the enormous palace along the Via del Proconsolo shades a bustling street but projects a sort of elegant tranquility. It can be hard to scrape away the centuries to imagine violent fires erupting through its rooms, rooms that had just days before hosted men plotting murder. War inevitably followed between Lorenzo, the pope, Naples, and others. But just when it seemed that the Pazzi War might create major changes in Florentine and Italian affairs, in 1480 the Ottoman Turks landed in Apulia and conquered the town of Otranto. King Ferrante, Pope Sixtus, and all other political powers agreed to temporarily set aside their own differences to free their resources and fight somebody else.[31] The Italian League returned.[32] Lorenzo remained in power. Now he turned to making sure he stayed that way.

Lorenzo used the Pazzi War to further strengthen his control over the Florentine state. A new group convened in April 1480 to propose new changes to the Florentine Republic. This time, the call was to create yet another council. This time, it was to be made up of seventy men. The Seventy would possess final approval on all matters submitted to other government offices. In addition, members of the Seventy would be picked to form two new sub-bodies. The *Otto di Pratica* would control Florentine external affairs. The *Dodici Procuratori* would oversee finances. Final approval of the actions of both groups, of course, lay with the Seventy. The Seventy would handpick members of the *Signoria*, which would continue as a central executive body. Finally, the Seventy would select men for the *Otto di Guardia,* which would serve as a political police force. Lorenzo naturally would handpick the composition of the Seventy. Every five years the body would need renewal. Each renewal would provide an opportunity to reevaluate the Seventy's membership. Such was the plan. But first, the Florentines had to approve of the changes.

Florentines yielded supremacy of their city to the Medici family slowly, in fits and starts, with reluctance, and often by the narrowest of margins even when facing the overt threat of physical violence. But in hindsight, the creation of the Seventy seems inevitable, especially in the spring of 1480. Lorenzo had been the quasi-ruler of Florence for over a decade: a strong foundation existed to expand his power. Lorenzo was riding a wave of success: he had just returned from Naples where he had personally helped negotiate a peace accord. Lorenzo had completed brutal reprisals against the Pazzi family and their key allies: opponents had recent reminders of the risks of rebellion. Even so, the law to establish the Seventy passed by a single vote! Narrow victory or not, from 1480 all elections, decisions, and discussions passed through Lorenzo's hands. From Lorenzo, matters moved to his handpicked allies for any further actions and/or approvals.[33]

Few Florentines were long-time members of the Medici inner circle. Few Florentines were interested in an extreme measure like the Pazzi. Even the more measured actions of Alamanno Rinuccini may have seemed too risky. Most Florentines sought to accommodate themselves and adjust their ambitions to the system presented to them. As in previous chapters, the Pandolfini provide a good example. After Pandolfo Pandolfini's death in 1464, Pandolfo's brother, Pierfilippo, became the patriarch of the family. Pierfilippo began a nearly unbroken series of diplomatic missions to the principal rulers in Italy. There, he left no doubt about his loyalties. He may have formally represented the will of the Florentine government abroad, but in practice he was Lorenzo's man.[34] It was not that Pierfilippo abandoned the familial ambitions that his brother Pandolfo had pursued within the Florentine political middle in previous decades. It was that the flexibility available to Pandolfo no longer existed for Pierfilippo in the 1480s. By that time the most ambitious men had to find ways into Lorenzo de' Medici's orbit.

Other Florentines made the same choice as Pierfilippo. In the 1440s and 1450s Donato Acciaiuoli had chummed around with Giannozzo Manetti and wished for the return of a more open government. In the early 1460s, he had supported Piero de' Pazzi's efforts to undermine the Italian League by assisting the Angevin War against King Ferrante in Naples. Yet, in 1464 it was Donato Acciaiuoli who declared the decision to dub Cosimo de' Medici *pater patriae* of Florence. By the early 1470s, Donato was filling key diplomatic missions on Lorenzo's behalf. Only Donato's premature death prevented him from reaching the same sort of trusted status in the Medici inner circle as Pierfilippo Pandolfini.[35] Giovanni Rucellai too saw the writing on the wall. Barred from office in the 1440s and 1450s, Giovanni married a daughter from the Medici family. His ban was removed. Subsequently, from the early 1460s, the Rucellai family returned to political office. In those offices, Rucellai men demonstrated their willingness to work under Lorenzo's gaze to maintain control of the government by the leading faction.[36]

Families that joined the Medici faction continued to use culture to profess their piety, power, and status. For example, newly empowered Giovanni Rucellai commissioned Leon Battista Alberti to finish the facade upon the church of Santa Maria Novella (Figure 21). It was a monumental undertaking. No major church in Florence possessed a finished facade in 1470: San Lorenzo, San Marco, Santa Maria del Fiore, Santa Maria del Carmine, Santa Croce, and Santa Maria Novella all presented bare bricks to visitors at their front doors. Moreover, Santa Maria Novella presented its own unique challenges. For one, it was so large that a facade would be prohibitively expensive. Moreover, no facade could be worthy of the visiting popes and emperors who periodically took up residence in the church's apartments. Giovanni Rucellai, thus,

Figure 21 Design (mostly) by Leon Battista Alberti. Facade of Santa Maria Novella.
Photo by Jebulon. Florence.

was not asking for Alberti to rebuild a church, like the Medici at San
Lorenzo and San Marco, but his efforts proved similarly awe-inspiring
to fifteenth-century onlookers.

For the facade Alberti used a range of classical models to create a
unique and influential design. For the broad bottom of the church Alberti
copied the shape of an ancient triumphant arch. The center of the arch
corresponds to the church's front door. Alberti's design required that the
facade change its style from earlier incomplete attempts: Alberti's round
arches still contrast with the earlier pointed arches near the bottom
of the facade. Atop the triumphant arch Alberti placed a design like a
classical temple with telltale triangular roof and columns. The temple was
centered upon both the triumphant arch and the church's central window.
Here was a religious building—a temple. Here was Christ's victory—a
triumphant arch. Next to the temple Alberti covered the church's slanted
side roofs with a circle and scroll design. Later buildings throughout
Europe and even the world drew inspiration from that innovation.
Finally, near the top of the facade an inscription proudly proclaimed its
patron: "Giovanni Rucellai, son of Paolo, in the year 1470."[37] By that

time, the Rucellai were expressing their piety, even as they were also professing the honor and status won by successfully entering the Medici's political circle through marriage, negotiation, wealth, and culture.

All around them Florentines and foreigners saw the collapse of power and politics around Lorenzo de' Medici. For example, public processions were a regular occurrence in Renaissance Florence. Traditionally, those processions had emphasized group solidarity. Different civic bodies, current-office holders, confraternities, religious organizations, guilds, and other bodies in the city each played a role in events designed to beseech divine favor. After all, in a city of consensus politics, the myth was that all enjoyed access to power. However, from the 1470s and especially the 1480s these processions began to emphasize Lorenzo de' Medici instead of collective consensus. The Medici coats of arms, Medici saints, the Medici *palle* all replaced guild imagery and other traditional symbols from Florentine history. When the city celebrated the feast day of St. John the Baptist the accompanying rituals were careful to denote Lorenzo as the primary patron. When diplomats arrived in Florence, Lorenzo greeted them personally and housed them in his country villas. When Lorenzo went in public he uniquely traveled with an entourage. The Florentine Republic, in short, now had its own symbolic king.[38]

Lorenzo had left behind the earlier notion that he was first among equals: instead, he was the first Florentine. As such, Lorenzo needed to look outside Florence to find marital matches of sufficient status. He tried to find a bride for his brother in Venice, but Giuliano's premature death killed any fruit from those labors.[39] Lorenzo had better luck with his children. Maddalena married the illegitimate son of Pope Innocent VIII. Lorenzo's eldest son Piero married Alfonsina Orsini from Naples. Another son Giovanni was made the first cardinal from Florence in decades. Then, Lorenzo matched his younger children—matches that carried somewhat less prestige—with other Florentine families.[40] This approach contrasted with standard Florentine marriage practice, where Florentines married other Florentines. It mirrored the trans-peninsular marital strategies pursued by Italian nobles.[41]

Lorenzo's rise also changed the roles of women in Florence. Under the republic, the law had formally excluded women from political roles, even as women like Alessandra Macinghi-Strozzi had participated in politics in more indirect ways.[42] Yet, the role of women in politics became increasingly overt from the 1460s. For example, Lorenzo's mother, Lucrezia Tornabuoni, worked to secure the match between her brother Giovanni Tornabuoni and Luca Pitti's daughter that helped end the uprising in

1466. Next, she tackled the match between her son Lorenzo and Clarice Orsini. In those negotiations, Piero de' Medici's constant illnesses meant that Lucrezia needed to take a leading role. After Piero died, as a widow Lucrezia became a property manager, cultural patron, and accomplished poet in her own right. She also served as a primary confidante to her son Lorenzo until her death.[43] Clarice Orsini exercised even more overt political power. At times Clarice conducted roles in Lorenzo's place, both in and outside of Florence.[44] These changes in gender roles brought Florence more in line with expectations in princely courts, where it was not unusual for women to rule in the stead of an absent husband.[45]

These changes were possible in part because of educational opportunities for women in Laurentian Florence. Already in the fourteenth century, Giovanni Villani had commented upon the thousands of girls receiving a rudimentary education in Florence. That tradition clearly continued over the next two centuries.[46] Humanist educators, for example, presented educational programs aimed specifically at women.[47] By the latter fifteenth century, some Florentine women were reaching the heights of learned culture. Alessandra Scala, daughter of the Florentine chancellor Bartolomeo, was an accomplished writer who also interacted regularly with the city's leading humanists.[48] Antonia Pulci and the aforementioned Lucrezia Tornabuoni both took leading roles in the city's growing fascination with vernacular poetry.[49] In fact, by the latter 1400s, elite families simply assumed that basic literacy was an ordinary part of life for women. Correspondents, for example, saw nothing unusual about the reading habits of the daughters of Clarice Orsini and Lorenzo de' Medici.[50]

The lives of nonelite women in Laurentian Florence may also have benefited from these changes, but in many ways these women had always enjoyed more independence than their wealthier counterparts. Women with more modest social standing still embodied the honors of their families. Thus, the importance of chastity for them remained just as it did for elite women. However, daily life forced nonelite women to more frequently take to the streets to help family businesses. Sequestration at home simply was not an option.[51] Elite and nonelite women alike joined the city's convents to devote their lives to God and to do a range of tasks around the city. In and around the convent their piety and abilities helped their families.[52] All Florentines, to varying degrees and in different ways, were coming to terms with life in a quasi-princely city.

Lorenzo treated other Florentines in ways that fit a man without local equals. For example, in 1432 Florence won a battle in their war against

Lucca. The artist Paolo Ucello painted an image to commemorate the victory. Throughout the mid-fifteenth century the patrons of the painting possessed and displayed it. Lorenzo desired it, but the family refused to yield it. Thus, Lorenzo forcibly took it. There were no consequences.[53] The image then joined Lorenzo's extensive collection of precious objects. Within the Medici Palace, Lorenzo brought together dozens of antiquities, vases, and gemstones. From the collection, Lorenzo tailored exhibitions to the interests of his visitors.[54] After passing through the fortified doors of the peerless palace, in short, visitors entered seemingly endless displays of Medici wealth, power, piety, and position.

Florentines increasingly measured social status by means of Lorenzo's favor, even at the expense of other traditional characteristics. Fifteenth-century consensus politics had measured social status by a person's wealth, family ancestry, and a history of office-holding. However, Lorenzo promoted loyal individuals to positions of prominence with or without those traditional markers. Certainly, sometimes Lorenzo's allies came from the most illustrious Florentine families. Donato Acciaiuoli and Tommaso Soderini, for example, possessed impeccable credentials. Pierfilippo Pandolfini also had enough traditional status to warrant his position in the city. At other times, however, Lorenzo's favor placed new men from humble backgrounds into power. Under Lorenzo, Matteo Palmieri held premier offices and filled leading diplomatic roles. Palmieri was the son of an apothecary, a humanist writer, and a quasi-heretic.[55] Bartolomeo Scala was the son of a miller and a humanist writer. In Lorenzo's Florence, Scala was the Florentine chancellor, officeholder, and diplomat. He even received a knighthood from Pope Innocent VIII![56] Republics measured status with office-holding. Monarchies measured status by a person's position at court.

Visual and literary arts reflected these changes within Florence. Lorenzo himself died too young to create a patronage oeuvre to match his grandfather. Lorenzo nevertheless left his mark on the visual arts.[57] For much of the fifteenth century patrons had paid for paintings featuring crowds of people. In these crowds, viewers could identify the likenesses of the patron, his and her family and allies, as well as others with whom the patron wanted a semi-permanent visual association. The patron made an argument for his soul's salvation and his social status through the quality of the painting, the expense of its materials, and the fantasy of attendance at a biblical or historical scene. At times painters included recognizable facial likenesses. At other times a person's dress and context helped identify more generic painted people.[58]

Under Lorenzo de' Medici, some patrons changed their images to emphasize proximity to the Medici family. For example, the Medici bank director Francesco Sassetti commissioned paintings for his family chapel within the Florentine Church of Santa Trinità. In one image, the Medici family tutor leads the Medici children up a staircase. Lorenzo de' Medici proudly looks on. Next to him stands loyal Francesco Sassetti. The message was clear: the Sassetti, important managers of the Medici bank, enjoyed prime access to Lorenzo himself, Lorenzo's inner circle, and even Lorenzo's household.[59] That proximity combined with their wealth and chapel to prove their cultural sophistication, their status, and the surely certain salvation of their eternal souls.

The content and styles of literary culture also reflected changes in Florence. As in previous decades, stories about the city's past had to be changed to explain the present. In the aftermath of the Pazzi Conspiracy, the humanist Angelo Polizano did just that. In the late Roman Republic, the Roman historian Sallust had written a work called *The War against Catiline*. In that work, Sallust told of a failed rebellion against the Roman Republic by the overly ambitious and morally suspect Catiline. Poliziano used Sallust's work as a model for his *Account of the Pazzi Conspiracy*. Poliziano's pen characterized the Pazzi as terrible villains, hellbent on slaying the magnanimous Medici and enslaving Florence under an aristocratic tyranny. Poliziano granted them no redeeming qualities. The Pazzi were not misguided: they were monsters.[60] In other words, the Pazzi did not fit into a long line of people opposed to Medici controls. Rather they bloodthirstily attacked, as a contemporary medallion proclaimed, the "*salus publica.*"[61]

Other writers crafted works to legitimate the Medici co-option of the Florentine Republic. In 1490 the humanist Aurelio Brandolini dedicated his work *Republics and Kingdoms Compared* to Lorenzo de' Medici. Brandolini had begun his work while living at the court of King Matthias of Hungary. In it, Brandolini planned to praise the king and argue for the superiority of one-person rule over republics. The king died, however, and thus Brandolini moved to Florence. There, he continued work on the book. He kept his earlier sections intact but added a new final section. In that new part Brandolini argued that only Lorenzo de' Medici kept the chaos standard in republics at bay in Florence. According to Brandolini, Whatever concord and felicity we enjoy, we have received from this one man; he is nevertheless so moderate and gentle that he arrogates to himself no more power or authority than is fair; indeed, he refuses much of what is righty owed him, so that he seems to be not a single individual controlling everyone, but a single individual obeying and serving everyone.[62] The language of Latin and humanism could potentially carry that argument far and wide. Lorenzo was undoubtedly flattered at the elegant packaging of his preferred fiction.

Other learned works began to reflect Lorenzo's quasi-princely rule. Many of the most innovative Florentine writers shifted their emphases from rhetoric and ethics toward more metaphysical questions.[63] It was not that traditional humanist studies on rhetoric, history, translation, and ethics went away. The success and prolific writings of Matteo Palmieri and Bartolomeo Scala show that they clearly did not. But Marsilio Ficino's often esoteric explorations of Neo-Platonic philosophy became some of the most popular and influential original works of the latter fifteenth century.[64] In another example, Pico della Mirandola earned a learned reputation that spanned Europe. Before he was yet thirty years of age, he proposed 900 points that he claimed could unify the arguments of multiple philosophical schools. He prefaced the work with a powerful statement on the potential of human beings.[65] Such changes happened in part because of changes in the interests and questions of learned men and women. The social and political world of Florence also helps explain this change in learned focus. Socially, with so many Florentines at least dabbling in humanist letters, knowledge of new philosophical topics became a way to demonstrate unusual learning and impress others.[66] Politically, that philosophy influenced and was influenced by the world around it. Some authors presented Lorenzo as the philosopher prince. Marsilio Ficino presented Lorenzo as an heir to a theocracy based on pre-Christian ideas.[67]

Finally, even the style and presentation of latter fifteenth-century Florentine literature could influence and be influenced by the city's changing political situation. Lorenzo de' Medici was an accomplished vernacular poet in the 1470s and 1480s. Simultaneously the Florentines more generally renewed their interest in vernacular writings.[68] Did this trend happen because people wished to produce works popular with Lorenzo? Did Lorenzo produce vernacular poetry because he was a part of a broader cultural trend? Regardless, Lorenzo's later fifteenth-century Florence was bursting with innovative Italian writings and renewed interests in older ones. The university professor Cristoforo Landino published an edition with extensive commentary on Dante's *Divine Comedy*. Readers also could enjoy illustrations by Sandro Botticelli, as well as the intermixing of Medici family and Florentine civic symbols.[69] Luigi Pulci penned his vernacular epic the *Morgante*.[70] Marsilio Ficino popularized his translations by creating vernacular versions of them.[71] By the early 1490s writers were arguing that emulating classical Latin styles remained important, but so was creating eloquent literary styles in Italian. As in so much else, Lorenzo was at the center of it.[72]

And, thus, it seemed that the things might remain. For nearly 150 years Florence's regional political focus had contrasted with the transnational languages of its culture. The Italian League seemed stronger than ever: no Italian power seemed interested in returning peninsular affairs to wider continental struggles. Plus, after sixty years of struggle, the Medici family could finally seem to claim unchallenged supremacy over Florence. The embrace of the vernacular seemed to reflect this regional strength and Medici power. Tuscan was a regional dialect that maybe could fit the city's regional ambitions. Maybe in the decades to come Florence would enjoy Medici rule, regional stability, and cultural forms that spoke Tuscan much more than broader continental languages. But, golden age or reign of a tyrant, nothing lasts forever.

In 1492, at only forty-three years of age, Lorenzo was nearing death. He had been sick for some time. Doctors had been called, but their treatments did not work. Lorenzo called for the popular Dominican preacher Girolamo Savonarola to hear his final confession. A later writer claimed that Savonarola demanded that Lorenzo yield his control over Florence in order to be absolved of his sins. In the story, Savonarola told Lorenzo that "First, you must have faith. Lorenzo said, I do, father. Second, you must return those things which you have unjustly taken. Then Lorenzo, thoughtful, was silent for a little bit. Then he said, on this question I will do this later, father, or if I cannot do it then my heirs will take care of what is left. Third he added, restore the liberty of your state, so that the Florentine Republic is arranged in its former condition. Because Lorenzo gave no response to those words Girolamo left a little later, and not long after Lorenzo left from life."[73]

It remains a popular story, even as it almost certainly is not true. Savonarola and Lorenzo were on good terms in the 1490s. Lorenzo did call the Dominican to his bedside. Last rites were an expected, even necessary part of the faith of fifteenth-century Florentines. Savonarola absolved the powerful man's sins.[74] As Lorenzo's breath grew shallow, did he anticipate the end with a clean conscience and a hope of salvation? Or did he fear that he would soon join other tyrants, would-be tyrants, and slayers of just rulers in a hell like Dante had so vividly described in his *Inferno*?

Some Florentines claimed that lightning struck Brunelleschi's dome when Lorenzo died.[75] Such a natural sign portended the passing of a great man, the end of an era. Most Florentines may have agreed with the first of those, even as they were probably less sure of the second. Lorenzo had built upon the foundations of his grandfather and father to construct a seemingly impenetrable political fortress to match the physical Medici palace. Like them, he had effectively used transcontinental languages of culture to worship, display cultural tastes, and to solidify his position. Now Lorenzo's son Piero seemed poised to take his place. Perhaps, all things being equal, he might have. But the French had not forgotten their lost territories in southern Italy. Nor had they forgotten their former friends in Florence. A fiery preacher inside the city was claiming the end times were coming, and Florence would have a key role to play. Armageddon may not have been at hand, but a change was coming to the city on the Arno. International culture would continue, but political regionalism was going to end. So was the Medici supremacy over Florence.

5

THE END OF THE REPUBLIC, 1493–1530

Piero di Lorenzo de' Medici seemed to inherit a solid position. His father had passed down more than twenty-five years of consolidated control over Florence. After so many failed attempts to dislodge the Medici from power, perhaps Florentines had begun to accept that power in their city was synonymous with the Medici and their inner circle. A peaceful transition to Piero seemed assured. Piero, then, could complete the transition of Florence from republic to monarchy. After all, most of Italy had already transitioned to princely politics. Florence just seemed late to the party. Florentines were adept at adopting their ambitions to new situations. Most of them had already adopted to the system that Piero inherited.

The French introduced a whirlwind of change across the Italian peninsula, including Florence. The talented friar Girolamo Savonarola convinced the Florentines that the scourge of God would arrive and establish a new Jerusalem in Florence. Then a large and seemingly unbeatable French army invaded Italy. The prophecy seemed true. The Medici fled the city. Subsequently, the French armies left the Italian League in tatters. Suddenly, Florence was professing the pro-French positions of its medieval heyday. The republic was reborn! But all was ephemeral. By 1512 the Medici had returned to Florence in triumph. By then the Medici family possessed too much power, too much wealth, and too many international connections to even pretend to be one Florentine family among many others. The French invasion and the Medici family's final push ended Florentine political regionalism. For the first time since the fourteenth century, the transcontinental languages of culture matched the continental political struggles enmeshing Florence. But the early modern Florence of 1530 was hardly seeking to become Rome reborn. It was one city of many trying to stay topside in the tempest of the Italian Wars.

After Lorenzo died in 1492 his son Piero tried to continue his father's manipulation of the Florentine government. At first, his father's allies transferred their loyalty to the son. Just over a week after Lorenzo had died the Florentine government passed two laws to confer to Piero the same offices held by his father. The same Council of Seventy was to continue. The same rules were to allow the *accoppiatori* to continue picking officeholders. Piero's allies seemed confident. Factions existed within the ruling regime, but the city had never been free of people forming groups to pursue paths for their own honors. People abroad plotted against him, but when had outsiders not plotted against the ruling regime? Piero pushed forward and turned to shoring up his support across the peninsula and beyond.[1] Maybe his transition could be as relatively smooth as his father's had been.

But things in 1492 were not the same as they had been decades before (Figure 22). Lorenzo de' Medici owed his success during the 1480s and early 1490s to his keen political abilities and his advantageous familial ties to a supportive pope. Lorenzo and Pope Innocent VIII had worked with Naples and Milan to uphold the strength of the Italian League and the Medici position in Florence. But Lorenzo's death was soon followed by that of the pope. The new pope—the still notorious Borgia Pope Alexander VI—had his own ambitions and plans, which hardly centered on the Medici relatives of his predecessor. Tensions consequently rose between the new pope and Piero's Florence. Additionally, problems were arising between Naples and Milan. The Italian League was springing leaks faster than anyone could plug them, let alone the young Piero de' Medici.[2]

To make matters worse, King Charles VIII in France began planning an invasion of the peninsula: he may have even blamed Lorenzo de' Medici for some of his grievances.[3] The prospect of a French presence in Italy was hardly new. But the situation in France was simply different in 1492 than it had been before. After the chaos of the Hundred Years' War (1337–1453) had ended, the French king Louis XI had consolidated the resources of his large kingdom.[4] Additionally, the Duke of Anjou had died and bequeathed his lands to the French crown.[5] Angevin claims to southern Italy, thus, joined the other claimed lands of the king of France. King Louis died without pressing the issue. His heir, King Charles VIII, took more interest.

Figure 22 William R. Shepherd. *Italy about 1494* (originally published in *The Historical Atlas of Europe*) (New York: Henry Hold and Company, 1923).

Things came to a head in 1494. Piero de' Medici's efforts to maintain the Italian League while offering lip service to French requests for support failed. The regent in Milan, Ludovico Sforza, and Pope Alexander VI both turned to France as a possible ally against Naples. Piero de' Medici, meanwhile, decided to lean into his alliance in Naples. When the requests from Sforza and the pope arrived in France, King Charles was just concluding a war against Brittany. Consequently, he boasted an army of restless veterans without a current conflict to satiate their bloodlust. Already generally interested, the people around King Charles further fanned his focus on his inherited claims in Italy.[6] Disenfranchised Florentines and members of Piero's own extended family assured the king that Florence was ready to remove the Medici, leave behind the regionalism of the Italian League, and return to its days of overt, tangible support for French causes.[7]

Charles pushed the deafening cannons of the French monarchy onto the stained Italian battlefields of the old Angevin dukes. His armies seemed invincible. Over the Alps, into Milan, farther south, they went. Their inexorable march reached Tuscany. There, Piero's youth, inexperience, and haughty personality worsened what was already a precarious, probably impossible situation.[8] Piero did not even pretend to work within the heavily corrupted republican system. Instead, he placed himself at the head of an embassy to negotiate terms with King Charles. It was a disaster. The Florentines had conquered and bought their regional state over the course of nearly four centuries. They were especially proud of their conquest of Pisa in 1406, which they compared to Rome's defeat over Carthage in Antiquity.[9] Nevertheless, Piero gave their cities to the king. He gave Pisa to the king.[10] Piero asked for nothing in return. When Piero's terms reached Florence the dishonor was too much for the men within the government. They refused to accept them. Piero was forced to flee the city in disgrace. The Florentines sent a different embassy, this one featuring the Dominican friar Girolamo Savonarola.[11]

Since 1490 Girolamo Savonarola had been preaching at San Marco about the end of the world. From his pulpit, Savonarola prophesized that a scourge of the Lord would soon descend upon Italy. This instrument of the Lord would conquer everything in his path. Savonarola urged his listeners to prepare by reforming their ways and demanding broader reforms in their Church. Savonarola began attracting a massive audience. Both he and his listeners noted the similarities between Savonarola's prophecies and Charles VIII's descent through the peninsula. After Piero's failures, the city turned to the prophet to save their city from

King Charles's terrifying armies. The mission went better than Piero's had gone. The French armed turned south without sacking Florence. Savonarola's reputation morphed from talented preacher and divine prophet to savior of the city.[12]

Savonarola and the collapse of the Italian League returned Florentine diplomacy to its old pro-French positions. For decades the Medici family had overseen policies that promoted regional insularity while only pretending to continue Florentine affinities for French causes. With the Medici gone the political pendulum ostensibly swung back in favor of France, even as, beneath the surface, things remained just as contested as before.[13] For example, in 1497, a group of young people in Florence were playing a game with two teams. One team took the name "the King," after the king of France. That team was made up of Florentines who supported Savonarola. The other team consisted of those opposed to the friar. They called themselves "the Duke," after the Duke of Milan.[14] The "King" was winning in the latter 1490s. But how long would it be before the "Duke" and his imperial allies regained the upper hand?

Savonarola combined pro-French policies with governmental changes that theoretically expanded direct access to political power. With Piero gone, the Florentines disbanded the government bodies that the Medici had used to maintain power. What would take their place? After much debate, the city settled upon a Great Council that both expanded access to political power while maintaining some control over who possessed political access. This new Great Council was open to any individual who had an ancestor or had himself been previously deemed eligible for the *Signoria*. That stipulation meant that the same basic sorts of people who had held office in previous decades could expect to continue to do so in the new system. Thus, there was continuity. But, unlike the previous facades of consensus politics, members of the Great Council possessed real power. In the system, legislation began with the *Signoria* and its colleges. A group of eighty then voted to advance that legislation to the Great Council for a final up or down vote. The 3,452 people within Great Council did not have to consent to others pulling the strings while they contented themselves with hollow, impotent offices.[15] Rather, a significant number of adult males had a direct say in the policies promoted in their city.

Once again, changes in the present necessitated a new Florentine past. Previous writers had justified Florence's politics and positions by tying the city to the Roman Republic, Julius Caesar, and/or Charlemagne. Savonarola preached that those classical and medieval foundation stories missed the point. For Savonarola, a classical foundation was secondary to Florence's special role in God's divine plan. In his sermons, Savonarola argued that Florence would become a new Jerusalem. In that role, Florence needed to purify itself of its sinful ways. Once purified, the Florentines would bring about the return of Christ and a new age. Florence, in short, was the central city in the story of Armageddon.[16] It was a twist that reflected a city enthralled by its charismatic preacher. But it also reflected the changed political realities of the city. Thrust back into a continental political exchange, few foresaw a forthcoming Florentine empire to rival that of Ancient Rome. Rather, people were starting to rate Florence as one of the weaker powers in Italy.[17] Who knew how God would turn things around for the weakened city? Clearly, He would: Florence might not recreate the Roman Empire, but its prophecies foretold of its central role in the age to come.

Florentines adjusted their transcontinental languages of culture to make new arguments about their new situations. It could not be otherwise: Florentines from all walks of life were drawn to Savonarola, and those people included many of Florence's leading writers, thinkers, and artists.[18] Here was Sandro Botticelli hearing a sermon and nodding his head with the friar's words.[19] Here was Marsilio Ficino listening to Savonarola, initially agreeing with him, and then ultimately rejecting his arguments.[20] Here was a young Michelangelo Buonarroti, struck so much by Savonarola's fiery words and delivery that he still recalled them years later.[21] Here was Pico della Mirandola, in another part of the nave, thinking it was God's work that had led Pico himself to convince Lorenzo de' Medici to bring Savonarola to San Marco. Pico's mind drifted from the friar's words: perhaps Pico should join Savonarola in the Dominican order? Here was Angelo Poliziano, fond of Pico, less sure about Savonarola.[22]

Savonarola both impacted and was impacted by Florentine culture. For example, in the 1470s and 1480s Sandro Botticelli painted works with classical themes. In the *Birth of Venus*, the goddess of love emerges from the sea upon a shell. She uses her hair to hide her nudity (Figure 23). In the *Primavera*, Botticelli created an enigmatic work based upon both vernacular and Latin poetical traditions (Figure 24). Such works had fit well in the esoteric and poetic cultural interests of Lorenzo de' Medici's Florence. However, in the 1490s, Botticelli became interested in Savonarola's message. At around the same time, he started painting more religious images to facilitate prayers. He may even had adopted a new abstract style to reflect his belief that the body was a corrupt vessel

Figure 23 Botticelli. *Birth of Venus*, 1482–5. Tempera on canvas (photo attributed to the Google Art Project). Uffizi Gallery, Florence.

Figure 24 Botticelli. *Primavera*, *c.* 1480. Tempera on panel (photo attributed to the Google Art Project). Uffizi Gallery, Florence.

separated from God.[23] Savonarola also influenced Florentine writers and thinkers. Pico della Mirandola had long been fascinated by astrology. As he gravitated toward Savonarola's orbit, he doubled down on that interest and crafted an in-depth attack upon that practice. Savonarola knew about the work and the two men talked about the topic. After Pico had died Savonarola wrote a condensed, vernacular, more religiously based version of Pico's text to help spread its arguments.[24]

Savonarola, like Piero di Lorenzo de' Medici, failed to navigate the tempestuous political waters of Europe during the 1490s. Problems grew at home and abroad. Divisions cracked across Florence. Some people became fanatical supporters of Savonarola and his reforms. Others became arch opponents of a person whom they viewed as a false prophet. Still others were both uncertain about Savonarola the prophet and reticent about his political ideas. Then others focused their efforts on bringing the Medici back into Florence.[25] As so often happened these internal developments played off external changes. Savonarola went too far in his condemnation of church figures and thus was excommunicated. He was ordered to stop preaching. And he did stop, for a while. But after several months, he began again in the spring of 1498. The city went under an Interdict, meaning that if Savonarola continued his sermons then all Florentines risked damnation. The Florentines split on the issue. Some were convinced of Savonarola's piety. Others were convinced he was a demon. Others were simply not sure. Nobody knew how things would turn out.[26]

The cross-town rivalry between the Franciscan and Dominican orders brought the crisis to a head. Franciscan friars from Santa Croce challenged the Dominican Savonarola to a test by fire. The idea was that, if Savonarola was God's prophet, then God would protect him as he walked through a blazing fire, while Savonarola's Franciscan opponents would be burned alive. If Savonarola was, by contrast, a heretic and blasphemer, then God would destroy him with the fire while protecting his Franciscan rivals. Were not the hagiographies full of such miraculous divine interventions? Savonarola probably did not have a chance to consider the matter before one of his more zealous supporters jumped at the chance to prove his prophet's piety. The event was to take place in front of the Palazzo Vecchio. It would settle things once and for all.

The day of the contest arrived. A huge crowd gathered in the Piazza della Signoria to see the miracle of Savonarola's salvation or the ignominy of his demise. Savonarola was not present and was instead represented by a proxy. The Franciscan challengers arrived. The two groups began to argue about the procedure: Who should go first? How should the contest unfold? They argued long enough that it started to rain. Maybe God had ordained that the contest not happen at all? Perhaps, but the event definitively turned the tide against Savonarola in the city. Angry citizens attacked San Marco. They seized Savonarola. They locked him in the tower cell in the Palazzo Vecchio. Civil and ecclesiastical trials followed. Savonarola and two key assistants were condemned. In May, Savonarola and the two followers were hanged and then their bodies were burned in the Piazza della Signoria. After the fire went out the charred remains were carefully collected and dumped in the Arno: there would be no relics for the pious to pray with or for entrepreneurs to sell.[27] Centuries later, the Florentines placed a commemorative marker in the Piazza della Signoria to remember the location of the pyre and to express regret about Savonarola's execution.

Just how far did Savonarola's impact reach? Was it Savonarola who brought changes to Pico and Botticelli's work? Did their works, by contrast, simply undergo a natural evolution in style as the two men grew older? It is impossible to say for sure. Ultimately, Savonarola may have aimed to purify Florence through things like a "bonfire of the vanities," but culture continued, and a lot of it lacked influence from the friar.[28] What about Savonarola's targets? For example, the friar Savonarola railed against homosexuality in Florence. Consequently, his followers instituted two periods of intense persecutions between 1495 and 1497. But those sorts of things didn't last.[29] Homosexuality had been and remained common in Renaissance Florence. Usually, an older man played a dominating role in a relationship with a younger, passive partner. Most men married women by their earlier thirties and then began a more strictly heterosexual stage of life.[30] There is much less evidence about lesbians in Renaissance Florence: people assumed that the female body was merely an imperfect imitation of male perfection. Thus, they scoffed at the idea that women could willingly look to each other for companionship. Even so, some such relationships still formed.[31] Some loving homosexual bonds may even have existed among Savonarola's followers. Pico and Poliziano, for example, may have reciprocated feelings stronger than platonic friendship.[32] Lovers or friends, the two men now rest next to each other within San Marco, where Pico's tomb leaves out that he died from arsenic poisoning.[33]

It is easier to identify Savonarola's long-term impacts on religion and politics. Far into the 1500s and beyond many Florentines believed in Savonarola and worked to enact his religious programs.[34] He even became seen as a harbinger of the Protestant Reformation. Beyond that, even when his post-mortem followers were not in power, Florence still felt Savonarola's political impact. For example, the Great Council survived him, even if in revised form. After Savonarola's death, some Florentines argued that the city needed more restrictive governing bodies that could limit the power of the Great Council. Others were opposed. In the end, they reached a compromise: the Great Council would keep its power, but the city would select a Standard Bearer of Justice to a lifetime appointment. That long-serving Standard Bearer, people thought, could provide an *ottimato* counterbalance to the popular-based Great Council. Around 2000 Florentines proposed and voted on candidates for the new lifetime position. They settled upon Piero Soderini. Soderini, it was thought, was not driven to enact more radical Savonarolan reforms, nor was he interested in the return of the Medici to Florence.[35] The hope was that he would govern somewhere in between.

The Soderini family had long enjoyed power within Florence. In recent decades, Piero's father Tommaso and his uncle Niccolò had been two of the most consequential Florentines between around 1460 to 1485. After the death of Cosimo de' Medici in 1464 Niccolò Soderini had plotted to end the electoral machinations on which the Medici had built their political position. He lost that fight. He was exiled. Niccolò's brother, Tommaso, by contrast, fared much better. Tommaso became a leading statesman and advisor to Lorenzo de' Medici by the early 1470s. Tommaso continued in that role until his death in late 1485.[36] After Tommaso, the next generation of Soderini men united in their support for a more open republic freed from Medici influence. Piero pushed those policies from his position as Standard Bearer of Justice for Life. He had powerful help abroad. Pope Alexander VI made Piero's brother Francesco a cardinal. Francesco, in turn, worked in Rome to maintain papal support for his brother back in Florence.[37]

Both Soderini brothers combined their efforts to drum up papal support to continue Florence's recent return to pro-French positions. Indeed, King Louis XII of France had helped get Francesco Soderini elected as a cardinal in the first place, and then Louis's successor, King Francis I, remained a key advocate for Soderini until the cardinal died in 1524.[38] The Guelf band of Florence, France, and the papacy was back together again, after a decades-long break-up from Medici-backed regionalism, papal conflicts, and lip service to French causes.[39] But appearances were deceiving. The complex chaos of the Italian Wars made an actual return to the Guelf positions of old impossible. The Spanish had invaded the Italian peninsula to drive out the French. The empire and the Spanish united their efforts. The papacy joined the Spanish; now the French; now the emperor; now someone else. All powers demanded Florentine allegiance. In the past the Florentines had tried to delay diplomatic crises so long that the issues had resolved themselves.[40] But Florence around 1500 was not a late medieval powerhouse negotiating with poor rulers who led small forces. Florence in 1500 was a regional power surrounded by the large, well-financed armies of others. The luxury of delay or consistent alliances was no longer permitted to them. The Florentines continually had to pick sides. It was only a matter of time before they picked wrong at the wrong time.

The loss of Pisa only made things worse. When Florence was still an insignificant town, medieval Pisa had risen to prominence as a major maritime power in the western Mediterranean Sea.[41] Florence and Pisa began to fight over Tuscany as Florence itself grew in population and power. After the hard decades in the mid-1300s, Pisa became subsumed into a large empire held by the Duke of Milan. When that duke died, his empire died with him. Florence seized its chance: after a brutal siege, Florence conquered Pisa in 1406. For nearly a century after, Pisa remained a key city within the Florentine territorial state.[42] By the 1470s, in fact, Lorenzo de' Medici selected Pisa as the place to which he wished to relocate much of the University of Florence.[43]

But the Pisans preferred liberty to subservience. The arrival of the French in 1494 provided them the opportunity to declare their independence. The Florentines appealed for help. The French promised to return the city to Florence just as soon as their work in Italy was complete. They lied. Time passed. Florence continued to try to retake Pisa by force. New ideas were needed. Some Florentines proposed redirecting the Arno River: the river left Florence, flowed through Tuscany, into Pisa, and then out to the Tyrrhenian Sea. Perhaps Pisa could be deprived of its central waterway? No less than Leonardo da Vinci and then Niccolò Machiavelli were brought in to engineer a plan. Despite the project's star power, it did not work. Pisa still stood.[44] Machiavelli tried a different idea. For centuries the Florentines had relied upon mercenaries to fight their wars. Machiavelli proposed that perhaps a standing citizen army could work better. Standing citizen armies are commonplace in the twenty-first century, but it was unusual for a time that tended to use mercenaries to fight conflicts.[45]

As the Florentines juggled competing, pressing external commitments with their burning desire to return Pisa to their control, within Florence they continued to use culture to make bold, transcontinental statements about their own power, piety, position, and status. In one example, the Florentine government-commissioned Michelangelo Buonarroti to create a new sculpture for Santa Maria del Fiore. By 1500 Michelangelo already was famous. He had fled the political problems in Florence in the 1490s and stayed in Bologna and then in Rome, sculpting as he went.[46] In Rome, he found patronage among cardinals. For one, he carved a nude and drunk Bacchus. Now, the work wows visitors to the museum in the Bargello. Then, the cardinal was unimpressed. For a different patron, Michelangelo carved a *Pietà*. In the work, a youthful Mary holds her sacrificed adult son. So polished and detailed is the carving that it seems only a matter of time before the Virgin's face wets with tears. Thousands of pilgrims to the church of Saint Peter's in Vatican City still silently weep with her.[47] After his *Pietà,* Michelangelo returned to Florence, where he was tasked with completing a partially finished work from a faulty piece of marble.[48]

By 1503 Michelangelo had completed his *David* (Figure 25). The Florentines quickly decided that it was better suited to the Piazza della Signoria than a high perch atop Santa Maria del Fiore. Most previous sculptors had depicted David at his moment of triumph: a confident youth was usually shown standing upright, his foot upon the decapitated head of his foe Goliath. Michelangelo changed the scene. In his *David*, a perfect male nude looks out at his implied adversary prior to their battle. David scowls slightly as he considers his enormous foe. He remains confident: he needs no armor; he feels no fear, for God's protection is stronger than any leather or steel. His sling stands ready for the forthcoming fight.[49] For 400 years *David* guarded the Palazzo Vecchio. In the latter nineteenth century the work was moved, and then in the early twentieth century a copy resumed *David*'s sentry. For over a century the original sculpture has rested a bit north in an interior space specifically designed to display it to visitors.[50]

It is hard today to imagine the impact of Michelangelo's giant *David* in the early sixteenth-century Piazza della Signoria. The copy today shares the Piazza with other huge works, most of which commemorate later rulers, their claims, and their accomplishments. Yet, strip away the other sculptures in the Piazza. Remove the later Uffizi Gallery. Return the *ringhiera* from which Florentine officials used to host important visitors, view events, and make announcements. What is the scene? David, long a symbol of the Florentine Republic, stood alone to protect the new Florentine Republic headed by Piero Soderini.[51] What a protector he

Figure 25 Michelangelo. *David*, 1503. Nineteenth-century copy showing original location. Marble sculpture. Photo by Txllxt TxllxT. Florence.

was! *David* called to mind not only the art of the ancient world but also the power of God to protect the pious. Here was a warrior capable of defending Florence from the continual onslaught of enemies and allies alike. It was a reassurance to the Florentines themselves. It was a reminder and a warning to all others outside the city of Florence's role in God's plan and its traditional claims to Antiquity.

Should an enemy pierce through *David*'s defenses then the Florentines also shored up their cultural guards within the Palazzo Vecchio itself. In the fifteenth century no room in the building could comfortably house the hundreds, even thousands of voting citizens of the Great Council. Thus, renovations were underway to create an adequate space. On the walls Leonardo da Vinci and Michelangelo Buonarotti were each

Figure 26 Leonardo da Vinci, copied and augmented by Peter Paul Rubens.
Battle of Anghiari. Sixteenth-century drawing (anonymous photo).
Wikimedia Commons

commissioned to paint a fresco commemorating a past Florentine military victory. Leonardo chose the Battle of Anghiari from 1440, at which Florentine forces overseen by Neri di Gino Capponi had defeated Milan. Leonardo planned a swirling image of violence and snarling horses (Figure 26). In the same room, Michelangelo depicted Florentine surprise at the Battle of Cascina in 1364. Naked men quickly jump from the river to arm themselves against their foes (Figure 27).[52] In the hours after the moment painted by Michelangelo, the Florentine forces recovered the advantage and defeated Pisa. Neither image was finished, but both would have dripped with contemporary significance.[53] Could Florence find victory again against Milan, their traditional nemesis before the Medici family and then an enemy again after the family had departed in 1494? Could they duplicate their historical success at Cascina by retaking the city of Pisa?

In the early sixteenth century a conquest of Milan by Florence was out of the question. But Pisa fell to the Florentines in 1509. The conquest reflected Florentine agency even as it also revealed the city's limitations on a larger European gameboard. Pisa was a city for other powers to use

Figure 27 Michelangelo Buonarroti. *Battle of Cascina*. Sixteenth-century copy by
Bastiano da Sangallo. Holkham Hall, England

to entice or attack Florence: ally with us, they seemed to say, or face our
support of the Pisans![54] Even after the Florentine conquest of the city that
situation continued. In 1509 wider European politics brought an end to
an alliance between the pope and France. By 1511 the French and the
papacy were at odds. The French wanted a church council to depose the
pope and explore church reforms aimed at pressuring their enemies. They
viewed Pisa as the perfect location.[55] The papacy, naturally, was opposed.
Florence had to choose. They chose the French. The pope responded by
calling his own council and declaring all conclusions from the Council of
Pisa null and void. A new alliance formed pitting much of Europe against
France and their lonely ally Florence.[56]

The Florentine balancing act between competing external powers
grew ever more precarious. Things were just as chaotic within the city's
walls. Piero Soderini's reign as lifetime Standard Bearer of Justice overlay
the same kinds of competing factional interests that had troubled the
Medici family and then Savonarola. Some Florentines were devoted to
Piero Soderini. They viewed the office of Standard Bearer for Life as
a good innovation, at least for now. Other families viewed Soderini as
not pursuing politics favorable enough to older families. Some families
remained loyal to Savonarola. Other families viewed the return of the
Medici family as their top political priority. Others focused on other
matters entirely.[57] Factions riddled the Florentine Republic from within,

111

powerful states shook the city from without. How long could Soderini manage such an untenable situation?

Even close-knit families split in the continually cracking political landscape of the early sixteenth century. The sons of Giannozzo Pandolfini, brothers of Pandolfo Pandolfini, introduced in Chapters 3 and 4, illustrate some of the complexity. Pierfilippo Pandolfini had become a primary support of the Medici family before 1494. After Piero de' Medici fled town, Pierfilippo maintained a powerful position within the new republican forms.[58] Pierfilippo's brother, Jacopo Pandolfini, was a prominent follower of Savonarola before changing heart and advocating to silence Savonarola in the spring of 1498. Then, after Savonarola's death, Jacopo was able to maintain his position in the new government.[59] Another brother, Niccolò Pandolfini, became a cardinal. In that role in Rome, he spoke ill of Piero Soderini's government and allied himself with Cardinal Giovanni de' Medici, who became the Medici patriarch after Piero's death in exile in 1503.[60] By contrast, a nephew of these Pandolfini brothers, Battista, was among the first people to seize assets from the Medici family after Piero's exit from Florence. Battista hosted Charles VIII as the king waited to enter Florence in 1494. Unlike his uncles, Battista was prevented from holding offices in the government. All these Pandolfini men used their resources, connections, and wits as tools to aggrandize themselves and their families in the complex early sixteenth century. Many of them professed their piety, position, power, and status through culture, like with their new chapel in the Badia, their classical renovations to their ancestral homes, and their new palace on the northside of town.[61] These Pandolfini provide but a handful of examples of the thousands of Florentines doing their best to prosper in the chaotic cinquecento.

The Medici themselves were a family looking out for ways to increase their power. After his exile, Piero de' Medici tried several times to finagle a means to return to his former position in Florence.[62] In 1503 he died, still trying. Leadership of the family passed to Piero's brother, Cardinal Giovanni. Giovanni continued Piero's efforts. Within a year, in September 1504, Giovanni hosted a gathering of forty Florentines in Rome. The event openly and intentionally disobeyed a law passed in Florence in 1497 that had prohibited the city's citizens from associating with the Medici family while abroad. Next, in 1509, Cardinal Giovanni arranged the marriage of his niece, Clarice di Piero de' Medici, to Filippo Strozzi, a young patriarch of the powerful Strozzi family.[63] It was a clear indication that nearly fifteen years after his brother's ignominious exit, Giovanni de' Medici's sights remained on Florence.

A culmination of crises in 1512 brought Cardinal Giovanni's plans to fruition. France and Florence were no match for a trans-European papal alliance. In June the French fled the peninsula, and with them went Florence's only ally. Matters deteriorated rapidly. On September 1 the papal armies with their Spanish allies opened Florence to Cardinal Giovanni's brother Giuliano. The Medici were back. On September 16 the Medici and their Spanish allies seized control of the Palazzo Vecchio. Three days later the Spanish relinquished control to Cardinal Giovanni and left town.[64] After nearly two decades fortune seemed to be smiling on the Medici family once again. In March 1513, Cardinal Giovanni was elected pope. He took the name Leo X. Based in Rome, Pope Leo appointed his nephew Lorenzo to rule Florence in his stead. Then, Leo turned to his marital ally Filippo Strozzi to help intermix papal, Florentine, and Medici monies. Florentine affairs joined papal ones. In that role, the city became part of the supporting cast in a play starring the French, the empire, the Spanish, and the papacy.[65]

Niccolò Machiavelli endured the return of the Medici family to Florence worse than most. Machiavelli derived from a family situated on the fringe of the governing elite. As such, he naturally received a humanist education. By 1498 he had joined the Florentine chancery as the "second chancellor." In that role, Machiavelli drafted documents, accompanied diplomats, and himself served as a diplomat on delicate missions. He became close to Piero Soderini. As a trusted confidant, he was granted unusual levels of responsibility and leeway in his field dispatches. Consequently, Machiavelli influenced Florentine politics more under Soderini than might be expected from his official position.[66] Consequently, when Soderini's regime fell to the Medici return, Machiavelli found himself in a dangerous position.

The new Medici-backed regime in 1512 eyed former Soderini supporters with suspicion. They had good reason to do so. In 1514 a group of Florentines sought to ferment a revolt against their rule. Machiavelli was implicated in the conspiracy. He was arrested. He was tortured with the *strappado*, a device where a torturer ties the condemned person's hands behind the back; pulls the rope through a raised pulley; and then lifts and drops the person. Machiavelli confessed very little. Was he innocent of the charges against him? Was he adept at resisting torture? Afterward, Machiavelli moved out of Florence to a nearby family farm. There, he pined about his misfortunes and boredom to his friend Francesco Vettori. Machiavelli told Vettori about days spent collecting country gossip at the local tavern. At night, however, he donned the formal clothes that he had used as a government official. He entered his study. He conversed with the ancients. Fortune may have removed Machiavelli from positions of political power, but the minds of Antiquity still welcomed him in their midst. With them, he was happy. With them, he wrote *The Prince*.[67]

Machiavelli's *Prince* illustrates the political and cultural changes gripping early sixteenth-century Florence. In his short treatise, Machiavelli sought to advise the new Medici rulers on how to govern a state. Each chapter presented a different political topic. In each scenario Machiavelli offered a pragmatic and at times seemingly amoral approach to problems. He brought in specific ancient and contemporary examples to prove his arguments. The text's ostensible simplicity masks its enigmatic complexities. Consequently, scholars have endlessly debated the significance, the meaning, the originality, the intention, and the language of *The Prince*. For most, Machiavelli has emerged neither as a Machiavellian cynic nor an unprecedented thinker. Rather, he was a man of his times. Machiavelli crafted beautiful Italian prose into original arguments. He divided society into conflicting social groups and sympathized with the people. He forcefully argued that rulers needed to focus on the pursuit, maintenance, and growth of their power. Ideally, the pursuit of power would also follow Christian morality. Occasionally, rulers needed to appear to act virtuously even as they did less upstanding things. It was and is a controversial work.[68] But it was also one whose arguments and examples resonated far beyond Florence. The use of the vernacular, meanwhile, continued the ongoing cultural shift in Florence toward greater acceptance of Italian as a literary language.

After the return of the Medici to Florence, the city's external affairs became intertwined with papal diplomacy. The head of the Medici family, after all, was the pope! Pope Leo initially returned Florence to the days of treating the French as one possible ally among others. After a French alliance failed to materialize, Pope Leo allied himself and Florence with the Spanish and the empire against the new French king Francis I in 1515. Pope Leo left his brother Giuliano and nephew Lorenzo to deal with Florentine opposition to his actions. Then, not long after, Leo changed tact. He mended fences with King Francis. Pope Leo's nephew Lorenzo married into the French royal family. A French noble needed his own kingdom! Thus, Pope Leo appointed the newly ennobled Lorenzo to be lord of the papal town of Urbino. Fortune unfortunately did not favor Leo's dynastic plans. In 1516 the pope's brother Giuliano died. In 1519 lord Lorenzo died. Leo tried to have his cousin Giulio tend to Florence. But Giulio was a cardinal, a creature of Rome. Thus, Medici cronies filled Florentine offices while executing directives issued from the Eternal City.[69] Pope Leo died in 1522, but the election of cardinal Giulio de' Medici as Pope Clement VII less than two years later meant that Florence's status as papal appendage continued.

The lives of women reflected the changing political circumstances of early sixteenth-century Florence. While Piero de' Medici had been in charge his Orsini wife and mother had often held leading roles in negotiations between their birth and marital families. Those negotiations, in turn, impacted policies in and outside Florence.[70] The ousting of Piero de' Medici had ended the quasi-monarchy in Florence and returned the city to republican forms. That change returned even the most elite women to indirect political roles. Women were among the most vocal and numerous supporters of Savonarola's preaching. Their support helped ensure the preacher's prevalence and influence. Even so, women were at times barred from attending certain sermons.[71] In Piero Soderini's republic, scandal ensued when Soderini's wife and family moved into the previously male-monopolized Palazzo Vecchio. Lines were blurring between where Soderini's house ended and where the governmental home of the Florentine Republic began.[72] Whoever was in charge, misogyny ruled. The Great Council opened political power to thousands of male Florentines. It did not grant a single vote to the female half of the city's population. The disenfranchisement of women was not oppressive enough. Additionally, the public spaces around Florence increasingly highlighted men and masculinity, even in some cases replacing images of heroic women with heroic men.[73]

The rise of Medici princes after 1512 reopened political spaces for women in Florence. For example, Medici women could serve as informal advocates for male relatives at the courts of both the Medici popes Leo X and Clement VII.[74] While Lorenzo de' Medici was ruling Florence in the 1510s, his mother Alfonsina Orsina encouraged him to consider himself above other Florentines.[75] Then, when Lorenzo was cultivating aristocratic ambitions in Urbino, Alfonsina was left to run Florence.[76] While in charge Alfonsina oversaw critical projects within the Florentine state. In one example, she issued orders to help prepare the city for a visit by Pope Leo X.[77] In another example, she oversaw the controversial draining of an artificial lake.[78] Florentines viewed this exercise of power with suspicion and malice. Alfonsina was battered by criticisms as much because she was a woman as for her specific policies.[79]

Alfonsina's agency fit into a consistent trend in Florentine history that permitted women to fill leadership roles when men were unable to do so:

when men were sick, out of town, etc. Under the republic the complete denial of political offices for women had been the exception to that rule. However, the transition of the city from a republic to a princely state tweaked that tradition. Other changes were also afoot. For example, religious reform movements began to emphasize enclosure as necessary for convents. After 1500 convents began to resemble fortresses and prisons more than the more fluid architecture of past centuries. Within those walls, the city's nuns were becoming major contributors to the city's silk business. They continued to own and rent property throughout Florence.[80] By the 1500s women were adding pharmacies to their entrepreneurial portfolios. It was a natural fit, as already women played essential roles in supplying, promoting, and mediating the health and health care of their families.[81]

In politics and gender, after 1512, the Medici were becoming more like princes than ever before. They boasted popes and royal relatives: a humble floor slab like Cosimo de' Medici's tomb in San Lorenzo simply no longer sufficed for their status.[82] Thus, Pope Leo and then Pope Clement sent Michelangelo to Florence to augment the church of San Lorenzo. For more than a century the rough exposed brick outside San Lorenzo had hidden the elegant beauty within. Michelangelo was ordered to complete the facade.[83] Michelangelo prepared a design. He procured marble. He began preliminary work. The pope changed his mind. Build a new tomb worthy of the Medici family, were his new instructions! Build a new library worthy of their learning! Michelangelo switched his focus from the exterior to the interior of San Lorenzo.

By 1520 Michelangelo had begun work on a new tomb to house the remains of the two recently deceased overseers of Florence: Giuliano and Lorenzo de' Medici.[84] Within the tomb allegories of Night, Day, Dawn, and Dusk observe visitors. Each contorted, muscular figure exemplifies the interests of early sixteenth-century people in the movement of the body: the so-called style of "mannerism." Above the allegories sit idealized male figures. For the tomb of Lorenzo, the sculpture wears the outfit of a Roman soldier (Figure 28). His surroundings evoke the classical past. On his lap rests the baton of command, a frequent symbol used to denote the political and especially military power of an individual. In the same room, Lorenzo's uncle Giuliano appears thoughtful (Figure 29). He too is surrounded by the trappings of classical architecture. He stares out. Perhaps he is contemplating what might have been had he or Lorenzo lived longer.[85] In symbol and expense, the Medici had left behind any pretense of equality with other Florentine families. Here was a tomb built

Figure 28 Michelangelo Buonarroti. *Tomb of Lorenzo de' Medici* (often titled Tomb of Giuliano de' Medici), 1523–34. Marble sculpture. San Lorenzo, Florence.

for nobility that used the transcontinental languages of style, materials, and iconography.

As he built the mausoleum Michelangelo also created a new library to house the Medici book collection. At its entrance three sets of stairs converge into a majestic staircase. The steps of the curious ascend to explore the treasures of one of Europe's first public libraries.[86] Today, modern visitors come for Michelangelo's architecture alone. The Medici manuscripts have long since been moved into the rare-book collection

Figure 29 Michelangelo Buonarroti. *Tomb of Giuliano de' Medici* (often titled *Tomb of Lorenzo de' Medici*), 1524–31. Marble sculpture. Photo by George M. Groutas, June 29, 2019. San Lorenzo, Florence.

of the modern Laurenzian Library located next door. For years a nondescript door opening to that modern reading room has contrasted with Michelangelo's majestic work. Yet, the modern library fulfills the same function: it houses the Medici collection, as well as countless other precious artifacts. Current readers now need not even enter through the plain door: the Medici treasures are almost all freely available for viewing online. Nearly five hundred years before the birth of that digital library, in 1534, Pope Clement VII died. Michelangelo left Florence, leaving his projects unfinished at San Lorenzo. He returned to Rome, never again to return to his birth city.[87] But he left enduring reminders of the Medici's open eclipse of other Florentine families and their use of transcontinental cultural languages to make their claims to piety, position, power, and status.

Those claims fit into a different political world than those made by earlier members of the Medici family. By the 1510s and 1520s, no breathtaking tomb could hide the fact that France, Spain, and the empire possessed much more plausible claims to be the heirs of Ancient Rome than Florence.[88] More than that, in theory the city remained independent and remained a republic, but the reality was that as the Medici papacies went, so went Florence. What had happened? What could be done about it? Niccolò Machiavelli tried to answer those questions in his *Florentine Histories*. Earlier histories of the city had begun with the foundation of Florence, or perhaps the creation of the world before moving onto the foundation of Florence. Machiavelli's work, by contrast, began with political powers other than the Florentines. He argued that recent papal calls for aid from transalpine powers had brought about the current chaotic situation across Italy. Gone are claims for the Florentine inheritance of Rome. In its place, Machiavelli's opening narrative makes Florence seem small: a city tossed helplessly across a narrative sea disturbed by the machinations of others.[89] It had not always been this way.

According to Machiavelli, once mighty Florence had lost its way because the city's *popolo* and *grandi* were unable to work together in a productive fashion. Machiavelli believed that successful republics needed at least two characteristics. A republic needed a direct voice for the city's lower orders. A city also needed strong checks on the insatiable appetites of the elites to oppress others. Florentine history, Machiavelli, argued, was driven by a series of fights between those social groups. Ultimately, unfortunately, the elites monopolized political power in the city. The lower social groups were disenfranchised.[90] A republic could not survive in that sort of situation. Unlike fifteenth-century official and semiofficial histories of Florence, Machiavelli told his tale of Florentine internal and external woes in the vernacular. Certainly, people far beyond Tuscany could still appreciate Machiavelli's set speeches, political assumptions, and classical references. But it was the muted trans-continentalism of a city humbled on the political stage, not the powerhouse with an unlimited future described by Giovanni Villani's vernacular chronicle two centuries before.[91]

The past facades of consensus politics or the equality of Florentine families could not encompass the new political realities: the Florentines had to keep adjusting. The prospects of a Medici-papal-French axis died with Lorenzo de' Medici and Pope Leo. In the years to come Giulio de' Medici as Pope Clement VII vacillated papal alliances across different rulers. Medici puppet rulers in Florence dragged the city along for the ride. Resentment grew about the relationship between Florence and Rome, the siphoning off of Florentine money, the men picked to run the city, and the disconnect between patrician expectations for political honors versus their muted, subordinate role in the Medici's republic.[92] In 1524, Clement VII picked the French as allies. The Spanish won a victory in 1525. Pope Clement switched to them. In 1526, it was back to the French again. By 1527, Charles V, who held the titles of both emperor and king of Spain, had had enough. One of his armies marched on Rome. His troops sacked it. Thus, the pope turned his support once again to the empire against the French. Back in Florence, the Florentines seized an opportunity of Medici's weakness. They took over the Palazzo Vecchio. By June a new Florentine Republic had been established.[93]

The new Florentine Republic tried to turn the clock back to the late fifteenth century. The governmental bodies dominated by the Medici and their allies were abolished. The Great Council was brought back. Political space was reopened for multiple groups: supporters of Savonarola, supporters of republican forms, supporters of one family or another. Many sought to chart a middle course between the fervent support of any one group.[94] The republic enacted revenge against the Medici family. The Florentines declared Pope Clement a debtor to their city. Pope Clement was ordered to repay the monies that he and his family had been seizing from the Florentine treasury in recent decades. Many Florentines embraced a return of Savonarola's ideas and a renewed belief in his prophecies. They even crowned Christ king of Florence.[95] Who knows? Had the Medici been only one family among many; had the Florentines inhabited the regional setting of the fifteenth century; had the French been more powerful; had Henry VIII in England had a son; had the Spanish ripped fewer resources from the Americas; then perhaps the republic could have created the start of a new age of republicanism in Florence.

But the Medici were no longer one family among many Florentine families, political regionalism had ended, and Florence was too important to ignore during the Italian Wars. After the sack of Rome Pope Clement had limited agency. Even had he wanted to fight against Emperor Charles V he could not have done so.[96] Pope Clement and Emperor Charles struck a deal. The pope wanted Florence back under his family's control. The emperor wanted visible papal support for his many causes. Among those causes, Charles wanted the pope to block a request being made by a different ruler. In distant England, Charles's aunt Catherine was married to King Henry VIII. Henry lacked a male heir and thus had petitioned the pope for a divorce. As part of his deal for Florence, Clement agreed to deny the request.[97] Pope Clement and Emperor Charles cemented their alliance through a marriage: the illegitimate daughter of the emperor, Margaret, married a relative of the pope, Alessandro de' Medici. It was all a far cry from the political regionalism of fifteenth-century Florence.

Things continued to get worse for Florence. In 1528 King Francis of France and Emperor Charles resumed hostilities. The Florentine Republic naturally favored the French against the Medici/papal-allied emperor. But the emperor's resources were seemingly without end. By the late 1520s Charles benefited from regular treasure ships carrying stolen wealth from the Americas. Charles defeated Francis. The ensuing Treaty of Cambrai ordered the French to vacate the Italian peninsula, leaving only the emperor and his allies. Charles and Clement turned to Florence. Bereft of allies, the city prepared for a siege. No less than Michelangelo helped prepare the city's defenses. In early 1530 the papal and imperial armies encamped outside of the thirteenth-century Florentine walls. For months the massive army starved the city. For months the city refused to yield. Tensions ran high as the government sought to seize assets from patricians deemed insufficiently loyal to the republic.[98] But hunger and hopelessness consume the souls of the strongest people. The city surrendered in mid-1530. The city's new masters paraded through streets soaked in the blood of possibly 30,000 dead Florentines—the besiegers had lost 14,000 of their own.[99] The Medici had returned once again, this time for good.

The end of the so-called Last Republic brought a symbolic end to the Florentine Renaissance. Since the mid-fourteenth century the city had juxtaposed its regional politics against its continental cultural claims. Florence had shifted their diplomatic outlooks between the French and the Spanish Empire. Although there were certainly exceptions, the Medici tended to favor Italian regionalism or the emperor, while Florentines looking to overturn Medici power tended to favor the French. Internally, the republic enabled Florentines to compete against each other. Most pursued their own ends somewhere in the political middle. But decades of changes matured after 1530. Politics rejoined culture with its continental scope, but both lacked the powerful position that they had enjoyed during the 1300s. Florence became a supporting player trying to balance the demands of far more powerful rulers outside the city against the desires and traditions of the Florentines themselves. After 1530 the imperial presence in Italy and family ties between the Medici and the empire determined decades of external affairs. The Latin supremacy of the fifteenth century gave way to a new focus on vernacular writings. Humanism yielded the intellectual limelight to other areas of study. New artistic styles were emerging. Within Florence, families and individuals continued to pursue their own interests, but the space for agency was rapidly collapsing. Political ambition ran through the Medici family and was measured by proximity to that family. One period of Florentine history had ended and another began.

6

EARLY MODERN FLORENCE AND THE MEDICI DUCHY, 1531–74

The armies of Charles V and Clement VII opened a new chapter in the history of Florence. By 1532 Pope Clement and Emperor Charles had installed their natural and marital relative, respectively, in Florence as the city's duke. It was the beginning of a duchy that lasted for over 200 years. Duke Alessandro, Duke Cosimo, Duke Francesco, and Duke Ferdinando each reigned in turn through the decades of the 1500s. Each ruler struck a balance between the preservation of Florentine independence and the increasing reality of Spanish hegemony in Italy. Most prominent Florentine families from before the duchy remained important in the city afterward. Florentines from the ducal family down the social hierarchy professed claims to power, position, piety, and status in transcontinental cultural languages. Thus, the duchy in some ways represented strong continuities with the past. Yet, in other ways the duchy marked more dramatic changes. A formal duchy was not a republic. Power and honors—within or outside of political office—emanated from the duke. Duke Cosimo successfully quelled most resistance to his rule. He established a stronger state apparatus than Florence had ever possessed before. Cultural expressions changed to reflect these new situations. Ultimately, under the duchy, the would-be heir to the might of Ancient Rome was becoming the shrine of Renaissance culture.

Superficial drama followed the conquest of Florence in 1530. Pope Clement had promised clemency for his rivals in Florence. He was true to his word. Certainly, his allies immediately returned to positions of power, but Clement limited reprisals to a few key adversaries. Moreover, the pope did not immediately install a member of the Medici family to oversee Florence.[1] Maybe a republic could continue! But it was only a matter of time. Pope Clement's relative Alessandro had spent 1531 in the entourage of the emperor. There, Alessandro jousted, served as a courtier, and worked to finalize his proposed marriage to Charles's illegitimate daughter Margaret.[2] Alessandro's appointment as interim head of Florence should have surprised no one, even if it was not uniformly supported. Alessandro entered the city in 1531. He began negotiations to determine a new government for Florence. Florentine men maneuvered to maintain some semblance of their past autonomy. Given the circumstances, they were remarkably successful. The new constitution on April 27, 1532, disbanded the Florentine *Signoria*. In its place, the government consisted of a new "Duke of the Florentine Republic," a small number of advisors, and two bigger councils filled with lifetime members. The board changed, but maybe the old game of jockeying for position and power by Florentine families could continue.[3]

The new Duke of the Florentine Republic, Alessandro de' Medici, was the first ruler of African descent in early modern Europe. Although not definitive, Alessandro's father was probably Lorenzo de' Medici, Duke of Urbino, while his mother was probably an African slave within the Medici household. Alessandro's darker skin complexion in a position of power was unusual, but his critics tended to focus more on his lowborn status than on his skin color (Figure 30).[4] Why? It was not because Florentines lacked exposure to people of African descent or prejudices toward them. In fact, Africa and Africans had long had a presence in Italy and in Florence. In Antiquity, northern Africa and the Middle East had formed as much a part of the Roman Empire as had areas like France and Italy. After Roman power collapsed, people continued to center their worlds on the Mediterranean Sea much more than on separate landmasses like "Europe" or "Africa." Much of Spain remained within Islamic empires for nearly 800 years, from just after 700 until just shy of 1500.[5]

Moreover, the African continent played a key role in the transmission of culture and the economy of Europe. During the 1100s, for example, Baghdad was a key cultural center. Learned people translated works from Antiquity into Arabic and wrote commentaries on them. Those Arabic works then traveled across the Islamic lands of North Africa into the Islamic Iberian Peninsula, which had several learned communities looking for classical books. In those centers of learning those Arabic works were translated into Latin. Those Latin versions, in turn, inspired a revival of classical studies in places like medieval France, England, the Holy Roman Empire, and the Italian peninsula.[6] In general, Europeans

Figure 30 Pontormo. *Portrait of Alessandro de' Medici*, 1534–5. Oil on canvas.
Photo from the Yorck project (2002). J. G. Johnson, Philadelphia.

viewed Africa as a mysterious place. It was a land in possession of gold
and riches, an ancient Christian kingdom, Islam, as well as people with
darker skin complexions to which Europeans attached a host of negative
stereotypes.[7] By the 1400s Florence coveted the wealth of Africa. In
1422 Florence purchased a new port town, Livorno, on the Tyrrhenian
Sea. They established a new governmental body, the Sea Councils, to
manage the development of Mediterranean maritime trade. Their first
action was to appoint diplomats and ships to sail to Africa—specifically
Alexandria, Egypt—to establish closer economic relations.[8]

   These sorts of interconnections combined with others to create a
regular flow of free and enslaved Africans and Europeans across the
Mediterranean Sea. Florence participated in this exchange to a limited
degree. Slavery, for example, existed in Florence. However, before the
1500s slavery was usually a condition based upon differences in religion
and prisoners of war, rather than an inherited servitude based upon
skin complexion. Nevertheless, enslaved Africans could be encountered
in the streets of the city. Wealthy Florentines purchased African slaves,
often women, as status symbols and to do domestic work. Benozzo

Gozzoli's *Adoration of the Magi*, discussed in Chapter 3, may depict the desirability of owning an African slave among the Florentine elite. There, an African male bowman walks between the horses of Cosimo de' Medici and Galeazzo Maria Sforza.[9] The presence of people of African descent increased during the 1500s. In the latter part of the century, ducal Florence invested heavily in their port city Livorno. In turn, Livorno became a key center for Mediterranean trade, including slaves.[10] Enslaved people from Africa became common human cargo on Florentine ships across the Mediterranean.[11]

The city of Florence, in fact, housed many kinds of people. People from across Europe immigrated to Florence. The largest stable community probably consisted of craftspeople originally from German lands.[12] Transitory guests to Florence could temporarily but dramatically shift the city's composition. The Council of Florence in 1439, for example, had brought thousands of people into the city.[13] Indeed, one visitor, the Patriarch of the Greek Church, remains interred within an extant wall tomb in Santa Maria Novella. Mercenaries knew no boundaries in their search for employment. Thus, soldiers from throughout Europe fought for or against Florence, in and around the city. English troops from the Hundred Years were especially prominent in Florentine struggles during the late 1300s.[14] During the sixteenth century Italian Wars, Florentines regularly ran into French, Imperial, and Swiss troops. These soldiers brought the languages, clothing, and customs of their homes. After around 1520 they might even bring their Protestant faiths. Most Florentines, certainly, rarely traveled far from their birth city, but encountering somebody who looked or sounded different from them must have been an almost quotidian experience.

A Jewish community also lived in Florence. Throughout the medieval, Renaissance, and early modern periods, relations between Jews and the dominant Christian society were fraught with tensions and perils. These tensions derived from antisemitism, and religious differences, and could be further exacerbated by some of the roles Jews filled in Florentine society. At times of crisis, it was common for the Florentines to single out Jews as scapegoats. Jewish people could have their property seized; their homes taken; and be killed or expelled from the city. Then, in 1571 Duke Cosimo forced Jews to relocate to a specific zone in the city, called the ghetto.[15] Throughout their history in Florence, Jews produced beautiful and learned cultural objects. Some Hebrew texts were intended only for the Jewish community itself. Other examples, however, spread through the porous boundaries of the city, its society, and its cultures. Some

Florentines even tried to learn Hebrew, even if their motivation often stemmed from an urge to convert Jews to Christianity.[16] Certainly, thus, Florentines in the 1530s possessed experiences with people from many different backgrounds and with many different physical appearances. The early modern city was neither homogenous nor accepting of such differences. In the example of Duke Alessandro, perhaps the focus by his contemporaries on his low-birth rather than his skin color reflects that racism too has a complex—and evil—history, in and outside of Florence.

The appointment of Alessandro continued the transition of the Florentine Republic to a ducal state. Under Alessandro, Florentines pursued ends and honors that could promote themselves, their families, and their allies. Alessandro's position obviously meant those honors and power emanated from proximity to his person. As such, ambitious men needed to excel as princely courtiers if they wanted to hold political offices. To accommodate changing circumstances, the meanings attached to key terms used to talk about status and power began to change.[17] Yet, even after almost twenty years as an appendage to the Medici in Rome; even after the disastrous republic between 1527 and 1530; even as the empire continued to consider a marriage alliance with the Medici, the Florentines still resisted the closure of their republic by a Medici prince.

No less than Filippo Strozzi, Pope Clement VII's friend, confidant, and banker, led the opposition. For years Filippo had built and spent fortunes in support of Pope Clement's efforts in Florence, Rome, and beyond. By 1532 Filippo's finances were inextricably tied to the Medici family.[18] Yet, Filippo and Alessandro de' Medici were neither friends nor allies. Consequently, Filippo opposed Alessandro's appointment in Florence. Pope Clement was able to paper over the differences between his crucial supporter and Alessandro, for a time. But Pope Clement died in 1534. Filippo sprang into action. The Florentine patrician Jacopo Nardi joined him. The two men found like-minded allies, including Florentine cardinals. They approached Charles V in both Naples and Barcelona about the prospect of replacing Alessandro with a different person and a new republican government in Florence. They suggested that perhaps Cardinal Ippolito de' Medici might serve as a suitable substitute as the new government's overlord. Emperor Charles listened to their ideas. Maybe he was receptive. After all, Pope Clement was dead. Charles had not yet formally invested Alessandro with the title of Duke. He had not yet agreed to his daughter's marriage to him. Maybe Ippolito could provide a more advantageous option.

Cardinal Ippolito's death in 1535 made the emperor's decision for him. Emperor Charles agreed to Alessandro's marriage to Margaret. It was consummated.[19] On April 29, 1536, the emperor arrived in Florence. Alessandro presented the keys to the city to him. The emperor, in turn, returned the keys to Alessandro, and thus ceremonially appointed him ruler of the city.[20] Filippo and his allies were hardly satisfied. By late 1536 they had determined to murder Alessandro and return Florence to its republican forms and practices, changes that would naturally also return them to greater positions of power. They awaited their opportunity.

On January 6, 1537, Alessandro's cousin Lorenzino told him that the husband of Caterina de' Ginori was out of town. Alessandro had been eying Caterina for an affair. Lorenzino told him that she could easily be persuaded to enjoy a nocturnal visit with the duke. Alessandro was interested. Lorenzino told him to go to his palace and wait. Lorenzino would go to talk with Caterina and then bring her to the palace. Alessandro went along with the plan. The duke was tired; Lorenzino was slow; and thus Alessandro fell asleep. Lorenzino met up with an ally and the two men entered the bedchamber with the snoozing duke. The first blow came from Lorenzino. His ally struck second. Alessandro resisted. A struggle ensued. Two armed men proved too much for the unarmed and unprepared Alessandro. He was killed. The body was hidden. The assassins fled. The new Florentine duchy was without a duke; the emperor was without a son-in-law.[21]

Florence danced between dangers. During Alessandro's rule, a large fortress had been built on the outskirts of the city. It was in imperial hands, and Charles intended to keep it that way. When his son-in-law was murdered, thus, imperial troops stood ready to impose direct imperial control over the city. Perhaps an imperial viceroy and more direct imperial leadership were needed to better control unruly Florence. The Florentines did not want to yield their local autonomy in such a way. However, Alessandro had no heir. Thus, there was no obvious Medici family member to take his place.

Florentine patricians feverishly explored options. Could they prevent more direct imperial rule while using the assassination to their advantage? Perhaps they could find a weak man who could appease the emperor while also obeying their instructions? The teenager Cosimo de' Medici, son of a popular mercenary captain and born to a different branch of the Medici family than Alessandro, seemed the perfect option. Cosimo's family name could offer a Medici to take Alessandro's place. Cosimo's youth and inexperience meant that older Florentine statesmen like Francesco Guicciardini and Francesco Vettori could shape him into whatever they wanted him to be. Cosimo would be a puppet ruler as other Florentines co-opted power for themselves. Young Cosimo might have been surprised to learn of his sudden rise in station, although his mother had already been advocating on his behalf for years.[22] He was tentatively appointed to succeed Alessandro.

Cosimo quickly dispelled patrician delusions that he would be their willing puppet. Cosimo immediately began negotiations to secure recognition for himself of the same titles and privileges possessed by Alessandro. He made clear to all that he intended for even the most powerful Florentines to occupy a position one step below that of the duke. Then he turned his eye toward his overt opposition. In the summer of 1537 Filippo Strozzi, his son, and other Florentines amassed troops in the nearby area of Montemurlo. Cosimo joined forces with the empire. Together, they met the opposition on August 2, 1537. Cosimo and his allies were victorious. His primary rivals were defeated. Most of them were captured and dragged in humiliation through the streets of Florence. Some were executed. Others imprisoned. The imperial forces determined that the captured leader, Filippo Strozzi, would be useful as a hostage. They imprisoned him within their fort in Florence. There he was to serve as a reminder that Cosimo ruled at the whim of Emperor Charles. Should Cosimo step too far out of line, then perhaps Filippo Strozzi might be more amenable to the emperor's wishes. The ploy only lasted a year: in 1538 Filippo Strozzi either committed suicide or was murdered.[23]

Filippo Strozzi's death symbolized both an end and a beginning in the history of Florence. It was an end. Filippo left a dramatic suicide note that compared his political actions and death to those of the Ancient Roman republican hero Cato. Like Cato, Filippo had fought and died for the republic that he cherished. Filippo left out of the note that, unlike Cato in Ancient Rome, Filippo had actively worked to subvert the Florentine Republic by financing Pope Clement's efforts to create the duchy in the first place! In other ways, Filippo's death changed nothing. The old ways of accruing honor and power in the Florentine Republic continued to yield to a world of courtiers in the Florentine duchy. In still other ways it was a beginning. Over the next thirty years, Cosimo de' Medici solidified Florentine independence and expanded his power in Tuscany. Florence no longer was a great European power, but Cosimo managed to secure a status for the early modern city that equaled other political units within the imperial sphere of influence.

That process began with Cosimo's consolidation of his rule over Florence. The emperor granted Cosimo's request for the same privileges possessed by Alessandro. Cosimo sought to further tie his political standing to the emperor by requesting a marriage with Margaret, Alessandro's widow who remained in the Spanish fortress in Florence. The emperor rejected that request but offered a different match with Eleonora di Toledo. Eleonora brought a Spanish noble family to the marriage. Even more, she was the daughter of the emperor's viceroy in Naples.[24] Through the connection, Cosimo's international fortunes were tied to the emperor and his representatives. In sixteenth-century Europe, it seemed a safe bet: Emperor Charles was ruling over one of the largest empires the world had ever seen. Cosimo's position, thus, seemed increasingly secure.

Simultaneously, Cosimo pushed for reforms to the Florentine governmental bureaucracy to strengthen his position at its head. He removed redundancies across different offices and looked for ways to tie subject communities closer to the Florentine center. For example, Cosimo oversaw changes to the enforcement and judication of law. After 1558 he moved many of the powers from the old *Otto di Guardia* to other agencies more dependent upon the will of the duke. He also reduced the *Otto's* budget and their financial backing to a new office more dependent upon Cosimo. He further cut into their power by establishing a rudimentary police force to monitor and investigate crime in the city.[25] Cosimo kept the appearance of several republican offices, but he ensured that he kept direct approval over each appointment for each vacancy. Over time he even secured a strong influence over appointments to ecclesiastical offices within his territories.[26] He appointed powerful Florentines as diplomats but made sure that loyal new men served as their secretaries. Those secretaries served as his eyes, ears, and advisors abroad.[27] Cosimo's actions created a more centralized and stable Florentine state centered upon the ducal person and his family.

Florentine changes toward increased centralized power reflected broader European developments. For example, in the past, European nobles had possessed enough resources to finance formidable fighting forces. The armies of Luca Pitti and Piero de' Medici in the 1460s serve as good examples. Such private forces had made it hard for the Florentine government to control its most powerful citizens. Yet, during the sixteenth century warfare was constant and constantly innovating. Above all, it was expensive to train soldiers in new techniques, outfit them with weaponry, and build fortifications to repulse attackers.[28] Individuals simply could not marshal the necessary resources to field a competitive army. Rulers refined administrative structures to collect taxes more efficiently. Bigger bureaucracies were formed to cope with more complex procedures. Workload increased even further with the availability of cheap paper and print. Cosimo's governmental reforms and his strengthened bureaucracy fit into these contexts. Those developments in turn helped pay to support and build new fortifications. In addition to the Fortezza da Basso, built by the Spanish then occupied by Cosimo after 1543, Cosimo's son Duke Ferdinand I later began a second defensive structure near the Boboli Gardens.[29]

The new ducal system finalized the process from republican honors to ducal ones threaded throughout the chapters of this book. Political space collapsed around the Medici duke. The fight for Cosimo's favor trumped or at the very least went together with the competition for government office. Consequently, ambitious people lacked the political flexibility of earlier decades. The options in the middle decreased. A person either advanced through a real or perceived pro-Medici position, or they rebelled against it through a real or perceived anti-Medici one. Certainly, most Florentines continued to try to stay out of such extremes. But now those choices meant they simply lacked access to positions of power. Florentines began to think differently about their position in the broader world. Florentines had always taken pride in their "liberty." During the fifteenth century, they defined liberty as their ability to chart a course for Florence without an external master and their ability to gain honor through holding political office. But that definition broke down after the city became run by the Medici in Rome and then by a Medici duke in Florence itself. Liberty came to mean independence and proximity to the prince, a proximity that office-holding could reflect.[30] More than just offices, nobles created arcane norms to set themselves off from other social groups. For example, the rabble ate with their hands and used their tablecloths as handkerchiefs. Nobles began using forks and small pieces of cloth.[31]

The transition from a republican to a courtly society meant new opportunities for women for formal political access. Eleonora of Toledo, wife of Duke Cosimo, served as regent over Florence in 1541. In that capacity, Eleonora oversaw all aspects of the state, including military and economic matters. In addition, Eleonora's noble upbringing and Spanish ancestry contrasted with the mercantile background of the Florentines, including, to a certain extent, Duke Cosimo himself. Thus, Eleonora was an invaluable negotiator with other rulers.[32] Ducal women continued to hold prominent political roles after Eleonora's death. Eleonora and Cosimo's daughter Isabella became a key intermediary to and for her father. She served as an advisor to Cosimo and often oversaw negotiations for marriage alliances. In each role, Isabella made use of an extensive network of women rulers, nobles, and powerful mothers from across Europe.[33] These trends continued after Duke Cosimo died in 1574. Joanna of Austria, wife of Cosimo's successor Francesco I, and Christine of Lorraine, wife of Franceso's successor Ferdinando I, both filled roles like Eleonora and Isabella. Christine took particular interest in reforming the educational norms within the ducal household.[34]

Life changed for women more broadly in ducal Florence. In the mid-1500s women made up around 55 percent of the city's population and headed about one in five households. Many of these women worked in the rising silk industry. The Medici dukes had begun encouraging the growth of silk trade and production after the more traditional wool industry lost its old markets. Consequently, silk became a primary driver of the Florentine economy. By 1663 women made up around 84 percent of silk workers. Their silk was often sold at local markets, rather than the more international focus of previous Florentine industries. Unfortunately, the increased integration of women into the workforce did not lead to quality-of-life improvements. Work in the silk industry required few special skills and paid little. Thus, education opportunities did not need to expand in order to hire women workers. The employment of women expanded, but the real income arriving to their families probably was less than it had been in previous decades.

Working conditions made the situation even worse. Much of the silk work took place within charitable organizations tasked with caring for poor women, children, and converted prostitutes. Those organizations argued that the women under their care should work without wages: their payment was the moral good created by doing honest work. Thus, financial profits failed to pass down to the workers themselves. In some situations, the work became a form of slavery. The charitable organization required women to work as a requirement for their room and board. Simultaneously, the women had no other options to turn to or, in some cases, were prevented from leaving.[35]

The histories that the Valori family wrote about themselves reveal the Florentine transition from republic to duchy. The Valori family had long enjoyed prominence in Florence. They had become especially noteworthy in the latter 1400s and early 1500s. In those years they had enjoyed close connections with the Florentine luminaries Marsilio Ficino and

Niccolò Machiavelli. However, during the same period, the Valori had at times opposed Medici rule in Florence and tied themselves to politically problematic people like Savonarola. Thus, writers of the history of the Valori family needed to smooth out the family's past. The past needed to align with the needs of Valori family members living under the Medici dukes.

Sixteenth-century writers used several tools to create a more useable history of the Valori family. Sometimes these writers simply omitted problematic past actions by Valori ancestors. When the family had been too prominent in problematic events to simply ignore it, then writers suggested that Valori family members had been defending the good republican government. The argument paralleled those made by the Medici dukes themselves. Initially, Duke Cosimo's cultural representations of himself had struck absolutist tones. However, as his rule solidified, Cosimo began stressing republican continuities between his reign and the Florentine past.[36] Additionally, Duke Cosimo required by law that officeholders wear clothes associated with officeholders during the fifteenth century.[37] The Valori family histories tapped into these sorts of ducal claims. Even more, the works often changed problematic past actions into a connection with the ruling family: Duke Cosimo continued the Florentine tradition of seeking out a good political order. The Valori family had always been ready to assist such efforts and stood ready to do so again.[38]

Ducal Florence also changed the stories that Florentines told about their collective past. After starting a history of Florence in his youth, from 1537 to 1540 Guicciardini penned his masterpiece, the *History of Italy*. Gone were claims to grand Florentine inheritance from Antiquity. Instead, Guicciardini pined for the days of the Italian League, particularly when Lorenzo the Magnificent had run Florence. In that time, Lorenzo's leadership had brought "peace and tranquility," "merchandise and riches," a "flourishing [of] men most skillful in the administration of public affairs and most nobly talented in all disciplines and distinguished and industrious in all the arts."[39] Now Italy lay in ruins. A comparison between accounts written by Leonardo Bruni in 1415 and Francesco Guicciardini in 1537 reveals just how far Guicciardini believed Florence had fallen. Writing ten years after the fact, Bruni compared the conquest of Pisa in 1406 to Rome's conquest of Carthage. By contrast, writing some twenty years after the reconquest of Pisa in 1509, Guicciardini wrote that the Florentines feared the power of the emperor Maximilian and of fortune in general. Consequently, they gave up their siege of the city. Instead, they "preferred to be certain of their victory under iniquitous treaty conditions" rather than "cast any part of their certainty once again into the lap of fortune."[40] Guicciardini, obviously, did not compare Florence's negotiated acquisition of Pisa in 1509 to any Ancient Roman accomplishments.

Benedetto Varchi's official *History of Florence* explicitly tied the city's past to its Medici masters. Varchi had been an ally of Filippo Strozzi and had opposed the consolidation of Cosimo's power during the 1530s. He was reconciled with the regime during the 1540s, lectured on Florentine literary greats, and was commissioned to write a history of Florence. Varchi opened his *History of Florence* with a declaration of the symbiosis between Florence and the Medici family: "The house of the Medici was exiled three times from Florence between 1433 and 1527. . . . And three times, as the heavens had destined, they returned always greater and more powerful than if they had not left."[41] He then proceeded to preface his history of Duke Cosimo's reign by briefly relating the rise of the Medici, beginning with Cosimo the elder's rise to power. From there, Varchi created a historical work predictably favorable to his patron Duke Cosimo and his ancestors, even as the work remained remarkably true to Varchi's republican sympathies.[42] Whatever its biases, Varchi's work symbolically equated the history of Florence as the same as the history of the Medici family.

Duke Cosimo took other steps to solidify the noble status of his family and their claims to political power. For example, on August 2, 1562—the same day he had triumphed at Montemurlo years earlier— Cosimo established the Order of St. Stefano. He modeled the order upon other knightly societies in courts across Europe. Cosimo claimed that he hoped the order could help unite his disparate realms in a new crusade against the Turks. He declared that members of the order had to attend court at regular intervals. People who wanted to join had to demonstrate their noble lineage. Cosimo admitted Florentines, people from Tuscany, and even people from farther afield. Members wore special tokens so that others could easily recognize their privileged position. People viewed members in the Order of St. Stefano as a sign of proximity to the duke. In the visual arts, Cosimo and his successors frequently celebrated the Order as a key accomplishment.[43] Onlookers of those artistic pieces received a reminder of the noble status of their Medici rulers and their unique position as heads of state.

Cosimo made the same sorts of arguments through new sculptures. The sculptor Baccio Bandinelli had already been hired by Pope Clement and then Duke Alessandro to create a heroic Hercules to accompany Michelangelo's *David* in the Piazza della Signoria. Duke Cosimo saw the work through to its completion. Bandinelli faced the unenviable task of creating a work that would help the *David* guard an entrance to the Palazzo Vecchio. Bandinelli's completed sculpture, unveiled in 1534, emphasized the extreme musculature of the classical hero and the bodily contortions of Hercules's fallen victim. (Figure 31)[44] The vanquished man looks up at his conqueror.[45] Not far away, some years later, Bandinelli's rival Benvenuto Cellini was hired to create a free-standing bronze sculpture of the classical hero Perseus (Figure 32). All viewers recognized the triumph of Perseus over Medusa, whose gory decapitated head drips bronze blood onto the piazza below. The most

Figure 31 Baccio Bandinelli. *Hercules and Cacus*, 1525–34. Marble sculpture. Photo by Jebulon, June 2, 2011. Florence.

Figure 32 Benvenuto Cellini. *Perseus*, 1545–54. Bronze sculpture. Photo by
Jordiferrer, August 8, 2016. Florence.

knowledgeable connoisseurs may have marveled at Cellini's technical
skills in forming such remarkable details in a difficult medium.[46] Did
some viewers, perhaps, see an irony? Michelangelo's David stood ready to
defend Soderini's Florentine Republic. David had failed. Now, Cosimo's
commissions celebrated the violent defeat and subjugation of his foes.

Cosimo used paintings to support his princely claims in Florence
and beyond. Portraiture, for example, exploded in popularity across
sixteenth-century Europe, including Florence. Each image of hundreds
of different Florentines projected a quasi-likeness carefully crafted to tell
viewers curated characteristics of the sitter. Across dozens of portraits,
Cosimo and his family used clothing and icons to project stability, links
to the Florentine past, and claims to power over the present.[47] Cosimo's

grandest expressions of power, undoubtedly, decorated the former meeting hall of the Great Council in the Palazzo Vecchio. There, Cosimo commissioned his court painter Giorgio Vasari to paint a series of large frescoes commemorating Cosimo's victories over his enemies. In the center of the room's ceiling, Cosimo sits in majesty. Dancing putti and coats of arms surround him. The ducal crown is held in wait. Flora, symbol of Florence, holds a crown of flowers above his head (Figure 33).[48] It was the quintessential expression of Cosimo's claim, like other European rulers but catered to the Florentine context, to a divine right to rule.[49]

Cosimo also solidified his power by defeating his rivals. At first, it seemed that Duke Cosimo might have to deal with the same sorts of resistance to his claims and the related unrest that his ancestors had

Figure 33 Giorgio Vasari. *Apotheosis of Cosimo de' Medici*, 1563–5. Oil painting on wood. Photo by Guillaume Piolle, July 4, 2010. Florence.

encountered. After all, his reign began with an attempted coup in 1537, and to contemporaries that coup could have seemed another chapter in a book with sections already devoted to 1433, 1434, 1458, 1466, 1478, 1494, 1498, 1512, 1527, 1530, and others. After Cosimo defeated Filippo Strozzi's forces in 1537, Filippo's allies continued seeking help for their cause abroad. From Rome in 1539, for example, Michelangelo sculpted a bust of Brutus for Florentines who were licking their wounds in exile. The bust expressed their belief that they were heirs to the classical, republican tradition, a tradition that included the possibility of tyrannicide.[50] Today, Michelangelo's *Brutus* is found in the Florentine Bargello. Its unfinished rough-hewn quality stands in stark contrast to the finished polish of Cellini's slightly later bust of Duke Cosimo in a nearby room.

There were other challenges. In addition to the possible rebels in Rome, Alessandro's murderer, Lorenzino de' Medici, remained at large and was rumored to be stirring trouble abroad. Emperor Charles repeatedly pressured Duke Cosimo to track down Lorenzino to avenge Lorenzino's affront to imperial honor. Cosimo often deferred and delayed action, even as news of Lorenzino's plots reached the duchy from abroad.[51] Perhaps Cosimo did not wish to rile up political sentiments at home. The drama of the Italian Wars also threatened Cosimo's position. Cosimo's victory at Montemurlo, for example, fit into broader struggles between the empire and France. Alliance with one offended the other. Cosimo's ties to Charles meant that the French did not even recognize his position in Florence before 1559.[52] In the meantime, who knew whom fortune would favor next – The French? The empire? The Ottomans? Someone else?

But things were changing. Cosimo's internal reforms during the 1540 and 1550s were bearing fruit. His alliance with the emperor provided a powerful ally. He expanded his state. He raised his international status. He monitored his enemies abroad in France and Venice using an intricate tapestry of transcontinental connections. Those enemies were losing power as the years passed and Cosimo's footing became more secure. All fortresses in Florence and Tuscany were returned to Cosimo in 1543. Those fortresses meant that Cosimo could better defend Florence. They also meant that he no longer shared his city with a foreign force fortified within impenetrable stone walls. He turned his gaze toward other issues. In 1552 the city of Siena expelled imperial forces from the city. They began assisting both the French and Florentine exiles. Cosimo's army defeated the Sienese and their allies in 1554 at Marciano. A year later

Siena surrendered. Emperor Charles granted the city to Cosimo as a fief. And thus Cosimo became master over all of Tuscany.[53]

Cosimo's *virtu* and fortune's favor brought more developments for ducal Florence. After Marciano, any remaining disaffected Florentines abroad lacked the power to challenge Cosimo's position. Then, the election of Pope Paul IV in 1555 brought a Medici ally to the throne of Saint Peter. The Peace of Cateau-Cambrésis in 1559 settled a general peace across Europe. Freed from the danger of picking the wrong side in the Italian Wars, Cosimo enjoyed greater flexibility to assert more agency in external affairs. He began supporting the religious reforms of Pope Paul's successor Pius IV and then Pius's successor, Pope Pius V. Cosimo supplied monetary aid to the French to fight against Protestants in their lands. As he supported the emperor's traditional enemies, Cosimo continued to profess imperial loyalty. He pressed the pope for the title of Grand Duke over his Tuscan lands. The request was granted in 1569. The title brought new prestige to the Medici duke. It also meant the ducal foundation rested now on papal authority in addition to the previous imperial investiture.[54]

The city's architecture reflected the increased stability of Florence and the Florentine state under Duke Cosimo. In 1559 Cosimo oversaw the destruction of buildings between the Palazzo Vecchio and the Arno river. In their place was constructed the Uffizi to house the growing state bureaucracy. Over the next twenty years, the immense and uniform building rose upward. Its elegant and open u-shaped structure, now home to a top art gallery, still contrasts with the fortress-like Palazzo Vecchio next door.[55] Snaking from the Uffizi, over the Ponte Vecchio, through the *oltrarno* quarter, and then arriving at the newly renovated Palazzo Pitti, where the Medici then lived, Vasari built a corridor to facilitate ducal access between these important political centers. The corridor not only made travel faster and easier, but it also helped Duke Cosimo to further separate himself from his Florentine subjects.[56] Other Florentines embraced the stability of the ducal state. In place of the rusticated fortresses of previous centuries, patricians built elegant, less defensible palaces that harkened back to classical models.[57] Those sixteenth and seventeenth-century palaces still abound in the modern city.

The Medici dukes were even able to wrestle some level of control over religion and religious institutions in their city. Since 1517 Protestants and Catholics had been killing each other over different interpretations of Christianity. Different religious groups sought to sway others to their points of view, across Europe, across Italy, and even in

Florence. Starting in 1545 the Catholic Church called the Council of Trent to discuss topics of reform and confirmation. In the years that followed, Cosimo became an active enforcer of the Council's decrees, both because of piety and because he wanted to keep the pope as a political ally. Even so, he seems to have been more accepting than others of heterodox religious views, especially before the 1560s, and strove to maintain independence from papal control. He and his successors at times worked with members of the Church, at times resisted enforcement of decrees, and at times the two groups tolerated each other. For example, the Council of Trent ordered the creation of lists of forbidden books. Cosimo and his successors worked with church authorities to help Florentine printers and writers while also promoting considerations of orthodoxy. By 1591 Duke Ferdinando I, in practice, possessed the final approval for texts printed in Florence.[58]

Better stability at home turned Florentine eyes toward participation in the sixteenth-century explosion in overseas trade and expansion. Duke Cosimo began investing capital to turn Livorno into a seaport. Over time the plan worked. Livorno became an important "free port," especially during the seventeenth century.[59] Duke Cosimo and his successors developed a Florentine navy to try to break into Ottoman markets in the eastern Mediterranean. In Egypt, they succeeded in establishing a strong mercantile presence. In other areas Florentine ambitions led to military actions. Battles were frequent in the later sixteenth and early seventeenth centuries.

Emboldened by ducal successes Florentines professed their continued centrality in European culture. Others already recognized Florence and Florentines as cultural leaders.[60] The artist Giorgio Vasari enhanced that reputation during the sixteenth century. Using a mixture of collected drawings, passed-down anecdotes, original research, and fantastical fabrications, Vasari, along with others, wrote long and short biographies of dozens of painters, sculptors, and architects from the late 1200s until his own day. Vasari's work claimed that individuals like Giotto had dispelled the veil of darkness from medieval art. In its place, those early artists had experimented with naturalism and classicism. Fifteenth-century artists had continued and built upon those trends. In the sixteenth century, art reached its perfection with the divine Michelangelo Buonarotti. Vasari crafted his progressive narrative around the art of Florentines. For Vasari, Florentine art, its styles, and its innovations, with few exceptions, were the standard against which all other visual expressions were compared.[61] Vasari's chronology, framework, and focus on Florence continues to influence popular conceptions of Renaissance art. Even today areas of artistic deviance from Florentine exempla are often unfairly judged as retrograde or of lesser quality, rather than examples of other tastes and styles from the period.

Despite its considerable strengths and cultural reputation, ducal Florence was still very much an early modern state. Cosimo did not possess absolutist control over the city of Florence or its subject cities. For example, Cosimo conquered the city of Siena in 1559. The new city and its former territories were permitted to continue with a special status within the government, rather than being absorbed into existing structures. Other cities in the Florentine state also enjoyed significant degrees of autonomy. Officeholders in Cosimo's Florence usually lacked the special training necessary to execute the demands of their positions. Thus, they relied upon long-serving bureaucrats. Corruption ran rampant in courts, where people used their social standing and connections to ensure favorable outcomes. Less wealthy, less connected people lacked such options: it was hardly the impartial system idealized by modern states.[62] Cosimo's Florence, in short, implemented many things that modern readers might find familiar, even positive. But the specifics of each change as well as the less teleological developments that accompanied them reflected the temporal distance between the twenty-first century and sixteenth-century Florence.

Moreover, the reputation of Florence as a cultural center overshadowed that much of the most innovative cultural production in Europe was happening elsewhere. Historians have long highlighted the increasing importance of northern European courts in the visual arts during the sixteenth and seventeenth centuries. In some cases, Italian artists made their careers abroad. The Venetian artist Titian, for example, found patronage with Charles V and his court. Many northern artists, like Albrecht Dürer and Hans Holbein, brought Italian styles back to transalpine patrons. Within the Italian peninsula, Rome became the cultural capital. Symbolically, Michelangelo left Florence for the last time in 1534. He spent the last thirty years of his life producing art and architecture in Rome, including his Last Judgement within the Sistine Chapel and a design for the original domed section of the rebuilt Saint Peter's Cathedral. As Rome grew as a political and religious center, cardinals invested their wealth in cultural expressions. Like the Florentines before them, culture became the currency in their competitions for piety, power, and position.

Written culture in Florence followed similar trends. During the fifteenth century, Florence was a cultural hub of manuscript culture.

The Florentines Niccolò Niccoli and Poggio Bracciolini had created new fonts to use when copying books.[63] People used their innovations. The Florentine manuscript dealer Vespasiano da Bisticci enjoyed clients as far away as the king of Hungary.[64] Yet Florence never established the same sort of importance in the world of printed books. The city did possess printing houses, yet those paled in comparison to printing presses in Venice, Rome, and transalpine cities like Basel.[65] During the sixteenth century, vernacular languages started to rival and even surpass Latin as key means for cultural expression.[66] The Medici dukes, consequently, oversaw formal academies to promote the Florentine vernacular.[67] They encouraged philosophers like Pier Vettori and historians like Benedetto Varchi to return to Florence.[68] They looked to revive the university at Pisa and promoted the printing of university materials within Florence itself.[69] At some level these efforts were a success. The Tuscan dialect, based upon the writings of Dante, Petrarch, and Boccaccio, became the standard accepted form of Italian across the fragmented peninsula. Yet, significantly, the key proponent of Tuscan Italian was Pietro Bembo, a Venetian. His debates with others about the primacy of the Italian used by the three crowned Florentine poets happened in the Veneto. It was largely Venetian printing presses that encouraged the use of a standard Italian based upon the Tuscan dialect.[70] Florence was losing its leadership role in cultural innovations, even as the perception of the city's cultural heritage remained unvarnished.

Other areas reflected the city's decreasing continental status. Florence had been a leader in the reintroduction of Ptolemy's astronomical and geographical knowledge to Latin Europe.[71] That work laid the foundation for many later constructions; yet it was mostly others who built those buildings. In astronomy, Nicholas Copernicus, Johannes Kepler, Tycho Brahe, and even Giordano Bruno were leading thinkers (Galileo Galilei in the 1600s was the obvious exception to that trend). In terms of geographical knowledge, the Florentine Paolo Toscanelli had been a key resource for Christopher Columbus.[72] The Florentine Amerigo Vespucci's book on the lands across the Atlantic proved so popular that their modern name derives from him.[73] Dukes Cosimo, Francesco, and Ferdinando all invested capital into the creation of a room in the Palazzo Vecchio to house an enormous globe and maps of everywhere in the known world. The room was also to proudly display rare objects possessed by the Medici family. It was to include over 200 portraits of famous men. Yet, after Duke Cosimo died his son Francesco scaled back the room's design. Leading experts associated with the project moved on to other things.

People chosen for their loyalty took their place. They finished the room in 1589, the style and conception of maps and decorations already out of date. The planned portraits were moved to the hallways of the Uffizi, where they remain today.[74] Ultimately, Florence played little direct role in the story of the overseas colonization and encounters between the Americas and other parts of Europe.[75] After the death of Duke Cosimo II (1609–21), Duke Ferdinando II (r. 1621–70) even sold off the Florentine naval fleet to focus more singularly on the port city of Livorno.[76]

Florence adopted the innovations of others in medicine too. All early modern Europeans took proactive measures to lead healthy lives. Museums are full of the artifacts that they used. For example, people took efforts to purify the air that they breathed. A fireplace could have an inscription that "it purges dirty things." A small metal ball could be used to burn perfumes as well as to warm a person's hands.[77] Like other governments, the Florentine ducal state monitored the outbreak of diseases in other places. They imposed measures to prevent those outbreaks from spreading into and through their territory. When they failed, the Florentine government and local church officials worked together to minimize the spread of the disease; to manage the outbreak; control panic; and end the disruption to life as soon as possible.[78] In these areas, Florence was typical of other early modern states. Like others, they imported the majority of major discoveries in health or innovations in public health from Venice, Rome, and beyond the Alps.[79]

After a reign of nearly three decades, Cosimo had solidified himself and his family as the hereditary dukes of Florence. The political space in the city had collapsed to an orbit around the Medici family. Power came from the duke. Honor came from the duke. Offices reflected proximity to the duke. Although he had been picked because of his youth and inexperience, Cosimo crushed his enemies and successfully maintained Florentine formal independence in a complex political and diplomatic environment. Even more, he maneuvered Florence into a respectable position among those areas formally and informally with the imperial sphere. His receipt of the Grand Ducal title from the pope accentuated his accomplishments. The title meant that both the empire and the pope— the supreme theoretical powers in Europe—recognized the Medici claim to rule Florence by law and by right. Although those powers recognized different claims and titles, it was, nevertheless, a strong foundation on which to continue to build an early modern state. Thus, it comes as little surprise that Cosimo's death led to the seamless transfer of power to his son Francesco in 1574.

The Medici duchy built upon the foundations of the Florentine Republic even as it inaugurated something new. The thirteenth-century dreams of continental empire drifted further away as Florence settled in as a secondary power in a political world dominated by others. Florentine families continued to jockey for power and influence, but the space between "Medici" and "anti-Medici" had collapsed so much that ambitions had to run the ruling family. Florence continued to vacillate its external loyalties: this time they allied with the emperor before moving back toward the pope and France later in the century. Florence maintained its reputation for cultural exceptionality, but that reputation increasingly rested upon the past. Culture kept tapping into transcontinental languages of visual and literary expression, even as the rising vernacular signaled broader intellectual and cultural changes happening in Europe. Early modern Florence, in short, combined strong continuities with the city's republican past with the new cultures, political structures, and styles of the early modern duchy. The city that had once dreamed of continental conquests had moved within the shadow of Brunelleschi's towering dome.

Epilogue, 1575–Present

Florence is famous for its golden age between about 1250 and 1550. This book has argued that good reasons remain for viewing those centuries as a unique period in the city's history. Beginning in the thirteenth century Florentine's political and cultural might unexpectedly exploded to continental proportions. Families jockeyed for access to real political power. They patronized cultural projects that made arguments for piety, position, power, and status using transcontinental languages. Their scope mirrored similar strengths in the city's economy and demographics. But things changed in the mid-fourteenth century. Demographic and economic collapse meant more limited political realities, even as the city's culture continued to profess the grandiose ambitions of previous decades. The unique juxtaposition between the cultural influence and political limits of Florence was born. Over time consensus politics fell to factional fighting. The Medici family emerged victorious. Families supported and resisted Medici's efforts to consolidate control. Many people avoided either extreme. The Medici moved the city away from its traditional French ties to the regionalism of the Italian League. Yet, transcontinental cultural arguments continued. During the sixteenth century, the Medici consolidated their power over the city. They forced ambitious men to become pro-Medici or leave politics or even Florence itself. Great culture continued but with less direct impact than before. Florence's cultural reputation, however, continued to increase. By the mid-sixteenth century the Renaissance period had ended. Early Modern Florence settled into secondary roles.

The 450 years between the rule of Duke Cosimo and the present have both changed and preserved the city that once proudly, perhaps at one time even realistically, proclaimed its rightful inheritance to the entirety of the old Roman Republic. The rule of Francesco and then his brother Ferdinando from 1587 continued the trends developed by their father Cosimo. Ferdinando's reign was particularly noteworthy. Ferdinando was a cardinal when his brother died without a male heir. He relinquished his red robes for a ducal crown. He married his distant relative Christine of Lorraine to strengthen Florentine ties with France, a kingdom then partly ruled by another relative, Catherine de' Medici. Ferdinando sought to build on his father and brother's investments in Livorno as an important port city. He built roads to better facilitate trade, travel, and unity across his Tuscan state. He continued to invest in the Florentine silk industry.[1] Like his ancestors and fellow Florentines, Ferdinando used culture for a variety of ends, including to legitimate and enhance his political power. Many sculpted likenesses survive, and the city still reflects his urban designs and developments.[2]

Ferdinando also built upon his father and brother's diplomatic efforts. Cosimo had maintained only a small court. Ferdinando brought to Florence his already substantial court as a cardinal and used it to augment the family's public displays. For example, approximately 2,800 guests attended the wedding between Ferdinando and Christine of Lorraine in 1589. Ferdinando continued to cultivate ties with France and through them England. By 1589 Florence was secretly keeping Queen Elizabeth in England informed about Spanish fleets. Simultaneously, Ferdinando maintained the strong ties that his family had developed with the Counter Reformation papacy. So began the seventeenth century, a century in which Florence looked more to consolidation than expansion, more contribution than creation.[3]

The 1600s brought a semi-stability to Italian peninsular political affairs. The French and Hapsburg fights over territory moved north of Florence. The Italian peninsula remained important in the minds of seventeenth-century political leaders, and Italian states participated in the Thirty Years' War. But the Italian theatre remained peripheral.[4] By the mid-seventeenth century Atlantic trade had decisively replaced the Mediterranean Sea as the premier economic zone of the continent. Italian states ruled by the Hapsburgs persisted the best that they could. Independent states like Venice suffered from the shift. Within this landscape, in Florence Ferdinando I was followed by his son Cosimo II and Cosimo by his son Ferdinando II. The Florentine economy suffered as trade and innovation moved elsewhere. Florence desperately tried to maintain neutrality amid conflicts far outside its modest means.[5]

Florence's most famous resident during the 1600s was undoubtedly Galileo Galilei. Galileo had spent parts of his life teaching at the University of Pisa. He was accused of teaching that the planets orbited around the sun in reality, not just in theory. Europeans had long considered the idea of a heliocentric universe. Nicholas Copernicus's posthumous publication of his astronomical studies had given new life to the idea during the latter 1500s and early 1600s. It was acceptable in Catholic Europe to use the heliocentric model as a tool to do theoretical thought experiments. The problem occurred when a person claimed, like Galileo, that heliocentrism was real; that the planets did in fact move; that the stars were mutable. Galileo was tried and condemned, but he was initially permitted to continue teaching. After about ten years he was denounced a second time for the same offenses. Galileo not only refused to yield his position, but he also presented his arguments in ways that antagonized his opponents. He was convicted. Galileo, as a relapsed heretic, was spared execution and permitted to live out his days in and near Florence.[6]

Otherwise, the most decisive trends and events in seventeenth-century Europe moved elsewhere. Europe's economic center had shifted north and west. Florentines continued to live and die in the duchy, and the city still bears their mark in some places. For example, slightly east and north of the Accademia gallery opens the Piazza Annunziata. An equestrian statue of Duke Ferdinando I watches visitors. The unified loggia of the square was completed with a new portico for the church of Santissima Annunziata around the turn of the seventeenth century.[7] In another part of town, the Pitti Palace was expanded as the ducal family continued to marry European nobles. Yet, few Baroque buildings occupy the modern city.[8] The days of Duke Cosimo flexing his might across Tuscany were becoming a distant memory. Florence was a political afterthought to events like the trading wars over the Atlantic between Spain, the Lowlands, and England.

After Ferdinando II, Duke Cosimo III ruled the city for over fifty years. His reign was marked by financial struggles, unsuccessful attempts to preserve the family line, and at times ill-advised neutral positions. He passed down this poor situation to his son Gian Gastone, who was unable to rectify these issues before his death in 1737. Lacking a male heir, the question of succession fell to external powers. Those northern European powers determined that Francis Stephen, Duke of Lorraine, should take Tuscany. When Francis died, Tuscany would be passed down through his family, separate from his other holdings.[9] At least Florence would remain marginally independent.

Gian Gastone's sister Anna Mara did not inherit her father and brother's state, but she did inherit the Medici family properties and collections. Before her death in 1743, she bequeathed the unparalleled collection of Medici art to the Florentine government on the condition that it never be sold. This collection, in turn, established the foundations of some of the most famous museums in Florence.[10] Within the Uffizi Gallery, the art of the Medici was installed in chronological rooms. Visitors to this day ascend a large staircase, walk briefly down a hallway flanked by ancient sculptures—any of which could be the prime piece in most museums—and enter a room proudly displaying giant altarpieces by Duccio, Cimabue, and Giotto. Through rooms dedicated to the fourteenth, the fifteenth, the sixteenth, the seventeenth, the eighteenth centuries and beyond, the galleries present a fraction of the Uffizi's true collection. At the Pitti Palace, so long the home of the Medici dukes, visitors view another massive slice of Maria's gift to the city. Countless paintings by the best early modern artists cover nearly all available wall space. The collection includes *Woman with a Veil* by Raphael, a work that visited the Chicago Institute of Art in the spring of 2000. There, the author of this book, then a 21-year-old undergraduate, saw it and simply had to learn more about the Italian Renaissance (Figure 34).

Figure 34 Raffaello Sanzio da Urbino, *Woman with a Veil*, 1512–15. Oil on canvas (photograph from A Treasury of Art Masterpieces: From the Renaissance to the Present Day, 29). Pitti Gallery, Florence.

More changes came to Florence. In the latter 1700s Pietro Leopold reformed the city's economy and judicial systems to conform with enlightenment ideals.[11] In the Napoleonic wars Florence opposed Napoleon on paper, but the city's weak military meant the city played little practical role in the conflicts. Napoleon temporarily conquered Italy. He entered Florence in mid-1796, his French troops came some three years later. After the French came a new Grand Duchy.[12] During the nineteenth century a new Italian unification movement was gaining momentum. By 1870 the powers of the peninsula had agreed to join together to form a single Italian state. The *Risorgimento,* on paper, was complete. The new state of Italy needed a capital. Piedmont had played a central role in the unification efforts. Thus, a new area was needed to increase state unity. The papal presence in Vatican City ruled out Rome as an option. Perhaps Florence could be a good option. After all, the Italian language helped unify the Italian people, and the Italian language had been born with the Florentine Dante.

The preparation for Florence as capital of Italy brought dramatic changes to the city's urban framework. Roads were straightened and widened to improve traffic. They tore down the long and obsolete city walls. Only a few towers and short sections were left to remind viewers of the power and ambition of late medieval Florence. An old market square and the Jewish ghetto were demolished. In their place, they built an open piazza and a grand archway that commemorated the city's modernization. The cathedral facade, long half-finished, was completed in its current form. The church of Santa Croce also gained a new facade to cover its previously rustic exterior.[13] Next to the new facade the city placed a statue of Dante to commemorate the 600th year of his birth.[14] Florence did not remain a capital for long, but the imprint of these urban changes still commemorates its short-lived status.

The strategic position of Florence along the north-south roads of the peninsula had historically served the city well. That location came to haunt the city in the Second World War. Initially an Axis power, after the overthrow of Benito Mussolini, in 1943 Italy joined the Allied forces. The German Axis armies occupied the state for a full year. Then, in the summer of 1944, the Allied armies began pushing north to expel their Axis enemies. Their path led through Florence. Street-fighting ensued. The retreating Germans tried to slow the Allied advances by destroying Florentine bridges. Only Ponte Vecchio was spared; an island of medieval heritage amid the carnage of twentieth-century war. Period photos reveal the rubble of buildings along the Arno bank. Streets that had resounded with church bells echoed the sounds of urban warfare and artillery fire.[15]

After the Second World War the city rebuilt its bombed bridges, cleaned out the rubble, and replaced burnt-out structures with new buildings. Yet destruction soon returned to the city. In November 1966, the fall rains filled the Arno past its banks. Nearly twenty-foot-deep water filled some areas of the city. The Piazza Santa Croce became a mud pit. Lives were lost. Property destroyed. Irreplaceable pieces of art irrevocably damaged.[16] At that time historians were just beginning to tap the vast resources of the Florentine state archive found within the Uffizi. The flood waters poured into the building like water from a faucet into a bottle. Records were lost or the waters removed the words from their pages. In partial response to these losses, a new and then state-of-the-art building was built on the outskirts of town, along the *viale* near the Piazza Cesare Beccaria.[17] Within that building, eager scholars still receive manuscripts filled with blank, washed-out pages. Back at the Uffizi, the lines of millions of tourists silently pass the stone "archivio di stato" sign that still marks the entrance to the old archive.

Over the more than fifty years since the flood, Florence has continued to grow as a tourist and study abroad destination. The Piazza della Repubblica now houses a carousel and food trucks. The piazze where premodern people could escape their cramped medieval streets now resemble packed concert crowds. Ironically, people now look for little-traveled, narrow side roads to avoid the hustle and bustle. The sounds of English of all accents fill the air. Recent changes to traffic patterns have created pedestrian-friendly zones in the most visited areas. Meanwhile, pedestrians, cars, and mopeds still battle at major sites like San Marco, the Accademia, the Piazzale Michelangelo, and others. Even the *oltrarno* feels the pinch. Most of that quarter lacks leading cultural sites. Consequently, it used to entertain few tourists and instead housed traditional artisanal shops. Yet, in recent years the quarter has become advertised as offering a more authentic Italian experience than the better-known sites in the city. Quiet walks become harder to find amid the curious crowds seeking the culture of Florence's past.

The city's present in some ways mirrors its Renaissance past. Like in the fifteenth century, the city possesses a disconnect between its outsized cultural inheritance versus its otherwise limited global reach. In 2021 the population of Florence was around 709,000 people. It was the eighth-largest city in Italy, far behind cities like Rome, Milan, Naples, and Turin.[18] Yet, Florence's cultural heritage defies its diminished global economic and political status. Nearly five million people visit Florence every year. Many of those visitors arrive at Florence's small but continually updated airport, named after Amerigo Vespucci. Many others come by train. Maybe they are coming for a day trip as they travel from Rome to Venice. Perhaps their cruise ship has docked near Pisa and threatened to leave them behind if they do not return by the appointed hour to disembark! Still others arrive by car: their hotel has a red number; the building they see has a black number, where is the building with the red number? However they visit, the moderate-sized modern city consistently houses enough tourists to rank near or among the top fifty most visited cities in the world.[19]

Looking out from San Miniato al Monte or the Piazzale Michelangelo it can be hard to imagine the modern city of Florence as an inconsequential Roman colony; or poised to take over the late medieval world; or the Renaissance and early modern city that struggled to fill its city walls (Figure 35). Brunelleschi's dome still towers over the old city. But, in the distance a modern judicial building seems to parallel its height and hovers over the low-lying suburbs. The judicial building makes it hard to imagine Brunelleschi's weathered dome as one of the tallest buildings in the world, or to recapture the awe that such a dome—surely a miracle from God!—could even exist. It can be hard to filter out the strange

Figure 35 Thomas Cole, *View of Florence*, 1837. Oil on canvas. Anonymous photo. Cleveland Museum of Art.

omnipresence of English, the mopeds, the buses, and the airplanes to imagine different background noises like church bells, an older version of Italian, Latin, domestic animals, and so many other premodern sounds lost in the modern city.

But that modern city is the heir to Florentines who housed popes, fought against emperors, and dreamed of an empire to mirror the fallen Roman one. It is the outcome of a republic of many families that slowly and in fits and starts changed to a monarchy revolving around the Medici. A once political powerhouse and cultural backwater became a regional power with unlimited cultural claims. What changes will the future bring? Will later readers view the Florentine Renaissance as the precursor to Italian dominance? Historians tell stories about the past and attach significance and meaning to otherwise unmanageable and innumerable strands of human existence. Only the future can tell what the past means and what people will find relevant about our present.

Notes

INTRODUCTION

1 See, for example, Fabio Martini, and Lucia Sarti, "Prima di Firenze: Dal paleolitico all'età del bronzo," in *Archeologia a Firenze: Città e territorio*, ed. Valeria d'Aquino et al. (Oxford: Archaeopress, 2015), 3–37.

2 Jacob Burckhardt, *The Civilization of the Renaissance in Italy* (London: Penguin Books, 1990), 65.

3 Burckhardt, *The Civilization of the Renaissance in Italy*, 114.

4 Burckhardt, *The Civilization of the Renaissance in Italy*, 257.

5 For an accessible summary of Burkhardt, his context, and his reception, see William Caferro, *Contesting the Renaissance* (Malden, MA: Wiley-Blackwell, 2011), passim. For a clear introduction to the Italian Renaissance, see Virginia Cox, *A Short History of the Italian Renaissance* (London: I.B. Tauris, 2016).

6 For interesting anecdotes about the Florentine archives during this period, see Anthony Molho, "The Closing of the Florentine Archive," *Journal of Modern History* 60, no. 2 (1988): 290–9, Gene Brucker, "The Uffizi Archives, 1952-1987: A Personal Memoir," in *Florence and Beyond. Culture, Society and Politics in Renaissance Italy*, ed. David S. Peterson and Daniel E. Bornstein (Toronto: CRRS, 2008), 51–9.

7 Colin Hardie, "The Origin and Plan of Roman Florence," *The Journal of Roman Studies* 55, no. 2 (1965): 128–34. On Etruscan Florence, see Giovannangelo Camporeale, "Gli Etruschi di Firenze," in *Archeologia a Firenze: Città e Territorio*, ed. Valeria d'Aquino et al. (Oxford: Archaeopress, 2015), passim. For more details, see Robert Davidsohn, *Storia di Firenze* (Florence: Sansoni, 1907), vol. 1, 1–16, esp. 10–16. See also Ferdinand Schevill, *Medieval and Renaissance Florence*, vol. 1: Medieval Florence (New York: Harper & Row, 1936), 4–7.

8 Hardie, "The Origin and Plan of Roman Florence," 135. On this theater, see also Monica Salvini et al., "Le premesse archeologiche alla Sala Grande," in *La Sala Grande di Palazzo Vecchio e la Battaglia di Anghiari di Leonardo da Vinci*, ed. Roberto Barsanti et al. (Florence: Leo S. Olschki, 2019), 71–95.

9 Giuseppina Carlotta Cianferoni, "Florentia," in *Archeologia a Firenze: Città e Territorio*, ed. Valeria d'Aquino et al. (Oxford: Archaeopress, 2015), passim. Davidsohn, *Storia di Firenze*, vol. 1, 23–4.

10 Camporeale, in *Archeologia a Firenze: Città e Territorio*, 39. See also Schevill, *Medieval and Renaissance Florence*, 7.

11 Schevill, *Medieval and Renaissance Florence*, 8–9, and 43, Davidsohn, *Storia di Firenze*, vol. 1, 48.

12 Schevill, *Medieval and Renaissance Florence*, 9–10. Despite civic tradition, Zenobius was probably not the city's first bishop. See Lorenzo Tanzini, *Firenze* (Spoleto: Fondazione Centro Italiano di Studi sull'Alto Medioevo, 2016), 35, Davidsohn, *Storia di Firenze*, vol. 1, 49–51 and 58–9. For further information on the cult of St. Zenobius in Florence, see George Dameron, *Florence and Its Church in the Age of Dante* (Philadelphia: University of Pennsylvania Press, 2005), 202–3, Maureen C. Miller, "The Saint Zenobius Dossal by the Master of the Bigallo and the Cathedral Chapter of Florence," in *The Haskins Society Journal 19*, ed. Stephen Morillo and William North (Woodbridge: Boydell Press, 2008), 65–70. Sally J. Cornelison, "When an Image Is a Relic: The St. Zenobius Panel from Florence Cathedral," in *Images, Relics, and Devotional Practices in Medieval and Renaissance Italy*, ed. Sally J. Cornelison and Scott B. Montgomery (Tempe, AZ: ACMRS, 2006), 95–113.

13 George Dameron, "Church and Community in a Medieval Italian City: The Place of San Lorenzo in Florentine Society from Late Antiquity to the Early Fourteenth Century," in *San Lorenzo. A Florentine Church*, ed. Robert W. Gaston and Louis A. Waldman (Villa I Tatti: Sheridan Books, 2017), 40–1. On San Lorenzo, see Paolo Viti, *Il Capitolo di San Lorenzo nel Quattrocento* (Florence: Leo S. Olschki, 2006), Robert W. Gaston, and Louis A. Waldman, eds., *San Lorenzo. A Florentine Church* (Villa I Tatti: Sheridan Books, 2017).

14 Hardie, "The Origin and Plan of Roman Florence," 135. Cianferoni, in *Archeologia a Firenze: Città e Territorio*, 59, places the desolation and abandonment of parts of the city in the 300s. For more information on Florence in the Roman Empire, see Davidsohn, *Storia di Firenze*, vol. 1, 21–36.

15 Hardie, "The Origin and Plan of Roman Florence," 135. Cf. Schevill, *Medieval and Renaissance Florence*, 29, which claims Totila is meant, not Attila. See also Davidsohn, *Storia di Firenze*, vol. 1, 77.

16 Schevill, *Medieval and Renaissance Florence*, 30–1. See also Francesco Maria Petrini, "Florentia 'ostrogota,'" in *Archeologia a Firenze: Città e Territorio*, ed.

Valeria d'Aquino et al. (Oxford: Archaeopress, 2015), 255–44, Davidsohn, *Storia di Firenze.*

17 Schevill, *Medieval and Renaissance Florence,* 31, Davidsohn, *Storia di Firenze,* vol. 1, 111–58.

18 Surveys of the medieval Florentine commune, for example, hardly even mention Florence before 1000. See, for example, Chris Wickham, *Early Medieval Italy: Central Power and Local Society, 400-1000* (Ann Arbor: University of Michigan Press, 1989), Philip Jones, *The Italian City-State: From Commune to Signoria* (Oxford: Clarendon Press, 1997). See also Davidsohn, *Storia di Firenze,* vol. 1, 158–84.

19 On the foundation of the Badia, see Anne Leader, *The Badia of Florence. Art and Observance in a Renaissance Monastery* (Bloomington: Indiana University Press, 2012), 11–13. On Ugo's tomb, see Shelley E. Zuraw, "The Public Commemorative Monument: Mino da Fiesole's Tombs in the Florentine Badia," *The Art Bulletin* 80, no. 3 (1998): 452–77, Schevill, *Medieval and Renaissance Florence,* 40–1, Tanzini, *Firenze,* 41. See also Davidsohn, *Storia di Firenze,* vol. 1, 171–3 and 81–2.

20 Francesco Gurrieri, "L'architettura," in *La Basilica di San Miniato al Monte a Firenze,* ed. Francesco Gurrieri, Luciano Berti, and Claudio Leonardi (Florence: Giunti, 1988), 15–22, Francesco Gurrieri, "San Miniato al Monte, la Basilica dell' 'Urbs perfecta,'" in *Dieci secoli per la Basilica di San Miniato al Monte,* ed. Francesco Gurrieri and Renzo Manetti (Florence: Polistampa, 2007). See also Davidsohn, *Storia di Firenze,* vol. 1, 196–9, Scott B. Montgomery, "*Quia venerabile corpus rediciti martyris ibi repositum:* Image and Relic in the Decorative Program of San Miniato al Monte," in *Images, Relics, and Devotional Practices in Medieval and Renaissance Italy,* ed. Sally J. Cornelison and Scott B. Montgomery (Tempe, AZ: ACMRS, 2006), 7-25.

21 See Scott B. Montgomery, "Securing the Sacred Head: Cephalophory and Relic Claims," in *Disembodied Heads in Medieval and Early Modern Culture,* ed. Barbara Baert, Anita Traninger, and Catrien Santing, (Leiden: Brill, 2013), 88–90, George Dameron, "The Cult of St. Minias and the Struggle for Power in the Diocese of Florence, 1011-1018," *Journal of Medieval History* 13 (1987): 125–41, Davidsohn, *Storia di Firenze,* vol. 1, 200–1. On the relative scarcity of documentation for these centuries, see also Enrico Faini, *Firenze nell'età romanica (1000-1211): L'espansione urbana, lo sviluppo istituzionale, il rapporto con il territorio* (Florence: Leo S. Olschki, 2010), 24.

22 On the Investiture Controversy, see Kathleen G. Cushing, *Reform and the Papacy in the Eleventh Century: Spiritual and Social Change* (Manchester: Manchester University Press, 2005), Uta-Renate Blumenthal, *The Investiture Controversy: Church and Monarchy from the Ninth to the Twelfth Century* (Philadelphia: University of Pennsylvania Press, 1988). See also Schevill,

Medieval and Renaissance Florence, 47, David J. Hay, *The Military Leadership of Matilda of Canossa 1046-1115* (Manchester: Manchester University Press, 2010), 30. For more details on Florence itself during this century of reform, see Davidsohn, *Storia di Firenze*, 206–455.

23 On this sculpture, see John Beldon Scott, "Papal Patronage in the Seventeenth Century: Urban VIII, Bernini, and the Countess of Matilda," in *L'âge d'or du mécénat (1598-1661)*, ed. Roland Mousnier and Jean Mesnard (Paris: Editions du CNRS, 1985), 119–27. See also C. D. Dickerson III, Ian Wardropper, and Tony Sigel, eds., *Bernini: Sculpting in Clay* (New Haven: Yale University Press, 2012), 131–5. However, those pages pertain to a bronze copy rather than the tomb itself. My thanks to Piers Baker-Bates and Pablo González Tornel for their help with this footnote.

24 Hay, *The Military Leadership of Matilda of Canossa 1046-1115*, Schevill, *Medieval and Renaissance Florence*, 55. See also Penelope Nash, *Empress Adelheid and Countess Matilda: Medieval Female Rulership and the Foundations of European Society* (New York: Palgrave Macmillan, 2017), 115.

25 Chris Wickham, *Courts and Conflict in Twelfth-Century Tuscany* (Oxford: Oxford University Press, 2003), 168–9. See also the comments at George Dameron, *Episcopal Power and Florentine Society, 1000-1320* (Cambridge, MA: Harvard University Press, 1991), 68.

26 Davidsohn, *Storia di Firenze*, 296–8 and 305.

27 Tanzini, *Firenze*, 42. See also Dameron, *Episcopal Power and Florentine Society, 1000-1320*, 65–7. More generally, see Faini, *Firenze nell'età romanica (1000-1211)*. For the broader context, see Jones, *The Italian City-State*. See also Davidsohn, *Storia di Firenze*, whose treatment of Matilda begins at vol. 1, 371.

28 The relationship between country and city, long characterized as highly antagonistic, probably was more "symbiotic rather than exploitive." As summed up at Dameron, *Episcopal Power and Florentine Society, 1000-1320*, 7, but passim. See also Tanzini, *Firenze*, 43–5, John M. Najemy, *A History of Florence, 1200-1575* (Malden, MA: Blackwell, 2006), 64.

29 Faini, *Firenze nell'età romanica (1000-1211)*, 51–4. For the growth of Florentine business on the Italian peninsula, see Richard A. Goldthwaite, *The Economy of Renaissance Florence* (Baltimore: Johns Hopkins University Press, 2009), 26.

30 Tanzini, *Firenze*, 46, Schevill, *Medieval and Renaissance Florence*, 78–9. On these early conquests, see Dameron, *Episcopal Power and Florentine Society, 1000-1320*, 69–77. See also Nicolai Rubinstein, *Studies in Italian History in the Middle Ages and the Renaissance*, ed. Giovanni Ciappelli (Roma: Edizioni di storia e letteratura, 2004), 1–35.

31 Faini, *Firenze nell'età romanica (1000-1211)*, 213–22, Tanzini, *Firenze*, 45–7.
    See also Wickham, *Courts and Conflict in Twelfth-Century Tuscany*, 168,
    Najemy, *A History of Florence, 1200-1575*, 64. For more detail, see Daniela
    De Rosa, *Alle origini della Repubblica Fiorentina dai consoli al "Primo
    Popolo" (1172-1260)* (Florence: Arnaud, 1995).

32 Schevill, *Medieval and Renaissance Florence*, 70–1, Dameron, *Episcopal
    Power and Florentine Society, 1000-1320*, 118–19. See also Carol Lansing,
    The Florentine Magnates: Lineage and Faction in a Medieval Commune
    (Princeton: Princeton University Press, 1991), Najemy, *A History of Florence,
    1200-1575*, Faini, *Firenze nell'età romanica (1000-1211)*, 161–9.

33 Tanzini, *Firenze*, 47–8. See also Najemy, *A History of Florence, 1200-1575*, 65–6.

34 Schevill, *Medieval and Renaissance Florence*, 86–8.

35 Rosa, *Alle origini della Repubblica Fiorentina dai consoli al "Primo Popolo,"*
    17 and 75. See also Faini, *Firenze nell'età romanica (1000-1211)*, 271–6.

36 Rosa, *Alle origini della Repubblica Fiorentina dai consoli al "Primo Popolo,"* 68.

37 Faini, *Firenze nell'età romanica (1000-1211)*, 23, 26–8, and 118–19. See also
    Lansing, *The Florentine Magnates*, 11.

38 Lansing, *The Florentine Magnates*.

39 Goldthwaite, *The Economy of Renaissance Florence*, 26–8.

40 Goldthwaite, *The Economy of Renaissance Florence*, 27–33, Rosa, *Alle
    origini della Repubblica Fiorentina dai consoli al "Primo Popolo,"* 203–4. For
    more details on earlier currencies used in Florence, see Faini, *Firenze nell'età
    romanica (1000-1211)*, 101–2.

41 Dameron, *Episcopal Power and Florentine Society, 1000-1320*, 122, Dameron,
    Florence and Its Church in the Age of Dante, 203–4, Montgomery, *"Quia
    venerabile corpus rediciti martyris ibi repositum."*

42 Tanzini, *Firenze*, 50–1.

43 Rosa, *Alle origini della Repubblica Fiorentina dai consoli al "Primo Popolo,"*
    179–80. See also Najemy, *A History of Florence, 1200-1575*, 69, with further
    leads therein.

44 Schevill, *Medieval and Renaissance Florence*, 106–16. On factions already
    in the twelfth century, see Faini, *Firenze nell'età romanica (1000-1211)*. On
    the outbreak of hostilities in 1216, see Enrico Faini, "Il convito fiorentino
    del 1216," in *Conflitti, paci e vendette nell'Italia comunale*, ed. Andrea
    Zorzi (Florence: Firenze University Press, 2009), 105–30. See also Dameron,
    Episcopal Power and Florentine Society, 1000-1320, 118–28, Najemy, *A
    History of Florence, 1200-1575*, 65.

45 Lansing, *The Florentine Magnates*, 11–12.

46 Najemy, *A History of Florence, 1200-1575*, 66–9. Tanzini, *Firenze*, 54.

47 Schevill, *Medieval and Renaissance Florence*, 116–8, Najemy, *A History of
    Florence, 1200-1575*, 66–8.

CHAPTER 1

1 Dameron, *Florence and Its Church in the Age of Dante*, 2.
2 Ann G. Carmichael, *Plague and the Poor in Renaissance Florence* (Cambridge: Cambridge University Press, 1986), 60–1.
3 Najemy, *A History of Florence, 1200-1575*, 70. On the Florin, see Goldthwaite, *The Economy of Renaissance Florence*, 48–57, with further references therein. On the reduction of the towers and more on the *Primo Popolo*, see Lansing, *The Florentine Magnates*, 17 and 193–5.
4 See Adrian W.B. Randolph, "Il Marzocco: Lionizing the Florentine State," in *Coming About . . . A Festschrift for John Shearman*, ed. Lars R. Jones and Louisa C. Matthew (Cambridge, MA: Harvard University Art Museums, 2001), 11–18, with further leads therein. See also Schevill, *Medieval and Renaissance Florence*, 123.
5 Beatrice Paolozzi Strozzi, "La storia del Bargello," in *La storia del Bargello: 100 capolavori da scoprire*, ed. Beatrice Paolozzi Strozzi (Milan: Silvana Editoriale, 2004), 13. In addition, the reader is pointed to two excellent, detailed guides to the Bargello and much of the city of Florence at Eve Borsook, *The Companion Guide to Florence*, 6th Revised ed. (Rochester, NY: Companion Guides, 1997), Alta Macadam, *Florence: Blue Guide*, Seventh ed. (London: A&C Black, 1998).
6 On the establishment of the museum at the Bargello, see Beatrice Paolozzi Strozzi, ed., *La storia del Bargello: 100 capolavori da scoprire* (Milan: Silvana Editoriale, 2004). See also Borsook, *The Companion Guide to Florence*, 74–6, Macadam, *Florence*, 209–18.
7 On these portraits, see Silvia Diacciati, "L'immagine di Dante nel Palazzo del Bargello," *Archivio storico italiano* 158, no. 1 (2020): 3–24, E. H. Gombrich, "Giotto's Portrait of Dante?," in *New Light on Old Masters*, ed. E. H. Gombrich (Chicago: University of Chicago Press, 1986), 11–31. John Pope-Hennessy, *The Portrait in the Renaissance* (New York: Pantheon Books, 1966), 4ff, Marco Santagata, *Dante: The Story of His Life*, trans. Richard Dixon (Cambridge, MA: Belknap Press of Harvard University Press, 2016), 5–7, Cristina Danti, Alberto Felici, and Paola Ilaria Mariotti, "La Cappella del Bargello. Vicende conservative delle pitture," in *La storia del Bargello. 100 capolavori da scoprire*, ed. Beatrice Paolozzi Strozzi (Milan: Silvana, 2004), 79–88. On the fresco, see George R. Bent, *Public Painting and Visual Culture in Early Republican Florence* (Cambridge: Cambridge University Press, 2016), 109–12.
8 Richard MacCracken, *The Dedication Inscription of the Palazzo del Podestà in Florence* (Florence: Leo S. Olschki, 2001), 3–4. Also on this inscription, see Najemy, *A History of Florence, 1200-1575*, 70, Tanzini, *Firenze*, 55.

9 MacCracken, *The Dedication Inscription of the Palazzo del Podestà in Florence*, 5–7. Translations from this text have been slightly altered.

10 MacCracken, *The Dedication Inscription of the Palazzo del Podestà in Florence*, 5.

11 MacCracken, *The Dedication Inscription of the Palazzo del Podestà in Florence*, 5.

12 The argument for Latini as author is made throughout MacCracken, *The Dedication Inscription of the Palazzo del Podestà in Florence*.

13 Giorgio Inglese, "Brunetto Latini," in *Dizionario Biografico degli Italiani*, vol. 64 (2005), accessed online at https://www.treccani.it/enciclopedia/brunetto -latini_%28Dizionario-Biografico%29/ (accessed July 11, 2022). For more detail, see Julia Bolton Holloway, *Twice-Told Tales: Brunetto Latino and Dante Alighieri* (New York: Peter Lang, 1993), 23–50. On Latini in general, see Julia Bolton Holloway, *Brunetto Latini: An Analytic Bibliography* (Valencia: Grant & Cutler Ltd, 1986). Inglese, *Brunetto Latini*.

14 Ronald G. Witt, *In the Footsteps of the Ancients: The Origins of Humanism from Lovato to Bruni* (Leiden: Brill, 2000), 178–9, Najemy, *A History of Florence, 1200-1575*, 71. On this battle, see Duccio Balestracci, *La battaglia di Montaperti* (Rome: Laterza, 2017).

15 A second key historical source for these events is published at Cesare Paoli, *Il Libro di Montaperti* (Florence: G.P. Vieusseux, 1889). See also Holloway, *Twice-Told Tales*, 39–40.

16 The image and many others can be viewed online at the Vatican Library Online (digivatlib), Chig.L.VIII.296 77r. (Chig.L.VIII.296 I DigiVatLib, accessed November 2, 2021). The image is by the workshop of Pacino di Buonaguida and appears in a copiously illustrated copy of Giovanni Villani's *Chronicle*. One other account of these events, with fictional speech, can be found at Leonardo Bruni, *History of the Florentine People*, trans. James Hankins, 3 vols. (Cambridge, MA: Harvard University Press, 2001-2007), 1.175–83. See also Giovanni Villani, *Cronica*, 8 vols. (Florence: Il Magheri, 1823), 2.116–18.

17 Holloway, *Twice-Told Tales*, 50–65, Witt, *In the Footsteps of the Ancients*, 178–9.

18 On these works, see Holloway, *Twice-Told Tales*, 56–65, 179ff, and passim. See also Brunetto Latini, *The Book of the Treasure (Li Livres dou Tresor)*, trans. Paul Barrette and Spurgeon Baldwin (New York: Garland Publishing, 1993), Brunetto Latini, *Il Tesoretto (The Little Treasure)*, ed. and trans. Julia Bolton Holloway (New York: Garland Publishing, Inc., 1981).

19 On the early Italian humanists, see in general Witt, *In the Footsteps of the Ancients*, Alexander Lee, *Humanism and Empire: The Imperial Ideal in Fourteenth-Century Italy* (Oxford: Oxford University Press, 2018),

Roberto Weiss, *Il primo secolo dell'umanesimo* (Rome: Edizione di storia e letteratura, 1949), Giuseppe Billanovich, *I primi umanisti e le tradizioni dei classici latini* (Fribourg: Edizioni universitarie, 1953).

20 The most prominent Tuscan humanist at that time was Geri d'Arezzo. On him, to start, see below. See also Patrizia Stoppacci and Claudia Cenni, *Geri d'Arezzo. Lettere e dialogo d'amore* (Pisa: Pacini, 2009), Simona Foà, "Geri d'Arezzo," in *Dizionario Biografico degli Italiani*, vol. 53 (2000), accessed online at https://www.treccani.it/enciclopedia/geri-d-arezzo_(Dizionario-Biografico) (accessed July 11, 2022). Ronald G. Witt, "Petrarch and Pre-Petrarchan Humanism: Stylistic Imitation and the Origins of Italian Humanism," in *Humanity and Divinity in Renaissance and Reformation*, ed. John W. O'Malley, Thomas M. Izbicki, and Gerald Christianson (Leiden: Brill, 1993), 73–100.

21 Najemy, *A History of Florence, 1200-1575*, 72–5. See also Holloway, *Twice-Told Tales*, 75–8. On Charles of Anjou, see also Jean Dunbabin, *Charles I of Anjou: Power, Kingship and State-Making in Thirteenth-Century Europe* (London: Routledge, 2014), David Abulafia, "Charles of Anjou Reassessed," *Journal of Medieval History* 26, no. 1 (2000): 93–114, Donald Matthew, *The Norman Kingdom of Sicily* (Cambridge: Cambridge University Press, 1992), 363–80.

22 Santagata, *Dante*, passim, but esp. 93–4 and 223–4. For more on Latini as Dante's teacher, see Holloway, *Twice-Told Tales*, 8–12 and 289–301.

23 Inglese, *Brunetto Latini*. The column is described at Borsook, *The Companion Guide to Florence*, 167, Macadam, *Florence*, 209. For more information on Latini during these later years, see Holloway, *Twice-Told Tales*, 147–67.

24 Najemy, *A History of Florence, 1200-1575*, 75–6, Tanzini, *Firenze*, 56–7, Nicola Ottokar, *Il Comune di Firenze alla fine del Dugento*, 2nd ed. (Torino: Giulio Einaudi, 1962), 33–47.

25 Guido Cariboni, "Symbolic Communication and Civic Values in Milan under the Early Visconti," in *Languages of Power in Italy (1300-1600)*, ed. Daniel Bornstein, Laura Gaffuri, and Brian Jeffrey Maxson (Turnhout: Brepols, 2017), 65–76, Jane Black, *Absolutism in Renaissance Milan: Plenitude of Power under the Visconti and the Sforza 1329-1535* (Oxford: Oxford University Press, 2009). On the Italian communes in general, see Daniel Waley and Trevor Dean, *The Italian City Republics*, 4 ed. (Abingdon: Routledge, 2009), Jones, *The Italian City-State*.

26 The classic study on the Sicilian Vespers is Steven Runciman, *The Sicilian Vespers. A History of the Mediterranean World in the Later Thirteenth Century* (Cambridge: Cambridge University Press, 2012). More recently, see Abulafia, "Charles of Anjou Reassessed."

27 These lines simplify a government that changed throughout the fourteenth century. See Najemy, *A History of Florence, 1200-1575*, 76–83. For the structure of the Ordinances of Justice, see Schevill, *Medieval and Renaissance Florence*, 157–9. Tanzini, *Firenze*, 56–8. Ottokar, *Il Comune di Firenze alla fine del Dugento*, John M. Najemy, *Corporatism and Consensus in Florentine Electoral Politics, 1280-1400* (Chapel Hill: University of North Carolina Press, 1982). Lansing, *The Florentine Magnates*, 201–11, Giuseppe Pampaloni, "Gli organi della Repubblica fiorentina per le relazioni con l'Estero," *Rivista di studi politici internazionali* 20 (1953): 260–96.

28 Najemy, *A History of Florence, 1200-1575*. On the Palazzo Vecchio, see Nicolai Rubinstein, *The Palazzo Vecchio, 1298-1532: Government, Architecture, and Imagery in the Civic Palace of the Florentine Republic* (Oxford: Clarendon Press, 1995). Rosa, 177–8. See also John M. Najemy, "Florentine Politics and Urban Spaces," in *Renaissance Florence: A Social History*, ed. Roger J. Crum and John T. Paoletti (Cambridge: Cambridge University Press, 2006), 19–54. Marvin Trachtenberg, "Founding the Palazzo Vecchio in 1299: The Corso Donati Paradox," *Renaissance Quarterly* 54, no. 4 (1999): 983–5.

29 Trachtenberg, "Founding the Palazzo Vecchio in 1299," 971–2. See also Najemy, in *Renaissance Florence: A Social History*, Rubinstein, *The Palazzo Vecchio, 1298-1532*, 13–14.

30 On Florentine Guelfs and Guelfism in these early years, see Gene Brucker, *Florentine Politics and Society 1343-1378* (Princeton: Princeton University Press, 1962), 74 and 102–3. On the integration of the Florentine Church and economics into papal networks, see Dameron, *Florence and Its Church in the Age of Dante*, 28, 58–60, and 74–7. See also Oren J. Margolis and Brian J. Maxson, "The 'Schemes' of Piero de' Pazzi and the Conflict with the Medici (1461-1462)," *Journal of Medieval History* 41, no. 4 (2015): 4–5.

31 For example, see the economic connections between the Florentines and the Angevins in the first half of the fourteenth century, at Dameron, *Florence and Its Church in the Age of Dante*, 111 and 224–6.

32 Trachtenberg, "Founding the Palazzo Vecchio in 1299," 969. See also Rubinstein, *The Palazzo Vecchio, 1298-1532*, 9.

33 See Najemy, *A History of Florence, 1200-1575*, esp. 5–64. On social groups in late medieval Florence, see also Lansing, *The Florentine Magnates*. Some recent political theorists have begun to reassess how Machiavelli may have viewed the distinctions between the *popolo* and the *grandi*. See, for example, Christopher Holman, *Machiavelli and the Politics of Democratic Innovation* (Toronto: University of Toronto Press, 2018).

34 On these struggles, see Najemy, *A History of Florence, 1200-1575*, 88–92, Santagata, *Dante*, Dino Compagni, *Chronicle of Florence*, ed. and trans.

Daniel E. Bornstein (Philadelphia: University of Pennsylvania Press, 1986), Randolph Starn, *Contrary Commonwealth: The Theme of Exile in Medieval and Renaissance Italy* (Berkeley: University of California Press, 1982). Teresa Pugh Rupp, "'If You Want Peace, Work for Justice': Dino Compagni's Compagni's *Cronica* and the Ordinances of Justice," in *Florence and Beyond. Culture, Society and Politics in Renaissance Italy*, ed. David S. Peterson and Daniel E. Bornstein (Toronto: CRRS, 2008), 323–37, with further leads therein. On these factions, see also Lansing, *The Florentine Magnates*, 231–4.

35 Santagata, *Dante*. On Dante in general, see Rachel Jacoff, *The Cambridge Companion to Dante* (Cambridge: Cambridge University Press, 1993), Zygmunt G. Baransky and Lino Pertile, eds., *Dante in Context* (Cambridge: Cambridge University Press, 2015), Joan M. Ferrante, *The Political Vision of the Divine Comedy* (Princeton: Princeton University Press, 1984), Giuseppe Mazzotta, *Reading Dante* (New Haven: Yale University Press, 2014).

36 On Emperor Henry VII in Italy, see William Bowsky, *Henry VII in Italy: The Conflict of Empire and City-State, 1310-1313* (Lincoln: University of Nebraska Press, 1960), Lee, *Humanism and Empire*.

37 See Dameron, *Florence and Its Church in the Age of Dante*, 48–9. See also Rona Goffen, *Spirituality in Conflict: Saint Francis and Giotto's Bardi Chapel* (University Park: Pennsylvania State University Press, 1987).

38 Jonathan Davies, *Florence and Its University during the Early Renaissance* (Leiden: Brill, 1998), 2.

39 Stoppacci and Cenni, *Geri d'Arezzo*, Foà, *Geri d'Arezzo*, Roberto Weiss, "Lineamenti per una storia del primo umanesimo fiorentino," *Rivista Storica Italiana* 60 (1948): 349–66, Helene Wieruszowski, *Politics and Culture in Medieval Spain and Italy* (Rome: Edizioni di storia e letteratura, 1971).

40 On this work and its reception, see Dante Alighieri, *Monarchy* (Cambridge: Cambridge University Press, 1996). For additional leads, see Santagata, *Dante*, 266–9, Anthony K. Cassell, *The Monarchia Controversy* (Washington, DC: Catholic University Press, 2004), Unn Falkeid, *The Avignon Papacy Contested: An Intellectual History from Dante to Catherine of Siena* (Cambridge, MA: Harvard University Press, 2017).

41 On Dante and early Italian humanists, see, for example, Santagata, *Dante*, Rino Modonutti and Enrico Zucchi, eds., *"Moribus antiquis sibi me fecere poetam." Albertino Mussato nel VII centenario dell'incoronazione poetica (Padova 1315-2015)* (Florence: SISMEL, 2017), Philip H. Wicksteed and Edmund G. Gardner, *Dante and Giovanni del Virgilio* (Westminster: Archibald Constable & Company, 1902).

42 Christopher S. Celenza, *The Intellectual World of the Italian Renaissance: Language, Philosophy, and the Search for Meaning* (Cambridge: Cambridge University Press, 2018).

43 Najemy, *A History of Florence, 1200-1575*, 124–9. For more detail, see Najemy, *Corporatism and Consensus in Florentine Electoral Politics, 1280-1400*, 43–119.

44 Najemy, *A History of Florence, 1200-1575*, 97, 100, and 13. This period corresponds to Florence's second economic phase, see Goldthwaite, *The Economy of Renaissance Florence*, 43 and passim.

45 Edwin S. Hunt, *The Medieval Super-Companies: A Study of the Peruzzi Company of Florence* (Cambridge: Cambridge University Press, 1994), 188–211. See also Najemy, *A History of Florence, 1200-1575*, 133–4.

46 On the Florentine state and its changes in the mid trecento, see Marvin B. Becker, *Florence in Transition*, 2 vols. (Baltimore: Johns Hopkins University Press, 1967–8). On the papacy in Avignon, see Joëlle Rollo-Koster, *Avignon and its Papacy, 1309-1417* (Lanham: Rowman & Littlefield, 2015).

47 Quoted in Brucker, *Florentine Politics and Society 1343-1378*, 3.

48 Najemy, *A History of Florence, 1200-1575*, 103. On construction in Florence more generally, see Richard A. Goldthwaite, *The Building of Renaissance Florence* (Baltimore: Johns Hopkins University Press, 1980).

49 Santagata, *Dante*, 334–5. On the building of the new cathedral in Florence, see Giuseppe Rocchi Coopmans de Yoldi, ed., *S. Maria del Fiore. Teorie e storie dell' archeologia e del restauro nella città delle fabbriche arnolfiane* (Florence: Alinea editrice, 2006).

50 On this image, see most recently Vittoria Camelliti, "La *Misericordia Domini* del Museo del Bigallo. Un *unicum* iconografico della pittura fiorentina dopo la Peste Nera?," *Studi di Storia dell'Arte* 26 (2015): 51–66. See also Howard Saalman, *The Bigallo. The Oratory and Residence of the Compagnia del Bigallo e della Misericorida in Florence* (New York: New York University Press, 1969). John Henderson, *Piety and Charity in Late Medieval Florence* (Chicago: University of Chicago Press, 1997).

51 Roger Aïm, *Le Dôme de Florence: Paradigme du projet* (Sarbonne: Hermann, 2010), 22. See also Mary Bergstein, "Marian Politics in Quattrocento Florence: The Renewed Dedication of Santa Maria del Fiore in 1412," *Renaissance Quarterly* 44, no. 4 (1991): 673–5.

52 For these dates, see Najemy, *A History of Florence, 1200-1575*, 105. See also Goldthwaite, *The Building of Renaissance Florence*, 8. Goffen, *Spirituality in Conflict*. Recent volumes edited by Timothy Verdon in the *Alla riscoperta delle chiesa di Firenze* series for Centro Di press pertain to both churches.

53 See Dameron, *Florence and Its Church in the Age of Dante*, 21, with more information on the financing of these churches at 45, 140–3, and 226–9.

54 Bent, *Public Painting and Visual Culture in Early Republican Florence*, 24–7 and 45–63.

55 Diane Finiello Zervas, *Orsanmichele a Firenze* (Modena: F. C. Panini, 1996), 56. On these early years and particularly the style of tabernacles that emerged

from them, see Enrica Neri Lusanna, "Andrea Pisano's Saint Stephen and the Genesis of Monumental Sculpture at Orsanmichele," in *Orsanmichele and the History and Preservation of the Civic Monument*, ed. Carl Brandon Strehlke (New Yaven: Yale, 2012), esp. 55–7.

56 Bruce Cole, *Giotto and Florentine Painting 1280-1375* (New York: Harper & Row, 1976), 22–6, Luciano Bellosi, *Cimabue* (New York: Abbeville Press, 1998).

57 Bellosi, *Cimabue*, Cole, *Giotto and Florentine Painting 1280-1375*, 30–1. For further leads on Cimabue, see Joseph Polzer, "Cimabue Reconsidered," *Arte medievale 5* (2015): 197–224. and Ada Labriola, "Lo stato degli studi su Cimabue e un libro recente," *Arte cristiana* 88 (2000): 341–52.

58 On Giotto, see Anne Derbes and Mark Sandona, eds., *The Cambridge Companion to Giotto* (Cambridge: Cambridge University Press, 2004), Cole, *Giotto and Florentine Painting 1280-1375*, Julian Gardner, *Giotto and His Publics: Three Paradigms of Patronage* (Cambridge, MA: Harvard University Press, 2011), Serena Romano, *La O di Giotto* (Milan: Electa, 2008), Carl Brandon Strehlke, "Review of Several Recent Works on Dante," *The Art Bulletin* 94, no. 3 (2012): 460–5.

59 The passage comes from *Purgatory*, Canto 11, verses 94–6.

60 On Forese, see Giovanni Ciappelli, "Forese da Rabatta," in *Dizionario Biografico degli Italiani*, vol. 48 (1997), accessed online at https://www .treccani.it/enciclopedia/forese-da-rabatta_%28Dizionario-Biografico%29/ (July 11, 2022).

61 Giovanni Boccaccio, *The Decameron*, trans. G. H. McWilliam, 2nd ed. (London: Penguin Books, 1995), 457–9. See also Derbes and Sandona, *The Cambridge Companion to Giotto*.

62 The scholarship on the Arena Chapel is vast. For leads, see Anne Derbes and Mark Sandona, *The Usurer's Heart: Giotto, Enrico Scrovengi, and the Arena Chapel in Padua* (University Park: Pennsylvania State University Press, 2008), Bruce Cole, *Giotto: The Scrovegni Chapel, Padua* (New York: George Braziller, 1993), Laura Jacobus, *Giotto and the Arena Chapel: Art, Architecture & Experience* (London: Harvey Miller Publishers, 2008), Andrew Ladis, *Giotto's O. Narrative, Figuration, and Pictorial Ingenuity in the Arena Chapel* (University Park, Pennsylvania: Pennsylvania State University Press, 2008). See also Derbes and Sandona, *The Cambridge Companion to Giotto*, Romano, *La O di Giotto*. and in English at Serena Romano, *Giotto's O* (Rome: Viella, 2015).

63 On Giotto's famous frescoes within the basilicas of San Francesco in Assisi and Santa Croce in Florence, in addition to the previously cited literature, see also Karen-Edis Barzman, "Islamic North Africa in Trecento Italy: Costume in the Assisi and Bardi Chapel Frescoes of Francis in Egypt," in

Power, Gender, and Ritual in Europe and the Americas, ed. Peter Arnade and Michael Rocke (Toronto: CRRS, 2008), 29–51. Goffen, *Spirituality in Conflict*, Leonetto Tintori and Eve Borsook, *Giotto. The Peruzzi Chapel* (New York: Harry N. Abrams, Inc., 1965).

64 The manuscript is in the Vatican Library, Chig L VIII, 296, which is available online at https://digi.vatlib.it/view/MSS_Chig.L.VIII.296 (accessed July 3, 2020). The image is at 12v. On Villani and his chronicle, as a start, see Paula Clarke, "The Villani Chronicles," in *Chronicling History: Chroniclers and Historians in Medieval and Renaissance Italy*, ed. Sharon Dale, Alison Williams Lewin, and Duane J. Osheim (University Park, PA: Pennsylvania State University Press, 2007), 113–43, with further leads therein. See also Franca Ragone, *Giovanni Villani e i suoi continuatori. La scrittura delle cronache a Firenze nel Trecento* (Rome: Istituto storico italiano per il Medio Evo, 1998).

65 The text appears in book 12, chapter 84, of Villani's *Nuova Cronica*. See Villani, *Cronica*, vol. 7, 196–9. An English version appears in Schevill, *Medieval and Renaissance Florence*, 239–40.

66 Compare the comments at Dameron, *Florence and Its Church in the Age of Dante*, 244. See also the description, based upon Giovanni Villani, at Brucker, *Florentine Politics and Society 1343-1378*, 4–5. Hunt, *The Medieval Super-Companies*, 247–8.

67 Najemy, *A History of Florence, 1200-1575*, 133–5; For further leads, see Hunt, *The Medieval Super-Companies*, Goldthwaite, *The Economy of Renaissance Florence*. Only the Acciaiuoli family remained with papal accounts.

68 On the years in politics leading up to 1342, see especially Najemy, *A History of Florence, 1200-1575*, 120–8.

69 Brucker, *Florentine Politics and Society 1343-1378*, 6–7.

70 On Walter of Brienne, the so-called Duke of Athens, see Najemy, *Corporatism and Consensus in Florentine Electoral Politics, 1280-1400*, Brucker, *Florentine Politics and Society 1343-1378*, 7–8 and 105–20, Najemy, *A History of Florence, 1200-1575*, 128–9. On the Florentine *monte*, see Anthony Molho, *Florentine Public Finances in the early Renaissance, 1400-1433* (Cambridge, MA: Harvard University Press, 1971). Becker, *Florence in Transition*, vol. 1, 151–200. For the political situation in the months after Walter's rule, see Najemy, *A History of Florence, 1200-1575*, 129–52.

71 Brucker, *Florentine Politics and Society 1343-1378*, 8. On politics, see Najemy, *A History of Florence, 1200-1575*, 152–8.

72 The most vivid description of the Plague in Florence comes from the Introduction to Boccaccio's *Decameron*. See also Brucker, *Florentine Politics and Society 1343-1378*, 8–9 and 120–4. More recently, see William Caferro,

Petrarch's War. Florence and the Black Death in Context (Cambridge: Cambridge University Press, 2018), with further references therein.

73 For a good sampling of these sorts of responses and explanations, see Rosemary Horrox, ed., *The Black Death* (Manchester: Manchester University Press, 1994), John Aberth, ed., *The Black Death, the Great Mortality of 1348-1350: A Brief History with Documents*, 2nd ed. (Boston: Bedford/St. Martin's, 2016).

74 On the return of the plague in subsequent years, see Carmichael, *Plague and the Poor in Renaissance Florence*, John Henderson, *Florence under Siege: Surviving Plague in an Early Modern City* (New Haven: Yale University Press, 2019).

75 Cf. Brucker, *Florentine Politics and Society 1343-1378*, 140 and 241–3. On the political situation, see Najemy, *A History of Florence, 1200-1575*, 166ff.

76 On the possible connections between Petrarch's father and Dante, see Santagata, *Dante*, Caferro, *Petrarch's War. Florence and the Black Death in Context*. On Ser Petracco's exile, see Laurence E. Hooper, "Exile and Petrarch's Reinvention of Authorship," *Renaissance Quarterly* 69, no. 4 (2016): 1217–56, Francesco Bettarini, "Petracco dall'Incisa," in *Dizionario Biografico degli Italiani*, vol. 82 (2015), accessed online at https://www .treccani.it/enciclopedia/petracco-dall-incisa_(Dizionario-Biografico) (accessed July 11, 2022), with further leads therein.

77 Deanna Shemek, "Verse," in *The Cambridge Companion to the Italian Renaissance*, ed. Michael Wyatt (Cambridge: Cambridge University Press, 2014), 182.

78 Cox, *A Short History of the Italian Renaissance*, 5, 122, 46, and 90–1. On Petrarch's poems more generally, as a start, see Petrarch, *Lyric Poems*, ed. and trans. Robert M. Durling (Cambridge, MA: Harvard University Press, 1976), Peter Hainsworth, *Petrarch the Poet. An Introduction to the Rerum Vulgarium Fragmenta* (London: Routledge, 1988), Thomas E. Peterson, *Petrarch's Fragmenta. The Narrative and Theological Unity of Rerum vulgarium fragmenta* (Toronto: University of Toronto Press, 2016), Aeleen A. Feng, *Writing Beloveds. Humanist Petrarchism and the Politics of Gender* (Toronto: University of Toronto Press, 2017), Victoria Kirkham and Armando Maggi, eds., *Petrarch: A Critical Guide to the Complete Works* (Chicago: University of Chicago Press, 2009).

79 Witt, *In the Footsteps of the Ancients*, 238–9. See also Witt, in *Humanity and Divinity in Renaissance and Reformation*. On Petrarch and Livy, see Giuseppe Billanovich, *La tradizione del testo di Livio e le origini dell' umanesimo*, 2 vols. (Padua: Antenore, 1981).

80 Witt, *In the Footsteps of the Ancients*, passim, esp. 275.

81 For some of Petrarch's humanist texts, see Ernst Cassirer, Paul Oskar Kristeller and John Herman Randall Jr., eds., *The Renaissance Philosophy of*

Man (Chicago: University of Chicago Press, 1948). See also several volumes in the *I Tatti Renaissance Library*.

82 For Petrarch's biography, see, with further leads, Christopher S. Celenza, *Petrarch: Everywhere a Wanderer* (London: Reaktion Books, 2017), Albert Russell Ascoli, ed., *Cambridge Companion to Petrarch* (Cambridge: Cambridge University Press, 2015), Francisco Rico and Luca Marcozzi, "Petrarca, Francesco," in *Dizionario Biografico degli Italiani*, vol. 82 (2015), accessed online at https://www.treccani.it/enciclopedia/francesco-petrarca_ (Dizionario-Biografico) (accessed July 11, 2022). Kirkham and Maggi, *Petrarch*, Ernest H. Wilkins, *The Life of Petrarch* (Chicago: University of Chicago Press, 1961).

83 Caferro, *Petrarch's War. Florence and the Black Death in Context*, 40. Davies, *Florence and its University during the Early Renaissance*.

84 On Boccacio's connections and the Naples that he knew, see Elizabeth Casteen, *From She-Wolf to Martyr: The Reign and Disputed Reputation of Johanna I of Naples* (Ithaca: Cornell University Press, 2015), Samantha Kelly, *The New Solomon: Robert of Naples (1309-1343) and Fourteenth-Century Kingship* (Leiden: Brill, 2003), Alessia Ronchetti, "Boccaccio Between Naples and Florence, or the Desire to Become Two: Gendering the Author's Past in the *Elegia di Madonna Fiammetta*," *Italian Studies* 72, no. 2 (2017): 205–17. On Boccaccio more generally, see Olivia Holmes and Dana E. Stewart, eds., *Reconsidering Boccaccio: Medieval Contexts and Global Intertexts* (Toronto: University of Toronto Press, 2018), Guyda Armstrong, Riannon Daniels and Stephen J. Milner, *The Cambridge Companion to Boccaccio* (Cambridge: Cambridge University Press, 2015), Valerio Cappozzo, Martin Eisner and Timothy Kircher, eds., *Boccaccio and His World*, a special issue of the journal *Heliotropa* 15 (2018), Victoria Kirkham, Michael Sherberg and Janet Levarie Smarr, *Boccaccio: A Critical Guide to the Complete Works* (Chicago: University of Chicago Press, 2013). But the literature is vast.

85 On the Decameron, as a start, see Armstrong, Daniels, and Milner, *The Cambridge Companion to Boccaccio*.

86 Boccaccio, *The Decameron*, 24–37.

87 Boccaccio, *The Decameron*, 655–8.

88 For these works, see Giovanni Boccaccio, *Famous Women*, ed. Virginia Brown (Cambridge, MA: Harvard University Press, 2001), Giovanni Boccaccio, *Genealogy of the Pagan Gods*, 2 vols. (Cambridge, MA: Harvard University Press, 2011-2017).

89 Antonia Mazza, "L'inventario della 'parva libraria' di Santo Spirito e la biblioteca del Boccaccio," *Italia medioevale e umanstica* 9 (1966): 1–74, Maddalena Signorini, "Considerazioni preliminari sulla biblioteca di Giovanni Boccaccio," *Studi sul Boccaccio* 29 (2011): 367–95.

90 Brucker, *Florentine Politics and Society 1343-1378*, 124–5.

91 Najemy, *A History of Florence, 1200-1575*, 145–8; See also Brucker, *Florentine Politics and Society 1343-1378*, 33–4, 124ff, and passim.

92 Margherita Datini, *Letters to Francesco Datini*, trans. Carolyn James and Antonio Pagliaro (Toronto: Centre for Reformation and Renaissance Studies, 2012), 47.

93 Brucker, *Florentine Politics and Society 1343-1378*, 77, with other similar examples at 128. On Datini more generally, see Iris Origo, *The Merchant of Prato: Francesco di Marco Datini* (Oxford: Alden Press, 1957), Ann Crabb, *The Merchant of Prato's Wife: Margherita Datini and Her World, 1360-1423* (Ann Arbor: Michigan University Press, 2015), Giampiero Nigro, ed., *Francesco di Marco Datini: The Man, the Merchant* (Florence: Firenze University Press, 2010).

94 Witt, *In the Footsteps of the Ancients*, 363–70, Brian Jeffrey Maxson, *The Humanist World of Renaissance Florence* (Cambridge: Cambridge University Press, 2014), 129–30.

95 Najemy, *A History of Florence, 1200-1575*, 148–51, Gene Brucker, *The Civic World of Early Renaissance Florence* (Princeton: Princeton University Press, 1977), 14–60, Susannah Foster Baxendale, "Exile in Practice: The Alberti Family In and Out of Florence 1401-1428," *Renaissance Quarterly* 44, no. 4 (1991): 720–56, Susannah F. Baxendale, "Alberti Kinship and Conspiracy in Late Medieval Florence," in *Florence and Beyond: Culture, Society and Politics in Renaissance Italy*, ed. David S. Peterson and Daniel E. Bornstein (Toronto: CRRS, 2008), 339–53. See also Najemy, *Corporatism and Consensus in Florentine Electoral Politics, 1280-1400*, 217–20.

96 Najemy, *A History of Florence, 1200-1575*, 194. On Florence and the Papal State during the 1350s, 1360s, and 1370s, see Brucker, *Florentine Politics and Society 1343-1378*, 172ff. See also Gene Brucker, *Florence, the Golden Age, 1138-1737*, 1st paperback ed. (New York: Abbeville Press, 1984), 170–4, William J. Connell and Andrea Zorzi, eds., *Florentine Tuscany: Structures and Practices of Power* (Cambridge: Cambridge University Press, 2000).

97 Compare Brucker, *Florentine Politics and Society 1343-1378*, 294–5. See also Alison Williams Lewin, *Negotiating Survival: Florence and the Great Schism, 1378-1417* (Madison, NJ: Fairleigh Dickinson University Press, 2003).

98 On the so-called War of Eight Saints, Lewin, *Negotiating Survival*, Ronald G. Witt, *Coluccio Salutati and His Public Letters* (Geneva: Librairie Droz, 1976), David S. Peterson, "The War of Eight Saints in Florentine Memory and Oblivion," in *Society & Individual in Renaissance Florence*, ed. William J. Connell (Berkeley: University of California Press, 2002), 173–214. Brucker, *Florentine Politics and Society 1343-1378*, 297ff. F. Thomas Luongo, *The Saintly Politics of Catherine of Siena* (Ithaca: Cornell University Press, 2006).

99 On the Great Schism, see Thomas M. Izbicki and Joëlle Rollo-Koster, *A Companion to the Great Western Schism (1378-1417)* (Leiden: Brill, 2009).

Rollo-Koster, *Avignon and its Papacy, 1309-1417*, John Holland Smith, *The Great Schism* (New York: Weybright and Talley, 1970).

100 Lewin, *Negotiating Survival*.

101 On Salvestro's term as Standard Bearer, see Brucker, *Florentine Politics and Society 1343-1378*, 358.

102 Brucker, *Florentine Politics and Society 1343-1378*, 384-6, Najemy, *A History of Florence, 1200-1575*, 164-5.

103 Najemy, *A History of Florence, 1200-1575*, 161-6. The literature on the Ciompi Revolt is vast. See, for example, Samuel Kline Cohn, *The Laboring Classes in Renaissance Florence* (New York: Academic Press, 1980), Patrick Lantschner, *The Logic of Political Conflict in Medieval Cities: Italy and the Southern Low Countries, 1370-1440* (Oxford: Oxford University Press, 2015), Niall Atkinson, *The Noisy Renaissance: Sound, Architecture, and Florentine Urban Life* (University Park, PA: Pennsylvania State University Press, 2017), with further leads therein. See also Najemy, *Corporatism and Consensus in Florentine Electoral Politics, 1280-1400*, 220ff.

CHAPTER 2

1 Gene Brucker, ed., *Two Memoirs of Renaissance Florence: The Diaries of Buonaccorso Pitti and Gregorio Dati* (Long Grove, IL: Waveland Press Inc, 1991), 49. Cf. the translation at Vittore Branca, ed., *Merchant Writers: Florentine Memoirs from the Middle Ages and Renaissance* (Toronto: University of Toronto Press, 2015), 282–83. Pitti's diary has also been published in its entirety in the original Italian. See Buonaccorso Pitti, *Ricordi*, ed. Veronica Vestri (Florence: Florence University Press, 2015).

2 Najemy, *A History of Florence, 1200-1575*, 182.

3 Najemy, *A History of Florence, 1200-1575*, 183-5. For more detail, see Najemy, *Corporatism and Consensus in Florentine Electoral Politics, 1280-1400*, 263–300.

4 Brucker, *The Civic World of Early Renaissance Florence*, Dale Kent, "The Florentine Reggimento in the Fifteenth Century," *Renaissance Quarterly* 28, no. 4 (1975): 575–638. More recently, see also Nicholas Scott Baker, *The Fruit of Liberty: Political Culture in the Florentine Renaissance, 1480-1550* (Cambridge, MA: Harvard University Press, 2013).

5 On dowries, as a start, see Julius Kirshner, *Marriage, Dowry, and Citizenship in Late Medieval and Renaissance Italy* (Toronto: University of Toronto Press, 2015).

6 Brucker, *Two Memoirs of Renaissance Florence*, 109–12. Brucker's edition does not include Dati's entry on his wedding to Bandecca. That entry can be found at Gregorio Dati, *Il libro segreto*, ed. Carlo Gargiolli (Bologna:

Gaetano Romagnoli, 1869), 15 and 21. On the status of the Berardi family, see Anthony Molho, *Marriage Alliance in Late Medieval Florence* (Cambridge, MA: Harvard University Press, 1994), 366. Lauro Martines, *The Social World of the Florentine Humanists 1390-1460* (Princeton: Princeton University Press, 1963), 360.

7 On Leonardo Dati, see Brucker, *Two Memoirs of Renaissance Florence*. See also Najemy, *Corporatism and Consensus in Florentine Electoral Politics, 1280-1400*, 301–4.

8 See John F. Padgett, "Open Elite? Social Mobility, Marriage, and Family in Florence, 1282-1494," *Renaissance Quarterly* 63 (2010): 357–411. Goldthwaite, *The Economy of Renaissance Florence*. For a contrasting view, see Molho, *Marriage Alliance in Late Medieval Florence*.

9 Goldthwaite, *The Economy of Renaissance Florence*, 561–2.

10 See, for example, the arguments at Richard A. Goldthwaite, *Wealth and the Demand for Art in Italy, 1300-1600* (Baltimore: Johns Hopkins University Press, 1993).

11 On Salutati in general with further leads, see the classic biography at Ronald G. Witt, *Hercules at the Crossroads: The Life, Works, and Thought of Coluccio Salutati* (Durham: Duke University Press, 1983). For more recent studies and bibliography, see Michael J. Hartwell and Brian Jeffrey Maxson, "Coluccio Salutati," in *Literature Criticism from 1400-1800*, ed. Lawrence J. Trudeau, vol. 256 (Farmington Hills: Gale Cengage, 2016), 85–246. See also Witt, *Coluccio Salutati and His Public Letters*.

12 On Salutati and Marsili, see Witt, *In the Footsteps of the Ancients*. Jerrold E. Seigel, *Rhetoric and Philosophy in Renaissance Humanism: The Union of Eloquence and Wisdom, Petrarch to Valla* (Princeton: Princeton University Press, 1968), 65–6, Paolo Falzone, "Luigi Marsili," in *Dizionario Biografico degli Italiani*, vol. 70 (2008), accessed online at https://www.treccani.it/enciclopedia/luigi-marsili_(Dizionario-Biografico) (accessed July 11, 2022). Maxson, "Coluccio Salutati," 306–8, Witt, *Hercules at the Crossroads*.

13 Davies, *Florence and Its University during the Early Renaissance*, 15. On Chrysoloras, see Giuseppe Cammelli, *I dotti bizantini e le origini dell'umanesimo*, vol. 1: *Manuele Crisolora* (Florence: Le Monnier, 1941), Ian Thomson, "Manuel Chrysoloras and the Early Italian Renaissance," *Greek, Roman, and Byzantine Studies* 7 (1966): 63–82.

14 On some of these early translations, see N. G. Wilson, *From Byzantium to Italy. Greek Studies in the Italian Renaissance*, 2nd ed. (London: Bloomsbury, 2017), James Hankins, *Humanism and Platonism in the Italian Renaissance*, vol. 1 (Rome: Edizioni di storia e letteratura, 2003), 243–91.

15 Clémence Revest, "Poggio's Beginnings at the Papal Curia: The Florentine Brain Drain and the Fashioning of the Humanist Movement," in *Florence in the Early Modern World*, ed. Nicholas Scott Baker and Brian Jeffrey

Maxson (Abingdon: Routledge, 2019), 189–212. Clémence Revest, *Romam veni: Humanisme et papauté à la fin du Grand Schisme* (Ceyzerieu: Champ Vallon, 2021). See also the classic study George Holmes, *The Florentine Enlightenment, 1400-1450* (London: Weidenfeld and Nicolson, 1969).

16 Maxson, *The Humanist World of Renaissance Florence.*

17 Craig Taylor, "The Ambivalent Influence of Italian Letters and the Rediscovery of the Classics in Late Medieval France," in *Humanism in Fifteenth-Century Europe*, ed. David Rundle (Oxford: The Society for the Study of Medieval Languages and Literature, 2012), 203–36. On similar themes, see Marina Belozerskaya, *Rethinking the Renaissance: Burgundian Arts across Europe* (Cambridge: Cambridge University Press, 2002), esp. 66–75.

18 John L. Flood, "Humanism in the German-Speaking Lands during the Fifteenth Century," in *Humanism in Fifteenth-Century Europe*, ed. David Rundle (Oxford: The Society for the Study of Medieval Languages and Literature, 2012), 79–80.

19 David Rundle, "Humanism across Europe: The Structure of Contacts," in *Humanism in Fifteenth-Century Europe*, ed. David Rundle (Oxford: The Society for the Study of Medieval Languages and Literature, 2012), 319–20.

20 For an introduction to Renaissance philosophy, see Brian Copenhaver and Charles B. Schmitt, *Renaissance Philosophy* (Oxford: Oxford University Press, 1992), James Hankins, ed., *The Cambridge Companion to Renaissance Philosophy* (Cambridge: Cambridge University Press, 2007). A more recent, thorough treatment can be found in the continually updated, online *Encyclopedia of Renaissance Philosophy,* edited by Marco Sgarbi.

21 Lewin, *Negotiating Survival.* On symbols of Guelfism in the late 1300s, see Zervas, *Orsanmichele a Firenze,* vol. 2, 319–29.

22 On the Romagna, see Luciano Piffanelli, "Nelle parti di Romagna: The Role and Influence of the Apennine Lords in Italian Renaissance Politics," in *Florence in the Early Modern World*, ed. Nicholas Scott Baker and Brian Jeffrey Maxson (London: Routledge, 2019), 117–41. On Florentine wars and diplomacy in general during these years, see Luciano Piffanelli, *Politica e diplomazia nell'Italia del primo Rinascimento* (Rome: École Française de Rome, 2020).

23 See Witt, *Coluccio Salutati and his Public Letters.*

24 On this text, see Ronald G. Witt, "The *De Tyranno* and Coluccio Salutati's View of Politics and Roman History," *Nuova Rivista Storica* 53 (1969): 434–74, Brian Jeffrey Maxson, "Kings and Tyrants: Leonardo Bruni's Translation of Xenophon's Hiero," *Renaissance Studies* 24, no. 2 (2010): 188–206. More recently, see Nikos Panou and Hester Schadee, eds., *Evil Lords. Theories and Representations of Tyranny from Antiquity to the Renaissance* (Oxford: Oxford University Press, 2018).

25 On this building in modern Florence, see Diane Finiello Zervas, "'Degno templo e tabernacolo santo': Remembering and Renewing Orsanmichele," in

Orsanmichele and the History and Preservation of the Civic Monument, ed. Carl Brandon Strehlke (New Haven: Yale University Press, 2012), 13.

26 On the importance of the building to city planning already in the late thirteenth century, see Maria Teresa Bartoli, "Designing Orsanmichele: The Rediscovered Rule," in *Orsanmichele and the History and Preservation of the Civic Monument*, ed. Carl Brandon Strehlke (New Haven: Yale University Press, 2012), 37–9. See also Blake Wilson, "If Monuments Could Sing: Image, Song, and Civic Devotion inside Orsanmichele," in *Orsanmichele and the History and Preservation of the Civic Monument*, ed. Carl Brandon Strehlke (New Haven: Yale University Press, 2012), 141–68.

27 Zervas, *Orsanmichele a Firenze*, 128, Diane Finello Zervas, *The Parte Guelfa, Brunelleschi & Donatello* (Locust Valley, NY: J.J. Augustin, 1987), 105.

28 Zervas, *Orsanmichele a Firenze*, 58 and 161.

29 Zervas, *Orsanmichele a Firenze*, 71–136. On the filling of these vaults, see Gert Kreytenberg, "The Limestone Tracery in the Arches of the Original Grain Loggia of Orsanmichele in Florence," in *Orsanmichele and the History and Preservation of the Civic Monument*, ed. Carl Brandon Strehlke (New Haven: Yale University Press, 2012), 112–24.

30 Zervas, *Orsanmichele a Firenze*, 187. Cf. Richard Krautheimer, *Lorenzo Ghiberti* (Princeton: Princeton University Press, 1982), 71–2.

31 Artur Rosenauer, "Orsanmichele: The Birthplace of Modern Sculpture," in *Orsanmichele and the History and Preservation of the Civic Monument*, ed. Carl Brandon Strehlke (New Haven: Yale University Press, 2012), 176–7. Cf. John Pope-Hennessy, *Donatello, Sculptor* (New York: Abbeville Press, 1993), 30.

32 Zervas, *Orsanmichele a Firenze*, vol. 1, 169 and 94–5. Lusanna, in *Orsanmichele and the History and Preservation of the Civic Monument*, 60.

33 The city had celebrated its first communal celebration of St. John in 1403. Zervas, *Orsanmichele a Firenze*, vol. 1, 196–7. Richard C. Trexler, *Public Life in Renaissance Florence* (Ithaca, NY: Cornell University Press, 1980), 289. Krautheimer, *Lorenzo Ghiberti*, 4 and 71–4, which also provides the rough comparison between bronze and stone. Cf. Henderson, *Piety and Charity in Late Medieval Florence*, 229. The connection between Florence and John the Baptist was, however, much older than the fifteenth century. See Christian Bec, "Il Mito di Firenze da Dante al Ghiberti," in *Lorenzo Ghiberti nel suo Tempo: Atti del Convegno Internazionale di Studi*, vol. 1 (Florence: Leo S. Olschki, 1980), 4–6.

34 Krautheimer, *Lorenzo Ghiberti*, 75–84, esp. 75–6.

35 Jeanne van Waadenoijen, "Ghiberti and the Origin of His International Style," in *Lorenzo Ghiberti nel suo Tempo: Atti del Convegno Internazionale di Studi*, vol. 1 (Florence: Leo S. Olschki, 1980), esp. 84 and 86–7. Cf. Krautheimer, *Lorenzo Ghiberti*, xxix. On the Spanish painter Starnina, see

Adele Condorelli, "Gherardo di Jacopo, detto lo Starnina," in *Dizionario Biografico degli Italiani*, vol. 53 (2000), accessed online at https://www .treccani.it/enciclopedia/gherardo-di-jacopo-detto-lo-starnina_(Dizionario-Biografico) (accessed July 11, 2022). For a different hypothesis about Ghiberti and the gothic, see Krautheimer, *Lorenzo Ghiberti*, xv–xvi and 54–67.

36 On Donatello, see, for example, Pope-Hennessy, *Donatello, Sculptor*, 12–14. James Beck, "Ghiberti Giovane e Donatello Giovanissimo," in *Lorenzo Ghiberti nel suo Tempo: Atti del Convegno Internazionale di Studi*, vol. 1 (Florence: Leo S. Olschki, 1980), 112–15. See also John T. Paoletti, "'Nella mia giovanile età mi partì . . . da Firenze,'" in *Lorenzo Ghiberti nel suo Tempo: Atti del Convegno Internazionale di Studi*, vol. 1 (Florence: Leo S. Olschki, 1980), 103.

37 On Ghiberti, historiography, and Orsanmichele, see Krautheimer, *Lorenzo Ghiberti*, xvi, xix–xxii, 16–28, esp. 20–8 and 84, 86–93. For another interesting work by Ghiberti at Orsanmichele, see Eleonora Luciano, "A More 'Modern' Ghiberti: The *Saint Matthew* for Orsanmichele," in *Orsanmichele and the History and Preservation of the Civic Monument*, ed. Carl Brandon Strehlke (New Haven: Yale University Press, 2012), 232–4. Giuliano Ercoli, "Il trecento senese nei *Commentari* di Lorenzo Ghiberti," in *Lorenzo Ghiberti nel suo Tempo: Atti del Convegno Internazionale di Studi*, vol. 2 (Florence: Leo S. Olschki, 1980), 325–34. Graziella Federici Vescovini, "Il problema delle fonti ottiche medievali del *Commentario terzo* di Lorenzo Ghiberti," in *Lorenzo Ghiberti nel suo Tempo: Atti del Convegno Internazionale di Studi*, vol. 2 (Florence: Leo S. Olschki, 1980), 349–87.

38 Zervas, *Orsanmichele a Firenze*, vol. 1, 198–202. See also Pope-Hennessy, *Donatello, Sculptor*, 34. For a different view, see H. W. Janson, *The Sculpture of Donatello* (Princeton: Princeton University Press, 1963), 16–21.

39 Henderson, *Piety and Charity in Late Medieval Florence*, 229. See also Luciano, in *Orsanmichele and the History and Preservation of the Civic Monument*. Carl Brandon Strehlke, "Orsanmichele before and after the Niche Sculptures: Making Decisions about Art in Renaissance Florence," in *Orsanmichele and the History and Preservation of the Civic Monument*, ed. Carl Brandon Strehlke (New Haven: Yale University Press, 2012), 26. Cf. Krautheimer, *Lorenzo Ghiberti*, 86, 93, and 95.

40 Pope-Hennessy, *Donatello, Sculptor*, 34–40.

41 On related themes, see Zervas, *The Parte Guelfa, Brunelleschi & Donatello*, 56–61. See also Gary M. Radke, "Masaccio's City: Urbanism, Architecture, and Sculpture in Early Fifteenth-Century Florence," in *The Cambridge Companion to Masaccio*, ed. Diane Cole Ahl (Cambridge: Cambridge University Press, 2002), 62, Patricia Lee Rubin, *Images and Identity in Fifteenth-Century Florence* (New Haven: Yale University Press, 2007), 50–5.

42 On the early history of the Guelf Party, see Zervas, *The Parte Guelfa, Brunelleschi & Donatello,* 13–38. See also Margolis and Maxson, "The 'Schemes' of Piero de' Pazzi and the Conflict with the Medici (1461-1462)," 3.

43 Zervas, *Orsanmichele a Firenze, 50.* Margolis and Maxson, "The 'Schemes' of Piero de' Pazzi and the Conflict with the Medici (1461-1462)," and the references therein. See also David Boffa, "Divine Illumination and the Portrayal of the Miraculous in Donatello's St. Louis of Toulouse," *Simiolus: Netherlands Quarterly for the History of Art* 31, no. 4 (2004-2005): 283, on Guelfism in Florence in general, see Oren Margolis, *The Politics of Culture in Quattrocento Europe: René of Anjou in Italy* (Oxford: Oxford University Press, 2016), 35–51.

44 Brian Jeffrey Maxson, "Establishing Independence: Leonardo Bruni's *History of the Florentine People* and Ritual in Fifteenth-Century Florence," in *Foundation, Dedication and Consecration in Early Modern Europe,* ed. Maarten Delbeke and Minou Schraven (Leiden: Brill, 2012), 80–2 and 94. On Bruni, see Gordon Griffiths, James Hankins and David Thompson, eds., *The Humanism of Leonardo Bruni* (Binghamton, NY: Medieval & Renaissance Texts and Studies, 1987). For a brief, recent summary of Bruni's life and works, see also Shaun Strohmer and Brian Jeffrey Maxson, "Leonardo Bruni," in *Literature Criticism from 1400-1800,* ed. Lawrence J. Trudeau, vol. 212 (Detroit: Gale Cengage, 2013), 87–260. Brian Jeffrey Maxson, "Leonardo Bruni," in *Encyclopedia of Renaissance Philosophy*, ed. Marco Sgarbi (New York: Springer, 2018), accessed online at https://link.springer.com/referencework/10.1007%2F978-3-319-02848-4 (accessed April 7, 2017). On Bruni's tax breaks to write the history, see Gary Ianziti, *Writing History in Renaissance Italy: Leonardo Bruni and the Uses of the Past* (Cambridge, MA: Harvard University Press, 2012), 188.

45 Najemy, *A History of Florence, 1200-1575,* 209. See also James Hankins, "Humanism in the Vernacular: The Case of Leonardo Bruni," in *Humanism and Creativity in the Renaissance: Essays in Honor of Ronald G. Witt,* ed. Christopher S. Celenza and Kenneth Gouwens (Leiden: Brill, 2006), 9–29. For a contrasting view, see James Hankins, *Virtue Politics: Soulcraft and Statecraft in Renaissance Italy* (Cambridge, MA: Harvard University Press, 2019).

46 See Riccardo Fubini, "La rivendicazione di Firenze della sovranità statale e il contributo delle '*Historiae*' di Leonardo Bruni," in *Storiografia dell'umanesimo in Italia da Leonardo Bruni ad Annio da Viterbo,* ed. Riccardo Fubini (Rome: Edizioni di Storia e Letteratura, 2003), 131–64. Maxson, "Establishing Independence."

47 Maxson, "Establishing Independence," 88–94.

48 On the Medici faction in Florence, see the classic Dale Kent, *The Rise of the Medici: Faction in Florence, 1426-1434* (Oxford: Oxford University Press,

1978), and more generally on the Medici, see Robert Black and John Law, eds., *The Medici: Citizens and Masters* (Florence: Villa I Tatti, 2015).

49 For a polycentric view of faction in fifteenth-century Florence, see Stefano U. Baldassarri and Brian Jeffrey Maxson, "Giannozzo Manetti's *Oratio in funere Iannotii Pandolfini*: Art, Humanism and Politics in Fifteenth-Century Florence," *Interpres* 34 (2016): esp. 79–80.

50 Baldassarri and Maxson, ""Giannozzo Manetti's *Oratio in funere Iannotii Pandolfini*," 82–6.

51 Zervas, *The Parte Guelfa, Brunelleschi & Donatello*, 55–6 and 62.

52 Zervas, *The Parte Guelfa, Brunelleschi & Donatello*, esp. 62–74. See also Alison Brown, "The Guelf Party in Fifteenth-Century Florence," in *The Medici in Florence: The Exercise and Language of Power*, ed. Alison Brown (Florence: Leo S. Olschki, 1992), 105–6.

53 Zervas, *Orsanmichele a Firenze*, 200, Zervas, *The Parte Guelfa, Brunelleschi & Donatello*, 134.

54 Zervas, *The Parte Guelfa, Brunelleschi & Donatello*, 57–9. A partial edition of these statutes can be found at Cesare Guasti, *Commissioni di Rinaldo degli Albizzi per il comune di Firenze dal MCCCXCIX al MCCCCXXXIII*, 3 vols. (Firenze: M. Cellini), vol. 3, 621–3. Bruni also dedicated a work, *On Knighthood*, to a leading Florentine statesman and Guelf partisan Rinaldo degli Albizzi. On these texts, see C.C. Bayley, *War and Society in Renaissance Florence: The De Militia of Leonardo Bruni* (Toronto: University of Toronto Press, 1961). Griffiths, Hankins, and Thompson, *The Humanism of Leonardo Bruni*, 48–9, 107–8, and 27–45, Hankins, *Virtue Politics*.

55 On the palace, see Howard Saalman, *Filippo Brunelleschi: The Buildings* (University Park: Pennsylvania State University Press, 1993), 287–337.

56 Their choice of Donatello was probably not coincidental: Donatello was the son of Niccolò di Betto Bardi, a man who had fled Florence after the Ciompi revolt; traveled with Buonaccorso Pitti in exile; and returned to prominence in the Guelf Party after his return to Florence in 1382. Pope-Hennessy, *Donatello, Sculptor*, 11–12. See also Zervas, *The Parte Guelfa, Brunelleschi & Donatello*, 13, 30–1, 87–91, 99–100, and 20–2.

57 Zervas, *The Parte Guelfa, Brunelleschi & Donatello*, 131–3.

58 Zervas, *The Parte Guelfa, Brunelleschi & Donatello*, 1–2, 4, 9–10, 34, 36, 91–3, 100–1, and 38–42, Boffa, "Divine Illumination and the Portrayal of the Miraculous in Donatello's St. Louis of Toulouse," 282–4. On this niche, see also Pope-Hennessy, *Donatello, Sculptor*, 48–52.

59 Boffa, "Divine Illumination and the Portrayal of the Miraculous in Donatello's St. Louis of Toulouse," 288–90. See also Zervas, *The Parte Guelfa, Brunelleschi & Donatello*, 2. On this sculpture, see also Janson, *The Sculpture of Donatello*, 44–56.

60 Zervas, *The Parte Guelfa, Brunelleschi & Donatello*. See also Boffa, "Divine Illumination and the Portrayal of the Miraculous in Donatello's St. Louis of Toulouse," 283.

61 Molho, *Florentine Public Finances in the early Renaissance, 1400-1433*, 79–87.

62 Brucker, *The Civic World of Early Renaissance Florence*, 483–6. For further leads, see Ugo Procacci, *Studio sul Catasto Fiorentino* (Florence: Leo S. Olschki, 1996), Bayley, *War and Society in Renaissance Florence*, 87–94.

63 Kent, *The Rise of the Medici: Faction in Florence, 1426-1434*, 22–3.

64 Kent, *The Rise of the Medici: Faction in Florence, 1426-1434*, 293–9 and 318.

65 Kent, *The Rise of the Medici: Faction in Florence, 1426-1434*, 311–29. For further leads on the role of Pope Eugenius IV as well as Francesco Sforza in these events, see Riccardo Fubini, "Il regime di Cosimo de' Medici al suo avvento al potere," in *Italia Quattrocentesca: Politica e diplomazia nell'etá di Lorenzo il Magnifico*, ed. Riccardo Fubini (Milan: FrancoAngeli, 1994), 80–4, Riccardo Fubini, and Sarah-Louise Raillard, "Cosimo de' Medici's Regime: His Rise to Power (1434)," *Revue française de science politique* 64, no. 6 (2014): 94–5.

66 Kent, *The Rise of the Medici: Faction in Florence, 1426-1434*, 305–6 and 28–44.

CHAPTER 3

1 On this anecdote, see Brian Jeffrey Maxson, "The *Certame Coronario* as Performative Ritual," in *Rituals of Politics and Culture in Early Modern Europe: Essays in Honour of Edward Muir*, ed. Mark Jurdjevic and Rolf Strøm-Olsen (Toronto: CRRS, 2016), 137–63.

2 Nicolai Rubinstein, *The Government of Florence under the Medici (1434-1494)*, 2nd ed. (Oxford: Clarendon Press, 1997), 1–59. On the despotic or constitutional nature of Medici rule, see Black and Law.

3 Rubinstein, *The Government of Florence under the Medici (1434-1494)*, 16–30 and 55–6.

4 On Neri Capponi, see Maxson, "The *Certame Coronario* as Performative Ritual," 140–4, with further leads therein.

5 On San Lorenzo, see Saalman, *Filippo Brunelleschi*, 107–209, David S. Peterson, "San Lorenzo, the Medici, and the Florentine Church in the Late Fourteenth and Early Fifteenth Centuries," in *San Lorenzo. A Florentine Church*, ed. Robert W. Gaston and Louis A. Waldman (Villa I Tatti: Sheridan Books, 2017), 86–7. See more generally Viti, *Il Capitolo di San Lorenzo nel Quattrocento*.

6 Saalman, *Filippo Brunelleschi*, 152ff. For Florentine responses to the construction site, see Emanuela Ferretti, "The Medici Palace, Cosimo the Elder, and Michelozzo: A Historiographical Survey," in *A Renaissance Architecture of Power: Princely Palaces in the Italian Quattrocento*, ed. Silvia Beltramo, Flavia Cantatore, and Marco Folin (Leiden: Brill, 2016), 264, with further leads therein.

7 On this altarpiece, see William Hood, *Fra Angelico at San Marco* (New Haven: Yale University Press, 1993), John T. Paoletti, "Fraternal Piety and Family Power: The Artistic Patronage of Cosimo and Lorenzo de' Medici," in *Cosimo 'il Vecchio' de' Medici, 1389-1464*, ed. Francis Ames-Lewis (Oxford: Clarendon Press, 1992), 195–219. But the literature is vast.

8 Martines, *The Social World of the Florentine Humanists 1390-1460*, 112–16, Vespasiano da Bisticci, *Renaissance Princes, Popes, and Prelates* (New York: Harper & Row, 1963), 397–8. The Italian version of Vespasiano's life of Niccolò Niccoli can be found at Vespasiano da Bisticci, *Le Vite*, ed. By Aulo Greco (Florence: Istituto Nazionale di Studi sul Rinascimento, 1976), vol. 2, 225–42, For further leads on Niccoli, see Maxson, *The Humanist World of Renaissance Florence*, 199.

9 Berthold L. Ullman and Philip A. Stadter, *The Public Library of Renaissance Florence: Niccolò Niccoli, Cosimo de' Medici and the Library of San Marco* (Padua: Editrice Antenore, 1972), 7–10, with the quotation on 7. The Latin is "omnes cives studiosi."

10 Ullman and Stadter, *The Public Library of Renaissance Florence*, 4–15.

11 Ullman and Stadter, *The Public Library of Renaissance Florence*, 303, cf. 13.

12 Howard Saalman, "Santa Maria del Fiore: 1294-1418," *The Art Bulletin* 46, no. 4 (1964): 473–90. Cf. Howard Saalman, *Filippo Brunelleschi: The Cupola of Santa Maria del Fiore* (London: A. Zwemmer Ltd, 1980), 32–41.

13 Aïm, *Le Dôme de Florence*, Saalman, "Santa Maria del Fiore," 492–3. For greater detail, see Saalman, *Filippo Brunelleschi*, 51–5.

14 Christine Smith and Joseph F. O'Connor, *Building the Kingdom: Giannozzo Manetti on the Material and Spiritual Edifice* (Tempe, AZ: ACMRS, 2006), 333.

15 Smith and O'Connor, *Building the Kingdom*, 338.

16 Giorgio Vasari, *Lives of the Artists*, trans. George Bull, vol. 1 (London: Penguin Books, 1965), 144. Cf the account at Antonio di Tuccio Manetti, *The Life of Brunelleschi*, ed. Howard Saalman, trans. Catherine Enggass (University Park: The Pennsylvania State University Press, 1970), 68 and 69. See also Ross King, *Brunelleschi's Dome, How a Renaissance Genius Reinvented Architecture* (New York: Walker & Company, 2000), 1 and 36–42. On Brunelleschi in general, see *Filippo Brunelleschi: La sua opera e il suo tempo*, 2 vols. (Florence: Centro Di, 1980).

17 On this competition, see also Saalman, *Filippo Brunelleschi*, 60–77.

18 Initially, Brunelleschi was appointed alongside Lorenzo Ghiberti and Battista d'Antonio, although it is unclear how much the two men contributed to Brunelleschi's clearly primary role. See Saalman, *Filippo Brunelleschi*, 68–70 and 186–90. On Ghiberti's role, see Krautheimer, *Lorenzo Ghiberti*.

19 Saalman, *Filippo Brunelleschi*, 80–97.

20 For a detailed summary of this construction based upon exhaustive archival research, see Saalman, *Filippo Brunelleschi*, 112–34, with machines at 48–64, and the great hoist at 54–8. See also Aïm, *Le Dôme de Florence*, 51–68. For the relationship between Brunelleschi's dome, earlier models, and especially other Tuscan examples, see Heinrich Klotz, *Filippo Brunelleschi: The Early Works and the Medieval Tradition* (New York: Rizzoli, 1990), 77–100.

21 Roger J. Crum, "Stepping Out of Brunelleschi's Shadow: The Consecration of Santa Maria del Fiore as International Statecraft in Medicean Florence," in *Foundation, Dedication and Consecration in Early Modern Europe*, ed. Maarten Delbeke and Minou Schraven (Leiden: Brill, 2012), 59. The Annunciation was, by law from 1412, the "principal holy day of the cathedral." See Bergstein, Bergstein, "Marian Politics in Quattrocento Florence," 675 and 79. For a copiously illustrated introduction to the Duomo, see Giovanni Fanelli and Michele Fanelli, *Brunelleschi's Cupola, Past and Present of an Architectural Masterpiece*, trans. Jeremy Carden et al. (Florence: Mandragora, 2004), King, *Brunelleschi's Dome, How a Renaissance Genius Reinvented Architecture*.

22 On these events, see the documents quoted at Stefano U. Baldassarri and Arielle Siber, eds., *Images of Quattrocento Florence* (New Haven: Yale University Press, 2000), 238–40. See also Marica Tacconi, *Cathedral and Civic Ritual in Late Medieval and Renaissance Florence: The Service Books of Santa Maria del Fiore* (Cambridge: Cambridge University Press, 2005), 3. The original Italian is found in Feo Belcari, *Lettere* (Florence: Il Magheri, 1825). See also Dale Kent, *Cosimo de' Medici and the Florentine Renaissance: The Patron's Oeuvre* (New Haven: Yale University Press, 2000), 124–8. My thanks to Margaret Hayden for her help with this footnote.

23 On the importance of religious piety in Cosimo's patronage, see Kent, *Cosimo de' Medici and the Florentine Renaissance*.

24 Gary Ianziti, "Leonardo Bruni, the Medici, and the Florentine Histories," *Journal of the History of Ideas* 69, no. 1 (2008): 1–22, passim. More broadly, see Ianziti, *Writing History in Renaissance Italy*. On Bruni's politics, see Arthur Field, "Leonardo Bruni, Florentine Traitor? Bruni, the Medici, and an Aretine Conspiracy of 1437," *Renaissance Quarterly* 51, no. 4 (1998): 1109–50. And more recently Arthur Field, *The Intellectual Struggle for Florence* (Oxford: Oxford University Press, 2017).

25 Paolo Viti, ed., *Firenze e il Concilio del 1439* (Florence: Leo S. Olschki, 1994). See also Biondo Flavio, *Historiam ab inclinatione romanorum imperii libri xxxi* (Basel, 1531), 551. On the council more generally, see Joseph Gill, *The Council of Florence* (Cambridge: Cambridge University Press, 1959).

26 On the role of Medici money, see Fubini, in *Italia Quattrocentesca: Politica e diplomazia nell'etá di Lorenzo il Magnifico*, 62. Republished in translation and in revised form at Fubini and Raillard, "Cosimo de' Medici's Regime." See also David S. Peterson, "The Albizzi, the Early Medici, and the Florentine Church, 1375-1460," in *The Medici: Citizens and Masters*, ed. Robert Black and John E. Law (Florence: Villa I Tatti, 2015), 178–9.

27 Maxson, "Establishing Independence," 88–94.

28 Eleonora Plebani, "Una fuga programmata. Eugenio IV e Firenze (1433-1434)," *Archivio storico italiano* 170, no. 2 (2012): 281–92.

29 On Eugenius's anger with Florence, see Maxson, "The *Certame Coronario* as Performative Ritual."

30 On Manetti, see David Marsh, *Giannozzo Manetti: The Life of a Florentine Humanist* (Cambridge, MA: Harvard University Press, 2019), Maxson, *The Humanist World of Renaissance Florence*, Stefano U. Baldassarri, ed., *Dignitas et excellentia hominis* (Florence: Le Lettere, 2008).

31 On this context, see Luca Boschetto, "L'esilio volontario di Manetti," in *Dignitas et excellentia hominis*, ed. Stefano U. Baldassarri (Florence: Le Lettere, 2008), 117–45. Stefano U. Baldassarri and Brian Jeffrey Maxson, "Giannozzo Manetti, the Emperor, and the Praise of a King in 1452," *Archivio storico italiano* 172, no. 3 (2014): 513–69. Brian Jeffrey Maxson, "The Letters of Giannozzo Manetti: Context and Chronology, with an Edition of Four New Letters," Bullettino dell'Istituto Storico Italiano per il Medio Evo 122 (2020): 203–52.

32 The text is newly edited and translated at Giannozzo Manetti, *On Human Worth and Excellence*, ed. and trans. Brian Copenhaver (Cambridge, MA: Harvard University Press, 2018). For a recent interpretation by a leading authority, see Stefano U. Baldassarri, "Reflections on Manetti's e Dignitate" and his "Vita Nicolai V," *Rivista di Letteratura Storiografica Italiana* 1 (2017): 31–45.

33 See Giuseppe Gianluca Cicco, "Benedetto Accolti e la diplomazia fiorentina all'indomani della conquista turca di Constantinopoli," *Schola Salernitana* 10 (2005): 251–67, Marios Philippides and Walter Hanak, *The Siege and the Fall of Constantinople in 1453: Historiography, Topography, and Military Studies* (Farnham: Ashgate, 2011), Robert Black, *Benedetto Accolti and the Florentine Renaissance* (Cambridge: Cambridge University Press, 1985).

34 On the Italian League and its implications, see Riccardo Fubini, "The Italian League and the Policy of the Balance of Power at the Accession of Lorenzo de'

Medici," *The Journal of Modern History* 67 (1995): 166–99, Riccardo Fubini, *Italia quattrocentesca: Politica e diplomazia nell'eta di Lorenzo il Magnifico* (Milan: FrancoAngeli, 1994), Serena Ferente, *La sfortuna di Jacopo Piccinino: Storia dei bracceschi in Italia, 1423-1465* (Florence: Leo S. Olsckhi, 2005), Margolis and Maxson, "The 'Schemes' of Piero de' Pazzi and the Conflict with the Medici (1461-1462)."

35 Brian Jeffrey Maxson, "The Letters of Giannozzo Manetti: Context and Chronology, with an Edition of Four New Letters," 227–8.

36 For these events, see Rubinstein, *The Government of Florence under the Medici (1434-1494)*, 99–153, esp. 99–17.

37 On Capponi as a possible Medici rival, see Maxson, "The *Certame Coronario* as Performative Ritual," 140–2. On the passage of the Council of 100, see Rubinstein, *The Government of Florence under the Medici (1434-1494)*, 117.

38 Brian Jeffrey Maxson, "Expressions of Power in Diplomacy in Fifteenth-Century Florence," in *Languages of Power in Italy (1300-1600)*, ed. Daniel Bornstein, Laura Gaffuri, and Brian Jeffrey Maxson (Turnhout: Brepols, 2017), 129–39.

39 On this situation, see Margolis and Maxson, "The 'Schemes' of Piero de' Pazzi and the Conflict with the Medici (1461-1462)."

40 For the identification of these figures, see Kent, *Cosimo de' Medici and the Florentine Renaissance: The Patron's Oeuvre*. On Gozzoli in general, see Diane Cole Ahl, *Benozzo Gozzoli* (New Haven: Yale University Press, 1996).

41 The painting also fit into the context of a confraternity devoted to this biblical story in which the Medici played a leading role. On this confraternity in Florence, see Rab Hatfield, "The Compagnia de' Magi," *Journal of the Warburg and Courtauld Institutes* 33 (1970): 107–61. More generally, see Richard C. Trexler, *The Journey of the Magi: Meanings in History of a Christian Story* (Princeton: Princeton University Press, 1997).

42 On the greeting of diplomats at the chapel, see Crum, in *Foundation, Dedication and Consecration in Early Modern Europe*, 74–5.

43 See the extant example by Leonardo Bruni delivered by Florentine diplomats to the emperor, published at Leonardo Bruni, *Opere letterarie e politiche*, ed. Paolo Viti (Torino: Unione tipografico-editrice torinese, 1996), 836–9. For an analysis, see Brian Jeffrey Maxson, "The Many Shades of Praise: Politics and Panegryics in Fifteenth-Century Florentine Diplomacy," in *Rhetorik in Mittelalter und Renaissance: Konzepte-Praxis-Diversität*, ed. Georg Strack and Julia Knödler (München: Herbert Utz, 2011), 406.

44 For these portraits, see Kent, *Cosimo de' Medici and the Florentine Renaissance*. The relationship between the Medici and the Sforza is well known. However, much less studied has been Cosimo's relations to the controversial Sigismondo Malatesta, who was famously reverse canonized

by Pope Pius II. On Sigismondo, see P. J. Jones, *The Malatesta of Rimini and the Papal State* (New York: Cambridge University Press, 2005), Anthony F. D'Elia, *Pagan Virtue in a Christian World: Sigismondo Malatesta and the Italian Renaissance* (Cambridge, MA: Harvard University Press, 2016). Pius II's consistent abuse of Sigismondo can be followed at Aeneas Silvius Pius II (Aeneas Silvius Piccolomini), *Commentaries*, ed. Margaret Meserve and Marcello Simonetta, 3 vols. (Cambridge, MA: Harvard University Press, 2003–18).

45 On Agnolo Acciaiuoli, see Serena Ferente, "The Ways of Practice: Angelo Acciaioli, 1450-1470," in *From Florence to the Mediterranean and Beyond: Essays in Honour of Anthony Molho*, ed. Diogo Ramada Curto et al., vol. 1 (Florence: Leo S. Olschki, 2009), 103–16.

46 See Margolis and Maxson, "The 'Schemes' of Piero de' Pazzi and the Conflict with the Medici (1461-1462)." Also on Piero de' Pazzi, see Claudia Tripodi, "Piero de' Pazzi," in *Dizionario Biografico degli Italiani*, vol. 82 (2015), accessed online at https://www.treccani.it/enciclopedia/piero-de-pazzi_ (Dizionario-Biografico) (accessed July 11, 2022).

47 On Niccolò Soderini, see Paula C. Clarke, *The Soderini and the Medici: Power and Patronage in Fifteenth-Century Florence* (Oxford: Clarendon Press, 1991), 46–51 and 80–94.

48 On Pandolfo Pandolfini, see Baldassarri and Maxson, "Giannozzo Manetti, the Emperor, and the Praise of a King in 1452."

49 On the Pandolfini family, see Baldassarri and Maxson, "Giannozzo Manetti's *Oratio in funere Iannotii Pandolfini.*"

50 On these relations, see F. W. Kent and Dale Kent, *Neighbours and Neighbourhood in Renaissance Florence: The District of the Red Lion in the Fifteenth Century* (Locust Valley, NY: J.J. Augustin, 1982).

51 Giovanni Rucellai, Alessandro Perosa and F. W. Kent, *Giovanni Rucellai ed il suo zibaldone*, 2 vols. (London: The Warburg Institute University of London, 1960).

52 Rubinstein, *The Government of Florence under the Medici (1434-1494)*, 51.

53 On the Rucellai palace, see Brenda Preyer, "The Rucellai Palace," in *Giovanni Rucellai ed il suo zibaldone*, ed. F. W. Kent et al., vol. 2 (The Warburg Institute: University of London, 1981), 155–207. Charles R. Mack, "The Rucellai Palace: Some New Proposals," *The Art Bulletin* 56 (1974): 517–29, Charles R. Mack, "The Palazzo Rucellai Reconsidered," in *Actas dell' XXIII congreso internacional de historia del arte (1973)*, vol. 2 (Grenada: Universidad Grenada, 1977), Richard Schofield, "A Local Renaissance: Florentine Quattrocento Palaces and *all' antica* styles," in *Local Antiquities, Local Identities: Art, Literature and Antiquarianism in Europe, c. 1400–1700*, ed. Kathleen Christian and Bianca de Divitiis (Manchester: Manchester University Press, 2019). See also Robert Tavernor, *On Alberti and the Art of*

Building (New Haven: Yale University Press, 1998), Anthony Grafton, *Leon Battista Alberti: Master Builder of the Italian Renaissance* (Cambridge, MA: Harvard University Press, 2002), 182–6, Allison Levy, *House of Secrets: The Many Lives of a Florentine Palazzo* (London: I.B. Tauris, 2019), Paul Balchin, *Urban Development in Renaissance Italy* (Chichester: John Wiley & Sons, 2008), 205.

54 But not always. On philosophy, especially in universities, see David A. Lines, *Aristotle's Ethics in the Italian Renaissance (ca. 1300-1650): The Universities and the Problem of Moral Education* (Leiden: Brill, 2002), Davies, *Florence and its University during the Early Renaissance*, Amos Edelheit, *Scholastic Florence: Moral Psychology in the Quattrocento* (Leiden: Brill, 2014), Paul Oskar Kristeller, *Renaissance Thought and Its Sources*, ed. Michael Mooney (Columbia: Columbia University Press, 1979), Celenza, *The Intellectual World of the Italian Renaissance*.

55 On these so-called Platonic academies, see Arthur Field, *The Origins of the Platonic Academy of Florence* (Princeton: Princeton University Press, 1988), James Hankins, "The Myth of the Platonic Academy of Florence," *Renaissance Quarterly* 44 (1991): 429–75. Still useful is Arnaldo della Torre, *Storia dell' Accademia platonica di Firenze* (Florence: Tip. G. Carnesecchi e figli, 1902).

56 On Hermes, the classic work is Frances A. Yates, *Giordano Bruno and the Hermetic Tradition* (Chicago: University of Chicago Press, 1964). More recently, see Denis J. J. Robichaud, "Ficino on Force, Magic, and Prayers: Neoplatonic and Hermetic Influences on Ficino's *Three Books on Life*," *Renaissance Quarterly* 70, no. 1 (2017): 44–87 with further leads therein, Massimiliano Malavasi, "Ficinus redivus. Su una nuova edizione della versione latina del *Pimander* e sui rapporti tra umanesimo e religione," *Rinascimento* 56 (2016): 327–58.

57 On Ficino, the classic work is Paul Oskar Kristeller, *The Philosophy of Marsilio Ficino* (New York: Columbia University Press, 1943). See more recently, Denis J. J. Robichaud, *Plato's Persona: Marsilio Ficino, Renaissance Humanism, and Platonic Traditions* (Philadelphia: University of Pennsylvania Press, 2018), Celenza, *The Intellectual World of the Italian Renaissance*, 241–87. Further leads to older scholarship can be found at Paul Oskar Kristeller, *Marsilio Ficino and His Work after Five Hundred Years* (Florence: Leo S. Olschki, 1987).

58 For this work, see Marsilio Ficino, *Platonic Theology*, ed. James Hankins, trans. Michael J. B. Allen, 6 vols. (Cambridge, MA: Harvard University, 2001-2006).

59 On medicinal practices and conceptions in Renaissance Italy, see Sandra Cavallo and Tessa Storey, *Healthy Living in late Renaissance Italy* (Oxford: Oxford University Press, 2013). For Florence specifically, see James Shaw

and Evelyn Welch, *Making and Marketing Medicine in Renaissance Florence* (Amsterdam: The Welcome Trust Centre for the History of Medicine at UCL, 2011). On doctors, see Katharine Park, *Doctors and Medicine in Early Renaissance Florence* (Princeton: Princeton University Press, 1985).

60 On spices, see especially Paul Freedman, *Out of the East: Spices and the Medieval Imagination* (New Haven: Yale University Press, 2008). On magic, see Brian Copenhaver, *Magic in Western Culture: From Antiquity to the Englightenment* (Cambridge: Cambridge University Press, 2015), Richard Kieckhefer, *Magic in the Middle Ages*, 2nd ed. (Cambridge: Cambridge University Press, 2014). While focused on later developments, useful are Brian Levack, *The Witch-Hunt in Early Modern Europe*, 4th ed. (London: Routledge, 2015) and Euan Cameron, *Enchanted Europe: Superstition, Reason, and Religion, 1250-1750* (Oxford: Oxford University Press, 2011).

61 This work is published at Marsilio Ficino, *Three Books on Life*, ed. Carol V. Kaske and John R. Clark (Arizona State University: Arizona Board of Regents, 1998).

62 On Alessandra and her family, see Ann Crabb, *The Strozzi of Florence: Widowhood and Family Solidarity in the Renaissance* (Ann Arbor: University of Michigan Press, 2000), Alessandra Macinghi-Strozzi, *Letters to Her Sons, 1447-1470*, ed. and trans. Judith Bryce, ed. Judith Bryce (Tempe: ACMRS, 2016). Lorenzo Fabbri, "Filippo Strozzi," in *Dizionario Biografico degli Italiani*, vol. 94 (2019), accessed online at https://www.treccani.it/enciclopedia /filippo-strozzi_(Dizionario-Biografico) (accessed July 11, 2022). Field, "Leonardo Bruni, Florentine Traitor? Bruni, the Medici, and an Aretine Conspiracy of 1437," Maxson, *The Humanist World of Renaissance Florence*, Fabbri, in *Dizionario Biografico degli Italiani*.

63 One shared acquaintance, for example, was probably Giannozzo Manetti. See Strozzi, *Letters to Her Sons, 1447-1470*, 85.

64 See Baldassarri and Maxson, "Giannozzo Manetti, the Emperor, and the Praise of a King in 1452," and the leads therein.

65 For an accessible translation of this much-studied work, see Leon Battista Alberti, *The Family in Renaissance Florence*, trans. Renee Neu Watkins (Long Grove, IL: Waveland Press, 1969). The scholarship on all or part of this work is vast. See, for example, the recent studies at Amyrose J. McCue, "Rereading *I libri della famiglia*: Leon Battista Alberti on Marriage, *Amicizia* and Conjugal Friendship," *California Italian Studies* 2 (2011), Hanan Yoran, "Glory, Passions and Money in Alberti's Della famiglia: A Humanist Reflects on the Foundations of Society," *The European Legacy* 20, no. 5 (2015): 527–42, Juliann Vitullo, "'Otium' and 'Negotium' in Alberti's 'I libri della famiglia,'" *Annali d'Italianistica* 32 (2014): 73–89, Timothy Kircher, *Living Well in Renaissance Italy: The Virtues of Humanism and Irony of Leon*

Battista Alberti (Tempe, AZ: ACMRS, 2012). Leon Battista Alberti enjoys great prominence in the scholarship and is even the focus of his own journal *Albertiana*. On the sequestering of women in the home and differences in socioeconomic class, see Natalie Tomas, "Did Women Have a Space?," in *Renaissance Florence. A Social History*, ed. Roger J. Crum and John T. Paoletti (Cambridge: Cambridge University Press, 2006), 311–28.

66 For gender and the history of women in fifteenth-century Florence, see, among many other studies, Sharon T. Strocchia, *Nuns and Nunneries in Renaissance Florence* (Baltimore: Johns Hopkins University Press, 2009). Christiane Klapisch-Zuber, *Women, Family, and Ritual in Renaissance Italy* (Chicago: University of Chicago Press, 1987), Natalie R. Tomas, *The Medici Women: Gender and Power in Renaissance Florence* (Burlington, VT: Ashgate, 2003), Crabb, *The Strozzi of Florence*. Tomas, in *Renaissance Florence. A Social History*.

67 On Renaissance marriages in general, see Kirshner, *Marriage, Dowry, and Citizenship in Late Medieval and Renaissance Italy*, Anthony F. D'Elia, *The Renaissance of Marriage in Fifteenth-Century Italy* (Cambridge, MA: Harvard University Press, 2004), Jacqueline Murray, ed., *Marriage in Premodern Europe: Italy and Beyond* (Toronto: CRRS, 2012), Thomas Kuehn, *Toward a Legal Anthropology of Renaissance Italy*, Rev. ed. (Chicago: University of Chicago Press, 1994), Thomas Kuehn, *Family and Gender in Renaissance Italy* (Cambridge: Cambridge University Press, 2017), Caroline Campbell, *Love and Marriage in Renaissance Florence* (London: Paul Holberton Publishing, 2009).

68 The famous negotiations of Filippo's marriage are scattered throughout Strozzi, *Letters to Her Sons, 1447-1470*.

69 This story is told at Gene Brucker, *Giovanni and Lusanna: Love and Marriage in Renaissance Florence* (Berkeley: University of California Press, 1986). Additional insights into the story can be found at Thomas Kuehn, "Reading Microhistory: The Example of Giovanni and Lusanna," *The Journal of Modern History* 61 (September 1989): 512–34. See also Tomas, *The Medici Women*.

70 On Florentine convents, see Strocchia, *Nuns and Nunneries in Renaissance Florence*.

71 On Cosimo's tomb in San Lorenzo, see Janis Clearfield, "The Tomb of Cosimo de' Medici In San Lorenzo," *Rutgers Art Review* 2 (1981): 13–32, Kent, *Cosimo de' Medici and the Florentine Renaissance*, Andrew Butterfield, *The Sculptures of Andrea del Verrocchio* (New Haven: Yale University Press, 1997), 37–44, Sharon Strocchia, *Death and Ritual in Renaissance Florence* (Baltimore: Johns Hopkins University Press, 1992), 184–5, Christine M. Sperling, "Verrocchio's Medici Tombs," in *Verrocchio and Late Quattrocento Italian Sculpture*, ed. Steven Bule, Alan Phipps Darr, and Fiorella Superbi

Gioffredi (Florence: Le Lettere, 1992), 51–61. Alison Brown, "De-Masking Renaissance Republicanism," in *Medicean and Savonarolan Florence: The Interplay of Politics, Humanism, and Religion*, ed. Alison Brown (Turnhout: Brepols, 2011), 237.

72 Alison Brown, "The Humanist Portrait of Cosimo de' Medici, Pater Patriae," *Journal of Warburg and Courtald Institutes* 24, no. 3/4 (1961): 186–221, Anthony Molho, "Cosimo de' Medici: *Pater Patriae* or *Padrino?*," in *Firenze nel Quattrocento, vol. 1: Politica e Fiscalità*, ed. Anthony Molho (Rome: Edizioni di Storia e Letteratura, 2006).

CHAPTER 4

1 Naemy, *A History of Florence, 1200-1575*, 341–2. See also Francesco Guicciardini, *The History of Italy*, ed. and trans. Sidney Alexander (Princeton: Princeton University Press, 1969), 4.

2 On Cosimo's death, see, for example, Mark Phillips, *The Memoir of Marco Parenti: A Life in Medici Florence* (Princeton: Princeton University Press, 1987), 3–19, Rubinstein, *The Government of Florence under the Medici (1434-1494)*, 155–9.

3 Rubinstein, *The Government of Florence under the Medici (1434-1494)*, 157–62.

4 Rubinstein, *The Government of Florence under the Medici (1434-1494)*, 179–88, Phillips, *The Memoir of Marco Parenti*, 190–8, Najemy, *A History of Florence, 1200-1575*, 301–4.

5 On this text, see Pitti, *Ricordi*, Brucker, *Two Memoirs of Renaissance Florence*, Peter Sposato, "The Chivalrous Life of Buonaccorso Pitti: Honor-Violence and the Profession of Arms in Late Medieval Florence and Italy," *Studies in Medieval and Renaissance History* 13 (2016): 141–76.

6 On Buonaccorso and this mission, see Margolis and Maxson, "The 'Schemes' of Piero de' Pazzi and the Conflict with the Medici (1461-1462)."

7 On the Pitti Palace, see M. Chiarini, ed., *Palazzo Pitti. L'arte e la storia* (Florence: Nardini, 2000), Adriano Marinazzo, "Palazzo Pitti: Dalla 'Casa vecchia' alla Reggia Granducale," *Bollettino della Società di Studi Fiorentini* 22 (2013): 299–306 with further leads therein. See also Laura Baldini Giusti and Fiorella Facchinetti Bottai, "Documento sulle prime fasi costruttive di Palazzo Pitti," in *Filippo Brunelleschi. La sua opera e il suo tempo*, vol. 2 (Florence: Centro Di, 1980), 703–31. Rubin, *Images and Identity in Fifteenth-Century Florence*, 11–12.

8 On the surviving images of the Palazzo Pitti prior to its changes in the sixteenth century, see F. Morandini, "Palazzo Pitti. La sua costruzione e i successivi ingrandimenti," *Commentari* 16 (1965): 38.

9 On this altarpiece, see Morandini, Henk Th. Van Veen, *Cosimo I de' Medici
   and His Self-Representation in Florentine Art and Culture*, trans. Andrew P.
   McCormick (Cambridge: Cambridge University Press, 2006), 209, Simona
   Lecchini Giovannoni, *Alessandro Allori* (Turin: Umberto Allemandi &
   C., 1991), 234, although the predella to the altarpiece is not discussed or
   reproduced. See also Jonathan Nelson and Richard J. Zeckhauser, eds.,
   The Patron's Payoff: Conspicuous Commissions in Italian Renaissance Art
   (Princeton: Princeton University Press, 2004).
10 See Phillips, *The Memoir of Marco Parenti.*
11 On this series of events, see Najemy, *A History of Florence, 1200-1575,*
   301–6. Another exciting narrative is found at Phillips, *The Memoir of Marco
   Parenti,* 189–216. For further leads and documents, see Nicolai Rubinstein,
   "La confessione di Francesco Neroni e la congiura antimedicea del 1466,"
   Archivio storico italiano 126, no. 304 (1968): 373–87, Ferente, in *From
   Florence to the Mediterranean and Beyond: Essays in Honour of Anthony
   Molho*, 112–13.
12 Clarke, *The Soderini and the Medici*, 154–71, Fubini, "The Italian League and
   the Policy of the Balance of Power at the Accession of Lorenzo de' Medici,"
   190–4. Najemy, *A History of Florence, 1200-1575,* 345.
13 On the Medici in the merchant's tribunal, see Andrew Butterfield,
   "Verrocchio's Christ and St. Thomas: Chronology, Iconography and Political
   Context," *The Burlington Magazine* 134, no. 1069 (1992): 228–32. On the
   Medici and the Guelf Party, see Brown, "The Guelf Party in Fifteenth-Century
   Florence," 103–50. On the Mercanzia more generally, see Goldthwaite, *The
   Economy of Renaissance Florence*, 109–14, with further leads therein, Luca
   Boschetto, "Writing the Vernacular at the Merchant Court of Florence,"
   in *Textual Cultures of Medieval Italy: Essays from the 41st Conference on
   Editorial Problems*, ed. William Robins (Toronto: University of Toronto
   Press, 2011), 217–62, Elena Maccioni and Sergio Tognetti, eds., *Tribunali di
   Mercanti e Giustizia Mercantile nel Tardo Medioevo* (Florence: Leo S. Olschki,
   2016).
14 Butterfield, "Verrocchio's Christ and St. Thomas: Chronology, Iconography
   and Political Context," 230–2. On this sculpture in general, see esp.
   Butterfield, *The Sculptures of Andrea del Verrocchio*, 47–80 and 209–12.
   On the replacement of the St. Toulouse sculpture at Orsanmichele with the
   Doubting Thomas, see Zervas, *Orsanmichele a Firenze*, 211ff, Butterfield, *The
   Sculptures of Andrea del Verrocchio*, 59.
15 Larry J. Feinberg, *The Young Leonardo: Art and Life in Fifteenth-Century
   Florence* (Cambridge: Cambridge University Press, 2011). For more
   information on Leonardo's family, see Anne Leader, "'In the Tomb of Ser
   Piero': Death and Burial in the Family of Leonardo da Vinci," *Renaissance
   Studies* 31, no. 3 (2017).

16 Feinberg, *The Young Leonardo*, 68–72.

17 Quoted in Ingeborg Walter, "Giuliano de' Medici," in *Dizionario Biografico degli Italiani*, vol. 73 (2009), accessed online at https://www.treccani.it/enciclopedia/giuliano-de-medici_res-f6ca07e6-dcde-11df-9ef0-d5ce3506d72e_ (Dizionario-Biografico) (accessed July 11, 2022). The Italian is "avessero addosso « d'adornamenti di perle e gioie il valsente di più di 60000 fiorini »."

18 On Simonetta Vespucci, see, to start, Ross Brooke Ettle, "The Venus Dilemma: Notes on Botticelli and Simonetta Cattaneo Vespucci," *Notes in the History of Art* 27, no. 4 (2008): 3–10, Judith Allan, "Lorenzo's Star and Savonarola's Serpent: Changing Representations of Simonetta Cattaneo Vespucci," *Italian Studies* 69, no. 1 (2014): 4–23. See also Judith Allan, "Simonetta Cattaneo Vespucci: Beauty, Politics, Literature and Art in Early Renaissance Florence" (Dissertation, University of Birmingham, 2014).

19 On this joust, see Feinberg, *The Young Leonardo*, 55–8, R. M. Ruggieri, "Letterati, poeti e pittori intorno alla giostra di Giuliano de' Medici," *Rinascimento* 10 (1959): 165–96, Paul Oskar Kristeller, "Un documento sconosciuto sulla giostra di Giuliano de' Medici," in *Studies in Renaissance Thought and Letters*, vol. 3 ed. Paul Oskar Kristeller (Rome: Edizioni di Storia e Letteratura, 1956), 437–50. See also Mark Davie, "Luigi Pulci and the Generation of '94," in *Italy in Crisis. 1494*, ed. Jane Everson and Diego Zancani (Oxford: European Humanities Research Centre, 2000), 63–79, Martin McLaughlin, "Poliziano's *Stanze per la giostra*: Postmodern Poetics in a Proto-Renaissance Poem," in *Italy in Crisis. 1494*, ed. Jane Everson and Diego Zancani (Oxford: European Humanities Research Centre, 2000), 129–51, Charles Dempsey, *Inventing the Renaissance Putto* (Chapel Hill: University of North Carolina Press, 2001).

20 For more details, see Rubinstein, *The Government of Florence under the Medici (1434-1494)*, 199–223.

21 On resistance to Lorenzo's rule in general, see Brown, "Lorenzo and Public Opinion in Florence: The Problem of Oppositions," in *Medicean and Savonarolan Florence: The Interplay of Politics, Humanism, and Religion*, ed. Alison Brown (Turhnout: Brepols, 2011), 87–111.

22 On Donato Acciaiuoli's previous unease with Medici power, see Margery Ganz, "Donato Acciaiuoli and the Medici: A Strategy for Survival in '400 Florence," *Rinascimento* 22 (1982): 33–73. On Pierfilippo's unease, see Baldassarri and Maxson, "Giannozzo Manetti's *Oratio in funere Iannotii Pandolfini*."

23 On this mission, see Riccardo Fubini, "Momenti di diplomazia medicea," in *Quattrocento fiorentino*, ed. Riccardo Fubini (Pisa: Pacini, 1996), 108–22. Many of the relevant diplomatic documents are found at Giuseppe Aiazzi, *Ricordi storici di Filippo di Cino Rinuccini dal 1282 al 1460 colla continuazione di Alamanno e Neri, suoi figli, fino al 1506, seguiti da altri*

monumenti inediti di storia patria estratti dai codici originali e preceduti dalla Storia genealogica della . . . (Florence: Stamperia Piatti, 1840), 225–50.

24 This dialogue has been translated into English. See Renee Neu Watkins, *Humanism and Liberty: Writings on Freedom from Fifteenth-Century Florence* (Columbia, South Carolina: University of South Carolina Press, 1978). See also Alamanno Rinuccini, *La Libertà Perduta/Dialogus de libertate*, ed. G. Civati (Monza: Vittone Editore, 2003), Brown, "Lorenzo and Public Opinion in Florence," 98–9.

25 On this diary, see Aiazzi, *Ricordi storici di Filippo di Cino Rinuccini dal 1282.*

26 Najemy, *A History of Florence, 1200-1575,* 347–52, with further leads therein. See also the greater detail at Rubinstein, *The Government of Florence under the Medici (1434-1494),* 205–13. Brown, "Lorenzo and Public Opinion in Florence," 93, Alison Brown, "The Language of Empire," in *Florentine Tuscany,* ed. William J. Connell and Andrea Zorzi (Cambridge: Cambridge University Press, 2000), 42–3.For similar trends toward Medici control in subject cities, see William J. Connell, "Appunti sui rapporti dei primi Medici con i comuni del territorio fiorentino," in *Machiavelli nel Rinascimento italiano,* ed. William J. Connell (Milan: FrancoAngeli, 2015), 194–210.

27 For this remark and further leads on the Pazzi, see Margolis and Maxson, "The 'Schemes' of Piero de' Pazzi and the Conflict with the Medici (1461-1462)." See also Lauro Martines, *April Blood: Florence and the Plot against the Medici* (Oxford and New York: Oxford University Press, 2003), 108–10. The letter is at Strozzi, *Letters to Her Sons,* 104–7.

28 Rubinstein, *The Government of Florence under the Medici (1434-1494),* 343–5.

29 On the extent of this conspiracy, see Marcello Simonetta, *The Montefeltro Conspiracy: A Renaissance Mystery Decoded* (New York: Doubleday, 2008), Riccardo Fubini, "Federico da Montefeltro e la congiura dei Pazzi: Immagine propagandistica e realtà politica," in *Italia Quattrocentesca,* ed. Riccardo Fubini (Milan: FrancoAngeli, 1994), 253–326. For leads on disputes within Florence, see Lorenzo Fabbri, "Women's Rights According to Lorenzo de' Medici: The Borromei-Pazzi Dispute and the *Lex de testamentis,*" in *The Art and Language of Power in Renaissance Florence: Essays for Alison Brown,* ed. Amy R. Bloch, Carolyn James, and Camilla Russell (Toronto: CRRS, 2019), 91–115.

30 See Simonetta, *The Montefeltro Conspiracy,* 160. For the history of portraits of condemned criminals in Florence, see Scott Nethersole, *Art and Violence in Early Renaissance Florence* (New Haven: Yale University Press, 2018), Samuel Edgerton, *Pictures and Punishment: Art and Criminal Prosecution during the Florentine Renaissance* (Ithaca: Cornell University Press, 1985). On these events, see Martines. The work of Tobias Daniels has added several

new accounts to the contemporary or near contemporary sources describing the conspiracy. See, for example, Tobias Daniels, "La congiura dei Pazzi nell'informazione e nella cronistica tedesca coeva," *Archivio storico italiano* 169 (2011): 23–76.

31 On the Pazzi War and its end, see Najemy, *A History of Florence, 1200-1575*, 357–61. For more detail, see Martines, *April Blood*, 186–96, Simonetta, *The Montefeltro Conspiracy*, 114ff.

32 On diplomacy, war, and peninsular politics between 1454 and 1494, see Fubini, "The Italian League and the Policy of the Balance of Power at the Accession of Lorenzo de' Medici."

33 On the Council of Seventy, see Rubinstein, *The Government of Florence under the Medici (1434-1494)*, 227–33.

34 Eleonora Plebani, "Pier Filippo Pandolfini," in *Dizionario Biografico degli Italiani*, vol. 80 (2014), accessed online at https://www.treccani.it/enciclopedia/pier-filippo-pandolfini_(Dizionario-Biografico) (accessed July 11, 2022).

35 For Donato's letters, see Maxson, "The Letters of Giannozzo Manetti." On Donato's support of Piero de' Pazzi, see Margolis and Maxson, "The 'Schemes' of Piero de' Pazzi and the Conflict with the Medici (1461-1462)." Oren J. Margolis, "The 'Gallic Crowd' at the 'Aragonese Doors': Donato Acciaiuoli's *Vita Caroli Magni* and the Workshop of Vespasiano da Bisticci," *I Tatti Studies in the Italian Renaissance* 17, no. 2 (2014): 241–82. For his oration, see Brown, "The Humanist Portrait of Cosimo de' Medici, Pater Patriae." On Donato's transition, see Ganz, "Donato Acciaiuoli and the Medici." In general, see also Eugenio Garin, "Donato Acciaiuoli, Citizen of Florence," in *Portraits from the Quattrocento*, ed. Eugenio Garin (New York: Harper & Row, 1963), 55–117.

36 On the Rucellai, see Rucellai, Perosa, and Kent, *Giovanni Rucellai ed il suo zibaldone*, F.W. Kent, *Household and Lineage in Renaissance Florence: The Family Life of the Capponi, Ginori, and Rucellai* (Princeton: Princeton University Press, 1977), Kent and Kent, *Neighbours and Neighbourhood in Renaissance Florence*.

37 On Alberti and Santa Maria Novella, see Tavernor, *On Alberti and the Art of Building*. On the facade of the church, see Brian E. Roy, "The Facade of Santa Maria Novella: Architecture, Context, Patronage and Meaning" (Dissertation, McGill University, 1997).

38 Trexler, *Public Life in Renaissance Florence*, 453.

39 Walter, in *Dizionario Biografico degli Italiani*.

40 Melissa Meriam Bullard, *Lorenzo il Magnifico: Image and Anxiety, Politics and Finance* (Florence: Leo S. Olschki, 1994), 61 and 136–40, Najemy, *A History of Florence, 1200-1575*, 372–4. See also Trexler, *Public Life in Renaissance Florence*, 455. On Giovanni's appointment as cardinal, see

Melissa Meriam Bullard, "Renaissance Spirituality and the Ethical Dimensions of Church Reform in the Age of Savonarola: The Dilemma of Cardinal Marco Barbo," in *The World of Savonarola: Italian Èlites and Perceptions of Crisis*, ed. Stella Fletcher and Christine Shaw (Aldershot: Ashgate, 2000), 83–8.

41 Molho, *Marriage Alliance in Late Medieval Florence*, passim.

42 See Tomas, in *Renaissance Florence. A Social History*. See also Virgina Cox, *Women's Writing in Italy 1400-1650* (Baltimore: Johns Hopkins University Press, 2008), 13–14.

43 Maria Grazia Pernis and Laurie Schneider Adams, *Lucrezia Tornabuoni de' Medici and the Medici Family in the Fifteenth Century* (New York: Peter Lang, 2006), 70–145.

44 Tomas, *The Medici Women*. More generally, see Giulia Calvi and Ricardo Spinelli, eds., *Le donne Medici nel sistema europeo delle corti* (Florence: Polistampa, 2008), Gabrielle Langdon, ed., *Medici Women: Portraits of Power, Love, and Betrayal in the Court of Duke Cosimo I* (Toronto: University of Toronto Press, 2006).

45 For example, see, with further leads therein, Sarah D. P. Cockram, *Isabella d'Este and Franceco Gonzaga. Power Sharing at the Italian Renaissance Court* (Farnham: Ashgate Publishing, 2013), Jennifer A. Cavalli, "The Learned Consort: Learning, Piety, and Female Political Authority in the Northern Courts," in *After Civic Humanism: Learning and Politics in Renaissance Italy*, ed. Nicholas Scott Baker and Brian Jeffrey Maxson (Toronto: CRRS, 2015), 173–92.

46 Lisa Kaborycha, "Brigida Baldinotti and Her Two Epistles in Quattrocento Florentine Manuscripts," *Speculum* 87, no. 3 (2012): 793–826. Judith Bryce, "Les livres des Florentines: Reconsidering Women's Literacy in Quattrocento Florence," in *At the Margins: Minority Groups in Premodern Italy*, ed. Stephen J. Milner (Minneapolis: University of Minnesota Press, 2005), 133–61, Najemy, *A History of Florence, 1200-1575*, Robert Black, *Education and Society in Florentine Tuscany* (Leiden: Brill, 2007). See also the further leads at William Robins, "The Study of Medieval Italian Textual Cultures," in *Textual Cultures of Medieval Italy: Essays from the 41st Conference on Editorial Problems*, ed. William Robins (Toronto: University of Toronto Press, 2011), 41–2.

47 See, for example, the text by Leonardo Bruni in Craig Kallendorf, ed., *Humanist Educational Treatises* (Cambridge, MA: Harvard University Press, 2002). On that work, see especially Virginia Cox, "Leonardo Bruni on Women and Rhetoric: *De studiis et litteris* Revisited," *Rhetorica: A Journal of the History of Rhetoric* 27, no. 1 (2009): 47–75.

48 On Alessandra Scala, see G. Pesenti, "Alessandra Scala: Una figurina della rinascenza fiorentina," *Giornale Storico della Letteratura Italiana* 85 (1923):

241–67, Margaret L. King, "Book-Lined Cells: Women and Humanism in the Italian Renaissance," in *Renaissance Humanism, Volume 1: Foundations, Forms, and Legacy*, ed. Albert Rabil (Philadelphia: University of Pennsylvania Press, 1988), 434–54, Lisa Jardine, "'O Decus Italiae Virgo,' or The Myth of the Learned Lady in the Renaissance," *The Historical Journal* 28, no. 4 (1985): 799–819, Alison Brown, *Bartolomeo Scala, 1430-1497, Chancellor of Florence: The Humanist as Bureaucrat* (Princeton, N.J.: Princeton University Press, 1979), 246–7. More generally, see Sarah Gwyneth Ross, *The Birth of Feminism: Woman as Intellect in Renaissance Italy and England* (Cambridge, MA: Harvard University Press, 2009).

49 Cox, *Women's Writing in Italy 1400-1650*. For some of their works, see Lucrezia Tornabuoni and Jane Tylus, *Sacred Narratives* (Chicago: University of Chicago Press, 2001); Antonia Pulci, James Wyatt Cook and Barbara Collier Cook, *Florentine Drama for Convent and Festival: Seven Sacred Plays* (Chicago: University of Chicago Press, 1996), Antonia Pulci, James Wyatt Cook and Elissa Weaver, *Saints' Lives and Bible Stories for the Stage* (Toronto: CRRS, 2010).

50 See the anecdotes from Piero's childhood found in Alison Brown, *Piero di Lorenzo de' Medici and the Crisis of Renaissance Italy* (Cambridge: Cambridge University Press, 2020).

51 Tomas, in *Renaissance Florence. A Social History*.

52 Strocchia, *Nuns and Nunneries in Renaissance Florence*.

53 F. W. Kent, *Lorenzo de' Medici and the Art of Magnificence* (Baltimore: Johns Hopkins University Press, 2004), 38. See also Francesco Caglioti, *Donatello e i Medici: Storia del 'David' e della 'Giuditta,'* 2 vols. (Florence: Leo S. Olschki, 2000), vol. 2, 266–81. The painting is listed among Lorenzo's possessions at Richard Stapleford, ed., *Lorenzo de' Medici at Home: The Inventory of the Palazzo Medici in 1492* (University Park, Pennsylvania: Pennsylvania State University Press, 2013), 71. For more details on Lorenzo the collector, see Laurie S. Fusco, and Gino Corti, eds., *Lorenzo de' Medici, Collector and Antiquarian* (Cambridge: Cambridge University Press, 2006).

54 Stapleford, with discussion of Lorenzo's guests at 8–9.

55 On Matteo Palmieri, see most recently Brian Jeffrey Maxson, "The Myth of the Renaissance Bubble: International Culture and Regional Politics in Fifteenth-Century Florence," in *Florence in the Early Modern World: New Perspectives*, ed. Nicholas Scott Baker and Brian Jeffrey Maxson (London: Routledge, 2020), 220–5.

56 On this diplomatic mission by Scala, see Maxson, *The Humanist World of Renaissance Florence*, 172–5. The foundational work on Scala remains Brown, Alison Brown, ed., *Bartolomeo Scala Humanistic and Political Writings* (Tempe, AZ: Medieval & Renaissance Texts & Studies, 1997). On

Lorenzo's new men more generally, see Brown, "Lorenzo de' Medici's New Men and Their Mores," in *Medicean and Savonarolan Florence: The Interplay of Politics, Humanism, and Religion*, ed. Alison Brown (Turnhout: Brepols, 2011), 1–38.

57 Kent, *Lorenzo de' Medici and the Art of Magnificence*, Bullard, *Lorenzo il Magnifico*.

58 Scholarship on Renaissance portraiture is vast. To start, see Keith Christiansen and Stefan Weppelmann, eds., *The Renaissance Portrait: From Donaello to Bellini* (New Haven: Yale University Press and the Metropolitan Museum of Art, 2011). See also the further leads in Piers Baker-Bates and Irene Brooke, eds., *Portrait Cultures of the Early Modern Cardinal* (Amsterdam: Amsterdam University Press, 2021).

59 On this, see the discussion and leads in Brian Jeffrey Maxson, "Visual and Verbal Portraits of Cardinals in Fifteenth-Century Florence," in *Portrait Cultures of the Early Modern Cardinal*, ed. Piers Baker-Bates and Irene Brooke (Amsterdam: Amsterdam University Press, 2021), 69–89.

60 The work has been translated into English at Benjamin G. Kohl, Ronald G. Witt and Eilzabeth B. Welles, *The Earthly Republic: Italian Humanists on Government and Society* (Philadelphia: University of Pennsylvania Press, 1978). For recent interpretations, see Marta Celati, "The Conflict after the Pazzi Conspiracy and Poliziano's 'Coniurationis commentarium': Literature, Law, and Politics," *Forum Italicum* 53, no. 2 (2019): 307–11, Celenza, *The Intellectual World of the Italian Renaissance*.

61 A copy of this medal is now in the National Gallery of Art in Washington D.C., with an image online at https://www.nga.gov/collection/art-object -page.70392.html (accessed September 4, 2019). On Bertoldo di Giovanni, see James Draper, *Bertoldo di Giovanni, Sculptor of the Medici Household* (Springfield, MO: University of Missouri Press, 1992), Aimee Ng, Alexander J. Noelle and Xavier F. Salomon, *Bertoldo di Giovanni: The Renaissance of Sculpture in Medici Florence* (New York: The Frick Collection, 2019).

62 Francesco Bausi, "The Medici: Defenders of Liberty in Fifteenth-Century Florence," in *The Medici: Citizens and Masters*, ed. Robert Black and John E. Law (Villa I Tatti: Sheridan Books, 2015), 247–51, with the quote found at p. 249. On this work in general, with both translation and edition, see Aurelio Lippo Brandolini, *Republics and Kingdoms Compared*, ed. and trans. James Hankins (Cambridge, MA: Harvard University Press, 2009).

63 On Lorenzo and philosophy, see James Hankins, "Lorenzo de' Medici as a Patron of Philosophy," *Rinascimento* 34 (1994): 15–53.

64 On Ficino, see Robichaud, *Plato's Persona: Marsilio Ficino, Renaissance Humanism, and Platonic Traditions*. See also the classic Kristeller, *The Philosophy of Marsilio Ficino*, Michael J. B. Allen and Valery Rees, eds.,

Marsilio Ficino: His Theology, His Philosophy, His Legacy (Leiden: Brill, 2002), Stephen Clucas, Peter J. Forshaw and Valery Rees, eds., *Laus platonici philosophi. Marsilio Ficino and His Influence* (Leiden: Brill, 2011).

65 On this work, see Brian P. Copenhaver, *Magic and the Dignity of Man: Pico della Mirandola and His Oration in Modern Memory* (Cambridge, MA: Harvard University Press, 2019), Giovanni Pico della Mirandola, *Syncretism in the West: Pico's 900 theses (1486)*, ed. and trans. S. A. Farmer (Tempe, AZ: Medieval & Renaissance Texts & Studies, 1998). Brown, "New Light on the Papal Condemnation on Pico's Theses," in *Medicean and Savonarolan Florence: The Interplay of Politics, Humanism, and Religion*, ed. Alison Brown (Turnhout: Brepols, 2011), 263–78.

66 Maxson, *The Humanist World of Renaissance Florence.*

67 Paolo Orvieto, "Religion and Literature in Oligarchic, Medicean, and Savonarolan Florence," in *The Medici. Citizens and Masters*, ed. Robert Black and John E. Law (Villa I Tatti: Sheridan Books, 2015), 192–200. See also Alison Brown, "Platonism in Fifteenth-Century Florence and Its Contribution to Early Modern Political Thought," *Journal of Modern History* 58, no. 2 (1986): 391–403. However, as James Hankins notes, Platonism was but one philosophical school associated with Lorenzo. See Hankins, "Lorenzo de' Medici as a Patron of Philosophy."

68 For Lorenzo's poetry, see Celenza, *The Intellectual World of the Italian Renaissance*, 294–5. See also Guido A. Guarino, ed. and trans., *The Complete Literary Works of Lorenzo de' Medici* (New York: Italica Press, 2016), with further leads therein, Lorenzo de' Medici, *Selected Poems and Prose*, ed. and trans. Jon Thiem (University Park: Pennsylvania State Press, 1992).

69 On Landino and this work, see Celenza, *The Intellectual World of the Italian Renaissance*, 298–9. Brown, "De-Masking Renaissance Republicanism," 239. Patricia Rubin has a short bibliographical essay on these illustrations at Rubin, *Images and Identity in Fifteenth-Century Florence*, 339–40.

70 On Pulci, see Celenza, *The Intellectual World of the Italian Renaissance*, 288–94, esp. 88–9. See also James K. Coleman and Andrea Moudares, eds., *Luigi Pulci in Renaissance Florence* (Turnhout: Brepols, 2018). Charles Dempsey, *The Early Renaissance and Vernacular Culture* (Cambridge, MA: Harvard University Press, 2012).

71 On these translations with further leads, see Simon Gilson, *Dante and Renaissance Florence* (Cambridge: Cambridge University Press, 2005), 141–6.

72 Celenza, *The Intellectual World of the Italian Renaissance*, 294, where Lorenzo is described as the "hub."

73 The anecdote is reported at Giovanni Francesco Pico della Mirandola, *Vita hieronymi savonarolae ferrariensis* (Paris: In palatio regio, 1674), Donald Weinstein, "The *Art of Dying Well* and Popular Piety in the Preaching and

Thought of Girolamo Savonarola," in *Life and Death in Fifteenth-Century Florence*, ed. Marcel Tetel, Ronald G. Witt, and Rona Goffen (Durham: Duke University Press, 1989). Translation from the Latin is my own.

74 Poliziano, for example, claimed that Lorenzo died well and that Savonarola accepted his confession. See Weinstein, in *Life and Death in Fifteenth-Century Florence*, 98. See also Nicolai Rubinstein, "Savonarola on the Government of Florence," in *The World of Savonarola: Italian Èlites and Perceptions of Crisis*, ed. Sella Fletcher and Christine Shaw (Aldershot: Ashgate, 2000), 49–51. For more, see Weinstein, in *Life and Death in Fifteenth-Century Florence*, 96–8. Nicholas Terpstra, ed., *The Art of Executing Well: Rituals of Execution in Renaissance Italy* (Kirksville, Missouri: Truman State University Press, 2008). Strocchia, *Nuns and Nunneries in Renaissance Florence*. Sharon Strocchia, *Death and Ritual in Renaissance Florence* (Baltimore: Johns Hopkins University Press, 1992); Marcel Tatel, Ronald G. Witt and Rona Goffen, eds., *Life and Death in Fifteenth-Century Florence* (Durham: Duke University Press, 1989).

75 Bullard, *Lorenzo il Magnifico*, 38.

CHAPTER 5

1 Rubinstein, *The Government of Florence under the Medici (1434-1494)*, 264–7, Alison Brown, "Piero in Power, 1492-1494," in *The Medici. Citizens and Masters*, ed. Robert Black and John E. Law (Villa I Tatti: Sheridan Books, 2015), 113–17. Brown, *Piero di Lorenzo de' Medici and the Crisis of Renaissance Italy*, 149–60. Alison Brown, "The Revolution of 1494 in Florence and Its Aftermath: A Reassessment," in *Italy in Crisis. 1494*, ed. Jane Everson and Diego Zancani (Oxford: European Humanities Research Center, 2000), 13–40.

2 Brown, *Piero di Lorenzo de' Medici and the Crisis of Renaissance Italy*, 160–79. For more on this diplomatic and political situation, see Michael Mallett and Christine Shaw, *The Italian Wars, 1494-1559*, 2nd ed. (London: Routledge, 2019), 11.

3 Brown, "Piero in Power, 1492-1494," 118. More generally, see Brown, *Piero di Lorenzo de' Medici and the Crisis of Renaissance Italy*. Donald Weinstein, *Savonarola and Florence: Prophecy and Patriotism in the Renaissance* (Princeton: Princeton University Press, 1970), 63. See also Michael Mallett and Christine Shaw, *The Italian Wars 1494-1559* (London: Routledge, 2012). On the French arrival in Italy, see David Abulafia, ed., *The French Descent into Renaissance Italy, 1494-95: Antecedents and Effects* (London: Routledge, 1995).

4   On the Hundred Years' War, see Michael Prestwich, *A Short History of the Hundred Years War* (London: I.B. Tauris, 2018), Jonathan Sumption, *The Hundred Years War*, 4 vols. (Philadelphia: University of Pennsylvania Press, 1999-2015). On Louis XI, see Paul Murray Kendall, *Louis XI, the Universal Spider* (New York: Norton & Company, 1971). On the War of the Roses, see Michael Hicks, *The Wars of the Roses* (New Haven: Yale University Press, 2012), Christine Carpenter, *The War of the Roses: Politics and Constitution in England, c. 1437-1509* (Cambridge: Cambridge University Press, 2008).

5   On this inheritance, see Mallett and Shaw, *The Italian Wars 1494-1559*, 8. On its role in helping to justify these conquests, see Andrew W. Devereux, *The Other Side of Empire: Just War in the Mediterranean and the Rise of Early Modern Spain* (Ithaca: Cornell University Press, 2020).

6   Mallett and Shaw, *The Italian Wars 1494-1559*, 6–12, Donald Weinstein, *Savonarola and Florence: Prophecy and Patriotism in the Renaissance* (Princeton: Princeton University Press, 1970), 9–11, Najemy, *A History of Florence, 1200-1575*, 376. On Piero de' Medici's role in these events, see Brown, *Piero di Lorenzo de' Medici and the Crisis of Renaissance Italy*.

7   Weinstein, *Savonarola and Florence*, 64, Najemy, *A History of Florence, 1200-1575*, 376–7, Brown, *Piero di Lorenzo de' Medici and the Crisis of Renaissance Italy*.

8   For more details, see Brown, *Piero di Lorenzo de' Medici and the Crisis of Renaissance Italy*, Mallett and Shaw, *The Italian Wars 1494-1559*.

9   Bruni, *History of the Florentine People*.

10 Brown, *Piero di Lorenzo de' Medici and the Crisis of Renaissance Italy*.

11 See most recently Brown, *Piero di Lorenzo de' Medici and the Crisis of Renaissance Italy*, 190–227, Najemy, *A History of Florence, 1200-1575*, 377–80, Michael Plaisance, *Florence in the Time of the Medici: Public Celebrations, Politics, and Literature in the Fifteenth and Sixteenth Centuries* (Toronto: CRRS, 2008), 41–2. Lauro Martines, *Fire in the City: Savonarola and the Struggle of the Soul of Renaissance Florence* (Oxford: Oxford University Press, 2006). On the cities, see also Rosemary Devonshire Jones, *Francesco Vettori: Florentine Citizen and Medici Servant* (London: Athlone Press, 1972), 10–11.

12 See Weinstein, *Savonarola and Florence*, Martines, *Fire in the City*, Stefano Dall'Aglio, *Savonarola and Savonarolism*, trans. John Gagné (Toronto: CRRS, 2010). See also Donald Weinstein, *Savonarola: The Rise and Fall of a Renaissance Prophet* (New Haven: Yale University Press, 2011).

13 On the new diplomatic emphasis, see, for example, the reception and welcome of King Charles in Florence described at Plaisance, *Florence in the Time of the Medici*, 41–53. See also Humfrey C. Butters, *Governors and Government in Early Sixteenth-Century Florence* (Oxford: Clarendon Press, 1985), 23–31. On these conflicts, see the elegant description at Martines, *Fire in the City*.

14 Plaisance, *Florence in the Time of the Medici*, 71.

15 Najemy, *A History of Florence, 1200-1575*, 382–90. Felix Gilbert, *Machiavelli and Guicciardini: Politics and History in Sixteenth-Century Florence* (New York: W.W. Norton & Company, 1965), Martines, *Fire in the City*.

16 Weinstein, *Savonarola and Florence*. See also Najemy, *A History of Florence, 1200-1575*, 390–4, Martines, *Fire in the City*.

17 Martines, *Fire in the City*. See also J. N. Stephens, *The Fall of the Florentine Republic, 1512-1530* (Oxford: Oxford University Press 1983), 35.

18 See Martines, *Fire in the City*. Dall'Aglio, *Savonarola and Savonarolism*. On an impact of Savonarola's preaching for intellectual history, see Peter Godman, *From Poliziano to Machiavelli: Florentine Humanism in the High Renaissance* (Princeton: Princeton University Press, 1998). Weinstein, *Savonarola and Florence*.

19 Dall'Aglio, *Savonarola and Savonarolism*, 79, Weinstein, *Savonarola and Florence*, 334–8.

20 Dall'Aglio, *Savonarola and Savonarolism*, 23, with further leads on 154–5. See also Lorenza Tromboni, "Ficinian Theories as Rhetorical Devices: The Case of Girolamo Savonarola," in *New Worlds and the Italian Renaissance*, ed. Andrea Moudarres and Christiana Thérèse Purdy Moudarres (Leiden: Brill, 2012), 143–71; Lorenza Tromboni, "La cultura filosofica di Girolamo Savonarola tra predicazione e umanesimo: Platone, Aristotele e la Sacra Scrittura," *Cahiers d'études italiennes* 29 (2019), Weinstein, *Savonarola and Florence*.

21 Rab Hatfield, "Trust in God: The Sources of Michelangelo's Frescos on the Sistine Ceiling," *Occasional Papers Published by Syracuse University, Florence, Italy* 1 (1991): 12–23.

22 Weinstein, *Savonarola and Florence*, 210.

23 As a start, see Dempsey, *Early Renaissance and Vernacular Culture*. See also Charles Dempsey, *The Portrayal of Love: Botticelli's Primavera and Humanist Culture at the Time of Lorenzo the Magnificent* (Princeton: Princeton University Press, 1992), Rebekah Compton, *Venus and the Arts of Love in Renaissance Florence* (Cambridge: Cambridge University Press, 2021), Daniel Arasse and Pierluigi De Vecchi, eds., *Botticelli: From Lorenzo the Magnificent to Savonarola* (Milan: Skira, 2003), Christopher Poncet, *La scelta di Lorenzo: La Primavera di Botticelli tra poesia e filosofia* (Pisa: Fabrizio Serra Editore, 2012), Ana Debenedetti and Caroline Elam, eds., *Botticelli Past and Present* (London: UCL Press, 2019).

24 Ovanes Akopyan, *Debating the Stars in the Italian Renaissance* (Leiden: Brill, 2020). See also Lorenza Tromboni, "Ficinian Theories as Rhetorical Devices: The Case of Girolamo Savonarola," in *New Worlds and the Italian Renaissance*," Remo Catani, "Astrological Polemics in the Crisis of the

1490s," in *Italy in Crisis. 1494.*, ed. Jane Everson and Diego Zancani (Oxford: European Humanities Research Centre, 2000), 41–62.

25 On some of these factions, see Brown, *Piero di Lorenzo de' Medici and the Crisis of Renaissance Italy.* See also Najemy, *A History of Florence, 1200-1575,* 394–8, Butters, *Governors and Government in Early Sixteenth-Century Florence,* Dall'Aglio, *Savonarola and Savonarolism,* Alison Brown, "Ideology and Faction in Savonarolan Florence," in *The World of Savonarola: Italian Élites and Perceptions of Crisis,* ed. Sella Fletcher and Christine Shaw (Aldershot: Ashgate, 2000), 22–41.

26 See the narrative at Martines, *Fire in the City.*

27 On these events, see Martines, *Fire in the City,* Najemy, *A History of Florence, 1200-1575,* 399–400.

28 In addition to the general literature on Savonarola, see Patrick Macey, *Bonfire Songs: Savonarola's Musical Legacy* (Oxford: Clarendon Press, 1998). Plaisance, *Florence in the Time of the Medici,* 55–84. For the potential influence of Lucretius on some cultural changes in the 1490s, for example, see Alison Brown, *The Return of Lucretius to Renaissance Florence* (Cambridge, MA: Harvard University Press, 2010).

29 Michael Rocke, *Forbidden Friendships: Homosexuality and Male Culture in Renaissance Florence* (Oxford: Oxford University Press, 1996), 216–21.

30 Rocke, *Forbidden Friendships.*

31 Judith C. Brown, *Immodest Acts: The Life of a Lesbian Nun in Renaissance Italy* (Oxford: Oxford University Press, 1986). Compare the exchange at Rudolph M. Bell, "Renaissance Sexuality and the Florentine Archives: An Exchange," *Renaissance Quarterly* 40, no. 3 (1987): 485–511. See also Patricia Simons, "Lesbian (In)visibility in Italian Renaissance Culture: Diana and Other Cases of donna con donna," *Journal of Homosexuality* 27, no. 1–2 (1994): 81–122.

32 Weinstein, *Savonarola,* 142. The letters between the two men are at Angelo Poliziano, *Letters,* trans. Shane Butler (Cambridge and London: Harvard University Press, 2006).

33 On Pico, Poliziano, and Savonarola, Weinstein, *Savonarola,* 79 and 142–4, Weinstein, *Savonarola and Florence.* Pico and Poliziano were also joined in a recent catalogue Paolo Viti, ed., *Pico, Poliziano e l'umanesimo di fine Quattrocento* (Florence: Leo S. Olschki, 1994). On Savonarola's disappointment that Pico did not join the Dominicans, see Catani, in *Italy in Crisis. 1494,* 53. On Pico's death, see Gianni Gallello et al., "Poisoning Histories in the Italian Renaissance: The Case of Pico della Mirandola and Angelo Poliziano," *Journal of Forensic and Legal Medicine* 56 (2018): 83–9. Poliziano, however, probably was not poisoned.

34 See Dall'Aglio, *Savonarola and Savonarolism.* One fascinating study about period religiosity can also be found at William J. Connell and Giles Constable,

Sacrilege and Redemption in Renaissance Florence: The Case of Antonio Rinaldeschi (Toronto: Centre for Reformation and Renaissance Studies, 2005).

35 Najemy, *A History of Florence, 1200-1575*, 400–7. For more details, see Butters, *Governors and Government in Early Sixteenth-Century Florence*, 34–46.

36 On the Soderini, see Clarke, *The Soderini and the Medici*.

37 On Tommaso's children and Francesco's efforts in Rome, see K. J. P. Lowe, *Church and Politics in Renaissance Italy: The Life and Career of Cardinal Francesco Soderini (1453-1524)* (Cambridge: Cambridge University Press, 1993). and Butters, *Governors and Government in Early Sixteenth-Century Florence*.

38 See Lowe, *Church and Politics in Renaissance Italy*.

39 See the comments found at Dall'Aglio, *Savonarola and Savonarolism*, 18.

40 Maxson, "Expressions of Power in Diplomacy in Fifteenth-Century Florence."

41 On Pisa's rise with particular regards to the Mediterranean, see David Abulafia, *The Great Sea: A Human History of the Mediterranean* (Oxford: Oxford University Press, 2011).

42 On Pisa, see Sergio Tognetti, ed., *Firenze e Pisa dopo il 1406: La creazione di una nuovo spazio regionale* (Florence: Leo S. Olschki, 2010), Michele Luzzati, *Estimi e catasti del contado di Pisa nel Quattrocento* (Pisa: Pacini, 1976), Michael Mallett, *Pisa and Florence in the Fifteenth Century: Aspects of the Period of the First Florentine Domination* (London: Faber & Faber, 1968), David Herlihy, *Pisa in the Early Renaissance* (New Haven: Yale University Press, 1958).

43 On this move, see Paul F. Grendler, *The Universities of the Italian Renaissance* (Baltimore: Johns Hopkins University Press, 2002), 70ff. See also Davies, *Florence and its University during the Early Renaissance*, 71–4 and 125–42.

44 Emanuela Ferretti, "Fra Leonardo, Machiavelli e Soderini. Ercole I d'Este e Biagio Rossetti nell'impresa <<del volgere l'Arno>> da Pisa," *Archivio storico italiano* 177, no. 2 (2019): 235–72. with further leads therein. For a more popular history, see Roger Masters, *Fortune Is a River: Leonardo da Vinci and Niccolò Machiavelli's Magnificent Dream to Change the Course of Florentine History* (New York: The Free Press, 1998). On forced labor for the project, see Suzanne B. Butters, "The Medici Dukes, *Comandati* and Pratolino: Forced Labour in Renaissance Florence," in *Communes and Despots in Medieval and Renaissance Italy*, ed. John E. Law and Bernadette Paton (Farnham: Ashgate, 2010), 254. For more details on the attempts to retake Pisa, see Mallett and Shaw, *The Italian Wars 1494-1559*.

45 Christopher S. Celenza, *Machiavelli: A Portrait* (Cambridge, MA: Harvard University Press, 2015), 40–51. See also Najemy, *A History of Florence, 1200-1575*, 410–13. More generally, see Corrado Vivanti, *Niccolo Machiavelli: An*

Intellectual Biography (Princeton: Princeton University Press, 2013), Robert Black, *Machiavelli* (London: Routledge, 2013). Alexander Lee, *Machiavelli: His Life and Times* (London: Picador, 2020).

46 On these early years, see William E. Wallace, *Michelangelo. The Artist, the Man, and His Times* (Cambridge: Cambridge University Press, 2010), 9–71. See also Michael Hirst, *Michelangelo: The Achievement of Fame, 1475-1534* (New Haven: Yale University Press, 2011), 1–26. William E. Wallace, ed., *Michelangelo. Selected Scholarship in English*, 5 vols. (New York: Garland, 1995), vol. 1.

47 Wallace, *Michelangelo. The Artist, the Man, and His Times*, 15–25, Hirst, *Michelangelo*, 31–7. See also Edgar Wind, "A Bacchic Mystery by Michelangelo," in *Pagan Mysteries in the Renaissance* (New Haven: Yale University Press, 1958; reprint, Wallace, ed., Michelangelo. *Selected Scholarship in English*, 201–16).

48 William E. Wallace, "An Impossible Task," in *Making and Moving Sculpture in Early Modern Italy*, ed. Kelley Helmstutler Di Dio (Farnham: Ashgate, 2015), 47–59.

49 On the David, see most recently John T. Paoletti, *Michelangelo's David: Florentine History and Civic Identity* (Cambridge: Cambridge University Press, 2015). Amy R. Bloch, "A Note on the Movement of Michelangelo's *David*," in *The Art and Language of Power in Renaissance Florence: Essays for Alison Brown*, ed. Amy R. Bloch, Carolyn James, and Camilla Russell (Toronto: CRRS, 2019), 205–19, Hirst, *Michelangelo*.

50 On the later history of the David and the Accademia, see Franca Falletti, ed., *The Accademia, Michelangelo, the Nineteenth Century* (Livorno: Sillabe, 1997), Paoletti, *Michelangelo's David*.

51 On these earlier depictions, see the leads in Paoletti, *Michelangelo's David*. See also the essays in Wallace, *Michelangelo. Selected Scholarship in English*. Brown, "De-Masking Renaissance Republicanism."

52 On this room and its frescoes, see the essays and further leads in Roberta Barsanti et al., eds., *La Sala Grande di Palazzo Vecchio e la Battaglia di Anghiari di Leonardo da Vinci* (Florence: Leo S. Olschki, 2019). On Michelangelo's proposed fresco, see Wallace, *Michelangelo. The Artist, the Man, and His Times*, 62–3, with further leads therein. See also the articles by Wilde and Gould found and republished in Wallace, *Michelangelo. Selected Scholarship in English*, vol. 1, Hirst, *Michelangelo*, 56–60.

53 Repeated efforts have been made to uncover the location of any remnants of Leonardo's fresco underneath Vasari's later frescoes. The most recent scholarship, however, suggests that he may not have ever started the fresco. See Barsanti et al., *La Sala Grande di Palazzo Vecchio e la Battaglia di Anghiari di Leonardo da Vinci*.

54　Brown, *Piero di Lorenzo de' Medici and the Crisis of Renaissance Italy*, 242. See also Butters, *Governors and Government in Early Sixteenth-Century Florence*, 133–8

55　On this council and politics, see Butters, *Governors and Government in Early Sixteenth-Century Florence*, 145ff. Additional leads can be found at J. H. Burns, "Angelo da Vallombrosa and the Pisan Schism," in *The Church, the Councils, & Reform. The Legacy of the Fifteenth Century*, ed. Gerald Christianson, Thomas M. Izbicki, and Christopher M. Bellitto (Washington, DC: Catholic University Press, 2008), 194–211. See also Christine Shaw, *Julius II. The Warrior Pope* (Oxford: Blackwell Publishers, 1993).

56　On these events, see Najemy, *A History of Florence, 1200-1575*, 407–13 and 19–20. On the Fifth Lateran Council, see Nelson H. Minnich, ed., *Alla ricerca di soluzioni, nuova luce sul Concilio Lateranense V* (Vatican City: Libreria Editrice Vaticana, 2019), Nelson H. Minnich, *The Decrees of the Fifth Lateran Council* (London: Routledge, 2016). Eric A. Constant, "A Reinterpretation of the Fifth Lateran Council Decree *Apostolici regiminis* (1513)," *Sixteenth Century Journal* 33, no. 2 (2002): 353–79.

57　On the political complexities of the period, see Butters, *Governors and Government in Early Sixteenth-Century Florence*. On the Savonarolans, see Lorenzo Polizzotto, *The Elect Nation: The Savonarolan Movement in Florence, 1494-1545* (Oxford: Clarendon Press, 1994).

58　On Pierfilippo, see Plebani, "Una fuga programmata. Eugenio IV e Firenze (1433-1434)," Maxson, *The Humanist World of Renaissance Florence*, Baldassarri and Maxson, "Giannozzo Manetti's *Oratio in funere Iannotii Pandolfini.*" Brown, *Piero di Lorenzo de' Medici and the Crisis of Renaissance Italy*. On his significance, see esp. Martines, *Fire in the City*, 200.

59　Martines, *Fire in the City*, 178 and 216. Guicciardini reported that Jacopo was among those leaders elected after Savonarola's downfall. See Francesco Guicciardini, *Storie fiorentine dal 1378 al 1509*, ed. Alessandro Castelvecchio (Milan: BUR, 1998). More generally, see Maxson, *The Humanist World of Renaissance Florence*, 32.

60　Butters, *Governors and Government in Early Sixteenth-Century Florence*, 207 and 13. Melissa Meriam Bullard, *Filippo Strozzi and the Medici: Favor & Finance in Sixteenth-Century Florence & Rome* (Cambridge: Cambridge University Press, 1980), 125. See also Louis A. Waldman, "The Patronage of a Favorite of Leo X: Cardinal Niccolò Pandolfini, Ridolfo Ghirlandaio and the Unfinished Tomb by Baccio da Montelupo," *Mitteilungen des Kunsthistorischen Institutes in Florenz* 48, no. 1/2 (2004): 105–28.

61　On the Palazzo Pandolfini, see Christoph Luitpold Frommel, "Palazzo Pandolfini: Problemi di datazione e di ricostruzione," in *Studi su Raffaello*, ed. Micaela Sambucco Hamoud (Urbino: Quattro Venti, 1987), 197–204 and 211–12, Kenneth Gouwens and Sheryl E. Reiss, eds., *The Pontificate of Clement VII: History, Politics, Culture* (Burlington, VT: Ashgate, 2005).On the Badia, see Eugenio Luporini, "Battista Pandolfini e Benedetto da Rovezzano nella Badia fiorentina. Documenti per la datazione," *Prospettiva* 33/36 (1983-1984): 112–23, Leader, *The Badia of Florence. Art and Observance in a Renaissance Monastery*, 284.

62 See especially Brown, *Piero di Lorenzo de' Medici and the Crisis of Renaissance Italy*.

63 On this marriage, see Bullard, *Filippo Strozzi and the Medici*, 45–60. See also Najemy, *A History of Florence, 1200-1575*, 414–16, Butters, *Governors and Government in Early Sixteenth-Century Florence*.

64 On these events, see Najemy, *A History of Florence, 1200-1575*, 419–21. Butters, *Governors and Government in Early Sixteenth-Century Florence*. See also Stephens, *The Fall of the Florentine Republic, 1512-1530*, 59–68. More generally, see Mallett and Shaw, *The Italian Wars 1494-1559*. From a different perspective with additional leads, see Edward Muir, "Was There Republicanism in the Renaissance Republics?," in *Venice Reconsidered. The History and Civilization of an Italian City-State*, ed. John Martin and Dennis Romano (Baltimore: Johns Hopkins University Press, 2000), 137–67.

65 Bullard, *Filippo Strozzi and the Medici*, Butters, *Governors and Government in Early Sixteenth-Century Florence*, Najemy, *A History of Florence, 1200-1575*, 428.

66 A number of good, recent biographies of Machiavelli exist. See, for example, Lee, *Machiavelli*, Black, *Machiavelli*, Celenza, *Machiavelli*, Vivanti, *Niccolo Machiavelli*. Although not strictly a biography, see also John M. Najemy, ed., *The Cambridge Companion to Machiavelli* (Cambridge: Cambridge University Press, 2010).

67 On Machiavelli's arrest, see Lee, *Machiavelli*. See also Black, *Machiavelli*. On Vettori, see Jones, *Francesco Vettori*, John M. Najemy, *Between Friends: Discourses of Power and Desire in the Machiavelli-Vettori Letters of 1513-1515* (Princeton: Princeton University Press, 1993).

68 See editions of the text at, for example, Niccolò Machiavelli, *The Prince*, ed. William J. Connell, 2nd ed. (Boston: Bedford/St. Martin's, 2005), Niccolò Machiavelli, *The Prince, Cambridge Texts in the History of Political Thought*, ed. Raymond Price and Quentin Skinner (Cambridge: Cambridge University Press, 1988). For Machiavelli's reception, see Humfrey C. Butters, "Conflicting Attitudes towards Machiavelli's Works in Sixteenth-Century Spain, Rome, and Florence," in *Communes and Despots in Medieval and Renaissance Italy*, ed. John E. Law and Bernadette Paton (Farnham: Ashgate, 2010), 75–87.

69 Najemy, *A History of Florence, 1200-1575*, 430–4. See also, Butters, *Governors and Government in Early Sixteenth-Century Florence*. For more

information on the structure of Florentine government during these years as well as Florentine agency, see Stephens, *The Fall of the Florentine Republic, 1512-1530.*

70 See especially their portrayal in Brown, *Piero di Lorenzo de' Medici and the Crisis of Renaissance Italy.*

71 See, for example, Lyn A. Blanchfield, "*Le Piagnoni:* The Weeping Women of Savonarola," in *Power, Gender, and Ritual in Europe and the Americas,* ed. Peter Arnade and Michael Rocke (Toronto: CRRS, 2008), 53–76. See also Polizzotto, *The Elect Nation.* Lorenzo Polizzotto, "When Saints Fall Out: Women and the Savonarolan Reform in Early Sixteenth-Century Florence," *Renaissance Quarterly* 46, no. 3 (1993): 486–525.

72 Amedeo Beluzzi, "Il gonfaloniere Soderini nel Palazzo dei Signori," in *La Sala Grande di Palazzo Vecchio e la Battaglia di Anghiari di Leonardo da Vinci,* ed. Roberta Barsanti et al. (Florence: Leo S. Olschki, 2019), 207–9.

73 Mary D. Garrard, "The Cloister and the Square," *Early Modern Women* 11, no. 1 (2016): 5–44.

74 Natalie Tomas, "All in the Family: The Medici Women and Pope Clement VII," in *The Pontificate of Clement VII. History, Politics, Culture,* ed. Kenneth Gouwens and Sheryl E. Reiss (Aldershot: Ashgate, 2005), 41–53.

75 Stephens, *The Fall of the Florentine Republic, 1512-1530,* 99.

76 Tomas, "Did Women Have a Space?," 326.

77 Butters, in *Communes and Despots in Medieval and Renaissance Italy,* 257–8.

78 Catherine Kovesi, "Muddying the Waters: Alfonsina Orsini de' Medici and the Lake of Fucecchio," in *Communes and Despots in Medieval and Renaissance Italy,* ed. John E. Law and Bernadette Paton (Farnham: Ashgate, 2010), 223–47. More generally, see Tomas, *The Medici Women,* Natalie Tomas, "Alfonsina Orsini de' Medici and the 'Problem' of a Female Ruler in Early Sixteenth-Century Florence," *Renaissance Studies* 14, no. 1 (2000): 70–90.

79 On critiques of Alfonsina and women in power more generally, see Tomas, *The Medici Women,* Giovanna Benadusi and Judith C. Brown, eds., *Medici Women: The Making of a Dynasty in Grand Ducal Tuscany* (Toronto: CRRS, 2015).

80 Strocchia, *Nuns and Nunneries in Renaissance Florence,* Saundra Weddle, "Identity and Alliance: Urban Presence, Spatial Privilege, and Florentine Renaissance Convents," in *Renaissance Florence. A Social History,* ed. Roger J. Crum and John T. Paoletti (Cambridge: Cambridge University Press, 2006), 394–412.

81 Sharon T. Strocchia, *Forgotten Healers. Women and the Pursuit of Health in Late Renaissance Italy* (Cambridge, MA: Harvard University Press, 2019).

82 On the Medici's lack of equals in Florence, see Stephens, *The Fall of the Florentine Republic, 1512-1530.*

83 On San Lorenzo, see most recently Gaston and Waldman, *San Lorenzo. A Florentine Church*, Viti, *Il Capitolo di San Lorenzo nel Quattrocento*, William E. Wallace, *Michelangelo at San Lorenzo: The Genius as Entrepreneur* (Cambridge: Cambridge University Press, 1994).

84 Wallace, *Michelangelo. The Artist, the Man, and His Times*. See also the articles in Wallace, *Michelangelo. Selected Scholarship in English*, vol. 3.

85 On these figures, see especially Richard Trexler and Mary Elizabeth Lewis, "Two Captains and Three Kings: New Light on the Medici Chapel," *Studies in Medieval and Renaissance History* 4 (1981): 91–177. On the *bastone*, see also Brian Jeffrey Maxson, "Humanism and the Ritual of Command in Fifteenth-Century Florence," in *After Civic Humanism: Learning and Politics in Renaissance Italy*, ed. Nicholas Scott Baker and Brian Jeffrey Maxson (Toronto: CRRS, 2015), 113–29.

86 Wallace, *Michelangelo. The Artist, the Man, and His Times*, 149–52. Hirst, *Michelangelo*, 208–16.

87 Wallace, *Michelangelo. The Artist, the Man, and His Times*. In general, see also Hirst, *Michelangelo*, 146–68 and 83–99, 208–16, and more generally Wallace, *Michelangelo. Selected Scholarship in English*, vol. 3.

88 See, for example, Thomas James Dandelet, *The Renaissance of Empire in Early Modern Europe* (Cambridge: Cambridge University Press, 2014).

89 Niccolò Machiavelli, *Florentine Histories*, trans. Jr. Laura F. Banfield and Harvey C. Mansfield (Princeton: Princeton University Press, 1988). For recent interpretations of this work, see, for example, John P. McCormick, *Reading Machiavelli. Scandalous Books, Suspect Engagements & the Virtue of Populist Politics* (Princeton: Princeton University Press, 2018), Mark Jurdjevic, *A Great & Wretched City. Promise and Failure in Machiavelli's Political Thought* (Cambridge, MA: Harvard University Press, 2014).

90 See, for example, with further leads, McCormick, Holman. More generally, see Anna Maria Cabrini, "Machiavelli's *Florentine Histories*," in *The Cambridge Companion to Machiavelli*, ed. John M. Najemy (Cambridge: Cambridge University Press, 2010), 128–43.

91 For other interpretations of the optimism or pessimism of the *Florentine Histories*, see Jurdjevic, *A Great & Wretched City*.

92 Baker, *The Fruit of Liberty*, 49–97.

93 Najemy, *A History of Florence, 1200-1575*, 447–9. For more detail, see Baker, *The Fruit of Liberty*, Cecil Roth, *The Last Florentine Republic* (London: Methuen & co. ltd., 1925), Stephens, *The Fall of the Florentine Republic, 1512-1530*.

94 On the factions in this republic, see Polizzotto "When Saints Fall Out," Baker, *The Fruit of Liberty*, Roth, *The Last Florentine Republic*, Dall'Aglio, *Savonarola and Savonarolism*.

95 See Najemy, *A History of Florence, 1200-1575*, 448–52. On the crowning of
   Christ, see Nicholas Scott Baker, "Discursive Republicanism in Renaissance
   Florence: Deliberation and Representation in the Early Sixteenth Century,"
   Past & Present 225 (2014): 47–77, Nicholas Scott Baker, "When Christ Was
   King in Florence: Religious Language and Political Paralysis during the Siege
   of Florence, 1529-30," in *Languages of Power in Italy (1300-1600)*, ed. Daniel
   Bornstein, Laura Gaffuri, and Brian Jeffrey Maxson (Turnhout: Brepols,
   2017), 215–28. For revenge against the Medici and their supporters, see
   Stephens, *The Fall of the Florentine Republic, 1512-1530*, 220–41.
96 On this sack, see Judith Hook, *The Sack of Rome, 1527* (London: Macmillan,
   1972), Kenneth Gouwens, *Remembering the Renaissance: Humanist
   Narratives of the Sack of Rome* (Leiden, Boston, Koln: Brill, 1998), Catherine
   Fletcher, *The Beauty and the Terror: The Italian Renaissance and the Rise of
   the West* (Oxford: Oxford University Press, 2020).
97 Najemy, *A History of Florence, 1200-1575*, 453. For more details about the
   negotiations behind this divorce, see Catherine Fletcher, *The Divorce of Henry
   VIII: The Untold Story* (London: Vintage Books, 2013).
98 Stephens, *The Fall of the Florentine Republic, 1512-1530*.
99 Najemy, *A History of Florence, 1200-1575*, 453–61. With more details at
   Roth, *The Last Florentine Republic*, Baker, *The Fruit of Liberty*, Stephens,
   The Fall of the Florentine Republic, 1512-1530. See also, with further leads,
   Pierre Nevejans, "An Ambassador as a Diversion? Giuliano Soderini and His
   Florentine Mission in France (1527–529)," *Legatio* 3 (2019): 5–38. Hirst,
   Michelangelo, 229–34.

CHAPTER 6

1 Catherine Fletcher, *The Black Prince of Florence* (Oxford: Oxford University
   Press, 2016), 61–4. On Clement VII more generally, see Gouwens and Reiss,
   The Pontificate of Clement VII.
2 Fletcher, *The Black Prince of Florence*.
3 Najemy, *A History of Florence, 1200-1575*, 454, 61, and 63–4, R. Burr
   Litchfield, *Emergence of a Bureaucracy. The Florentine Patricians 1530-1790*
   (Princeton: Princeton University Press, 1986), Fletcher, *The Black Prince of
   Florence*, Baker, *The Fruit of Liberty*.
4 Fletcher, *The Black Prince of Florence*, 14–19, John K. Brackett, "Race and
   Rulership: Alessandro de' Medici, First Medici Duke of Florence, 1529-1537,"
   in *Black Africans in Renaissance Europe*, ed. T. F. Earle and K. J. P. Lowe
   (Cambridge: Cambridge University Press, 2005), 303–25.
5 See recent studies on the Mediterranean, such as Abulafia, *The Great Sea*,
   Monique O'Connell, and Eric Dursteler, *The Mediterranean World: From the*

Fall of Rome to the Rise of Napoleon (Baltimore: Johns Hopkins University Press, 2016). See also Chris Wickham, *The Inheritance of Rome. A History of Europe from 400 to 1000* (New York: Penguin, 2009).

6 The classic study of the Twelfth-Century Renaissance is Charles Homer Haskins, *The Renaissance of the Twelfth Century* (Cambridge, MA: Harvard University Press, 1928). A more recent introduction is at R. N. Swanson, *The Twelfth-Century Renaissance* (Manchester: Manchester University Press, 1999).

7 See, for example, Kate Lowe, "The Stereotyping of Black Africans in Renaissance Europe," in *Black Africans in Renaissance Europe*, ed. T. F. Earle and K. J. P. Lowe (Cambridge: Cambridge University Press, 2005), 17–47, Matteo Salvadore, *The African Prester John and the Birth of Ethiopian-European Relations* (London: Routledge, 2017).

8 On this mission, see Michael E. Mallett, *The Florentine Galleys in the Fifteenth Century* (Oxford: Clarendon Press, 1967), Nicholas Eckstein, *Painted Glories: The Brancacci Chapel in Renaissance Florence* (New Haven: Yale University Press, 2014), Mahnaz Yousefzadeh, *Florence's Embassy to the Sultan of Egypt. An English Translation of Felice Brancacci's Diary* (London: Palgrave Macmillan, 2018), Dante Catellacci, "Diario di Felice Brancacci Ambasciatore con Carlo Federighi al Cairo per il comune di Firenze," *Archivio storico italiano*, Fourth Series, vol. 8 (1881).

9 Sergio Tognetti, "The Trade in Black African Slaves in Fifteenth-Century Florence," in *Black Africans in Renaissance Europe*, ed. T. F. Earle and K. J. P. Lowe (Cambridge: Cambridge University Press, 2005), 213–46, Paul H.D. Kaplan, "Isabella d'Este and Black African Women," in *Black Africans in Renaissance Europe*, ed. T. F. Earle and K. J. P. Lowe, 125–54 (Cambridge: Cambridge University Press, 2005).

10 Corey Tazzara, *The Free Port of Livorno and the Transformation of the Mediterranean World* (Oxford: Oxford University Press, 2017), Stephanie Nadalo, "Negotiating Slavery in a Tolerant Frontier: Livorno's Turkish *Bagno* (1547-1747)," *Mediaevalia* 32, no. 1 (2011). Florence also continued its long tradition of forced labor among people in its territories. See Butters, in *Communes and Despots in Medieval and Renaissance Italy*.

11 Tognetti, "The Trade in Black African Slaves in Fifteenth-Century Florence," 223. See also F. Angiolini, "Slaves and Slavery in Early Modern Tuscany," *Journal of Italian History and Culture* 3 (1997): 67–86, Steven A. Epstein, *Speaking of Slavery. Color, Ethnicity, & Human Bondage in Italy* (Ithaca: Cornell University Press, 2001).

12 Katalin Prajda, *Network and Migration in Early Renaissance Florence, 1378-1433* (Amsterdam: Amsterdam University Press, 2018), 9. David Rosenthal, "The Spaces of Plebeian Ritual and the Boundaries of Transgression," in *Renaissance Florence. A Social History*, ed. Roger J. Crum and John T. Paoletti

(Cambridge: Cambridge University Press, 2006), 168, Lorenz Böninger, *Die deutsche Einwanderung nach Florenz im Spätmittelalter* (Leiden: Brill, 2006), Daniels.

13 Seven hundred visitors came from Byzantium alone. See Lilia Campana, "Sailing into Union: The Byzantine Naval Convoy for the Council of Ferrara-Florence (1438–1439)," *Dumbarton Oaks Papers* 73 (2019): 103–26. See also Gill, *The Council of Florence.*

14 On the most famous of these, John Hawkwood, see William Caferro, *John Hawkwood: An English Mercenary in Fourteenth-Century Italy.* (Baltimore: Johns Hopkins University Press, 2006).

15 On Jews in Florence, see Stefanie B. Siegmund, *The Medici State and the Ghetto of Florence: The Construction of an Early Modern Jewish Community* (Stanford: Stanford University Press, 2006). Roberto G. Salvadori, *The Jews of Florence* (Florence: Giutina, 2001), Edward L. Goldberg, *Jews and Magic in Medici Florence. The Secret World of Benedetto Blanis* (Toronto: University of Toronto Press, 2011). On the later period, see Francesca Bregoli, *Mediterranean Enlightenment: Livornese Jews, Tuscan Culture, and Eighteenth-Century Reform* (Stanford: Stanford University Press, 2014), Francesca Trivellato, *The Familiarity of Strangers: The Sephardic Diaspora, Livorno, and Cross-Cultural Trade in the Early Modern Period* (New Haven: Yale University Press, 2009).

16 See, for example, Daniel Stein Kokin, "The Josephan Renaissance: Flavius Josephus and His Writings in Italian Humanist Discourse," *Viator* 47, no. 2 (2016): 205–48, Yakov Z. Mayer, "Crying at the Florence Baptistery Entrance: A Testimony of a Traveling Jew," *Renaissance Studies* 33, no. 3 (2019): 441–57, Stefano U. Baldassarri, and Fabrizio Lelli, eds., *Umanesimo e cultura ebraica nel Rinascimento italiano* (Florence: Angelo Pontecorboli, 2016), Giannozzo Manetti, *Against the Jews and Gentiles*, ed. Stefano U. Baldassarri and Daniela Pagliara, trans. David Marsh, vol. 1 (Cambridge, MA: Harvard University Press, 2017), Giannozzo Manetti, *A Translator's Defense*, ed. Myron McShane, trans. Mark Young (Cambridge, MA: Harvard University Press, 2016), Ilana Zinguer, Abraham Melamed, and Zur Shalev, eds., *Hebraic Aspects of the Renaissance* (Leiden: Brill, 2011), with further leads therein.

17 Litchfield, *Emergence of a Bureaucracy*, Baker, *The Fruit of Liberty*, Najemy, *A History of Florence, 1200-1575*, 478.

18 Bullard, *Filippo Strozzi and the Medici.*

19 Bullard, *Filippo Strozzi and the Medici*, 174–6, Najemy, *A History of Florence, 1200-1575*, Fletcher, *The Black Prince of Florence*, 179–230, Dall'Aglio, *Savonarola and Savonarolism*, 121–2, Brackett, in *Black Africans in Renaissnace Europe*, 322–3.

20 Najemy, *A History of Florence, 1200-1575*, 465–6. See also Fletcher, *The Black Prince of Florence*, 221–8.

21 For this narrative, see Fletcher, *The Black Prince of Florence*, 3–5. For more detail, see Stefano Dall'Aglio, *The Duke's Assassin: Exile and Death of Lorenzino de' Medici*, trans. Donald Weinstein (New Haven: Yale University Press, 2015), 3–12.

22 Najemy, *A History of Florence, 1200-1575*, 466–7, Litchfield, *Emergence of a Bureaucracy*, Baker, *The Fruit of Liberty*. See also Eric Cochrane, *Florence in the Forgotten Centuries, 1527-1800. A History of Florence and the Florentines in the Age of the Grand Dukes* (Chicago: University of Chicago Press, 1973), 13–21, Tomas, "All in the Family," 50–2.

23 On these events, see Bullard, *Filippo Strozzi and the Medici*, 176, Cochrane, *Florence in the Forgotten Centuries, 1527-1800*, Najemy, *A History of Florence, 1200-1575*, 467.

24 On this match, see Langdon, *Medici Women*, 6, Cochrane, *Florence in the Forgotten Centuries, 1527-1800*, 38–9. On Eleonora more generally, see Konrad Eisenbichler, ed., *The Cultural World of Eleonora di Toledo* (Aldershot: Ashgate, 2004).

25 John K. Brackett, *Criminal Justice and Crime in Late Renaissance Florence, 1537-1609* (Cambridge: Cambridge University Press, 1992).

26 Litchfield, *Emergence of a Bureaucracy*, 67–83, Najemy, *A History of Florence, 1200-1575*, 469–78, Cochrane, *Florence in the Forgotten Centuries, 1527-1800*.

27 Alessandra Contini, "Aspects of Medicean Diplomacy in the Sixteenth Century," in *Politics and Diplomacy in Early Modern Italy: The Structure of Diplomatic Practice, 1450-1800*, ed. Daniela Frigo (Cambridge: Cambridge University Press, 2000), 63–71. Cf. Najemy, *A History of Florence, 1200-1575*, 469ff.

28 Geoffrey Parker, *The Military Revolution: Military Innovation and the Rise of the West, 1500-1800*, 2nd ed. (Cambridge: Cambridge University Press, 1996).

29 Balchin, *Urban Development in Renaissance Italy*, 280–3, J. R. Hale, "The End of Florentine Liberty: The Fortezza da Basso," in *Florentine Studies. Politics and Society in Renaissance Florence*, ed. Nicolai Rubinstein (London: Faber and Faber, 1968), 501–32, Najemy, *A History of Florence, 1200-1575*, 464–8, Baker, *The Fruit of Liberty*, 193.

30 Baker, *The Fruit of Liberty*, Litchfield, *Emergence of a Bureaucracy*. Duke Cosimo built on recent Medici practices. See Stephens, *The Fall of the Florentine Republic, 1512-1530*, 147–54.

31 As famously argued at Norbert Elias, *The Civilizing Process*, vol. 2 (Oxford: Blackwell, 1978–1982).

32 Tomas, *The Medici Women*.

33 Elisabetta Mori, "Isabella de' Medici: Unraveling the Legend," in *Medici Women: The Making of a Dynasty in Grand Ducal Tuscany*, ed. Giovanna Benadusi and Judith C. Brown (Toronto: CRRS, 2015), 90–127. See also

Caroline Murphy, *Murder of a Medici Princess* (Cambridge: Cambridge University Press, 2009).

34 See the essays and further leads on each of these women at Benadusi and Brown, *Medici Women*.

35 Nicholas Terpstra, "Mapping Gendered Labor in the Textile Industry of Early Modern Florence," in *Florence in the Early Modern World. New Perspectives*, ed. Nicholas Scott Baker and Brian Jeffrey Maxson (London: Routledge, 2020), 68–91. For more on women and work during this period, see Goldthwaite, *The Economy of Renaissance Florence*, Strocchia, *Nuns and Nunneries in Renaissance Florence*.

36 Veen, *Cosimo I de' Medici and his Self-Representation in Florentine Art and Culture*.

37 Elizabeth Currie, *Fashion and Masculinity in Renaissance Florence* (London: Bloomsbury, 2016). On clothing in general, see Carole Collier Frick, *Dressing Renaissance Florence: Families, Fortunes, and Fine Clothing* (Baltimore: The John Hopkins University Press, 2002).

38 On the Valori family histories, see Mark Jurdjevic, *Guardians of Republicanism: The Valori Family in the Florentine Renaissance* (Oxford: Oxford University Press, 2008).

39 Guicciardini, *The History of Italy*, 4.

40 Guicciardini, *The History of Italy*, 206. On this work, see also Gilbert, *Machiavelli and Guicciardini*, Mark Phillips, *Francesco Guicciardini: The Historian's Craft* (Toronto: University of Toronto Press, 1977).

41 Benedetto Varchi, *Storia fiorentina*, ed. Lelio Arbib, vol. 1 (Florence: Editrice delle storie del Nardi e del Varchi, 1843), 55. Translation from the Italian is my own.

42 On Varchi, see Cochrane, *Florence in the Forgotten Centuries, 1527-1800*, Annalisa Andreoni, *La via della dottrina: Le lezioni accademiche di Benedetto Varchi* (Pisa: ETS, 2012), Dario Brancato, and Salvatore Lo Re, "Per una nuova edizione della *"Storia"* del Varchi: Il problema storico e testuale," *Annali della Scuola Normale Superiore di Pisa. Classe di Lettere e Filosofia* Series 5 7, no. 1 (2015): 201–31 and 71–72, Richard S. Samuels, "Benedetto Varchi, the Accademia degli Infiammati, and the Origins of the Italian Academic Movement," *Renaissance Quarterly* 29, no. 4 (1976): 599–634, Dario Brancato, "'Narrar la sustanzia in poche parole.' Cosimo I e Baccio Baldini correttori della *Storia fiorentina* di Benedetto Varchi," *Giornale Italiano di Filologia* 67 (2015): 323–33, Raymond Carlson, "'Eccellentissimo poeta et amatore divinissimo': Benedetto Varchi and Michelangelo's Poetry at the Accademia Fiorentina," *Italian Studies* 69, no. 1–2 (2014): 169–88. But the literature is vast.

43 Najemy, *A History of Florence, 1200-1575*, 479–80, Litchfield, *Emergence of a Bureaucracy*, 34-7, Katherine Poole-Jones, "The Medici, Maritime Empire,

and the Enduring Legacy of the Cavalieri di Santo Stefano," in *Florence in Early Modern Europe. New Perspectives*, ed. Nicholas Scott Baker and Brian Jeffrey Maxson (London: Routledge, 2020), 156–86, Currie, *Fashion and Masculinity in Renaissance Florence.*

44 On mannerism, the classic account is John Shearman, *Mannerism* (New York: Penguin, 1967). More recently, see David Franklin, *Painting in Renaissance Florence, 1500-1550* (New Haven: Yale University Press, 2001), Louisa C. Matthew, and Lars R. Jones, eds., *Coming About . . . A Festschrift for John Shearman* (Cambridge, MA: Harvard University Art Museums, 2001).

45 On Bandinelli, see Detlef Heikamp, and Beatriche Paolozzi Strozzi, eds., *Baccio Bandinelli. Scultore e maestro (1493-1560)* (Florence: Giunti, 2014), Louis A. Waldman, *Baccio Bandinelli and Art at the Medici Court* (Philadelphia: American Philosophical Society, 2004), Virginia L. Bush, "Bandinelli's 'Hercules and Cacus' and Florentine Traditions," *Memoirs of the American Academy in Rome* 35 (1980): 163–206.

46 On Cellini, see, with further leads therein, Benvenuto Cellini, *Autobiography*, trans. George Bull (New York: Penguin, 1999), Christine Corretti, *Cellini's Perseus and Medusa and the Loggia dei Lanzi. Configurations of the Body of State* (Leiden: Brill, 2015), Margaret A. Gallucci, and Paolo L. Rossi, eds., *Benvenuto Cellini: Sculptor, Goldsmith, Writer* (Cambridge: Cambridge University Press, 2004), John Pope-Hennessy, *Cellini* (London: Macmillan, 1985).

47 On these portraits, see Carl B. Strehlke, ed., *Pontormo, Bronzino, and the Medici: The Transformation of the Renaissance Portrait in Florence* (Philadelphia: Philadelphia Museum of Art, 2004), Andrea M. Gáldy, ed., *Agnolo Bronzino: Medici Court Artist in Context* (Newcastle upon Tyne: Cambridge Scholars Publishing, 2013), Dana V. Hogan, "Constructing the Image of a Cardinal-Prince: Child Portraits of Giovanni de' Medici by Bronzino and Salviati," *Comitatus: A Journal of Medieval and Renaissance Studies* 50, no. 1 (2019): 139–75, Langdon, *Medici Women*. On the importance of clothing see Megan Moran, "Young Women Negotiating Fashion in Early Modern Florence," in *The Youth of Early Modern Women*, ed. Elizabeth S. Cohen and Margaret Reeves (Toronto: CRRS, 2018), 179–94. More generally, see Konrad Eisenbichler, ed., *The Cultural Politics of Duke Cosimo I de' Medici* (Aldershot: Ashgate, 2001), Veen, *Cosimo I de' Medici and his Self-Representation in Florentine Art and Culture*. A new study, Keith Christiansen, and Carlo Falciani, eds., *The Medici: Portraits and Politics, 1512-1570* (New Haven: Yale University Press, 2021), appeared too late to be included in this book.

48 On Vasari's frescoes, see Eisenbichler, *The Cultural Politics of Duke Cosimo I de' Medici*, Veen, *Cosimo I de' Medici and his Self-Representation in Florentine Art and Culture*, Ugo Muccini, *Il Salone dei Cinquecento in*

Palazzo Vecchio (Florence: Le Lettere, 1990). Donatella Fratini, "Due disegni di Giorgio Vasari provenienti dall'eredità del cavalier Francesco Maria Vasari per il Salone dei Cinquecento in Palazzo Vecchio," *Mitteilungen des Kunsthistorischen Institutes in Florenz* 57, no. 3 (2015): 350–60.

49 Gregory Murry, *The Medicean Succession: Monarchy and Sacral Politics in Duke Cosimo dei Medici's Florence* (Cambridge, MA: Harvard University Press, 2014).

50 On the Brutus bust, see the articles by D. J. Gordon and Thomas Martin in Wallace, *Michelangelo. Selected Scholarship in English*, vol. 4, 159–76 and 77–93.

51 Dall'Aglio, *The Duke's Assassin*.

52 Contini, in *Politics and Diplomacy in Early Modern Italy*, 57 and 63. Najemy, *A History of Florence, 1200-1575*, 468. On the Italian Wars more generally, see Mallett and Shaw, *The Italian Wars, 1494-1559*, Fletcher, *The Beauty and the Terror*.

53 Contini, in *Politics and Diplomacy in Early Modern Italy*, 71–5. Najemy, *A History of Florence, 1200-1575*, 482–5, Mallett and Shaw, *The Italian Wars, 1494-1559*, esp. 248–55.

54 Contini, in *Politics and Diplomacy in Early Modern Italy*.

55 On the Uffizi, see Roger J. Crum, "'Cosmos, the World of Cosimo': The Iconography of the Uffizi Façade," *The Art Bulletin* 71, no. 2 (1989): 237–53, Leon Satkowski, and Roger J. Crum, "On the Iconography of the Uffizi Façade," *The Art Bulletin* 72, no. 1 (1990): 131–35, Lindsay Alberts, "Francesco I's Museum. Cultural Politics at the Galleria degli Uffizi," *Journal of the History of Collections* 30, no. 2 (2018): 203–16, Paula Findlen, "The Eighteenth-Century Invention of the Renaissance: Lessons from the Uffizi," *Renaissance Quarterly* 66, no. 1 (2013): 1–34., Paola Barocchi, and Giovanna Ragionieri, eds., *Gli Uffizi: Quattro secoli di una galleria*, 2 vols. (Florence: Leo S. Olschki, 1983). See also Cochrane, *Florence in the Forgotten Centuries, 1527-1800*, 107, Balchin, *Urban Development in Renaissance Italy*, 297–8.

56 Paul N. Balchin, *Urban Development in Renaissance Italy* (Chichester: John Wiley & Sons, 2008), 298–9. For more information, see Francesca Funis, *Il Corridoio vasariano. Una strada sopra la città* (Florence: Sillabe, 2018).

57 Balchin, *Urban Development in Renaissance Italy*. For more details, see Franco Borsi, *Firenze del Cinquecento* (Rome: Editalia, 1974), Giorgio Spini, *Architettura e politica da Cosimo I a Ferdinando I* (Florence: Leo S. Olschki, 1976).

58 On these relationships, see Kathleen Comerford, *Jesuit Foundations and Medici Power, 1532-1621* (Leiden: Brill, 2016). Plaisance, *Florence in the Time of the Medici*, 141–73. See also Abigail Sarah Brundin, and Matthew Treherne, eds., *Forms of Faith in Sixteenth-Century Italy* (Aldershot: Ashgate,

2009), Najemy, *A History of Florence, 1200-1575*, 481–2, Stephen J.
Campbell, "Counter Reformation Polemic and Mannerist Counter-Aesthetics:
Bronzino's 'Martyrdom of St. Lawrence' in San Lorenzo," *RES: Anthropology
and Aesthetics* 46 (2004): 98–119, Butters, "Conflicting Attitudes towards
Machiavelli's Works in Sixteenth-Century Spain, Rome, and Florence," 79.
Murphy, *Murder of a Medici Princess*, 71–2.

59 Tazzara, *The Free Port of Livorno and the Transformation of the
Mediterranean World*. See also Bregoli, *Mediterranean Enlightenment*.

60 On Florence's early modern reputation, see Sarah Gwyneth Ross, "New
Perspectives on *Patria*. The Adreini Performance of Florentine Citizenship,"
in *Florence in the Early Modern World. New Perspectives*, ed. Nicholas Scott
Baker and Brian Jeffrey Maxson (London: Routledge, 2020), 236–55. Ann
E. Moyer, *The Intellectual World of Sixteenth-Century Florence* (Cambridge:
Cambridge University Press, 2020).

61 On this text, see Marco Ruffini, "Sixteenth-Century Paduan Annotations to
the First Edition of Vasari's Vite (1550)," *Renaissance Quarterly* 62, no. 3
(2009): 748–808, Marco Ruffini, *Art Without an Author: Vasari's Lives and
Michelangelo's Death* (New York: Fordham University Press, 2011), Marco
Ruffini, "Per la genesi delle "Vite." Il quaderno di Yale," *Mitteilungen des
Kunsthistorischen Institutes in Florenz* 58, no. 3 (2016): 376–401, David J.
Cast, ed., *The Ashgate Companion to Giorgio Vasari* (Farnham: Ashgate,
2014), Philip Jacks, ed., *Vasari's Florence: Artists and Literati at the Medicean
Court* (Cambridge: Cambridge University Press, 1998).

62 Brackett, *Criminal Justice and Crime in Late Renaissance Florence, 1537-
1609*. See also Giovanna Benadusi, *A Provincial Elite in Early Modern
Tuscany: Family and Power in the Creation of the State* (Baltimore: Johns
Hopkins University Press, 1996).

63 Albinia de la Mare, "New Research on Humanistic Scribes in Florence," in
Miniatura fiorentina del Rinascimento 1440-1525, ed. Annarosa Garzelli, vol.
1 (Florence: Giunta Regionale Toscana, 1985), 393–600, Albinia de la Mare,
The Handwriting of Italian Humanists (Oxford: Oxford University Press,
1973).

64 On Vespasiano, see Albinia Catherine de la Mare, "Vespasiano da Bisticci,
Historian and Bookseller" (Dissertation, University of London, 1966),
Giuseppe M. Cagni, *Vespasiano da Bisticci e il suo epistolario* (Rome: Edizioni
di Storia e Letteratura, 1969), Maxson, *The Humanist World of Renaissance
Florence*.

65 Brian Richardson, *Print Culture in Renaissance Italy* (Cambridge: Cambridge
University Press, 1994); On the introduction of print, the continuation of
manuscript culture, and related themes see Brian Richardson, *Manuscript
Culture in Renaissance Italy* (Cambridge: Cambridge University Press,

2009), Angela Nuovo, *The Book Trade in the Italian Renaissance*, trans. Lydia G. Cochrane (Leiden: Brill, 2013). Brian Richardson, *Printing, Writers and Readers in Renaissance Italy* (Cambridge: Cambridge University Press, 1999). D. E. Rhodes, ed., *La stampa a Firenze (1471-1550). Omaggio a Roberto Ridolfi* (Florence: Leo S. Olschki, 1984), D. E. Rhodes et al., "Note e discussioni. La stampa a Firenze (1471-1550). Omaggio a Roberto Ridolfi," *La Bibliofilia* 87, no. 1 (1985): 59–64, Roberto Ridolfi, *La stampa in Firenze nel secolo xv* (Florence: Leo S. Olschki, 1958).

66 Celenza, *The Intellectual World of the Italian Renaissance*, with further leads therein. Moyer, *The Intellectual World of Sixteenth-Century Florence*.

67 Najemy, *A History of Florence, 1200-1575*, 481.

68 Cochrane, *Florence in the Forgotten Centuries, 1527-1800*, 67–73. On Pier Vettori, most recently, with further leads, Davide Baldi, *Il greco a Firenze e Pier Vettori (1499-1585)* (Alessandria: Edizioni dell'Orso, 2014).

69 Brian Richardson, *Print Culture in Renaissance Italy: The Editor and the Vernacular Text, 1470-1600* (Cambridge: Cambridge University Press, 1994), Cochrane, *Florence in the Forgotten Centuries, 1527-1800*, 69, Jonathan Davies, *Culture and Power. Tuscany and its Universities 1537-1609* (Leiden: Brill, 2009).

70 Richardson, *Print Culture in Renaissance Italy*. On these literary debates, as a start see Celenza, *The Intellectual World of the Italian Renaissance*.

71 Sean Roberts, *Printing a Mediterranean World: Florence, Constantinople, and the Renaissance of Geography* (Cambridge, MA: Harvard University Press, 2013), with further leads therein. See also Margolis, *The Politics of Culture in Quattrocento Europe*.

72 On Columbus and Toscanelli, see John Larner, "The Church and the Quattrocento Renaissance in Geography," *Renaissance Studies* 12, no. 1 (1998): 26–39, Edgerton, *Pictures and Punishment*. Eric Apfelstadt, "Christopher Columbus, Paolo dal Pozzo Toscanelli and Fernão de Roriz: New Evidence for a Florentine Connection," *Nuncius* 7, no. 2 (1992): 69–80. Although largely accepted as authentic, some historians dispute Toscanelli's influence. See Miles H. Davidson, "The Toscanelli Letters: A Dubious Influence on Columbus," *Colonial Latin American Historical Review* 5, no. 3 (1996): 287–310. Toscanelli was friends with Leon Battista Alberti, see Grafton, *Leon Battista Alberti*.

73 On Vespucci, see Giuliano Pinto, Leonardo Rombai, and Claudia Tripodi, eds., *Vespucci, Firenze e le Americhe* (Florence: Leo S. Olschki, 2014), Davide Baldi, "The Young Amerigo Vespucci's Latin Exercises," *Humanistica Lovaniensia* 65 (2016): 39–48, Lia Markey, *Imagining the Americas in Medici Florence* (University Park, Pennyslvania: Penn State University Press, 2016).

74 Mark Rosen, *The Mapping of Power in Renaissance Italy* (Cambridge: Cambridge University Press, 2015), 106–12.

75 On Florence and the New World, see Markey, *Imagining the Americas in Medici Florence*. More generally, see Elizabeth Horodowich, and Lia Markey, eds., *The New World in Early Modern Italy, 1492-1750* (Cambridge: Cambridge University Press, 2017).

76 Brian Brege, "The Advantages of Stability: Medici Tuscany's Ambitions in the Eastern Mediterranean," in *Florence in the Early Modern World. New Perspectives*, ed. Nicholas Scott Baker and Brian Jeffrey Maxson (London: Routledge, 2020), 142–55.

77 Cavallo and Storey, *Healthy Living in late Renaissance Italy*, 94–103; see also Strocchia, *Forgotten Healers. Women and the Pursuit of Health in Late Renaissance Italy*.

78 Henderson, *Florence under Siege*.

79 Hannah Marcus, *Forbidden Knowledge: Medicine, Science, and Censorship in Early Modern Italy* (Chicago: University of Chicago Press, 2020).

EPILOGUE, 1575–PRESENT

1 J. R. Hale, *Florence and the Medici* (London: Phoenix, 1977), 149–51. On the Florentine silk industry more generally, see Goldthwaite, *The Economy of Renaissance Florence*.

2 Marta Caroscio, "Shaping the City and the Landscape: Politics, Public Space, and Innovation under Ferdinando I de' Medici," in *Florence in the Early Modern World. New Perspectives*, ed. Nicholas Scott Baker and Brian Jeffrey Maxson (London: Routledge, 2020), 92–113.

3 Contini, in *Politics and Diplomacy in Early Modern Italy*, 86–94.

4 David Parrott, "Richelieu, Mazarin and Italy (1635-59): Statesmanship in Context," in *Secretaries and Statecraft in the Early Modern World*, ed. Paul Dover (Edinburgh: Edinburgh University Press, 2016), 155–76. Gregory Hanlon, *Italy 1636. Cemetery of Armies* (Oxford: Oxford University Press, 2016). More generally, see John A. Marino, ed., *Early Modern Italy 1550-1796* (Oxford: Oxford University Press, 2002), Gregory Hanlon, *Early Modern Italy, 1550-1800* (New York: St. Martin's Press, 2000).

5 Hale, *Florence and the Medici*, 179–84, Cochrane, *Florence in the Forgotten Centuries, 1527-1800*.

6 The literature on Galileo is vast. As a start, Maurice A. Finocchiaro, *The Trial of Galileo. Essential Documents* (Indianapolis: Hackett Publishing Company, 2014).

7 On the Piazza di SS. Annunziata and its church, see Valeria Tomasi, "L'organizzazione dei cantieri in epoca rinascimentale: I loggiati su Piazza SS. Annunziata a Firenze," *Mélanges de l'Ecole française de Rome* 119, no. 2 (2007): 299–319, Marcello Fantoni, "Il culto dell'Annunziata e la sacralità del

potere mediceo," *Archivio storico italiano* 147, no. 4 (1989): 513–69, Suzanne B. Butters, "Ferdinando de' Medici and the Art of the Possible," in *The Medici, Michelangelo, and the Art of Late Renaissance Florence* (New Haven: Yale University Press), 72, C. Sisi, *La Basilica della Santissima Annunziata dal duecento al cinquecento* (Florence: Pacini, 2013), Borsook, *The Companion Guide to Florence*, 212–16.

8 Balchin, *Urban Development in Renaissance Italy*, 441–2.

9 See Hale, *Florence and the Medici*, 185–91, Cochrane, *Florence in the Forgotten Centuries, 1527-1800*, Litchfield, *Emergence of a Bureaucracy*. See also Marcello Verga, "Between Dynastic Strategies and Civic Myth: Anna Maria Luisa de' Medici and Florence as the New Athens," in *Medici Women: The Making of a Dynasty in Grand Ducal Tuscany*, ed. Giovanna Benadusi and Judith C. Brown (Toronto: CRRS, 2015), 347–71.

10 Stefano Casciu, "Anna Maria Luisa, Electress Palatine: Last Art Patron and Collector of the Medici Dynasty," in *Medici Women: The Making of a Dynasty in Grand Ducal Tuscany*, ed. Giovanna Benadusi and Judith C. Brown (Toronto: CRRS, 2015), 323–46. Verga, in *Medici Women*.

11 Cochrane, *Florence in the Forgotten Centuries, 1527-1800*, Litchfield, *Emergence of a Bureaucracy*, Harry Hearder, *Italy in the Age of the Risorgimento 1790-1870* (London: Routledge, 2013).

12 Hearder, *Italy in the Age of the Risorgimento 1790-1870*.

13 Gene Brucker, *Renaissance Florence*, Rev. ed. (Berkeley: University of California Press, 1983), 8. For more details on this period, see Monika Poettinger, and Piero Rogg, eds., *Florence. Capital of the Kingdom of Italy, 1865-71* (London: Bloomsbury, 2018), Franco Borsi, *La capitale a Firenze e l'opera di G. Poggi* (Bologna: Colombo, 1970). But the literature is vast.

14 On this event, see Mahnaz Yousefzadeh, "Anti-Hegemonic Nationalism: The Dante Centenary of 1865," in *Power, Gender, and Ritual in Europe and the Americas*, ed. Peter Arnade and Michael Rocke (Toronto: CRRS, 2008), 339–52. Guy P. Raffa, "Bones of Contention: Ravenna's and Florence's Claims to Dante's Remains," *Italica* 92, no. 3 (2015): 565–81. See also Borsook, *The Companion Guide to Florence*.

15 On Florence and Italy in the Second World War, see, as a start, Tom Behan, *The Italian Resistance. Fascists, Guerrillas and the Allies* (London: Pluto Press, 2009), 85–92, Victoria C. Belco, *War, Massacre, and Recovery in Central Italy 1943-1948* (Toronto: University of Toronto Press, 2010), Philip Morgan, *The Fall of Mussolini* (Oxford: Oxford University Press, 2007).

16 On this flood and its aftermath, see Paul Conway and Martha O'Hara Conway, eds., *Flood in Florence, 1966: A Fifty-Year Retrospective* (Ann Arbor: Michigan Publishing, University of Michigan Library, 2018). This title is available in open-access format at *Flood in Florence, 1966: A Fifty-Year Retrospective*, hosted by the University of Michigan (accessed April 9, 2021).

17 Molho, "The Closing of the Florentine Archive," Brucker, "The Uffizi Archives, 1952-1987."

18 As reported at worldpopulationreview.com, based upon data compiled by the United Nations. See https://worldpopulationreview.com/world-cities/florence -population (accessed April 1, 2021).

19 As reported by worlddata.info. See https://www.worlddata.info/europe/italy/ tourism.php (accessed April 1, 2021).

Bibliography

Aberth, John, ed. *The Black Death, the Great Mortality of 1348–1350: A Brief History with Documents*. 2nd ed. Boston: Bedford/St. Martin's, 2016.

Abulafia, David. "Charles of Anjou Reassessed." *Journal of Medieval History* 26, no. 1 (2000): 93–114.

Abulafia, David, ed. *The French Descent into Renaissance Italy, 1494–95: Antecedents and Effects*. London: Routledge, 1995.

Abulafia, David. *The Great Sea: A Human History of the Mediterranean*. Oxford: Oxford University Press, 2011.

Ahl, Diane Cole. *Benozzo Gozzoli*. New Haven: Yale University Press, 1996.

Aiazzi, Giuseppe. *Ricordi storici di Filippo di Cino Rinuccini dal 1282 al 1460 colla continuazione di Alamanno e Neri, suoi figli, fino al 1506, seguiti da altri monumenti inediti di storia patria estratti dai codici originali e preceduti dalla Storia genealogica. . . .* Florence: Stamperia Piatti, 1840.

Aïm, Roger. *Le Dôme de Florence: Paradigme du projet*. Sarbonne: Hermann, 2010.

Akopyan, Ovanes. *Debating the Stars in the Italian Renaissance*. Leiden: Brill, 2020.

Alberti, Leon Battista. *The Family in Renaissance Florence*. Translated by Renee Neu Watkins. Long Grove, IL: Waveland Press, 1969.

Alberts, Lindsay. "Francesco I's Museum. Cultural Politics at the Galleria degli Uffizi." *Journal of the History of Collections* 30, no. 2 (2018): 203–16.

Alighieri, Dante. *Monarchy*. Cambridge: Cambridge University Press, 1996.

Allan, Judith. "Lorenzo's Star and Savonarola's Serpent: Changing Representations of Simonetta Cattaneo Vespucci." *Italian Studies* 69, no. 1 (2014): 4–23.

Allan, Judith. "Simonetta Cattaneo Vespucci: Beauty, Politics, Literature and Art in Early Renaissance Florence." Dissertation, University of Birmingham, 2014.

Allen, Michael J.B., and Valery Rees, eds. *Marsilio Ficino: His Theology, His Philosophy, His Legacy*. Leiden: Brill, 2002.

Andreoni, Annalisa. *La via della dottrina: Le lezioni accademiche di Benedetto Varchi*. Pisa: ETS, 2012.

Angiolini, F. "Slaves and Slavery in Early Modern Tuscany." *Journal of Italian History and Culture* 3 (1997): 67–86.

Apfelstadt, Eric. "Christopher Columbus, Paolo dal Pozzo Toscanelli and Fernão de Roriz: New Evidence for a Florentine Connection." *Nuncius* 7, no. 2 (1992): 69–80.

Arasse, Daniel, and Pierluigi De Vecchi, eds. *Botticelli: From Lorenzo the Magnificent to Savonarola*. Milan: Skira, 2003.

Armstrong, Guyda, Riannon Daniels, and Stephen J. Milner. *The Cambridge Companion to Boccaccio*. Cambridge: Cambridge University Press, 2015.

Ascoli, Albert Russell, ed. *Cambridge Companion to Petrarch*. Cambridge: Cambridge University Press, 2015.

Atkinson, Niall. *The Noisy Renaissance: Sound, Architecture, and Florentine Urban Life*. University Park: Pennsylvania State University Press, 2017.

Baker, Nicholas Scott. "Discursive Republicanism in Renaissance Florence: Deliberation and Representation in the Early Sixteenth Century." *Past & Present* 225 (2014): 47–77.

Baker, Nicholas Scott. *The Fruit of Liberty: Political Culture in the Florentine Renaissance, 1480–1550*. Cambridge, MA: Harvard University Press, 2013.

Baker, Nicholas Scott. "When Christ Was King in Florence: Religious Language and Political Paralysis during the Siege of Florence, 1529–30." In *Languages of Power in Italy (1300–1600)*, edited by Daniel Bornstein, Laura Gaffuri, and Brian Jeffrey Maxson, 215–18. Turnhout: Brepols, 2017.

Baker-Bates, Piers, and Irene Brooke, eds. *Portrait Cultures of the Early Modern Cardinal*. Amsterdam: Amsterdam University Press, 2021.

Balchin, Paul N. *Urban Development in Renaissance Italy*. Chichester: John Wiley & Sons, 2008.

Baldassarri, Stefano U., ed. *Dignitas et excellentia hominis*. Florence: Le Lettere, 2008.

Baldassarri, Stefano U. "Reflections on Manetti's e Dignitate' and his 'Vita Nicolai V.'" *Rivista di Letteratura Storiografica Italiana* 1 (2017): 31–45.

Baldassarri, Stefano U., and Fabrizio Lelli, eds. *Umanesimo e cultura ebraica nel Rinascimento italiano*. Florence: Angelo Pontecorboli, 2016.

Baldassarri, Stefano U., and Brian Jeffrey Maxson. "Giannozzo Manetti's Oratio in funere Iannotii Pandolfini: Art, Humanism and Politics in Fifteenth-Century Florence." *Interpres* 34 (2016): 79–142.

Baldassarri, Stefano U., and Brian Jeffrey Maxson. "Giannozzo Manetti, the Emperor, and the Praise of a King in 1452." *Archivio storico italiano* 172, no. 3 (2014): 513–69.

Baldassarri, Stefano U., and Arielle Siber, eds. *Images of Quattrocento Florence.* New Haven: Yale University Press, 2000.

Baldi, Davide. *Il greco a Firenze e Pier Vettori (1499–1585).* Alessandria: Edizioni dell'Orso, 2014.

Baldi, Davide. "The Young Amerigo Vespucci's Latin Exercises." *Humanistica Lovaniensia* 65 (2016): 39–48.

Balestracci, Duccio. *La battaglia di Montaperti.* Rome: Laterza, 2017.

Baransky, Zygmunt G., and Lino Pertile, eds. *Dante in Context.* Cambridge: Cambridge University Press, 2015.

Barocchi, Paola, and Giovanna Ragionieri, eds. *Gli Uffizi: Quattro secoli di una galleria.* Florence: Leo S. Olschki, 1983.

Barsanti, Roberta, Gianluca Belli, Emanuela Ferretti, and Cecilia Forsinini, eds. *La Sala Grande di Palazzo Vecchio e la Battaglia di Anghiari di Leonardo da Vinci.* Florence: Leo S. Olschki, 2019.

Bartoli, Maria Teresa. "Designing Orsanmichele: The Rediscovered Rule." In *Orsanmichele and the History and Preservation of the Civic Monument,* edited by Carl Brandon Strehlke, 35–52. New Haven: Yale University Press, 2012.

Barzman, Karen-Edis. "Islamic North Africa in Trecento Italy: Costume in the Assisi and Bardi Chapel Frescoes of Francis in Egypt." In *Power, Gender, and Ritual in Europe and the Americas,* edited by Peter Arnade and Michael Rocke, 29–51. Toronto: CRRS, 2008.

Bausi, Francesco. "The Medici: Defenders of Liberty in Fifteenth-Century Florence." In *The Medici: Citizens and Masters,* edited by Robert Black and John E. Law, 239–51. Villa I Tatti: Sheridan Books, 2015.

Baxendale, Susannah Foster. "Alberti Kinship and Conspiracy in Late Medieval Florence." In *Florence and Beyond: Culture, Society and Politics in Renaissance Italy,* edited by David S. Peterson and Daniel E. Bornstein, 339–53. Toronto: CRRS, 2008.

Baxendale, Susannah Foster. "Exile in Practice: The Alberti Family In and Out of Florence 1401–1428." *Renaissance Quarterly* 44, no. 4 (1991): 720–56.

Bayley, C C. *War and Society in Renaissance Florence: The De Militia of Leonardo Bruni.* Toronto: University of Toronto Press, 1961.

Bec, Christian. "Il Mito di Firenze da Dante al Ghiberti." In *Lorenzo Ghiberti nel suo Tempo: Atti del Convegno Internazionale di Studi*, vol. 1, 3–26. Florence: Leo S. Olschki, 1980.

Beck, James. "Ghiberti Giovane e Donatello Giovanissimo." In *Lorenzo Ghiberti nel suo Tempo: Atti del Convegno Internazionale di Studi*, vol. 1, 111–34. Florence: Leo S. Olschki, 1980.

Becker, Marvin B. *Florence in Transition*. 2 vols. Baltimore: Johns Hopkins University Press, 1967–68.

Behan, Tom. *The Italian Resistance. Fascists, Guerrillas and the Allies*. London: Pluto Press, 2009.

Belcari, Feo. *Lettere*. Florence: Il Magheri, 1825.

Belco, Victoria C. *War, Massacre, and Recovery in Central Italy 1943–1948*. Toronto: University of Toronto Press, 2010.

Bell, Rudolph M. "Renaissance Sexuality and the Florentine Archives: An Exchange." *Renaissance Quarterly* 40, no. 3 (1987): 485–511.

Bellosi, Luciano. *Cimabue*. New York: Abbeville Press, 1998.

Belozerskaya, Marina. *Rethinking the Renaissance: Burgundian Arts across Europe*. Cambridge: Cambridge University Press, 2002.

Beluzzi, Amedeo. "Il gonfaloniere Soderini nel Palazzo dei Signori." In *La Sala Grande di Palazzo Vecchio e la Battaglia di Anghiari di Leonardo da Vinci*, edited by Roberta Barsanti, Gianluca Belli, Emanuela Ferretti, and Cecilia Fosinini, 205–22. Florence: Leo S. Olschki, 2019.

Benadusi, Giovanna. *A Provincial Elite in Early Modern Tuscany: Family and Power in the Creation of the State*. Baltimore: Johns Hopkins University Press, 1996.

Benadusi, Giovanna, and Judith C. Brown, eds. *Medici Women: The Making of a Dynasty in Grand Ducal Tuscany*. Toronto: CRRS, 2015.

Bent, George R. *Public Painting and Visual Culture in Early Republican Florence*. Cambridge: Cambridge University Press, 2016.

Bergstein, Mary. "Marian Politics in Quattrocento Florence: The Renewed Dedication of Santa Maria del Fiore in 1412." *Renaissance Quarterly* 44, no. 4 (1991): 673–719.

Bettarini, Francesco. "Petracco dall'Incisa." In *Dizionario Biografico degli Italiani*, vol. 82, 2015. Accessed online at https://www.treccani .it/enciclopedia/petracco-dall-incisa_(Dizionario-Biografico) (July 11, 2022).

Billanovich, Giuseppe. *I primi umanisti e le tradizioni dei classici latini*. Fribourg: Edizioni universitarie, 1953.

Billanovich, Giuseppe. *La tradizione del testo di Livio e le origini dell' umanesimo*. 2 vols. Padua: Antenore, 1981.

Bisticci, Vespasiano da. *Le Vite*. Edited by Aulo Greco. 2 Vols. Florence: Istituto Nazionale di Studi sul Rinascimento, 1976.

Bisticci, Vespasiano da. *Renaissance Princes, Popes, and Prelates*. New York: Harper & Row, 1963.

Black, Jane. *Absolutism in Renaissance Milan: Plenitude of Power under the Visconti and the Sforza 1329–1535*. Oxford: Oxford University Press, 2009.

Black, Robert. *Benedetto Accolti and the Florentine Renaissance*. Cambridge: Cambridge University Press, 1985.

Black, Robert. *Education and Society in Florentine Tuscany*. Leiden: Brill, 2007.

Black, Robert. *Machiavelli*. London: Routledge, 2013.

Black, Robert, and John Law, eds. *The Medici: Citizens and Masters*. Villa I Tatti: Sheridan Books, 2015.

Blanchfield, Lyn A. "Le Piagnoni: The Weeping Women of Savonarola." In *Power, Gender, and Ritual in Europe and the Americas*, edited by Peter Arnade and Michael Rocke, 53–76. Toronto: CRRS, 2008.

Bloch, Amy R. "A Note on the Movement of Michelangelo's *David*." In *The Art and Language of Power in Renaissance Florence: Essays for Alison Brown*, edited by Amy R. Bloch, Carolyn James, and Camilla Russell, 205–19. Toronto: CRRS, 2019.

Blumenthal, Uta-Renate. *The Investiture Controversy: Church and Monarchy from the Ninth to the Twelfth Century*. Philadelphia: University of Pennsylvania Press, 1988.

Boccaccio, Giovanni. *The Decameron*. Translated by G.H. McWilliam. 2nd ed. London: Penguin Books, 1995.

Boccaccio, Giovanni. *Famous Women*. Edited by Virginia Brown. Cambridge, MA: Harvard University Press, 2001.

Boccaccio, Giovanni. *Genealogy of the Pagan Gods*. 2 vols. Cambridge, MA: Harvard University Press, 2011–2017.

Boffa, David. "Divine Illumination and the Portrayal of the Miraculous in Donatello's St. Louis of Toulouse." *Simiolus: Netherlands Quarterly for the History of Art* 31, no. 4 (2004–2005): 279–91.

Böninger, Lorenz. *Die deutsche Einwanderung nach Florenz im Spätmittelalter*. Leiden: Brill, 2006.

Borsi, Franco. *Firenze del Cinquecento*. Rome: Editalia, 1974.

Borsi, Franco. *La capitale a Firenze e l'opera di G. Poggi*. Bologna: Colombo, 1970.

Borsook, Eve. *The Companion Guide to Florence*. *Sixth* Revised ed. Rochester, NY: Companion Guides, 1997.

Boschetto, Luca. "L'esilio volontario di Manetti." In *Dignitas et excellentia hominis*, edited by Stefano U. Baldassarri, 117–45. Florence: Le Lettere, 2008.

Boschetto, Luca. "Writing the Vernacular at the Merchant Court of Florence." In *Textual Cultures of Medieval Italy: Essays from the 41st Conference on Editorial Problems*, edited by William Robins, 217–62. Toronto: University of Toronto Press, 2011.

Bowsky, William. *Henry VII in Italy: The Conflict of Empire and City-State, 1310–1313*. Lincoln: University of Nebraska Press, 1960.

Brackett, John K. *Criminal Justice and Crime in Late Renaissance Florence, 1537–1609*. Cambridge: Cambridge University Press, 1992.

Brackett, John K. "Race and Rulership: Alessandro de' Medici, First Medici Duke of Florence, 1529–1537." In *Black Africans in Renaissance Europe*, edited by T.F. Earle and K.J.P. Lowe, 303–25. Cambridge: Cambridge University Press, 2005.

Branca, Vittore, ed. *Merchant Writers: Florentine Memoirs from the Middle Ages and Renaissance*. Translated by Murtha Baca. Toronto: University of Toronto Press, 2015.

Brancato, Dario. ""Narrar la sustanzia in poche parole." Cosimo I e Baccio Baldini correttori della *Storia fiorentina* di Benedetto Varchi." *Giornale Italiano di Filologia* 67 (2015): 323–33.

Brancato, Dario, and Salvatore Lo Re. "Per una nuova edizione della 'Storia' del Varchi: Il problema storico e testuale." *Annali della Scuola Normale Superiore di Pisa. Classe di Lettere e Filosofia Series 5* 7, no. 1 (2015): 201–31 and 71–72.

Brandolini, Aurelio Lippo. *Republics and Kingdoms Compared*. Edited and translated by James Hankins. Cambridge, MA: Harvard University Press, 2009.

Brege, Brian. "The Advantages of Stability: Medici Tuscany's Ambitions in the Eastern Mediterranean." In *Florence in the Early Modern World. New Perspectives*, edited by Nicholas Scott Baker and Brian Jeffrey Maxson, 142–55. London: Routledge, 2020.

Bregoli, Francesca. *Mediterranean Enlightenment: Livornese Jews, Tuscan Culture, and Eighteenth-Century Reform*. Stanford: Stanford University Press, 2014.

Brown, Alison, ed. *Bartolomeo Scala Humanistic and Political Writings*. Tempe, AZ: Medieval & Renaissance Texts & Studies, 1997.

Brown, Alison. *Bartolomeo Scala, 1430–1497, Chancellor of Florence: The Humanist as Bureaucrat*. Princeton: Princeton University Press, 1979.

Brown, Alison. "De-Masking Renaissance Republicanism." In *Medicean and Savonarolan Florence: The Interplay of Politics, Humanism, and Religion*, edited by Alison Brown, 225–46. Turnhout: Brepols, 2011.

Brown, Alison. "The Guelf Party in Fifteenth-Century Florence." In *The Medici in Florence: The Exercise and Language of Power*, edited by Alison Brown, 103–50. Florence: Leo S. Olschki, 1992.

Brown, Alison. "The Humanist Portrait of Cosimo de' Medici, Pater Patriae." *Journal of Warburg and Courtald Institutes* 24, no. 3/4 (1961): 186–221.

Brown, Alison. "Ideology and Faction in Savonarolan Florence." In *The World of Savonarola: Italian Élites and Perceptions of Crisis*, edited by Sella Fletcher and Christine Shaw, 22–41. Aldershot: Ashgate, 2000.

Brown, Alison. "The Language of Empire." In *Florentine Tuscany*, edited by William J. Connell and Andrea Zorzi, 32–47. Cambridge: Cambridge University Press, 2000.

Brown, Alison. "Lorenzo and Public Opinion in Florence: The Problem of Oppositions." In *Medicean and Savonarolan Florence: The Interplay of Politics, Humanism, and Religion*, edited by Alison Brown, 87–111. Turhnout: Brepols, 2011.

Brown, Alison. "Lorenzo de' Medici's New Men and Their Mores." In *Medicean and Savonarolan Florence: The Interplay of Politics, Humanism, and Religion*, edited by Alison Brown, 1–38. Turnhout: Brepols, 2011.

Brown, Alison. "New Light on the Papal Condemnation on Pico's Theses." In *Medicean and Savonarolan Florence: The Interplay of Politics, Humanism, and Religion*, edited by Alison Brown, 263–78. Turnhout: Brepols, 2011.

Brown, Alison. *Piero di Lorenzo de' Medici and the Crisis of Renaissance Italy*. Cambridge: Cambridge University Press, 2020.

Brown, Alison. "Piero in Power, 1492–1494." In *The Medici. Citizens and Masters*, edited by Robert Black and John E. Law, 113–25. Florence: Villa I Tatti: Sheridan Books, 2015.

Brown, Alison. "Platonism in Fifteenth-Century Florence and Its Contribution to Early Modern Political Thought." *Journal of Modern History* 58, no. 2 (1986): 383–413.

Brown, Alison. *The Return of Lucretius to Renaissance Florence*. Cambridge, MA: Harvard University Press, 2010.

Brown, Alison. "The Revolution of 1494 in Florence and its Aftermath: A Reassessment." In *Italy in Crisis. 1494*, edited by Jane Everson and Diego Zancani, 13–40. Oxford: European Humanities Research Center, 2000.

Brown, Judith C. *Immodest Acts: The Life of a Lesbian Nun in Renaissance Italy*. Oxford: Oxford University Press, 1986.

Brucker, Gene. *The Civic World of Early Renaissance Florence*. Princeton: Princeton University Press, 1977.

Brucker, Gene. *Florence, the Golden Age, 1138–1737*. 1st paperback ed. New York: Abbeville Press, 1984.

Brucker, Gene. *Florentine Politics and Society 1343–1378*. Princeton: Princeton University Press, 1962.

Brucker, Gene. *Giovanni and Lusanna: Love and Marriage in Renaissance Florence*. Berkeley: University of California Press, 1986.

Brucker, Gene. *Renaissance Florence*. Rev. ed. Berkeley: University of California Press, 1983. Originally published in 1969.

Brucker, Gene, ed. *Two Memoirs of Renaissance Florence: The Diaries of Buonaccorso Pitti and Gregorio Dati*. Translated by Julia Martines. Long Grove, IL: Waveland Press Inc, 1991.

Brucker, Gene. "The Uffizi Archives, 1952–1987: A Personal Memoir." In *Florence and Beyond. Culture, Society and Politics in Renaissance Italy*, edited by David S. Peterson and Daniel E. Bornstein, 51–9. Toronto: CRRS, 2008.

Brundin, Abigail Sarah, and Matthew Treherne, eds. *Forms of Faith in Sixteenth-Century Italy*. Aldershot: Ashgate, 2009.

Bruni, Leonardo. *History of the Florentine People*. Translated by James Hankins. 3 vols. Cambridge, MA: Harvard University Press, 2001–2007.

Bruni, Leonardo. *Opere letterarie e politiche*. Edited by Paolo Viti. Torino: Unione tipografico-editrice torinese, 1996.

Bryce, Judith. "Les livres des Florentines: Reconsidering Women's Literacy in Quattrocento Florence." In *At the Margins: Minority Groups in Premodern Italy*, edited by Stephen J. Milner, 133–61. Minneapolis: University of Minnesota Press, 2005.

Bullard, Melissa Meriam. *Filippo Strozzi and the Medici: Favor & Finance in Sixteenth-Century Florence & Rome*. Cambridge: Cambridge University Press, 1980.

Bullard, Melissa Meriam. *Lorenzo il Magnifico: Image and Anxiety, Politics and Finance*. Florence: Leo S. Olschki, 1994.

Bullard, Melissa Meriam. "Renaissance Spirituality and the Ethical Dimensions of Church Reform in the Age of Savonarola: The Dilemma of Cardinal Marco Barbo." In *The World of Savonarola: Italian Èlites and Perceptions of Crisis*, edited by Stella Fletcher and Christine Shaw, 65–89. Aldershot: Ashgate, 2000.

Burckhardt, Jacob. *The Civilization of the Renaissance in Italy*. London: Penguin Books, 1990.

Burns, J.H. "Angelo da Vallombrosa and the Pisan Schism." In *The Church, the Councils, & Reform. The Legacy of the Fifteenth Century*, edited by

Gerald Christianson, Thomas M. Izbicki, and Christopher M. Bellitto, 194–211. Washington, DC: Catholic University Press, 2008.

Bush, Virginia L. "Bandinelli's 'Hercules and Cacus' and Florentine Traditions." *Memoirs of the American Academy in Rome* 35 (1980): 163–206.

Butterfield, Andrew. *The Sculptures of Andrea del Verrocchio.* New Haven: Yale University Press, 1997.

Butterfield, Andrew. "Verrocchio's Christ and St. Thomas: Chronology, Iconography and Political Context." *The Burlington Magazine* 134, no. 1069 (1992): 225–33.

Butters, Humfrey C. "Conflicting Attitudes towards Machiavelli's Works in Sixteenth-Century Spain, Rome, and Florence." In *Communes and Despots in Medieval and Renaissance Italy*, edited by John E. Law and Bernadette Paton, 75–87. Farnham: Ashgate, 2010.

Butters, Humfrey C. *Governors and Government in Early Sixteenth-Century Florence.* Oxford: Clarendon Press, 1985.

Butters, Suzanne B. "Ferdinando de' Medici and the Art of the Possible." In *The Medici, Michelangelo, and the Art of Late Renaissance Florence*, 67–75. New Haven: Yale University Press, 2002.

Butters, Suzanne B. "The Medici Dukes, *Comandati* and Pratolino: Forced Labour in Renaissance Florence." In *Communes and Despots in Medieval and Renaissance Italy*, edited by John E. Law and Bernadette Paton, 249–77. Farnham: Ashgate, 2010.

Cabrini, Anna Maria. "Machiavelli's *Florentine Histories*." In *The Cambridge Companion to Machiavelli*, edited by John M. Najemy, 128–43. Cambridge: Cambridge University Press, 2010.

Caferro, William. *Contesting the Renaissance.* Malden, MA: Wiley-Blackwell, 2011.

Caferro, William. *John Hawkwood: An English Mercenary in Fourteenth-Century Italy.* Baltimore: Johns Hopkins University Press, 2006.

Caferro, William. *Petrarch's War. Florence and the Black Death in Context.* Cambridge: Cambridge University Press, 2018.

Caglioti, Francesco. *Donatello e i Medici: Storia del "David" e della "Giuditta."* 2 vols. Florence: Leo S. Olschki, 2000.

Cagni, Giuseppe M. *Vespasiano da Bisticci e il suo epistolario.* Rome: Edizioni di Storia e Letteratura, 1969.

Calvi, Giulia, and Ricardo Spinelli, eds. *Le donne Medici nel sistema europeo delle corti.* Florence: Polistampa, 2008.

Camelliti, Vittoria. "La Misericordia *Domini* del Museo del Bigallo. Un *unicum* iconografico della pittura fiorentina dopa la Peste Nera?" *Studi di Storia dell'Arte* 26 (2015): 51–66.

Cameron, Euan. *Enchanted Europe: Superstition, Reason, and Religion, 1250–1750.* Oxford: Oxford University Press, 2011.

Cammelli, Giuseppe. *I dotti bizantini e le origini dell'umanesimo: Manuele Crisolora*, vol. 1. Florence: Le Monnier, 1941.

Campana, Lilia. "Sailing into Union: The Byzantine Naval Convoy for the Council of Ferrara-Florence (1438–1439)." *Dumbarton Oaks Papers* 73 (2019): 103–26.

Campbell, Caroline. *Love and Marriage in Renaissance Florence.* London: Paul Holberton Publishing, 2009.

Campbell, Stephen J. "Counter Reformation Polemic and Mannerist Counter-Aesthetics: Bronzino's "Martyrdom of St. Lawrence" in San Lorenzo." *RES: Anthropology and Aesthetics* 46 (2004): 98–119.

Camporeale, Giovannangelo. "Gli Etruschi di Firenze." In *Archeologia a Firenze: Città e Territorio*, edited by Valeria d'Aquino, Guido Guarducci, Silvia Nencetti, and Stefano Valentini, 39–54. Oxford: Archaeopress, 2015.

Cappozzo, Valerio, Martin Eisner, and Timothy Kircher, eds. *Boccaccio and His World.* A Special issue of *Heliotropia* , 2018.

Cariboni, Guido. "Symbolic Communication and Civic Values in Milan under the Early Visconti." In *Languages of Power in Italy (1300–1600)*, edited by Daniel Bornstein, Laura Gaffuri, and Brian Jeffrey Maxson, 65–76. Turnhout: Brepols, 2017.

Carlson, Raymond. "'Eccellentissimo poeta et amatore divinissimo': Benedetto Varchi and Michelangelo's Poetry at the Accademia Fiorentina." *Italian Studies* 69, no. 1–2 (2014): 169–88.

Carmichael, Ann G. *Plague and the Poor in Renaissance Florence.* Cambridge: Cambridge University Press, 1986.

Caroscio, Marta. "Shaping the City and the Landscape: Politics, Public Space, and Innovation under Ferdinando I de' Medici." In *Florence in the Early Modern World. New Perspectives*, edited by Nicholas Scott Baker and Brian Jeffrey Maxson, 92–113. London: Routledge, 2020.

Carpenter, Christine. *The War of the Roses: Politics and Constitution in England, c. 1437–1509.* Cambridge: Cambridge University Press, 2008.

Casciu, Stefano. "Anna Maria Luisa, Electress Palatine: Last Art Patron and Collector of the Medici Dynasty." In *Medici Women: The Making of a Dynasty in Grand Ducal Tuscany*, edited by Giovanna Benadusi and Judith C. Brown, 323–46. Toronto: CRRS, 2015.

Cassell, Anthony K. *The Monarchia Controversy.* Washington, DC: Catholic University Press, 2004.

Cassirer, Ernst, Paul Oskar Kristeller, and John Herman Randall Jr., eds. *The Renaissance Philosophy of Man*. Chicago: University of Chicago Press, 1948.

Cast, David J., ed. *The Ashgate Companion to Giorgio Vasari*. Farnham: Ashgate, 2014.

Casteen, Elizabeth. *From She-Wolf to Martyr: The Reign and Disputed Reputation of Johanna I of Naples*. Ithaca, NY: Cornell University Press, 2015.

Catani, Remo. "Astrological Polemics in the Crisis of the 1490s." In *Italy in Crisis. 1494*, edited by Jane Everson and Diego Zancani, 41–62. Oxford: European Humanities Research Centre, 2000.

Catellacci, Dante. "Diario di Felice Brancacci Ambasciatore con Carlo Federighi al Cairo per il comune di Firenze." *Archivio storico italiano Fourth Series* 8 (1881): 157–88.

Cavalli, Jennifer A. "The Learned Consort: Learning, Piety, and Female Political Authority in the Northern Courts." In *After Civic Humanism: Learning and Politics in Renaissance Italy*, edited by Nicholas Scott Baker and Brian Jeffrey Maxson, 173–92. Toronto: CRRS, 2015.

Cavallo, Sandra, and Tessa Storey. *Healthy Living in late Renaissance Italy*. Oxford: Oxford University Press, 2013.

Celati, Marta. "The Conflict after the Pazzi Conspiracy and Poliziano's 'Coniurationis commentarium': Literature, Law, and Politics." *Forum Italicum* 53, no. 2 (2019): 327–49.

Celenza, Christopher S. *The Intellectual World of the Italian Renaissance: Language, Philosophy, and the Search for Meaning*. Cambridge: Cambridge University Press, 2018.

Celenza, Christopher S. *Machiavelli: A Portrait*. Cambridge, MA: Harvard University Press, 2015.

Celenza, Christopher S. *Petrarch: Everywhere a Wanderer*. London: Reaktion Books, 2017.

Cellini, Benvenuto. *Autobiography*. Translated by George Bull. New York: Penguin, 1999.

Chiarini, M., ed. *Palazzo Pitti. L'arte e la storia*. Florence: Nardini, 2000.

Christiansen, Keith, and Carlo Falciani, eds. *The Medici: Portraits and Politics, 1512–1570*. New Haven: Yale University Press, 2021.

Christiansen, Keith, and Stefan Weppelmann, eds. *The Renaissance Portrait: From Donaello to Bellini*. New Haven: Yale University Press and the Metropolitan Museum of Art, 2011.

Cianferoni, Giuseppina Carlotta. "Florentia." In *Archeologia a Firenze: Città e Territorio*, edited by Valeria d'Aquino, Guido Guarducci, Silvia Nencetti, and Stefano Valentini, 55–70. Oxford: Archaeopress, 2015.

Ciappelli, Giovanni. "Forese da Rabatta." In *Dizionario Biografico degli Italiani*, vol. 48, 1997. Accessed online at https://www.treccani.it/enciclopedia/forese-da-rabatta_%28Dizionario-Biografico%29/ (accessed July 11, 2022).

Cicco, Giuseppe Gianluca. "Benedetto Accolti e la diplomazia fiorentina all'indomani della conquista turca di Constantinopoli." *Schola Salernitana* 10 (2005): 251–67.

Clarke, Paula. "The Villani Chronicles." In *Chronicling History: Chroniclers and Historians in Medieval and Renaissance Italy*, edited by Sharon Dale, Alison Williams Lewin, and Duane J. Osheim, 113–43. University Park: Pennsylvania State University Press, 2007.

Clarke, Paula C. *The Soderini and the Medici: Power and Patronage in Fifteenth-Century Florence*. Oxford: Clarendon Press, 1991.

Clearfield, Janis. "The Tomb of Cosimo de' Medici In San Lorenzo." *Rutgers Art Review* 2 (1981): 13–32.

Clucas, Stephen, Peter J. Forshaw, and Valery Rees, eds. *Laus platonici philosophi. Marsilio Ficino and his Influence*. Leiden: Brill, 2011.

Cochrane, Eric. *Florence in the Forgotten Centuries, 1527–1800. A History of Florence and the Florentines in the Age of the Grand Dukes*. Chicago: University of Chicago Press, 1973.

Cockram, Sarah D.P. *Isabella d'Este and Franceco Gonzaga. Power Sharing at the Italian Renaissance Court*. Farnham: Ashgate Publishing, 2013.

Cohn, Samuel Kline. *The Laboring Classes in Renaissance Florence*. New York: Academic Press, 1980.

Cole, Bruce. *Giotto and Florentine Painting 1280–1375*. New York: Harper & Row, 1976.

Cole, Bruce. *Giotto: The Scrovegni Chapel, Padua*. New York: George Braziller, 1993.

Coleman, James K., and Andrea Moudares, eds. *Luigi Pulci in Renaissance Florence*. Turnhout: Brepols, 2018.

Comerford, Kathleen. *Jesuit Foundations and Medici Power, 1532–1621*. Leiden: Brill, 2016.

Compagni, Dino. *Chronicle of Florence*. Edited and translated by Daniel E. Bornstein. Philadelphia: University of Pennsylvania Press, 1986.

Compton, Rebekah. *Venus and the Arts of Love in Renaissance Florence*. Cambridge: Cambridge University Press, 2021.

Condorelli, Adele. "Gherardo di Jacopo, detto lo Starnina." In *Dizionario Biografico degli Italiani*, vol. 53, 2000. Accessed online at https://www.treccani.it/enciclopedia/gherardo-di-jacopo-detto-lo-starnina_(Dizionario-Biografico) (July 11, 2022).

Connell, William J. "Appunti sui rapporti dei primi Medici con i comuni del territorio fiorentino." In *Machiavelli nel Rinascimento italiano*, edited by William J. Connell, 194–210. Milan: FrancoAngeli, 2015.

Connell, William J, and Giles Constable. *Sacrilege and Redemption in Renaissance Florence: The Case of Antonio Rinaldeschi*. Toronto: Centre for Reformation and Renaissance Studies, 2005.

Connell, William J, and Andrea Zorzi, eds. *Florentine Tuscany: Structures and Practices of Power*. Cambridge: Cambridge University Press, 2000.

Constant, Eric A. "A Reinterpretation of the Fifth Lateran Council Decree *Apostolici regiminis* (1513)." *Sixteenth Century Journal* 33, no. 2 (2002): 353–79.

Contini, Alessandra. "Aspects of Medicean Diplomacy in the Sixteenth Century." In *Politics and Diplomacy in Early Modern Italy: The Structure of Diplomatic Practice, 1450–1800*, edited by Daniela Frigo, 49–94. Cambridge: Cambridge University Press, 2000.

Conway, Paul, and Conway Martha O'Hara, eds. *Flood In Florence, 1966: A Fifty-Year Retrospective*. Ann Arbor: Michigan Publishing, University of Michigan Library, 2018.

Copenhaver, Brian. *Magic in Western Culture: From Antiquity to the Englightenment*. Cambridge: Cambridge University Press, 2015.

Copenhaver, Brian P. *Magic and the Dignity of Man: Pico della Mirandola and his Oration in Modern Memory*. Cambridge, MA: Harvard University Press, 2019.

Copenhaver, Brian P., and Charles B. Schmitt. *Renaissance Philosophy*. Oxford: Oxford University Press, 1992.

Cornelison, Sally J. "When an Image is a Relic: The St. Zenobius Panel from Florence Cathedral." In *Images, Relics, and Devotional Practices in Medieval and Renaissance Italy,* edited by Sally J. Cornelison and Scott B. Montgomery, 95–113. Tempe, AZ: ACMRS, 2006.

Corretti, Christine. *Cellini's Perseus and Medusa and the Loggia dei Lanzi. Configurations of the Body of State*. Leiden: Brill, 2015.

Cox, Virginia. "Leonardo Bruni on Women and Rhetoric: *De studiis et litteris* Revisited." *Rhetorica: A Journal of the History of Rhetoric* 27, no. 1 (2009): 47–75.

Cox, Virginia. *A Short History of the Italian Renaissance*. London: I.B. Tauris, 2016.

Cox, Virgina. *Women's Writing in Italy 1400–1650*. Baltimore: Johns Hopkins University Press, 2008.

Crabb, Ann. *The Merchant of Prato's Wife: Margherita Datini and Her World, 1360–1423*. Ann Arbor: Michigan University Press, 2015.

Crabb, Ann. *The Strozzi of Florence: Widowhood and Family Solidarity in the Renaissance*. Ann Arbor: University of Michigan Press, 2000.

Crum, Roger J. ""Cosmos, the World of Cosimo": The Iconography of the Uffizi Façade." *The Art Bulletin* 71, no. 2 (1989): 237–53.

Crum, Roger J. "Stepping Out of Brunelleschi's Shadow: The Consecration of Santa Maria del Fiore as International Statecraft in Medicean Florence." In *Foundation, Dedication and Consecration in Early Modern Europe*, edited by Maarten Delbeke and Minou Schraven, 59–77. Leiden: Brill, 2012.

Currie, Elizabeth. *Fashion and Masculinity in Renaissance Florence*. London: Bloomsbury, 2016.

Cushing, Kathleen G. *Reform and the Papacy in the Eleventh Century: Spiritual and Social Change*. Manchester: Manchester University Press, 2005.

D'Elia, Anthony F. *Pagan Virtue in a Christian World: Sigismondo Malatesta and the Italian Renaissance*. Cambridge, MA: Harvard University Press, 2016.

D'Elia, Anthony F. *The Renaissance of Marriage in Fifteenth-Century Italy*. Cambridge, MA: Harvard University Press, 2004.

d'Ossat, Guglielmo de Angelis, Franco Borsi, and Pina Ragionieri, eds. *Filippo Brunelleschi: La sua opera e il suo tempo*. Florence: Centro Di, 1980.

Dall'Aglio, Stefano. *The Duke's Assassin: Exile and Death of Lorenzino de' Medici*. Translated by Donald Weinstein. New Haven: Yale University Press, 2015.

Dall'Aglio, Stefano. *Savonarola and Savonarolism*. Translated by John Gagné. Toronto: CRRS, 2010.

Dameron, George. "Church and Community in a Medieval Italian City: The Place of San Lorenzo in Florentine Society from Late Antiquity to the Early Fourteenth Century." In *San Lorenzo. A Florentine Church*, edited by Robert W. Gaston and Louis A. Waldman, 40–50. Villa I Tatti: Sheridan Books, 2017.

Dameron, George. "The Cult of St. Minias and the Struggle for Power in the Diocese of Florence, 1011–1018." *Journal of Medieval History* 13 (1987): 125–41.

Dameron, George. *Episcopal Power and Florentine Society, 1000–1320*. Cambridge, MA: Harvard University Press, 1991.

Dameron, George. *Florence and its Church in the Age of Dante*. Philadelphia: University of Pennsylvania Press, 2005.

Dandelet, Thomas James. *The Renaissance of Empire in Early Modern Europe*. Cambridge: Cambridge University Press, 2014.

Daniels, Tobias. "La congiura dei Pazzi nell'informazione e nella cronistica tedesca coeva." *Archivio storico italiano* 169 (2011): 23–76.

Danti, Cristina, Alberto Felici, and Paola Ilaria Mariotti. "La Cappella del Bargello. Vicende conservative delle pitture." In *La storia del Bargello. 100 capolavori da scoprire*, edited by Beatrice Paolozzi Strozzi, 79–88. Milan: Silvana, 2004.

Dati, Gregorio. *Il libro segreto*. Edited by Carlo Gargiolli. Bologna: Gaetano Romagnoli, 1869.

Datini, Margherita. *Letters to Francesco Datini*. Translated by Carolyn James and Antonio Pagliaro. Toronto: Centre for Reformation and Renaissance Studies, 2012.

Davidsohn, Robert. *Storia di Firenze*. Florence: Sansoni, 1907.

Davidson, Miles H. "The Toscanelli Letters: A Dubious Influence on Columbus." *Colonial Latin American Historical Review* 5, no. 3 (1996): 287–310.

Davie, Mark. "Luigi Pulci and the Generation of '94." In *Italy in Crisis. 1494*, edited by Jane Everson and Diego Zancani, 63–79. Oxford: European Humanities Research Centre, 2000.

Davies, Jonathan. *Culture and Power. Tuscany and its Universities 1537–1609*. Leiden: Brill, 2009.

Davies, Jonathan. *Florence and its University during the Early Renaissance*. Leiden: Brill, 1998.

Debenedetti, Ana, and Caroline Elam, eds. *Botticelli Past and Present*. London: UCL Press, 2019.

Dempsey, Charles. *The Early Renaissance and Vernacular Culture*. Cambridge, MA: Harvard University Press, 2012.

Dempsey, Charles. *Inventing the Renaissance Putto*. Chapel Hill: University of North Carolina Press, 2001.

Dempsey, Charles. *The Portrayal of Love: Botticelli's Primavera and Humanist Culture at the Time of Lorenzo the Magnificent*. Princeton: Princeton University Press, 1992.

Derbes, Anne, and Mark Sandona, eds. *The Cambridge Companion to Giotto*. Cambridge: Cambridge University Press, 2004.

Derbes, Anne, and Mark Sandona. *The Usurer's Heart: Giotto, Enrico Scrovengi, and the Arena Chapel in Padua*. University Park: Pennsylvania State University Press, 2008.

Devereux, Andrew W. *The Other Side of Empire: Just War in the Mediterranean and the Rise of Early Modern Spain*. Ithaca: Cornell University Press, 2020.

Diacciati, Silvia. "L'immagine di Dante nel Palazzo del Bargello." *Archivio storico italiano* 158, no. 1 (2020): 3–24.

Dickerson, III, C.D., Ian Wardropper, and Tony Sigel, eds. *Bernini: Sculpting in Clay*. New Haven: Yale University Press, 2012.

Draper, James. *Bertoldo di Giovanni, Sculptor of the Medici Household*. Springfield, MO: University of Missouri Press, 1992.

Dunbabin, Jean. *Charles I of Anjou: Power, Kingship and State-Making in Thirteenth-Century Europe*. London: Routledge, 2014.

Eckstein, Nicholas. *Painted Glories: The Brancacci Chapel in Renaissance Florence*. New Haven: Yale University Press, 2014.

Edelheit, Amos. *Scholastic Florence: Moral Psychology in the Quattrocento*. Leiden: Brill, 2014.

Edgerton, Samuel. *Pictures and Punishment: Art and Criminal Prosecution during the Florentine Renaissance*. Ithaca: Cornell University Press, 1985.

Eisenbichler, Konrad, ed. *The Cultural Politics of Duke Cosimo I de' Medici*. Aldershot: Ashgate, 2001.

Eisenbichler, Konrad, ed. *The Cultural World of Eleonora di Toledo*. Aldershot: Ashgate, 2004.

Elias, Norbert. *The Civilizing Process*. 2 vols. Oxford: Blackwell, 1978–1982.

Epstein, Steven A. *Speaking of Slavery. Color, Ethnicity, & Human Bondage in Italy*. Ithaca: Cornell University Press, 2001.

Ercoli, Giuliano. "Il trecento senese nei *Commentari* di Lorenzo Ghiberti." In *Lorenzo Ghiberti nel suo Tempo*, vol. 2, 317–41. Florence: Leo S. Olschki, 1980.

Ettle, Ross Brooke. "The Venus Dilemma: Notes on Botticelli and Simonetta Cattaneo Vespucci." *Notes in the History of Art* 27, no. 4 (2008): 3–10.

Fabbri, Lorenzo. "Filippo Strozzi." In *Dizionario Biografico degli Italiani*, vol. 94, 2019. Accessed online at https://www.treccani.it/enciclopedia/filippo -strozzi_(Dizionario-Biografico) (accessed July 11, 2022).

Fabbri, Lorenzo. "Women's Rights According to Lorenzo de' Medici: The Borromei-Pazzi Dispute and the *Lex de testamentis*." In *The Art and Language of Power in Renaissance Florence: Essays for Alison Brown*, edited by Amy R. Bloch, Carolyn James, and Camilla Russell, 91–115. Toronto: CRRS, 2019.

Faini, Enrico. *Firenze nell'età romanica (1000–1211): L'espansione urbana, lo sviluppo istituzionale, il rapporto con il territorio*. Florence: Leo S. Olschki, 2010.

Faini, Enrico. "Il convito fiorentino del 1216." In *Conflitti, paci e vendette nell'Italia comunale*, edited by Andrea Zorzi, 105–30. Florence: Firenze University Press, 2009.

Falkeid, Unn. *The Avignon Papacy Contested: An Intellectual History from Dante to Catherine of Siena*. Cambridge, MA: Harvard University Press, 2017.

Falletti, Franca, ed. *The Accademia, Michelangelo, the Nineteenth Century*. Livorno: Sillabe, 1997.

Falzone, Paolo. "Luigi Marsili." In *Dizionario Biografico degli Italiani*, vol. 70, 2008. Accessed online at https://www.treccani.it/enciclopedia/luigi-marsili_(Dizionario-Biografico) (July 11, 2022).

Fanelli, Giovanni, and Michele Fanelli. *Brunelleschi's Cupola, Past and Present of an Architectural Masterpiece*. Translated by Jeremy Carden, Michele Fanelli, Andrea Paoleti, and Mark Roberts. Florence: Mandragora, 2004.

Fantoni, Marcello. "Il culto dell'Annunziata e la sacralità del potere mediceo." *Archivio storico italiano* 147, no. 4 (1989): 771–93.

Feinberg, Larry J. *The Young Leonardo: Art and Life in Fifteenth-Century Florence*. Cambridge: Cambridge University Press, 2011.

Feng, Aeleen A. *Writing Beloveds. Humanist Petrarchism and the Politics of Gender*. Toronto: University of Toronto Press, 2017.

Ferente, Serena. *La sfortuna di Jacopo Piccinino: Storia dei bracceschi in Italia, 1423–1465*. Florence: Leo S. Olsckhi, 2005.

Ferente, Serena. "The Ways of Practice: Angelo Acciaioli, 1450–1470." In *From Florence to the Mediterranean and Beyond: Essays in Honour of Anthony Molho*, edited by Diogo Ramada Curto, Eric R. Dursteler, Julius Kirshner, Francesca Trivellato, and with Niki Koniordos, vol. 1, 103–16. Florence: Leo S. Olschki, 2009.

Ferrante, Joan M. *The Political Vision of the Divine Comedy*. Princeton: Princeton University Press, 1984.

Ferretti, Emanuela. "Fra Leonardo, Machiavelli e Soderini. Ercole I d'Este e Biagio Rossetti nell'impresa <<del volgere l'Arno>> da Pisa." *Archivio storico italiano* 177, no. 2 (2019): 235–72.

Ferretti, Emanuela. "The Medici Palace, Cosimo the Elder, and Michelozzo: A Historiographical Survey." In *A Renaissance Architecture of Power: Princely Palaces in the Italian Quattrocento*, edited by Silvia Beltramo, Flavia Cantatore, and Marco Folin, 263–89. Leiden: Brill, 2016.

Ficino, Marsilio. *Platonic Theology*. Edited by James Hankins. Translated by Michael J.B. Allen. 6 vols. Cambridge, MA: Harvard University, 2001–06.

Ficino, Marsilio. *Three Books on Life*. Edited by Carol V. Kaske and John R. Clark. Arizona State University: Arizona Board of Regents, 1998.

Field, Arthur. *The Intellectual Struggle for Florence*. Oxford: Oxford University Press, 2017.

Field, Arthur. "Leonardo Bruni, Florentine Traitor? Bruni, the Medici, and an Aretine Conspiracy of 1437." *Renaissance Quarterly* 51, no. 4 (1998): 1109–50.

Field, Arthur. *The Origins of the Platonic Academy of Florence.* Princeton: Princeton University Press, 1988.

Findlen, Paula. "The Eighteenth-Century Invention of the Renaissance: Lessons from the Uffizi." *Renaissance Quarterly* 66, no. 1 (2013): 1–34.

Finocchiaro, Maurice A. *The Trial of Galileo. Essential Documents.* Indianapolis: Hackett Publishing Company, 2014.

Flavio, Biondo. *Historiam ab inclinatione romanorum imperii libri xxxi.* Basel, 1531.

Fletcher, Catherine. *The Beauty and the Terror: The Italian Renaissance and the Rise of the West.* Oxford: Oxford University Press, 2020.

Fletcher, Catherine. *The Black Prince of Florence.* Oxford: Oxford University Press, 2016.

Fletcher, Catherine. *The Divorce of Henry VIII: The Untold Story.* London: Vintage Books, 2013.

Flood, John L. "Humanism in the German-Speaking Lands during the Fifteenth Century." In *Humanism in Fifteenth-Century Europe*, edited by David Rundle, 79–117. Oxford: The Society for the Study of Medieval Languages and Literature, 2012.

Foà, Simona. "Geri d'Arezzo." In *Dizionario Biografico degli Italiani*, vol. 53, 2000. Accessed online at https://www.treccani.it/enciclopedia/geri-d-arezzo_(Dizionario-Biografico) (accessed July 11, 2022).

Franklin, David. *Painting in Renaissance Florence, 1500–1550.* New Haven: Yale University Press, 2001.

Fratini, Donatella. "Due disegni di Giorgio Vasari provenienti dall'eredità del cavalier Francesco Maria Vasari per il Salone dei Cinquecento in Palazzo Vecchio." *Mitteilungen des Kunsthistorischen Institutes in Florenz* 57, no. 3 (2015): 350–60.

Freedman, Paul. *Out of the East: Spices and the Medieval Imagination.* New Haven: Yale University Press, 2008.

Frick, Carole Collier. *Dressing Renaissance Florence: Families, Fortunes, and Fine Clothing.* Baltimore: The John Hopkins University Press, 2002.

Frommel, Christoph Luitpold. "Palazzo Pandolfini: Problemi di datazione e di ricostruzione." In *Studi su Raffaello*, edited by Micaela Sambucco Hamoud, 197–204 and 211–12. Urbino: Quattro Venti, 1987.

Fubini, Riccardo. "Federico da Montefeltro e la congiura dei Pazzi: Immagine propagandistica e realtà politica." In *Italia Quattrocentesca*, edited by Riccardo Fubini, 253–326. Milan: FrancoAngeli, 1994.

Fubini, Riccardo. "Il regime di Cosimo de' Medici al suo avvento al potere." In *Italia Quattrocentesca: Politica e diplomazia nell'etá di Lorenzo il Magnifico*, edited by Riccardo Fubini, 62–86. Milan: FrancoAngeli, 1994.

Fubini, Riccardo. *Italia quattrocentesca: Politica e diplomazia nell'eta di Lorenzo il Magnifico*. Milan: FrancoAngeli, 1994.

Fubini, Riccardo. "The Italian League and the Policy of the Balance of Power at the Accession of Lorenzo de' Medici." *The Journal of Modern History* 67 (1995): 166–99.

Fubini, Riccardo. "La rivendicazione di Firenze della sovranità statale e il contributo delle "*Historiae*" di Leonardo Bruni." In *Storiografia dell'umanesimo in Italia da Leonardo Bruni ad Annio da Viterbo*, edited by Riccardo Fubini, 131–64. Rome: Edizioni di Storia e Letteratura, 2003.

Fubini, Riccardo. "Momenti di diplomazia medicea." In *Quattrocento fiorentino*, edited by Riccardo Fubini, 108–22. Pisa: Pacini, 1996.

Fubini, Riccardo, and Sarah-Louise Raillard. "Cosimo de' Medici's Regime: His Rise to Power (1434)." *Revue française de science politique* 64, no. 6 (2014): 81–97.

Funis, Francesca. *Il Corridoio vasariano. Una strada sopra la città*. Florence: Sillabe, 2018.

Fusco, Laurie S., and Gino Corti, eds. *Lorenzo de' Medici, Collector and Antiquarian*. Cambridge: Cambridge University Press, 2006.

Gáldy, Andrea M., ed. *Agnolo Bronzino: Medici Court Artist in Context*. Newcastle upon Tyne: Cambridge Scholars Publishing, 2013.

Gallello, Gianni, Elisabetta Cilli, Fulvio Bartoli, Massimo Andretta, Lucio Calcagnile, Agustin Pastor, Miguel de la Guardia, Patrizia Serventi, Alberto Marino, Stefano Benazzi, and Giorgio Gruppioni. "Poisoning Histories in the Italian Renaissance: The Case of Pico della Mirandola and Angelo Poliziano." *Journal of Forensic and Legal Medicine* 56 (2018): 83–9.

Gallucci, Margaret A., and Paolo L. Rossi, eds. *Benvenuto Cellini: Sculptor, Goldsmith, Writer*. Cambridge: Cambridge University Press, 2004.

Ganz, Margery. "Donato Acciaiuoli and the Medici: A Strategy for Survival in '400 Florence." *Rinascimento* 22 (1982): 33–73.

Gardner, Julian. *Giotto and His Publics: Three Paradigms of Patronage*. Cambridge, MA: Harvard University Press, 2011.

Garin, Eugenio. "Donato Acciaiuoli, Citizen of Florence." In *Portraits from the Quattrocento*, edited by Eugenio Garin, 55–117. New York: Harper & Row, 1963.

Garrard, Mary D. "The Cloister and the Square." *Early Modern Women* 11, no. 1 (2016): 5–44.

Gaston, Robert W., and Louis A. Waldman, eds. *San Lorenzo. A Florentine Church*. Villa I Tatti: Sheridan Books , 2017.

Gilbert, Felix. *Machiavelli and Guicciardini: Politics and History in Sixteenth-Century Florence*. New York: W.W. Norton & Company, 1965.

Gill, Joseph. *The Council of Florence*. Cambridge: Cambridge University Press, 1959.

Gilson, Simon. *Dante and Renaissance Florence*. Cambridge: Cambridge University Press, 2005.

Giovannoni, Simona Lecchini. *Alessandro Allori*. Turin: Umberto Allemandi & C., 1991.

Giusti, Laura Baldini, and Fiorella Facchinetti Bottai. "Documento sulle prime fasi costruttive di Palazzo Pitti." In *Filippo Brunelleschi. La sua opera e il suo tempo*, vol. 2, 703–31. Florence: Centro Di, 1980.

Godman, Peter. *From Poliziano to Machiavelli: Florentine Humanism in the High Renaissance*. Princeton: Princeton University Press, 1998.

Goffen, Rona. *Spirituality in Conflict: Saint Francis and Giotto's Bardi Chapel*. University Park: Pennsylvania State University Press, 1987.

Goldberg, Edward L. *Jews and Magic in Medici Florence. The Secret World of Benedetto Blanis*. Toronto: University of Toronto Press, 2011.

Goldthwaite, Richard A. *The Building of Renaissance Florence*. Baltimore: Johns Hopkins University Press, 1980.

Goldthwaite, Richard A. *The Economy of Renaissance Florence*. Baltimore: Johns Hopkins University Press, 2009.

Goldthwaite, Richard A. *Wealth and the Demand for Art in Italy, 1300–1600*. Baltimore: Johns Hopkins University Press, 1993.

Gombrich, E.H. "Giotto's Portrait of Dante?" In *New Light on Old Masters*, edited by E. H. Gombrich, 11–31. Chicago: University of Chicago Press, 1986.

Gouwens, Kenneth. *Remembering the Renaissance: Humanist Narratives of the Sack of Rome*. Leiden, Boston, Koln: Brill, 1998.

Gouwens, Kenneth, and Sheryl E. Reiss, eds. *The Pontificate of Clement VII: History, Politics, Culture*. Burlington, VT: Ashgate, 2005.

Grafton, Anthony. *Leon Battista Alberti: Master Builder of the Italian Renaissance*. Cambridge, MA: Harvard University Press, 2002.

Grendler, Paul F. *The Universities of the Italian Renaissance*. Baltimore: Johns Hopkins University Press, 2002.

Griffiths, Gordon, James Hankins, and David Thompson, eds. *The Humanism of Leonardo Bruni*. Binghamton, NY: Medieval & Renaissance Texts and Studies, 1987.

Guarino, Guido A. ed. and trans. *The Complete Literary Works of Lorenzo de' Medici*. New York: Italica Press, 2016.

Guasti, Cesare. *Commissioni di Rinaldo degli Albizzi per il comune di Firenze dal MCCCXCIX al MCCCCXXXIII.* 3 vols. Firenze: M. Cellini.

Guicciardini, Francesco. *The History of Italy.* Edited and translated by Sidney Alexander. Princeton: Princeton University Press, 1969.

Guicciardini, Francesco. *Storie fiorentine dal 1378 al 1509.* Edited by Alessandro Castelvecchio. Milan: BUR, 1998.

Gurrieri, Francesco. "L'architettura." In *La Basilica di San Miniato al Monte a Firenze,* edited by Francesco Gurrieri, Luciano Berti, and Claudio Leonardi, 15–127. Florence: Giunti, 1988.

Gurrieri, Francesco. "San Miniato al Monte, la Basilica dell' 'Urbs perfecta.'" In *Dieci secoli per la Basilica di San Miniato al Monte,* edited by Francesco Gurrieri and Renzo Manetti, 11–16. Florence: Polistampa, 2007.

Hainsworth, Peter. *Petrarch the Poet. An Introduction to the Rerum Vulgarium Fragmenta.* London: Routledge, 1988.

Hale, J.R. "The End of Florentine Liberty: The Fortezza da Basso." In *Florentine Studies. Politics and Society in Renaissance Florence,* edited by Nicolai Rubinstein, 501–32. London: Faber and Faber, 1968.

Hale, J.R. *Florence and the Medici.* London: Phoenix, 1977.

Hankins, James, ed. *The Cambridge Companion to Renaissance Philosophy.* Cambridge: Cambridge University Press, 2007.

Hankins, James. *Humanism and Platonism in the Italian Renaissance,* vol. 1. Rome: Edizioni di storia e letteratura, 2003.

Hankins, James. "Humanism in the Vernacular: The Case of Leonardo Bruni." In *Humanism and Creativity in the Renaissance: Essays in Honor of Ronald G. Witt,* edited by Christopher S. Celenza and Kenneth Gouwens, 9–29. Leiden: Brill, 2006.

Hankins, James. "Lorenzo de' Medici as a Patron of Philosophy." *Rinascimento* 34 (1994): 15–53.

Hankins, James. "The Myth of the Platonic Academy of Florence." *Renaissance Quarterly* 44 (1991): 429–75.

Hankins, James. *Virtue Politics: Soulcraft and Statecraft in Renaissance Italy.* Cambridge, MA: Harvard University Press, 2019.

Hanlon, Gregory. *Early Modern Italy, 1550–1800.* New York: St. Martin's Press, 2000.

Hanlon, Gregory. *Italy 1636. Cemetery of Armies.* Oxford: Oxford University Press, 2016.

Hardie, Colin. "The Origin and Plan of Roman Florence." *The Journal of Roman Studies* 55, no. 2 (1965): 122–40.

Hartwell, Michael J., and Brian Jeffrey Maxson. "Coluccio Salutati." In *Literature Criticism from 1400–1800*, vol. 256, edited by Lawrence J. Trudeau, 85–246. Farmington Hills, MI: Gale Cengage, 2016.

Haskins, Charles Homer. *The Renaissance of the Twelfth Century.* Cambridge, MA: Harvard University Press, 1928.

Hatfield, Rab. "The Compagnia de' Magi." *Journal of the Warburg and Courtauld Institutes* 33 (1970): 107–61.

Hatfield, Rab. "Trust in God: The Sources of Michelangelo's Frescos on the Sistine Ceiling." *Occasional Papers Published by Syracuse University, Florence, Italy* 1 (1991): 1–23.

Hay, David J. *The Military Leadership of Matilda of Canossa 1046–1115.* Manchester: Manchester University Press, 2010.

Hearder, Harry. *Italy in the Age of the Risorgimento 1790–1870.* London: Routledge, 2013.

Heikamp, Detlef, and Beatriche Paolozzi Strozzi, eds. *Baccio Bandinelli. Scultore e maestro (1493–1560).* Florence: Giunti, 2014.

Henderson, John. *Florence under Siege: Surviving Plague in an Early Modern City.* New Haven: Yale University Press, 2019.

Henderson, John. *Piety and Charity in Late Medieval Florence.* Chicago: University of Chicago Press, 1997.

Herlihy, David. *Pisa in the Early Renaissance.* New Haven: Yale University Press, 1958.

Hicks, Michael. *The Wars of the Roses.* New Haven: Yale University Press, 2012.

Hirst, Michael. *Michelangelo: The Achievement of Fame, 1475–1534.* New Haven: Yale University Press, 2011.

Hogan, Dana V. "Constructing the Image of a Cardinal-Prince: Child Portraits of Giovanni de' Medici by Bronzino and Salviati." *Comitatus: A Journal of Medieval and Renaissance Studies* 50, no. 1 (2019): 139–75.

Holloway, Julia Bolton. *Brunetto Latini: An Analytic Bibliography.* Valencia: Grant & Cutler Ltd, 1986.

Holloway, Julia Bolton. *Twice-Told Tales: Brunetto Latino and Dante Alighieri.* New York: Peter Lang, 1993.

Holman, Christopher. *Machiavelli and the Politics of Democratic Innovation.* Toronto: University of Toronto Press, 2018.

Holmes, George. *The Florentine Enlightenment, 1400–1450.* London: Weidenfeld and Nicolson, 1969.

Holmes, Olivia, and Dana E. Stewart, eds. *Reconsidering Boccaccio: Medieval Contexts and Global Intertexts.* Toronto: University of Toronto Press, 2018.

Hood, William. *Fra Angelico at San Marco*. New Haven: Yale University Press, 1993.

Hook, Judith. *The Sack of Rome, 1527*. London: Macmillan, 1972.

Hooper, Laurence E. "Exile and Petrarch's Reinvention of Authorship." *Renaissance Quarterly* 69, no. 4 (2016): 1217–56.

Horodowich, Elizabeth, and Lia Markey, eds. *The New World in Early Modern Italy, 1492–1750*. Cambridge: Cambridge University Press, 2017.

Horrox, Rosemary, ed. *The Black Death*. Manchester: Manchester University Press, 1994.

Hunt, Edwin S. *The Medieval Super-Companies: A Study of the Peruzzi Company of Florence*. Cambridge: Cambridge University Press, 1994.

Ianziti, Gary. "Leonardo Bruni, the Medici, and the Florentine Histories." *Journal of the History of Ideas* 69, no. 1 (2008): 1–22.

Ianziti, Gary. *Writing History in Renaissance Italy: Leonardo Bruni and the Uses of the Past*. Cambridge, MA: Harvard University Press, 2012.

Inglese, Giorgio. "Brunetto Latini." In *Dizionario Biografico degli Italiani*, vol. 64. 2005. Accessed online at https://www.treccani.it/enciclopedia /brunetto-latini_%28Dizionario-Biografico%29/ (accessed July 11, 2022).

Izbicki, Thomas M., and Joëlle Rollo-Koster. *A Companion to the Great Western Schism (1378–1417)*. Leiden: Brill, 2009.

Jacks, Philip, ed. *Vasari's Florence: Artists and Literati at the Medicean Court*. Cambridge: Cambridge University Press, 1998.

Jacobus, Laura. *Giotto and the Arena Chapel: Art, Architecture & Experience*. London: Harvey Miller Publishers, 2008.

Jacoff, Rachel. *The Cambridge Companion to Dante*. Cambridge: Cambridge University Press, 1993.

Janson, H.W. *The Sculpture of Donatello*. Princeton: Princeton University Press, 1963.

Jardine, Lisa. "'O Decus Italiae Virgo,' or The Myth of the Learned Lady in the Renaissance." *The Historical Journal* 28, no. 4 (1985): 799–819.

Jones, P. J. *The Malatesta of Rimini and the Papal State*. New York: Cambridge University Press, 2005.

Jones, Philip. *The Italian City-State: From Commune to Signoria*. Oxford: Clarendon Press, 1997.

Jones, Rosemary Devonshire. *Francesco Vettori: Florentine Citizen and Medici Servant*. London: Athlone Press, 1972.

Jurdjevic, Mark. *A Great & Wretched City. Promise and Failure in Machiavelli's Political Thought*. Cambridge, MA: Harvard University Press, 2014.

Bibliography

Jurdjevic, Mark. *Guardians of Republicanism: The Valori Family in the Florentine Renaissance*. Oxford: Oxford University Press, 2008.

Kaborycha, Lisa. "Brigida Baldinotti and Her Two Epistles in Quattrocento Florentine Manuscripts." *Speculum* 87, no. 3 (2012): 793–826.

Kallendorf, Craig, ed. *Humanist Educational Treatises*. Cambridge, MA: Harvard University Press, 2002.

Kaplan, Paul H.D. "Isabella d'Este and Black African Women." In *Black Africans in Renaissance Europe*, edited by T.F. Earle and K.J.P. Lowe, 125–54. Cambridge: Cambridge University Press, 2005.

Kelly, Samantha. *The New Solomon: Robert of Naples (1309–1343) and Fourteenth-Century Kingship*. Leiden: Brill, 2003.

Kendall, Paul Murray. *Louis XI, the Universal Spider*. New York: Norton & Company, 1971.

Kent, Dale. *Cosimo de' Medici and the Florentine Renaissance: The Patron's Oeuvre*. New Haven: Yale University Press, 2000.

Kent, Dale. "The Florentine Reggimento in the Fifteenth Century." *Renaissance Quarterly* 28, no. 4 (1975): 575–638.

Kent, Dale. *The Rise of the Medici: Faction in Florence, 1426–1434*. Oxford: Oxford University Press, 1978.

Kent, F.W. *Household and Lineage in Renaissance Florence: The Family Life of the Capponi, Ginori, and Rucellai*. Princeton: Princeton University Press, 1977.

Kent, F.W. *Lorenzo de' Medici and the Art of Magnificence*. Baltimore: Johns Hopkins University Press, 2004.

Kent, F.W., and Dale Kent. *Neighbours and Neighbourhood in Renaissance Florence: The District of the Red Lion in the Fifteenth Century*. Locust Valley: J.J. Augustin, 1982.

Kieckhefer, Richard. *Magic in the Middle Ages*. 2 ed. Cambridge: Cambridge University Press, 2014.

King, Margaret L. "Book-Lined Cells: Women and Humanism in the Italian Renaissance." In *Renaissance Humanism, Volume 1: Foundations, Forms, and Legacy,* edited by Albert Rabil, 434–54. Philadelphia: University of Pennsylvania Press, 1988.

King, Ross. *Brunelleschi's Dome, How a Renaissance Genius Reinvented Architecture*. New York: Walker & Company, 2000.

Kircher, Timothy. *Living Well in Renaissance Italy: The Virtues of Humanism and Irony of Leon Battista Alberti*. Tempe, AZ: ACMRS, 2012.

Kirkham, Victoria, and Armando Maggi, eds. *Petrarch: A Critical Guide to the Complete Works*. Chicago: University of Chicago Press, 2009.

Kirkham, Victoria, Michael Sherberg, and Janet Levarie Smarr. *Boccaccio: A Critical Guide to the Complete Works*. Chicago: University of Chicago Press, 2013.

Kirshner, Julius. *Marriage, Dowry, and Citizenship in Late Medieval and Renaissance Italy*. Toronto: University of Toronto Press, 2015.

Klapisch-Zuber, Christiane. *Women, Family, and Ritual in Renaissance Italy*. Chicago: University of Chicago Press, 1987.

Klotz, Heinrich. *Filippo Brunelleschi: The Early Works and the Medieval Tradition*. New York: Rizzoli, 1990.

Kohl, Benjamin G., Ronald G. Witt, and Eilzabeth B. Welles. *The Earthly Republic: Italian Humanists on Government and Society*. Philadelphia: University of Pennsylvania Press, 1978.

Kokin, Daniel Stein. "The Josephan Renaissance: Flavius Josephus and his Writings in Italian Humanist Discourse." *Viator* 47, no. 2 (2016): 205–48.

Kovesi, Catherine. "Muddying the Waters: Alfonsina Orsini de' Medici and the Lake of Fucecchio." In *Communes and Despots in Medieval and Renaissance Italy*, edited by John E. Law and Bernadette Paton, 223–47. Farnham: Ashgate, 2010.

Krautheimer, Richard. *Lorenzo Ghiberti*. Princeton: Princeton University Press, 1982.

Kreytenberg, Gert. "The Limestone Tracery in the Arches of the Original Grain Loggia of Orsanmichele in Florence." In *Orsanmichele and the History and Preservation of the Civic Monument*, edited by Carl Brandon Strehlke, 112–24. New Haven: Yale University Press, 2012.

Kristeller, Paul Oskar. *Marsilio Ficino and His Work after Five Hundred Years*. Florence: Leo S. Olschki, 1987.

Kristeller, Paul Oskar. *The Philosophy of Marsilio Ficino*. New York: Columbia University Press, 1943.

Kristeller, Paul Oskar. *Renaissance Thought and its Sources*. Edited by Michael Mooney. Columbia: Columbia University Press, 1979.

Kristeller, Paul Oskar. "Un documento sconosciuto sulla giostra di Giuliano de' Medici." In *Studies in Renaissance Thought and Letters*, edited by Paul Oskar Kristeller, vol. 3, 437–50. Rome: Edizioni di Storia e Letteratura, 1956.

Kuehn, Thomas. *Family and Gender in Renaissance Italy*. Cambridge: Cambridge University Press, 2017.

Kuehn, Thomas. "Reading Microhistory: The Example of Giovanni and Lusanna." *The Journal of Modern History* 61 (September 1989): 512–34.

Kuehn, Thomas. *Toward a Legal Anthropology of Renaissance Italy*. Rev. ed. Chicago: University of Chicago Press, 1994.

Labriola, Ada. "Lo stato degli studi su Cimabue e un libro recente." *Arte cristiana* 88 (2000): 341–52.

Ladis, Andrew. *Giotto's O. Narrative, Figuration, and Pictorial Ingenuity in the Arena Chapel*. University Park: Pennsylvania State University Press, 2008.

Langdon, Gabrielle, ed. *Medici Women: Portraits of Power, Love, and Betrayal in the Court of Duke Cosimo I*. Toronto: University of Toronto Press, 2006.

Lansing, Carol. *The Florentine Magnates: Lineage and Faction in a Medieval Commune*. Princeton: Princeton University Press, 1991.

Lantschner, Patrick. *The Logic of Political Conflict in Medieval Cities: Italy and the Southern Low Countries, 1370–1440*. Oxford: Oxford University Press, 2015.

Larner, John. "The Church and the Quattrocento Renaissance in Geography." *Renaissance Studies* 12, no. 1 (1998): 26–39.

Latini, Brunetto. *The Book of the Treasure (Li Livres dou Tresor)*. Translated by Paul Barrette and Spurgeon Baldwin. New York: Garland Publishing, 1993.

Latini, Brunetto. *Il Tesoretto (The Little Treasure)*. Edited and translated by Julia Bolton Holloway. New York: Garland Publishing, Inc., 1981.

Leader, Anne. *The Badia of Florence. Art and Observance in a Renaissance Monastery*. Bloomington: Indiana University Press, 2012.

Leader, Anne. "'In the Tomb of Ser Piero': Death and Burial in the Family of Leonardo da Vinci." *Renaissance Studies* 31, no. 3 (2017): 324–45.

Lee, Alexander. *Humanism and Empire: The Imperial Ideal in Fourteenth-Century Italy*. Oxford: Oxford University Press, 2018.

Lee, Alexander. *Machiavelli: His Life and Times*. London: Picador, 2020.

Levack, Brian. *The Witch-Hunt in Early Modern Europe*. 4 ed. London: Routledge, 2015.

Levy, Allison. *House of Secrets: The Many Lives of a Florentine Palazzo*. London: I.B. Tauris, 2019.

Lewin, Alison Williams. *Negotiating Survival: Florence and the Great Schism, 1378–1417*. Madison, NJ: Fairleigh Dickinson University Press, 2003.

Lines, David A. *Aristotle's Ethics in the Italian Renaissance (ca. 1300–1650): The Universities and the Problem of Moral Education*. Leiden: Brill, 2002.

Litchfield, R. Burr. *Emergence of a Bureaucracy. The Florentine Patricians 1530–1790*. Princeton: Prineton University Press, 1986.

Lowe, K.J.P. *Church and Politics in Renaissance Italy: The Life and Career of Cardinal Francesco Soderini (1453–1524)*. Cambridge: Cambridge University Press, 1993.

Lowe, Kate. "The Stereotyping of Black Africans in Renaissance Europe." In *Black Africans in Renaissance Europe*, edited by T.F. Earle and K.J.P. Lowe, 17–47. Cambridge: Cambridge University Press, 2005.

Luciano, Eleonora. "A More "Modern" Ghiberti: The *Saint Matthew* for Orsanmichele." In *Orsanmichele and the History and Preservation of the Civic Monument*, edited by Carl Brandon Strehlke, 213–42. New Haven: Yale University Press, 2012.

Luongo, F. Thomas. *The Saintly Politics of Catherine of Siena*. Ithaca: Cornell University Press, 2006.

Luporini, Eugenio. "Battista Pandolfini e Benedetto da Rovezzano nella Badia fiorentina. Documenti per la datazione." *Prospettiva* 33/36 (1983–1984): 112–23.

Lusanna, Enrica Neri. "Andrea Pisano's Saint Stephen and the Genesis of Monumental Sculpture at Orsanmichele." In *Orsanmichele and the History and Preservation of the Civic Monument*, edited by Carl Brandon Strehlke, 53–74. New Haven: Yale University Press, 2012.

Luzzati, Michele. *Estimi e catasti del contado di Pisa nel Quattrocento*. Pisa: Pacini, 1976.

Macadam, Alta. *Florence: Blue Guide*. 7th ed. London: A&C Black, 1998.

Maccioni, Elena, and Sergio Tognetti, eds. *Tribunali di Mercanti e Giustizia Mercantile nel Tardo Medioevo*. Florence: Leo S. Olschki, 2016.

MacCracken, Richard. *The Dedication Inscription of the Palazzo del Podestà in Florence*. Florence: Leo S. Olschki, 2001.

Macey, Patrick. *Bonfire Songs: Savonarola's Musical Legacy*. Oxford: Clarendon Press, 1998.

Machiavelli, Niccolo. *Florentine Histories*. Translated by Jr. Laura F. Banfield and Harvey C. Mansfield. Princeton: Princeton University Press, 1988.

Machiavelli, Niccolo. *The Prince*. Cambridge Texts in the History of Political Thought, edited by Raymond Price and Quentin Skinner. Cambridge: Cambridge University Press, 1988.

Machiavelli, Niccolò. *The Prince*. Edited by William J. Connell. 2nd ed. Boston: Bedford/St. Martin's, 2005.

Mack, Charles R. "The Palazzo Rucellai Reconsidered." In *Actas dell' XXIII congreso internacional de historia del arte (1973)*, vol. 2. Grenada: Universidad Grenada, 1977.

Mack, Charles R. "The Rucellai Palace: Some New Proposals." *The Art Bulletin* 56 (1974): 517–29.

Malavasi, Massimiliano. "Ficinus redivus. Su una nuova edizione della versione latina del *Pimander* e sui rapporti tra umanesimo e religione." *Rinascimento* 56 (2016): 327–58.

Mallett, Michael E. *The Florentine Galleys in the Fifteenth Century*. Oxford: Clarendon Press, 1967.

Mallett, Michael E. *Pisa and Florence in the Fifteenth Century: Aspects of the Period of the First Florentine Domination*. London: Faber & Faber, 1968.

Mallett, Michael, and Christine Shaw. *The Italian Wars, 1494–1559*. 2nd ed. London: Routledge, 2019.

Manetti, Antonio di Tuccio. *The Life of Brunelleschi*. Edited by Howard Saalman. Translated by Catherine Enggass. University Park: The Pennsylvania State University Press, 1970.

Manetti, Giannozzo. *Against the Jews and Gentiles*, vol. 1. Edited by Stefano U. Baldassarri and Daniela Pagliara. Translated by David Marsh. Cambridge, MA: Harvard University Press, 2017.

Manetti, Giannozzo. *On Human Worth and Excellence*. Edited and translated by Brian Copenhaver. Cambridge, MA: Harvard University Press, 2018.

Manetti, Giannozzo. *A Translator's Defense*. Edited by Myron McShane. Translated by Mark Young. Cambridge, MA: Harvard University Press, 2016.

Marcus, Hannah. *Forbidden Knowledge: Medicine, Science, and Censorship in Early Modern Italy*. Chicago: University of Chicago Press, 2020.

Mare, Albinia Catherine de la. "Vespasiano da Bisticci, Historian and Bookseller." Dissertation, University of London, 1966.

Mare, Albinia de la. *The Handwriting of Italian Humanists*. Oxford: Oxford University Press, 1973.

Mare, Albinia de la. "New Research on Humanistic Scribes in Florence." In *Miniatura fiorentina del Rinascimento 1440–1525*, edited by Annarosa Garzelli, vol. 1, 393–600. Florence: Giunta Regionale Toscana, 1985.

Margolis, Oren J. "The 'Gallic Crowd' at the "Aragonese Doors": Donato Acciaiuoli's *Vita Caroli Magni* and the Workshop of Vespasiano da Bisticci." *I Tatti Studies in the Italian Renaissance* 17, no. 2 (2014): 241–82.

Margolis, Oren J. *The Politics of Culture in Quattrocento Europe: René of Anjou in Italy*. Oxford: Oxford University Press, 2016.

Margolis, Oren J., and Brian J. Maxson. "The 'Schemes' of Piero de' Pazzi and the Conflict with the Medici (1461–62)." *Journal of Medieval History* 41, no. 4 (2015): 484–503.

Marinazzo, Adriano. "Palazzo Pitti: Dalla 'Casa vecchia' alla Reggia Granducale." *Bollettino della Società di Studi Fiorentini* 22 (2013): 299–306.

Marino, John A., ed. *Early Modern Italy 1550–1796*. Oxford: Oxford University Press, 2002.

Markey, Lia. *Imagining the Americas in Medici Florence*. University Park: Penn State University Press, 2016.

Marsh, David. *Giannozzo Manetti: The Life of a Florentine Humanist*. Cambridge, MA: Harvard University Press, 2019.

Martines, Lauro. *April Blood: Florence and the Plot against the Medici*. Oxford and New York: Oxford University Press, 2003.

Martines, Lauro. *Fire in the City: Savonarola and the Struggle of the Soul of Renaissance Florence*. Oxford: Oxford University Press, 2006.

Martines, Lauro. *The Social World of the Florentine Humanists 1390–1460*. Princeton: Princeton University Press, 1963.

Martini, Fabio, and Lucia Sarti. "Prima di Firenze: Dal paleolitico all'età del bronzo." In *Archeologia a Firenze: Città e territorio*, edited by Valeria d'Aquino, Guido Guarducci, Silvia Nencetti, and Stefano Valentini, 3–37. Oxford: Archaeopress, 2015.

Masters, Roger. *Fortune Is a River: Leonardo da Vinci and Niccolò Machiavelli's Magnificent Dream to Change the Course of Florentine History*. New York: The Free Press, 1998.

Matthew, Donald. *The Norman Kingdom of Sicily*. Cambridge: Cambridge University Press, 1992.

Matthew, Louisa C., and Lars R. Jones, eds. *Coming About . . . A Festschrift for John Shearman*. Cambridge, MA: Harvard University Art Museums, 2001.

Maxson, Brian Jeffrey. "The *Certame Coronario* as Performative Ritual." In *Rituals of Politics and Culture in Early Modern Europe: Essays in Honour of Edward Muir*, edited by Mark Jurdjevic and Rolf Strøm-Olsen, 137–63. Toronto: CRRS, 2016.

Maxson, Brian Jeffrey. "Establishing Independence: Leonardo Bruni's *History of the Florentine People* and Ritual in Fifteenth-Century Florence." In *Foundation, Dedication and Consecration in Early Modern Europe*, edited by Maarten Delbeke and Minou Schraven, 79–98. Leiden: Brill, 2012.

Maxson, Brian Jeffrey. "Expressions of Power in Diplomacy in Fifteenth-Century Florence." In *Languages of Power in Italy (1300–1600)*, edited by Daniel Bornstein, Laura Gaffuri, and Brian Jeffrey Maxson, 129–39. Turnhout: Brepols, 2017.

Maxson, Brian Jeffrey. "Humanism and the Ritual of Command in Fifteenth-Century Florence." In *After Civic Humanism: Learning and Politics in Renaissance Italy*, edited by Nicholas Scott Baker and Brian Jeffrey Maxson, 113–29. Toronto: CRRS, 2015.

Maxson, Brian Jeffrey. *The Humanist World of Renaissance Florence*. Cambridge: Cambridge University Press, 2014.

Maxson, Brian Jeffrey. "Kings and Tyrants: Leonardo Bruni's Translation of Xenophon's Hiero." *Renaissance Studies* 24, no. 2 (2010): 188 –206.

Maxson, Brian Jeffrey. "Leonardo Bruni." In *Encyclopedia of Renaissance Philosophy*, edited by Marco Sgarbi. New York: Springer, 2018. Accessed online at https://link.springer.com/referencework/10.1007%2F978-3-319 -02848-4 (accessed April 7, 2017).

Maxson, Brian Jeffrey. "The Letters of Giannozzo Manetti: Context and Chronology, with an Edition of Four New Letters." *Bullettino dell'Istituto Storico Italiano per il Medio Evo* 122 (2020): 203–52.

Maxson, Brian Jeffrey. "The Many Shades of Praise: Politics and Panegryics in Fifteenth-Century Florentine Diplomacy." In *Rhetorik in Mittelalter und Renaissance: Konzepte-Praxis-Diversität*, edited by Georg Strack and Julia Knödler, 393–412. München: Herbert Utz, 2011.

Maxson, Brian Jeffrey. "The Myth of the Renaissance Bubble: International Culture and Regional Politics in Fifteenth-Century Florence." In *Florence in the Early Modern World: New Perspectives*, edited by Nicholas Scott Baker and Brian Jeffrey Maxson, 213–35. London: Routledge, 2020.

Maxson, Brian Jeffrey. "Visual and Verbal Portraits of Cardinals in Fifteenth-Century Florence." In *Portrait Cultures of the Early Modern Cardinal*, edited by Piers Baker-Bates and Irene Brooke, 69–89. Amsterdam: Amsterdam University Press, 2021.

Mayer, Yakov Z. "Crying at the Florence Baptistery Entrance: A Testimony of a Traveling Jew." *Renaissance Studies* 33, no. 3 (2019): 441–57.

Mazza, Antonia. "L'inventario della "parva libraria" di Santo Spirito e la biblioteca del Boccaccio." *Italia medioevale e umanstica* 9 (1966): 1–74.

Mazzotta, Giuseppe. *Reading Dante*. New Haven: Yale University Press, 2014.

McCormick, John P. *Reading Machiavelli. Scandalous Books, Suspect Engagements & the Virtue of Populist Politics*. Princeton: Princeton University Press, 2018.

McCue, Amyrose J. "Rereading *I libri della famiglia*: Leon Battista Alberti on Marriage, *Amicizia* and Conjugal Friendship." *California Italian Studies* 2 (2011).

McLaughlin, Martin. "Poliziano's *Stanze per la giostra*: Postmodern Poetics in a Proto-Renaissance Poem." In *Italy in Crisis. 1494*, edited by Jane Everson and Diego Zancani, 129–51. Oxford: European Humanities Research Centre, 2000.

Medici, Lorenzo de'. *Selected Poems and Prose*. Edited and translated by Jon Thiem. University Park: Pennsylvania State Press, 1992.

Miller, Maureen C. "The Saint Zenobius Dossal by the Master of the Bigallo and the Cathedral Chapter of Florence." In *The Haskins Society Journal 19*, edited by Stephen Morillo and William North, 65–81. Woodbridge: Boydell Press, 2008.

Minnich, Nelson H., ed. *Alla ricerca di soluzioni, nuova luce sul Concilio Lateranense V*. Vatican City: Libreria Editrice Vaticana, 2019.

Minnich, Nelson H. *The Decrees of the Fifth Lateran Council*. London: Routledge, 2016.

Mirandola, Giovanni Francesco Pico della. *Vita hieronymi savonarolae ferrariensis*. Paris: In palatio regio, 1674.

Mirandola, Giovanni Pico della. *Syncretism in the West: Pico's 900 theses (1486)*. Edited and translated by S.A. Farmer. Tempe, AZ: Medieval & Renaissance Texts & Studies, 1998.

Modonutti, Rino, and Enrico Zucchi, eds. *"Moribus antiquis sibi me fecere poetam." Albertino Mussato nel VII centenario dell'incoronazione poetica (Padova 1315–2015)*. Florence: SISMEL, 2017.

Molho, Anthony. "The Closing of the Florentine Archive." *Journal of Modern History* 60, no. 2 (1988): 290–99.

Molho, Anthony. "Cosimo de' Medici: *Pater Patriae* or *Padrino?*" In *Firenze nel Quattrocento. vol. 1: Politica e Fiscalità*, edited by Anthony Molho. Rome: Edizioni di Storia e Letteratura, 2006.

Molho, Anthony. *Florentine Public Finances in the early Renaissance, 1400–1433*. Cambridge. MA: Harvard University Press, 1971.

Molho, Anthony. *Marriage Alliance in Late Medieval Florence*. Cambridge, MA: Harvard University Press, 1994.

Montgomery, Scott B. "Quia venerabile corpus rediciti martyris ibi repositum: Image and Relic in the Decorative Program of San Miniato al Monte." In *Images, Relics, and Devotional Practices in Medieval and Renaissance Italy*, edited by Sally J. Cornelison and Scott B. Montgomery, 7–25. Tempe, AZ: ACMRS, 2006.

Montgomery, Scott B. "Securing the Sacred Head: Cephalophory and Relic Claims." In *Disembodied Heads in Medieval and Early Modern Culture*, edited by Barbara Baert, Anita Traninger, and Catrien Santing, 77–115. Leiden: Brill, 2013.

Moran, Megan. "Young Women Negotiating Fashion in Early Modern Florence." In *The Youth of Early Modern Women*, edited by Elizabeth S. Cohen and Margaret Reeves, 179–94. Toronto: CRRS, 2018.

Morandini, F. "Palazzo Pitti. La sua costruzione e i successivi ingrandimenti." *Commentari* 16 (1965): 35–46.

Morgan, Philip. *The Fall of Mussolini*. Oxford: Oxford University Press, 2007.

Mori, Elisabetta. "Isabella de' Medici: Unraveling the Legend." In *Medici Women: The Making of a Dynasty in Grand Ducal Tuscany*, edited by Giovanna Benadusi and Judith C. Brown, 90–127. Toronto: CRRS, 2015.

Moyer, Ann E. *The Intellectual World of Sixteenth-Century Florence*. Cambridge: Cambridge University Press, 2020.

Muccini, Ugo. *Il Salone dei Cinquecento in Palazzo Vecchio*. Florence: Le Lettere, 1990.

Muir, Edward. "Was There Republicanism in the Renaissance Republics?" In *Venice Reconsidered. The History and Civilization of an Italian City-State*, edited by John Martin and Dennis Romano, 137–67. Baltimore: Johns Hopkins University Press, 2000.

Murphy, Caroline. *Murder of a Medici Princess*. Cambridge: Cambridge University Press, 2009.

Murray, Jacqueline, ed. *Marriage in Premodern Europe: Italy and Beyond*. Toronto: CRRS, 2012.

Murry, Gregory. *The Medicean Succession: Monarchy and Sacral Politics in Duke Cosimo dei Medici's Florence*. Cambridge, MA: Harvard University Press, 2014.

Nadalo, Stephanie. "Negotiating Slavery in a Tolerant Frontier: Livorno's Turkish *Bagno* (1547–1747)." *Mediaevalia* 32, no. 1 (2011): 275–324.

Najemy, John M. *Between Friends: Discourses of Power and Desire in the Machiavelli-Vettori Letters of 1513–1515*. Princeton: Princeton University Press, 1993.

Najemy, John M., ed. *The Cambridge Companion to Machiavelli*. Cambridge: Cambridge University Press, 2010.

Najemy, John M. *Corporatism and Consensus in Florentine Electoral Politics, 1280–1400*. Chapel Hill: University of North Carolina Press, 1982.

Najemy, John M. "Florentine Politics and Urban Spaces." In *Renaissance Florence: A Social History*, edited by Roger J. Crum and John T. Paoletti, 19–54. Cambridge: Cambridge University Press, 2006.

Najemy, John M. *A History of Florence, 1200–1575*. Malden, MA: Blackwell, 2006.

Nash, Penelope. *Empress Adelheid and Countess Matilda: Medieval Female Rulership and the Foundations of European Society*. New York: Palgrave Macmillan, 2017.

Nelson, Jonathan, and Richard J. Zeckhauser, eds. *The Patron's Payoff: Conspicuous Commissions in Italian Renaissance Art*. Princeton: Princeton University Press, 2004.

Nethersole, Scott. *Art and Violence in Early Renaissance Florence*. New Haven: Yale University Press, 2018.

Nevejans, Pierre. "An Ambassador as a Diversion? Giuliano Soderini and his Florentine Mission in France (1527–29)." *Legatio* 3 (2019): 5–38.

Ng, Aimee, Alexander J. Noelle, and Xavier F. Salomon. *Bertoldo di Giovanni: The Renaissance of Sculpture in Medici Florence*. New York: The Frick Collection, 2019.

Nigro, Giampiero, ed. *Francesco di Marco Datini: The Man, the Merchant*. Florence: Firenze University Press, 2010.

Nuovo, Angela. *The Book Trade in the Italian Renaissance*. Translated by Lydia G. Cochrane. Leiden: Brill, 2013.

O'Connell, Monique, and Eric Dursteler. *The Mediterranean World: From the Fall of Rome to the Rise of Napoleon*. Baltimore: Johns Hopkins University Press, 2016.

Origo, Iris. *The Merchant of Prato: Francesco di Marco Datini*. Oxford: Alden Press, 1957.

Orvieto, Paolo. "Religion and Literature in Oligarchic, Medicean, and Savonarolan Florence." In *The Medici. Citizens and Masters*, edited by Robert Black and John E. Law, 189–203. Villa I Tatti: Sheridan Books, 2015.

Ottokar, Nicola. *Il Comune di Firenze alla fine del Dugento*. 2nd ed. Torino: Giulio Einaudi, 1962.

Padgett, John F. "Open Elite? Social Mobility, Marriage, and Family in Florence, 1282–1494." *Renaissance Quarterly* 63 (2010): 357–411.

Pampaloni, Giuseppe. "Gli organi della Repubblica fiorentina per le relazioni con l'Estero." *Rivista di studi politici internazionali* 20 (1953): 260–96.

Panou, Nikos, and Hester Schadee, eds. *Evil Lords. Theories and Representations of Tyranny from Antiquity to the Renaissance*. Oxford: Oxford University Press, 2018.

Paoletti, John T. "Fraternal Piety and Family Power: The Artistic Patronage of Cosimo and Lorenzo de' Medici." In *Cosimo 'il Vecchio' de' Medici, 1389–1464*, edited by Francis Ames-Lewis, 195–219. Oxford: Clarendon Press, 1992.

Paoletti, John T. *Michelangelo's David: Florentine History and Civic Identity*. Cambridge: Cambridge University Press, 2015.

Paoletti, John T. "'Nella mia giovanile età mi partì . . . da Firenze.'" In *Lorenzo Ghiberti nel suo Tempo: Atti del Convegno Internazionale di Studi*, vol. 1, 99–110. Florence: Leo S. Olschki, 1980.

Paoli, Cesare. *Il Libro di Montaperti*. Florence: G.P. Vieusseux, 1889.

Park, Katharine. *Doctors and Medicine in Early Renaissance Florence.* Princeton: Princeton University Press, 1985.

Parker, Geoffrey. *The Military Revolution: Military Innovation and the Rise of the West, 1500–1800.* 2nd ed. Cambridge: Cambridge University Press, 1996.

Parrott, David. "Richelieu, Mazarin and Italy (1635–59): Statesmanship in Context." In *Secretaries and Statecraft in the Early Modern World,* edited by Paul Dover, 115–76. Edinburgh: Edinburgh University Press, 2016.

Pernis, Maria Grazia, and Laurie Schneider Adams. *Lucrezia Tornabuoni de' Medici and the Medici Family in the Fifteenth Century.* New York: Peter Lang, 2006.

Pesenti, G. "Alessandra Scala: Una figurina della rinascenza fiorentina." *Giornale Storico della Letteratura Italiana* 85 (1923): 241–67.

Peterson, David S. "The Albizzi, the Early Medici, and the Florentine Church, 1375–1460." In *The Medici: Citizens and Masters,* edited by Robert Black and John E. Law, 171–87. Villa I Tatti: Sheridan Books, 2015.

Peterson, David S. "San Lorenzo, the Medici, and the Florentine Church in the Late Fourteenth and Early Fifteenth Centuries." In *San Lorenzo. A Florentine Church,* edited by Robert W. Gaston and Louis A. Waldman, 62–102. Villa I Tatti: Sheridan Books, 2017.

Peterson, David S. "The War of Eight Saints in Florentine Memory and Oblivion." In *Society & Individual in Renaissance Florence,* edited by William J. Connell, 173–214. Berkeley: University of California Press, 2002.

Peterson, Thomas E. *Petrarch's Fragmenta. The Narrative and Theological Unity of Rerum vulgarium fragmenta.* Toronto: University of Toronto Press, 2016.

Petrarch. *Lyric Poems.* Edited and translated by Robert M. Durling. Cambridge, MA: Harvard University Press, 1976.

Petrini, Francesco Maria. "Florentia 'ostrogota.'" In *Archeologia a Firenze: Città e Territorio,* edited by Valeria d'Aquino, Guido Guarducci, Silvia Nencetti, and Stefano Valentini, . Oxford: Archaeopress, 2015.

Philippides, Marios, and Walter Hanak. *The Siege and the Fall of Constantinople in 1453: Historiography, Topography, and Military Studies.* Farnham: Ashgate, 2011.

Phillips, Mark. *Francesco Guicciardini: The Historian's Craft.* Toronto: University of Toronto Press, 1977.

Phillips, Mark. *The Memoir of Marco Parenti: A Life in Medici Florence.* Princeton: Princeton University Press, 1987.

Bibliography

Piccolomini, Aeneas Silvius (Pope Pius II). *Commentaries*. Edited by Margaret Meserve and Marcello Simonetta. 3 vols. Cambridge, MA: Harvard University Press, 2003–2018.

Piffanelli, Luciano. "Nelle parti di Romagna: The Role and Influence of the Apennine Lords in Italian Renaissance Politics." In *Florence in the Early Modern World*, edited by Nicholas Scott Baker and Brian Jeffrey Maxson, 117–41. London: Routledge, 2019.

Piffanelli, Luciano. *Politica e diplomazia nell'Italia del primo Rinascimento*. Rome: École Française de Rome, 2020.

Pinto, Giuliano, Leonardo Rombai, and Claudia Tripodi, eds. *Vespucci, Firenze e le Americhe*. Florence: Leo S. Olschki, 2014.

Pitti, Buonaccorso. *Ricordi*. Edited by Veronica Vestri. Florence: Florence University Press, 2015.

Plaisance, Michael. *Florence in the Time of the Medici: Public Celebrations, Politics, and Literature in the Fifteenth and Sixteenth Centuries*. Toronto: CRRS, 2008.

Plebani, Eleonora. "Pier Filippo Pandolfini." In *Dizionario Biografico degli Italiani*, vol. 80. 2014. Accessed online at https://www.treccani.it /enciclopedia/pier-filippo-pandolfini_(Dizionario-Biografico) (July 11, 2022).

Plebani, Eleonora. "Una fuga programmata. Eugenio IV e Firenze (1433–1434)." *Archivio storico italiano* 170, no. 2 (2012): 285–310.

Poettinger, Monika, and Piero Rogg, eds. *Florence. Capital of the Kingdom of Italy, 1865–71*. London: Bloomsbury, 2018.

Poliziano, Angelo. *Letters*. Translated by Shane Butler. Cambridge, MA and London: Harvard University Press, 2006.

Polizzotto, Lorenzo. *The Elect Nation: The Savonarolan Movement in Florence, 1494–1545*. Oxford: Clarendon Press, 1994.

Polizzotto, Lorenzo. "When Saints Fall Out: Women and the Savonarolan Reform in Early Sixteenth-Century Florence." *Renaissance Quarterly* 46, no. 3 (1993): 486–525.

Polzer, Joseph. "Cimabue Reconsidered." *Arte medievale* 5 (2015): 197–224.

Poncet, Christopher. *La scelta di Lorenzo: La Primavera di Botticelli tra poesia e filosofia*. Pisa: Fabrizio Serra Editore, 2012.

Poole-Jones, Katherine. "The Medici, Maritime Empire, and the Enduring Legacy of the Cavalieri di Santo Stefano." In *Florence in Early Modern Europe. New Perspectives*, edited by Nicholas Scott Baker and Brian Jeffrey Maxson, 156–86. London: Routledge, 2020.

Pope-Hennessy, John. *Cellini*. London: Macmillan, 1985.

Pope-Hennessy, John. *Donatello, Sculptor*. New York: Abbeville Press, 1993.

Pope-Hennessy, John. *The Portrait in the Renaissance*. New York: Pantheon Books, 1966.

Prajda, Katalin. *Network and Migration in Early Renaissance Florence, 1378–1433*. Amsterdam: Amsterdam University Press, 2018.

Prestwich, Michael. *A Short History of the Hundred Years War*. London: I.B. Tauris, 2018.

Preyer, Brenda. "The Rucellai Palace." In *Giovanni Rucellai ed il suo Zibaldone*, edited by F.W. Kent, Alessandro Perosa, Brenda Preyer, Piero Sanpaolesi, Roberto Salvini, and Nicholai Rubinstein, vol. 2, 155–207. The Warburg Institute: University of London, 1981.

Procacci, Ugo. *Studio sul Catasto Fiorentino*. Florence: Leo S. Olschki, 1996.

Pulci, Antonia, James Wyatt Cook, and Barbara Collier Cook. *Florentine Drama for Convent and Festival: Seven Sacred Plays*. Chicago: University of Chicago Press, 1996.

Pulci, Antonia, James Wyatt Cook, and Elissa Weaver. *Saints' Lives and Bible Stories for the Stage*. Toronto: CRRS, 2010.

Radke, Gary M. "Masaccio's City: Urbanism, Architecture, and Sculpture in Early Fifteenth-Century Florence." In *The Cambridge Companion to Masaccio*, edited by Diane Cole Ahl, 40–63. Cambridge: Cambridge University Press, 2002.

Raffa, Guy P. "Bones of Contention: Ravenna's and Florence's Claims to Dante's Remains." *Italica* 92, no. 3 (2015): 565–81.

Ragone, Franca. *Giovanni Villani e i suoi continuatori. La scrittura delle cronache a Firenze nel Trecento*. Rome: Istituto storico italiano per il Medio Evo, 1998.

Randolph, Adrian W.B. "Il Marzocco: Lionizing the Florentine State." In *Coming About . . . A Festschrift for John Shearman* edited by Lars R. Jones and Louisa C. Matthew, 11–18. Cambridge, MA: Harvard University Art Museums, 2001.

Revest, Clémence. "Poggio's Beginnings at the Papal Curia: The Florentine Brain Drain and the Fashioning of the Humanist Movement." In *Florence in the Early Modern World*, edited by Nicholas Scott Baker and Brian Jeffrey Maxson, 189–212. Abingdon: Routledge, 2019.

Revest, Clémence. *Romam veni: Humanisme et papauté à la fin du Grand Schisme*. Ceyzerieu: Champ Vallon, 2021.

Rhodes, D.E., ed. *La stampa a Firenze (1471–1550). Omaggio a Roberto Ridolfi*. Florence: Leo S. Olschki, 1984.

Rhodes, D.E., Eugenio Garin, Maria J. Minicucci, and Alessandro Olschki. "Note e discussioni. La stampa a Firenze (1471–1550). Omaggio a Roberto Ridolfi." *La Bibliofilia* 87, no. 1 (1985): 59–64.

Richardson, Brian. *Manuscript Culture in Renaissance Italy*. Cambridge: Cambridge University Press, 2009.

Richardson, Brian. *Print Culture in Renaissance Italy: The Editor and the Vernacular Text, 1470–1600*. Cambridge: Cambridge University Press, 1994.

Richardson, Brian. *Printing, Writers and Readers in Renaissance Italy*. Cambridge: Cambridge University Press, 1999.

Rico, Francisco, and Luca Marcozzi. "Petrarca, Francesco." In *Dizionario Biografico degli Italiani*, vol. 82, 2015. Accessed online at https://www.treccani.it/enciclopedia/francesco-petrarca_(Dizionario-Biografico) (July 11, 2022).

Ridolfi, Roberto. *La stampa in Firenze nel secolo xv*. Florence: Leo S. Olschki, 1958.

Rinuccini, Alamanno. *La Libertà Perduta/Dialogus de libertate*. Edited by G. Civati. Monza: Vittone Editore, 2003.

Roberts, Sean. *Printing a Mediterranean World: Florence, Constantinople, and the Renaissance of Geography*. Cambridge, MA: Harvard University Press, 2013.

Robichaud, Denis J.J. "Ficino on Force, Magic, and Prayers: Neoplatonic and Hermetic Influences on Ficino's *Three Books on Life*." *Renaissance Quarterly* 70, no. 1 (2017): 44–87.

Robichaud, Denis J.J. *Plato's Persona: Marsilio Ficino, Renaissance Humanism, and Platonic Traditions*. Philadelphia: University of Pennsylvania Press, 2018.

Robins, William. "The Study of Medieval Italian Textual Cultures." In *Textual Cultures of Medieval Italy: Essays from the 41st Conference on Editorial Problems*, edited by William Robins, 11–49. Toronto: University of Toronto Press, 2011.

Rocke, Michael. *Forbidden Friendships: Homosexuality and Male Culture in Renaissance Florence*. Oxford: Oxford University Press, 1996.

Rollo-Koster, Joëlle. *Avignon and its Papacy, 1309–1417*. Lanham: Rowman & Littlefield, 2015.

Romano, Serena. *Giotto's O*. Rome: Viella, 2015.

Romano, Serena. *La O di Giotto*. Milan: Electa, 2008.

Ronchetti, Alessia. "Boccaccio Between Naples and Florence, or the Desire to Become Two: Gendering the Author's Past in the *Elegia di Madonna Fiammetta*." *Italian Studies* 72, no. 2 (2017): 205–17.

Rosa, Daniela de. *Alle origini della Repubblica Fiorentina dai consoli al 'Primo Popolo' (1172–1260)*. Florence: Arnaud, 1995.

Rosen, Mark. *The Mapping of Power in Renaissance Italy*. Cambridge: Cambridge University Press, 2015.

Rosenauer, Artur. "Orsanmichele: The Birthplace of Modern Sculpture." In *Orsanmichele and the History and Preservation of the Civic Monument*, edited by Carl Brandon Strehlke, 169–78. New Haven: Yale University Press, 2012.

Rosenthal, David. "The Spaces of Plebeian Ritual and the Boundaries of Transgression." In *Renaissance Florence. A Social History*, edited by Roger J. Crum and John T. Paoletti, 161–81. Cambridge: Cambridge University Press, 2006.

Ross, Sarah Gwyneth. *The Birth of Feminism: Woman as Intellect in Renaissance Italy and England*. Cambridge, MA: Harvard University Press, 2009.

Ross, Sarah Gwyneth. "New Perspectives on *Patria*. The Adreini Performance of Florentine Citizenship." In *Florence in the Early Modern World. New Perspectives*, edited by Nicholas Scott Baker and Brian Jeffrey Maxson, 236–55. London: Routledge, 2020.

Roth, Cecil. *The Last Florentine Republic*. London: Methuen & co. ltd., 1925.

Roy, Brian E. "The Facade of Santa Maria Novella: Architecture, Context, Patronage and Meaning." Dissertation, McGill University, 1997.

Rubin, Patricia Lee. *Images and Identity in Fifteenth-Century Florence*. New Haven: Yale University Press, 2007.

Rubinstein, Nicolai. *The Government of Florence under the Medici (1434–1494)*. 2nd ed. Oxford: Clarendon Press, 1997.

Rubinstein, Nicolai. "La confessione di Francesco Neroni e la congiura antimedicea del 1466." *Archivio storico italiano* 126, no. 304 (1968): 373–87.

Rubinstein, Nicolai. *The Palazzo Vecchio, 1298–1532 : Government, Architecture, and Imagery in the Civic Palace of the Florentine Republic*. Oxford: Clarendon Press, 1995.

Rubinstein, Nicolai. "Savonarola on the Government of Florence." In *The World of Savonarola: Italian Èlites and Perceptions of Crisis*, edited by Sella Fletcher and Christine Shaw, 42–54. Aldershot: Ashgate, 2000.

Rubinstein, Nicolai. *Studies in Italian history in the Middle Ages and the Renaissance*. Edited by Giovanni Ciappelli. Roma: Edizioni di storia e letteratura, 2004.

Rucellai, Giovanni, Alessandro Perosa, and F. W. Kent. *Giovanni Rucellai ed il suo zibaldone*. 2 vols. London: The Warburg Institute University of London, 1960.

Ruffini, Marco. *Art Without an Author: Vasari's Lives and Michelangelo's Death*. New York: Fordham University Press, 2011.

Ruffini, Marco. "Per la genesi delle "Vite." Il quaderno di Yale." *Mitteilungen des Kunsthistorischen Institutes in Florenz* 58, no. 3 (2016): 376–401.

Ruffini, Marco. "Sixteenth-Century Paduan Annotations to the First Edition of Vasari's Vite (1550)." *Renaissance Quarterly* 62, no. 3 (2009): 748–808.

Ruggieri, R.M. "Letterati, poeti e pittori intorno alla giostra di Giuliano de' Medici." *Rinascimento* 10 (1959): 165–96.

Runciman, Steven. *The Sicilian Vespers. A History of the Mediterranean World in the Later Thirteenth Century.* Cambridge: Cambridge University Press, 2012.

Rundle, David. "Humanism across Europe: The Structure of Contacts." In *Humanism in Fifteenth-Century Europe*, edited by David Rundle, 307–35. Oxford: The Society for the Study of Medieval Languages and Literature, 2012.

Rupp, Teresa Pugh. "'If You Want Peace, Work for Justice': Dino Compagni's Compagni's *Cronica* and the Ordinances of Justice." In *Florence and Beyond. Culture, Society and Politics in Renaissance Italy*, edited by David S. Peterson and Daniel E. Bornstein, 323–37. Toronto: CRRS, 2008.

Saalman, Howard. *The Bigallo. The Oratory and Residence of the Compagnia del Bigallo e della Misericorida in Florence.* New York: New York University Press, 1969.

Saalman, Howard. *Filippo Brunelleschi: The Buildings.* University Park: Pennsylvania State University Press, 1993.

Saalman, Howard. *Filippo Brunelleschi: The Cupola of Santa Maria del Fiore.* London: A. Zwemmer Ltd, 1980.

Saalman, Howard. "Santa Maria del Fiore: 1294–1418." *The Art Bulletin* 46, no. 4 (1964): 471–500.

Salvadore, Matteo. *The African Prester John and the Birth of Ethiopian-European Relations.* London: Routledge, 2017.

Salvadori, Roberto G. *The Jews of Florence.* Florence: Giutina, 2001.

Salvini, Monica, Susanna Bianchi, Paolo Lelli, Valeria Montanarini, Riccardo Santoni, and Pasquino Pallecchi. "Le premesse archeologiche alla Sala Grande." In *La Sala Grande di Palazzo Vecchio e la Battaglia di Anghiari di Leonardo da Vinci,* edited by Roberto Barsanti, Gianluca Belli, Emanuela Ferretti, and Cecilia Fosinini, 71–95. Florence: Leo S. Olschki, 2019.

Samuels, Richard S. "Benedetto Varchi, the Accademia degli Infiammati, and the Origins of the Italian Academic Movement." *Renaissance Quarterly* 29, no. 4 (1976): 599–634.

Santagata, Marco. *Dante: The Story of His Life.* Translated by Richard Dixon. Cambridge, MA: Belknap Press of Harvard University Press, 2016.

Satkowski, Leon, and Roger J. Crum. "On the Iconography of the Uffizi Façade." *The Art Bulletin* 72, no. 1 (1990): 131–35.

Schevill, Ferdinand. *Medieval and Renaissance Florence. vol. 1: Medieval Florence*. New York: Harper & Row, 1936.

Schofield, Richard. "A Local Renaissance: Florentine Quattrocento Palaces and *all' antica* styles." In *Local Antiquities, Local Identities: Art, Literature and Antiquarianism in Europe, c. 1400–1700*, edited by Kathleen Christian and Bianca de Divitiis, 13–36. Manchester: Manchester University Press, 2019.

Scott, John Beldon. "Papal Patronage in the Seventeenth Century: Urban VIII, Bernini, and the Countess of Matilda." In *L'âge d'or du mécénat (1598–1661)*, 119–27. Paris: Editions du CNRS, 1985.

Seigel, Jerrold E. *Rhetoric and Philosophy in Renaissance Humanism: The Union of Eloquence and Wisdom, Petrarch to Valla*. Princeton: Princeton University Press, 1968.

Shaw, Christine. *Julius II. The Warrior Pope*. Oxford: Blackwell Publishers, 1993.

Shaw, James, and Evelyn Welch. *Making and Marketing Medicine in Renaissance Florence*. Amsterdam: The Welcome Trust Centre for the History of Medicine at UCL, 2011.

Shearman, John. *Mannerism*. New York: Penguin, 1967.

Shemek, Deanna. "Verse." In *The Cambridge Companion to the Italian Renaissance*, edited by Michael Wyatt, 179–201. Cambridge: Cambridge University Press, 2014.

Siegmund, Stefanie B. *The Medici State and the Ghetto of Florence: The Construction of an Early Modern Jewish Community*. Stanford: Stanford University Press, 2006.

Signorini, Maddalena. "Considerazioni preliminari sulla biblioteca di Giovanni Boccaccio." *Studi sul Boccaccio* 29 (2011): 367–95.

Simonetta, Marcello. *The Montefeltro Conspiracy: A Renaissance Mystery Decoded*. New York: Doubleday, 2008.

Simons, Patricia. "Lesbian (In)Visibility in Italian Renaissance Culture: Diana and Other Cases of donna con donna." *Journal of Homosexuality* 27, no. 1–2 (1994): 81–122.

Sisi, C. *La Basilica della Santissima Annunziata dal duecento al cinquecento*. Florence: Pacini, 2013.

Smith, Christine, and Joseph F. O'Connor. *Building the Kingdom: Giannozzo Manetti on the Material and Spiritual Edifice*. Tempe, AZ: ACMRS, 2006.

Smith, John Holland. *The Great Schism*. New York: Weybright and Talley, 1970.

Sperling, Christine M. "Verrocchio's Medici Tombs." In *Verrocchio and Late Quattrocento Italian Sculpture*, edited by Steven Bule, Alan Phipps Darr, and Fiorella Superbi Gioffredi, 51–61. Florence: Le Lettere, 1992.

Spini, Giorgio. *Architettura e politica da Cosimo I a Ferdinando I*. Florence: Leo S. Olschki, 1976.

Sposato, Peter. "The Chivalrous Life of Buonaccorso Pitti: Honor-Violence and the Profession of Arms in Late Medieval Florence and Italy." *Studies in Medieval and Renaissance History* 13 (2016): 141–76.

Stapleford, Richard, ed. *Lorenzo de' Medici at Home: The Inventory of the Palazzo Medici in 1492*. University Park: Pennsylvania State University Press, 2013.

Starn, Randolph. *Contrary Commonwealth: The Theme of Exile in Medieval and Renaissance Italy*. Berkeley: University of California Press, 1982.

Stephens, J.N. *The Fall of the Florentine Republic, 1512–1530*. Oxford: Oxford University Press, 1983.

Stoppacci, Patrizia, and Claudia Cenni. *Geri d'Arezzo. Lettere e dialogo d'amore*. Pisa: Pacini, 2009.

Strehlke, Carl Brandon. "Orsanmichele before and after the Niche Sculptures: Making Decisions about Art in Renaissance Florence." In *Orsanmichele and the History and Preservation of the Civic Monument*, edited by Carl Brandon Strehlke, 21–34. New Haven: Yale University Press, 2012.

Strehlke, Carl Brandon, ed. *Pontormo, Bronzino, and the Medici: The Transformation of the Renaissance Portrait in Florence*. Philadelphia: Philadelphia Museum of Art, 2004.

Strehlke, Carl Brandon. "Review of Several Recent Works on Dante." *The Art Bulletin* 94, no. 3 (2012): 460–65.

Strocchia, Sharon T. *Death and Ritual in Renaissance Florence*. Baltimore: Johns Hopkins University Press, 1992.

Strocchia, Sharon T. *Forgotten Healers. Women and the Pursuit of Health in Late Renaissance Italy*. Cambridge, MA: Harvard University Press, 2019.

Strocchia, Sharon T. *Nuns and Nunneries in Renaissance Florence*. Baltimore: Johns Hopkins University Press, 2009.

Strohmer, Shaun, and Brian Jeffrey Maxson. "Leonardo Bruni." In *Literature Criticism from 1400–1800*, edited by Lawrence J. Trudeau, vol. 212, 87–260. Detroit: Gale Cengage, 2013.

Strozzi, Alessandra Macinghi. *Letters to Her Sons, 1447–1470*. Edited and translated by Judith Bryce, edited by Judith Bryce. Tempe: ACMRS, 2016.

Strozzi, Beatrice Paolozzi. "La storia del Bargello." In *La storia del Bargello: 100 capolavori da scoprire*, edited by Beatrice Paolozzi Strozzi, 11–78. Milan: Silvana Editoriale, 2004.

Strozzi, Beatrice Paolozzi, ed. *La storia del Bargello: 100 capolavori da scoprire*. Milan: Silvana Editoriale, 2004.

Sumption, Jonathan. *The Hundred Years War*. 4 vols. Philadelphia: University of Pennsylvania Press, 1999–2015.

Swanson, R.N. *The Twelfth-Century Renaissance*. Manchester: Manchester University Press, 1999.

Tacconi, Marica. *Cathedral and Civic Ritual in Late Medieval and Renaissance Florence: The Service Books of Santa Maria del Fiore*. Cambridge: Cambridge University Press, 2005.

Tanzini, Lorenzo. *Firenze*. Spoleto: Fondazione Centro Italiano di Studi sull'Alto Medioevo, 2016.

Tatel, Marcel, Ronald G. Witt, and Rona Goffen, eds. *Life and Death in Fifteenth-Century Florence*. Durham: Duke University Press, 1989.

Tavernor, Robert. *On Alberti and the Art of Building*. New Haven: Yale University Press, 1998.

Taylor, Craig. "The Ambivalent Influence of Italian Letters and the Rediscovery of the Classics in Late Medieval France." In *Humanism in Fifteenth-Century Europe*, edited by David Rundle, 203–36. Oxford: The Society for the Study of Medieval Languages and Literature, 2012.

Tazzara, Corey. *The Free Port of Livorno and the Transformation of the Mediterranean World*. Oxford: Oxford University Press, 2017.

Terpstra, Nicholas, ed. *The Art of Executing Well: Rituals of Execution in Renaissance Italy*. Kirksville, MO: Truman State University Press, 2008.

Terpstra, Nicholas. "Mapping Gendered Labor in the Textile Industry of Early Modern Florence." In *Florence in the Early Modern World. New Perspectives*, edited by Nicholas Scott Baker and Brian Jeffrey Maxson, 68–91. London: Routledge, 2020.

Thomson, Ian. "Manuel Chrysoloras and the Early Italian Renaissance." *Greek, Roman, and Byzantine Studies* 7 (1966): 63–82.

Tintori, Leonetto, and Eve Borsook. *Giotto. The Peruzzi Chapel*. New York: Harry N. Abrams, Inc., 1965.

Tognetti, Sergio, ed. *Firenze e Pisa dopo il 1406: La creazione di una nuovo spazio regionale*. Florence: Leo S. Olschki, 2010.

Tognetti, Sergio. "The Trade in Black African Slaves in Fifteenth-Century Florence." In *Black Africans in Renaissance Europe*, edited by T.F. Earle and K.J.P. Lowe, 213–46. Cambridge: Cambridge University Press, 2005.

Tomas, Natalie. "Alfonsina Orsini de' Medici and the 'Problem' of a Female Ruler in Early Sixteenth-Century Florence." *Renaissance Studies* 14, no. 1 (2000): 70–90.

Tomas, Natalie. "All in the Family: The Medici Women and Pope Clement VII." In *The Pontificate of Clement VII. History, Politics, Culture*, edited by Kenneth Gouwens and Sheryl E. Reiss, 41–53. Aldershot: Ashgate, 2005.

Tomas, Natalie. "Did Women Have a Space?" In *Renaissance Florence. A Social History*, edited by Roger J. Crum and John T. Paoletti, 311–28. Cambridge: Cambridge University Press, 2006.

Tomas, Natalie R. *The Medici Women: Gender and Power in Renaissance Florence*. Burlington, VT: Ashgate, 2003.

Tomasi, Valeria. "L'organizzazione dei cantieri in epoca rinascimentale: I loggiati su Piazza SS. Annunziata a Firenze." *Mélanges de l'Ecole française de Rome* 119, no. 2 (2007): 299–319.

Tornabuoni, Lucrezia, and Jane Tylus. *Sacred Narratives*. Chicago: University of Chicago Press, 2001.

Torre, Arnaldo della. *Storia dell' Accademia platonica di Firenze*. Florence: Tip. G. Carnesecchi e figli, 1902.

Trachtenberg, Marvin. "Founding the Palazzo Vecchio in 1299: The Corso Donati Paradox." *Renaissance Quarterly* 54, no. 4 (1999): 966–93.

Trexler, Richard C. *The Journey of the Magi: Meanings in History of a Christian Story*. Princeton: Princeton University Press, 1997.

Trexler, Richard C. *Public Life in Renaissance Florence*. Ithaca: Cornell University Press, 1980.

Trexler, Richard C., and Mary Elizabeth Lewis. "Two Captains and Three Kings: New Light on the Medici Chapel." *Studies in Medieval and Renaissance History* 4 (1981): 91–177.

Tripodi, Claudia. "Piero de' Pazzi." In *Dizionario Biografico degli Italiani*, vol. 82, 2015. Accessed online at https://www.treccani.it/enciclopedia/piero-de-pazzi_(Dizionario-Biografico) (July 11, 2022).

Trivellato, Francesca. *The Familiarity of Strangers: The Sephardic Diaspora, Livorno, and Cross-Cultural Trade in the Early Modern Period*. New Haven: Yale University Press, 2009.

Tromboni, Lorenza. "Ficinian Theories as Rhetorical Devices: The Case of Girolamo Savonarola." In *New Worlds and the Italian Renaissance*, edited by Andrea Moudarres and Christiana Thérèse Purdy Moudarres, 143–71. Leiden: Brill, 2012.

Tromboni, Lorenza. "La cultura filosofica di Girolamo Savonarola tra predicazione e umanesimo: Platone, Aristotele e la Sacra Scrittura." *Cahiers d'études italiennes* 29 (2019).

Ullman, Berthold L., and Philip A. Stadter. *The Public Library of Renaissance Florence: Niccolò Niccoli, Cosimo de' Medici and the Library of San Marco*. Padua: Editrice Antenore, 1972.

Varchi, Benedetto. *Storia fiorentina*, vol. 1. Edited by Lelio Arbib. Florence: Editrice delle storie del Nardi e del Varchi, 1843.

Vasari, Giorgio. *Lives of the Artists*, vol. 1. Translated by George Bull. London: Penguin Books, 1965.

Veen, Henk Th. Van. *Cosimo I de' Medici and his Self-Representation in Florentine Art and Culture*. Translated by Andrew P. McCormick. Cambridge: Cambridge University Press, 2006.

Verga, Marcello. "Between Dynastic Strategies and Civic Myth: Anna Maria Luisa de' Medici and Florence as the New Athens." In *Medici Women: The Making of a Dynasty in Grand Ducal Tuscany*, edited by Giovanna Benadusi and Judith C. Brown, 347–71. Toronto: CRRS, 2015.

Vescovini, Graziella Federici. "Il problema delle fonti ottiche medievali del *Commentario terzo* di Lorenzo Ghiberti." In *Lorenzo Ghiberti nel suo Tempo*, vol. 2, 349–87. Florence: Leo S. Olschki, 1980.

Villani, Giovanni. *Cronica*. 8 vols. Florence: Il Magheri, 1823.

Viti, Paolo, ed. *Firenze e il Concilio del 1439*. Florence: Leo S. Olschki, 1994.

Viti, Paolo. *Il Capitolo di San Lorenzo nel Quattrocento*. Florence: Leo S. Olschki, 2006.

Viti, Paolo, ed. *Pico, Poliziano e l'umanesimo di fine Quattrocento*. Florence: Leo S. Olschki, 1994.

Vitullo, Juliann. "'Otium' and 'Negotium' in Alberti's 'I libri della famiglia.'" *Annali d'Italianistica* 32 (2014): 73–89.

Vivanti, Corrado. *Niccolo Machiavelli: An Intellectual Biography*. Princeton: Princeton University Press, 2013.

Waadenoijen, Jeanne van. "Ghiberti and the Origin of His International Style." In *Lorenzo Ghiberti nel suo Tempo: Atti del Convegno Internazionale di Studi*, vol. 1, 81–7. Florence: Leo S. Olschki, 1980.

Waldman, Louis A. *Baccio Bandinelli and Art at the Medici Court*. Philadelphia: American Philosophical Society, 2004.

Waldman, Louis A. "The Patronage of a Favorite of Leo X: Cardinal Niccolò Pandolfini, Ridolfo Ghirlandaio and the Unfinished Tomb by Baccio da Montelupo." *Mitteilungen des Kunsthistorischen Institutes in Florenz* 48, no. 1/2 (2004): 105–28.

Waley, Daniel, and Trevor Dean. *The Italian City Republics*. 4 ed. Abingdon: Routledge, 2009.

Wallace, William E. "An Impossible Task." In *Making and Moving Sculpture in Early Modern Italy*, edited by Kelley Helmstutler Di Dio, 47–59. Farnham: Ashgate, 2015.

Wallace, William E. *Michelangelo at San Lorenzo: The Genius as Entrepreneur*. Cambridge: Cambridge University Press, 1994.

Wallace, William E., ed. *Michelangelo. Selected Scholarship in English.*
5 vols. New York: Garland, 1995.

Wallace, William E. *Michelangelo. The Artist, the Man, and his Times.*
Cambridge: Cambridge University Press, 2010.

Walter, Ingeborg. "Giuliano de' Medici." In *Dizionario Biografico degli
Italiani*, vol. 73, 2009. Accessed online at https://www.treccani
.it/enciclopedia/giuliano-de-medici_res-f6ca07e6-dcde-11df-9ef0
-d5ce3506d72e_(Dizionario-Biografico) (accessed July 11, 2022).

Watkins, Renée Neu. *Humanism and Liberty: Writings on Freedom from
Fifteenth-Century Florence*. Columbia: University of South Carolina Press,
1978.

Weddle, Saundra. "Identity and Alliance: Urban Presence, Spatial Privilege,
and Florentine Renaissance Convents." In *Renaissance Florence. A
Social History*, edited by Roger J. Crum and John T. Paoletti, 394–412.
Cambridge: Cambridge University Press, 2006.

Weinstein, Donald. "The *Art of Dying* Well and Popular Piety in the
Preaching and Thought of Girolamo Savonarola." In *Life and
Death in Fifteenth-Century Florence*, edited by Marcel Tetel,
Ronald G. Witt, and Rona Goffen, 88–104. Durham: Duke University
Press, 1989.

Weinstein, Donald. *Savonarola and Florence: Prophecy and Patriotism in the
Renaissance*. Princeton: Princeton University Press, 1970.

Weinstein, Donald. *Savonarola: The Rise and Fall of a Renaissance Prophet.*
New Haven: Yale University Press, 2011.

Weiss, Roberto. *Il primo secolo dell'umanesimo*. Rome: Edizione di storia e
letteratura, 1949.

Weiss, Roberto. "Lineamenti per una storia del primo umanesimo fiorentino."
Rivista Storica Italiana 60 (1948): 349–66.

Wickham, Chris. *Courts and Conflict in Twelfth-Century Tuscany*. Oxford:
Oxford University Press, 2003.

Wickham, Chris. *Early Medieval Italy: Central Power and Local Society,
400–1000*. Ann Arbor: University of Michigan Press, 1989.

Wickham, Chris. *The Inheritance of Rome. A History of Europe from 400 to
1000*. New York: Penguin, 2009.

Wicksteed, Philip H., and Edmund G. Gardner. *Dante and Giovanni del
Virgilio*. Westminster: Archibald Constable & Company, 1902.

Wieruszowski, Helene. *Politics and Culture in Medieval Spain and Italy.*
Rome: Edizioni di storia e letteratura, 1971.

Wilkins, Ernest H. *The Life of Petrarch*. Chicago: University of Chicago Press,
1961.

Wilson, Blake. "If Monuments Could Sing: Image, Song, and Civic Devotion inside Orsanmichele." In *Orsanmichele and the History and Preservation of the Civic Monument*, edited by Carl Brandon Strehlke, 141–68. New Haven: Yale University Press, 2012.

Wilson, N.G. *From Byzantium to Italy. Greek Studies in the Italian Renaissance.* 2nd ed. London: Bloomsbury, 2017.

Wind, Edgar. "A Bacchic Mystery by Michelangelo." In *Pagan Mysteries in the Renaissance.* New Haven: Yale University Press, 1958. Reprint, William E. Wallace, ed., Michelangelo. *Selected Scholarship in English*, 201–16.

Witt, Ronald G. *Coluccio Salutati and His Public Letters.* Geneva: Librairie Droz, 1976.

Witt, Ronald G. "The *De Tyranno* and Coluccio Salutati's View of Politics and Roman History." *Nuova Rivista Storica* 53 (1969): 434–74.

Witt, Ronald G. *Hercules at the Crossroads: The Life, Works, and Thought of Coluccio Salutati.* Durham: Duke University Press, 1983.

Witt, Ronald G. *In the Footsteps of the Ancients: The Origins of Humanism from Lovato to Bruni.* Leiden: Brill, 2000.

Witt, Ronald G. "Petrarch and Pre-Petrarchan Humanism: Stylistic Imitation and the Origins of Italian Humanism." In *Humanity and Divinity in Renaissance and Reformation*, edited by John W. O'Malley, Thomas M. Izbicki, and Gerald Christianson, 73–100. Leiden: Brill, 1993.

Yates, Frances A. *Giordano Bruno and the Hermetic Tradition.* Chicago: University of Chicago Press, 1964.

Yoldi, Giuseppe Rocchi Coopmans de, ed. *S. Maria del Fiore. Teorie e storie dell' archeologia e del restauro nella città delle fabbriche arnolfiane.* Florence: Alinea editrice, 2006.

Yoran, Hanan. "Glory, Passions and Money in Alberti's Della famiglia: A Humanist Reflects on the Foundations of Society." *The European Legacy* 20, no. 5 (2015): 527–42.

Yousefzadeh, Mahnaz. "Anti-Hegemonic Nationalism: The Dante Centenary of 1865." In *Power, Gender, and Ritual in Europe and the Americas*, edited by Peter Arnade and Michael Rocke, 339–52. Toronto: CRRS, 2008.

Yousefzadeh, Mahnaz. *Florence's Embassy to the Sultan of Egypt. An English Translation of Felice Brancacci's Diary.* London: Palgrave Macmillan, 2018.

Zervas, Diane Finiello. "'Degno templo e tabernacolo santo': Remembering and Renewing Orsanmichele." In *Orsanmichele and the History and Preservation of the Civic Monument*, edited by Carl Brandon Strehlke, 9–20. New Haven: Yale University Press, 2012.

Zervas, Diane Finiello. *Orsanmichele a Firenze*. Modena: F. C. Panini, 1996.

Zervas, Diane Finello. *The Parte Guelfa, Brunelleschi & Donatello*. Locust Valley: J.J. Augustin, 1987.

Zinguer, Ilana, Abraham Melamed, and Zur Shalev, eds. *Hebraic Aspects of the Renaissance*. Leiden: Brill, 2011.

Zuraw, Shelley E. "The Public Commemorative Monument: Mino da Fiesole's Tombs in the Florentine Badia." *The Art Bulletin* 80, no. 3 (1998): 452–77.

Index

Index